Interpersonal Communication

Concepts, Components, and Contexts

Interpersonal Communication

Concepts, Components, and Contexts

Second Edition

Judy Cornelia Pearson
Ohio University, Athens

Brian H. Spitzberg
University of North Texas

 Wm. C. Brown Publishers

Book Team

Editor *Stan Stoga*
Developmental Editor *Jane F. Lambert*
Production Editor *Harry Halloran*
Art Editor *Gayle A. Salow*
Photo Editor *Carrie Burger*
Permissions Editor *Karen L. Storlie*
Visuals Processor *Andé Meyer*

 Wm. C. Brown Publishers

President *G. Franklin Lewis*
Vice President, Publisher *George Wm. Bergquist*
Vice President, Publisher *Thomas E. Doran*
Vice President, Operations and Production *Beverly Kolz*
National Sales Manager *Virginia S. Moffat*
Advertising Manager *Ann M. Knepper*
Marketing Manager *Kathleen Nietzke*
Production Editorial Manager *Colleen A. Yonda*
Production Editorial Manager *Julie A. Kennedy*
Publishing Services Manager *Karen J. Slaght*
Manager of Visuals and Design *Faye M. Schilling*

Cover and interior design by John R. Rokusek

The credits section for this book begins on page 401, and is considered an extension of the copyright page.

Printed in the United States of America by Wm. C. Brown Publishers, 2460 Kerper Boulevard, Dubuque, IA 52001

10 9 8 7 6 5 4 3 2 1

Contents

Preface

As teachers of the introductory Interpersonal Communication course, we believe that the course is most successful when theoretical material is combined with a skills orientation. *Interpersonal Communication: Concepts, Components, and Contexts* provides this combination.

Interpersonal Communication: Concepts, Components, and Contexts has a point of view. The book begins with a discussion of basic concepts. It continues by being organized around the components of expressiveness, composure, other-orientation, and conversational coordination. These components are examined in the contexts of communication with strangers, acquaintances, and friends, communication with intimates, family communication, and communication in the interview.

The first three chapters are concerned with the most basic concepts of interpersonal communication. They cover those topics and terms that are prerequisite to understanding interpersonal communication. The first chapter provides a broad-based introduction to the study of interpersonal communication. In this chapter you will discover what distinguishes interpersonal communication from other forms of communication. In addition, general considerations regarding personal enhancement of communication are examined.

The second chapter introduces you to interpersonal relationships. All interpersonal communication influences your relationship with someone in some way. The characteristics of interpersonal relationships, their values, and typical patterns of the evolution of interpersonal relationships are briefly explained. You will find that most interpersonal relationships develop in similar ways across a similar set of stages.

The third chapter concerns the process of perception. The obvious importance of this subject is easily demonstrated when you try to consider the possibility of communication without perception. The nature of perception is explained in terms of the factors that influence the process of perception and the ways in which perception influences interpretation.

Over the next eight chapters, we examine the skills that can enhance communicative competence. These particular skills will be best understood in the context of a general model of communicative competence. Motivation, knowledge, and skills are all basic. Across most conversations, the more motivated you are to communicate well, the more knowledgeable you are about conversation, and the more skilled you are in your behavior, the more competent you are likely to be in your communication.

The particular skills that comprise competent interpersonal transactions are covered under four general areas: expressiveness, composure, other-orientation, and conversational coordination. Expressiveness concerns the ways in which we use behavior to express ideas and meanings. Composure concerns confidence in our manner and assertion of our rights. Other-orientation means that you show interest and concern for the other person in the conversation. Conversational coordination involves the processes of turn-taking and topic management. Whereas composure promotes the self, other-orientation promotes the other person. And while expressiveness projects one's own intentions and meanings, conversational coordination helps assure that these meanings are enacted in a manner specifically adapted to the rules and norms of the other person. Thus, these skills represent both the importance of the self and the importance of the other.

Learning about interpersonal communication does not help you much if you do not know when and where to apply what you have learned. The third section covers four of the most important contexts in which the skills you have been learning can be applied. The first context includes those relationships you have with others that tend to be casual, nonintimate, and nonromantic in orientation. Strangers, acquaintances, and friends may comprise the majority of people adolescents and adults communicate with on a day-to-day basis, especially those who work full-time, who are students, or who are not married or cohabiting. The similarities and differences among these types of relationships and their communication are explained.

The second context examines intimate relationships and communication. Intimate relationships in this sense refers to those relationships that contain a romantic or sexual dimension to them. The various motivations and values of intimacy are discussed, and the characteristics of intimate communication are identified. Ways of improving communication in intimate contexts are also reviewed.

The third context is one that prevails as a social institution despite the trends examined in chapter 1. The family represents one of the most primary and influential contexts in which our identity is formed. The characteristics that distinguish the family from other social systems are found to also significantly affect forms of communication. Ways of improving family communication and systems are analyzed.

The final context is the interview context. While this context may seem very different from the others, it is similar in terms of its importance to quality of life. Few contexts can be so clearly and unambiguously identified that bear so significant an influence on your quality of life as the job interview.

This book has a number of key features. Concrete first-person dialogues, collected from students, colleagues, friends, and family, clarify the more theoretical material. These transcripted interactions allow students to directly apply the ideas they have learned and encourage them to experiment with new and useful behaviors. Each chapter is previewed in an outline and an introduction and reviewed in a summary. A variety of application exercises are strategically placed throughout the chapters so you can immediately determine if you understand the concepts discussed in that section. Items from contemporary culture, such as cartoons, song lyrics, and quotations, are included in each chapter to illustrate and underscore the content in an interesting and relevant form. Additional sources are listed at the end of each chapter for those of you who want to study the topics in greater depth.

New Material

This text was originally published as *Interpersonal Communication: Clarity, Confidence, Concern.* A number of significant changes have been made from that book. First, three entirely new chapters have been added. Chapter 3 on the role of perception in interpersonal communication clarifies the role of perception in communication, defines perception, explains why differences occur in perception, and details the activities that are involved in perception. Chapter 10 considers the role of communication rules. The nature of rules is examined in relationship to norms, conventions, morals, and laws. The importance of rules is highlighted as is clarification concerning competence in using communication rules. Chapter 11 provides information on conversational coordination. The nature of conversational coordination introduces the chapter. Basic terms and definitions, basic behaviors and processes such as components of turn-exchange and turn-exchange rules, and the role of knowledge in conversational coordination are provided. The chapter details the importance of conversational coordination and concludes with a discussion of competence in conversational coordination.

Major new sections have been added to other chapters. The first section of the text, which considers basic concepts, has been expanded. Discussions of alienation and anomie add relevance to chapter 1. Additional information on changes in the family, increased mobility, and changes in the labor force has been added. In chapter 2, information on interpersonal relationships has been provided that distinguishes relationships as complementary, symmetrical, noncomplementary, or anticomplementary. Three kinds of attraction—task attraction, social attraction, and physical attraction—are considered. More information on attachment is present in this edition. Discussions of exclusivity, commitment, and interdependence also mark this book.

The second section on components includes new sections in existing chapters as well as the new chapters highlighted above. In chapter 4, information on verbal expressiveness is added concerning the way in which words accrue meaning from their context. A new section on indexing—including the four levels of content, actor, coactor, and context indexing—is presented. Chapter 5, which considers nonverbal expressiveness, adds new materials that recommend that competent communicators avoid extreme levels of behavior and that they seek to adapt their nonverbal communication to the expectations of the context. Self-disclosure is discussed in chapter 6, and the role of self-concept, basic to self-disclosure, has been added. Self-assertion, the topic of chapter 7, includes additional information including several specific types of assertive messages that are identified and distinguished. Listening is further examined in chapter 8 with an exploration of contemporary research. The role of listening in contemporary organizations is highlighted. Research shows that married couples may also benefit by learning listening skills.

Changes have been added to the context section as well. The role of first impressions and prototypes are added to chapter 12, which considers communication among strangers, acquaintances, and friends. The communication characteristics of friendship are identified and described. Basic rules of friendship behavior are also elucidated. Why are we attracted to those with whom we become intimate? Chapter 13 identifies some of those factors. The relational state that is borne of particular individuals in a relational system is also described. A new Intimacy Behaviors Activity completes this section. Chapter 15 on Interviewing has an added organizational pattern to describe effective and appropriate interviewing behavior.

Finally, current research studies on which this book is based have been examined and included as appropriate. The reader will find updated reading lists at the end of each chapter. In general, the text reflects our contemporary understanding of interpersonal communication theorizing and skill development, some of which has emerged since the first edition of this book.

Instructor's Manual

A detailed Instructor's Manual will help the instructor use this book in the Interpersonal Communication course. It includes teaching strategies, course syllabi, major long-term assignments, additional teaching activities, a glossary of terms, suggested audiovisual resources for each chapter, and a section containing multiple-choice, true–false, and essay examination questions.

Acknowledgments

Interpersonal Communication: Concepts, Components, and Contexts reflects a collaboration with professors, colleagues, publishers, editors, reviewers, and students. Judy Pearson's undergraduate professors at St. Cloud State University; graduate professors at Indiana University in Bloomington; colleagues at Bradley University, Indiana-Purdue University at Fort Wayne, Iowa State University, Michigan State University, and Ohio University; friends in the Midwest Basic Course Directors Conference and throughout the country; and family and friends all deserve acknowledgment in the construction of this text. Brian Spitzberg's undergraduate professors at the University of Texas at Arlington; graduate professors at University of Southern California; colleagues at the University of Wisconsin–Madison, University of North Texas, and San Diego State University; and family and friends all served a role, however indirectly, in the development of this text. We wish to thank Mary Pearson, Sue Manderick, and Patricia Cambridge for their contributions. The people at Wm C. Brown also provided support and encouragement. We are grateful for the assistance of Stan Stoga who contributed in special ways to the book. We also want to thank the reviewers for their careful reading of the manuscript for the first edition and their sensitive suggestions for improvement: Phil Backlund, Central Washington University; Sue DeWine, Ohio University; Paul Friedman, University of Kansas; Jo-Ann Graham, Bronx Community College; Richard Kaough, Southern Oregon State College; Larry Miller, Indiana University; Sue Pendell, Colorado State University; and Jack Sterk, Los Angeles Valley College. In addition, the reviewers for the second edition deserve equal thanks: Phil Backlund (again!); Roy Beck, Western Michigan University; Mary Anne Fitzpatrick, University of Wisconsin–Madison; Lon Green, Ferris State University; Larry Hugenberg, Youngstown State University; Alan L. Sillars, University of Montana; and Mary Trimbo, Vincennes University.

Interpersonal communication is fascinating because of its pervasiveness and complexity. No single textbook can provide all of the information necessary to become a more effective interpersonal communicator. *Interpersonal Communication: Concepts, Components, and Contexts* comes from our own commitment to the improvement of communication skills and our enthusiasm for teaching. We hope that it will provide important information about interpersonal communication that enables people to interact more effectively with others.

Judy Cornelia Pearson
Brian H. Spitzberg

Interpersonal Communication

Concepts, Components, and Contexts

Concepts

The first three chapters are concerned with the most basic concepts of interpersonal communication. Before you can run, you must learn to walk. These first few chapters cover those topics and terms that are necessary to understanding almost anything else that concerns interpersonal communication.

The first chapter provides a broad-based introduction to the study of interpersonal communication. The study of interpersonal communication is still a relatively recent phenomenon. In this chapter you will discover what distinguishes interpersonal communication from other forms of communication. In addition, general considerations regarding personal enhancement of communication are examined.

The second chapter introduces you to interpersonal relationships. While you may not think about it often in this way, all interpersonal communication influences your relationship with someone in some way. The characteristics of interpersonal relationships, their values, and typical patterns of evolution are briefly explained. You will find that most interpersonal relationships develop in similar ways across a similar set of stages.

The third chapter concerns the process of perception. The obvious importance of this subject is easily demonstrated when you try to consider the possibility of communication without perception. The nature of perception is explained in terms of the factors that influence the process of perception and the ways in which perception influences interpretation.

Together, these three chapters only scratch the surface, yet they are essential to set the stage for what is to come. A general understanding of the process of interpersonal communication, interpersonal relationships, and perception will provide a foundation from which the other chapters build. If understanding is a necessary prelude to learning, then Part One becomes particularly important to the value of the remainder of the textbook.

An Introduction to Interpersonal Communication

HeRe SHe COMeS NOW...
...WONDeR iF i SHOULD SAY HELLO??
iF i SPeAK FiRST SHe MAY THiNK
i'M TOO FORWARD... THeN AGAiN, iF i
WAiT TiLL SHe SPeAKS, MAYBe SHe'LL
THiNK i DON'T LiKe HeR!!
...AND iF SHe THiNKS i DON'T LiKe
HeR, THeN SHe MAY NOT SPeAK TO Me
...WORSe YeT, SHe MAY NOT LiKe Me...
AND iF i SPeAK TO HeR...SHe MAY
TELL Me SO...

???

...i'LL PReTeND
i DON'T See HeR!

2/11 Tom Wilson

©1974 Universal Press Syndicate

ZIGGY COPYRIGHT 1974 Ziggy and Friends, Inc. Distributed by UNIVERSAL PRESS SYNDICATE.

Ziggy, in this cartoon, expresses thoughts that each of us has had at one time or another. We have analyzed the simplest of interpersonal encounters and recognized the many choices that we have and the even greater number of interpretations that a simple comment like "Hello," may be given. Perhaps you can recall experiences in which you hesitated in entering into a conversation with another person because you were afraid of your own responses, you felt you could not communicate clearly to the other person, or you did not know how to express understanding. When you have completed this book, you should be able to communicate confidently, clearly, and with concern.

Interpersonal communication pervades all aspects of our lives. Our social and family relationships, our work experiences, and our day-to-day encounters with others are facilitated by interpersonal communication. Perhaps because interpersonal communication is so commonplace, we sometimes fail to focus on it in the same way that we take the air we breathe, the water we drink, and the space through which we move for granted.

Ironically, when we do consider interpersonal interactions it may be because of some difficulty that we are having, such as when a friend walks away in anger, when a business associate explains that we don't present ourselves well in professional interviews, or when we are faced with the termination of a love relationship. The amount of time that we spend considering successful interpersonal communication and improving our relationships with others may be minimal. Brown and Van Riper suggest that the usual pedagogy in teaching a baby to talk is so poor that if people were taught to read by the same crude methods, we would be a nation of illiterates.[1] How many of us are functionally illiterate at interpersonal communication?

Most of us would not like to admit to illiteracy in anything, especially something we do every day of our lives. We assume that because people do not run in fear when they see us coming, that people do not consistently slap us in the face in reaction to our comments, and that we seem to have at least a modicum of success at sustaining acquaintanceships, that we therefore must be fully competent at the complex process called communication. In other words, since we are not commonly experiencing clear-cut failure in our encounters, it becomes easy to assume our own success. Further, in those instances in which failure does occur, conditions are usually ambiguous enough to allow us to find blame in others rather than ourselves.

We would like to suggest that the first step to increasing your own interpersonal communication competence is to realize there is always room for improvement in your own communication skills. Think of your skills as existing on a continuum, from very unskilled to very skilled. At the unskilled end of the continuum would be people you really do actively try systematically to avoid. Such persons might be considered overly opinionated or overly equivocal, overly boorish or overly boring, overly anxious or overly methodical, overly talkative or overly quiet, overly argumentative or overly submissive. Persons at this end of the continuum are likely to experience difficulty initiating, establishing, maintaining, and exiting both conversations and relationships. Interacting with them is consistently unrewarding.

At the other end of the continuum are people with whom interaction is consistently rewarding. These people are the ones whom you meet for only a few minutes, yet may think about and remember them for months thereafter. Such persons seem to always have something to say, and, when they are not saying something, seem intensely interested in what you have to say. Such persons seem to move comfortably through varieties of social encounters with no apparent problems in adaptation. Such persons are likely to be popular, engaged in numerous relationships at all times, and successful in accomplishing their personal goals in the interpersonal world.

Obviously these two ends of the continuum are hypothetical in nature. In actuality, few people ever achieve these extremes, and if they do, probably achieve these states for relatively brief periods of time during their life. But the *idea* of these hypothetical ends of the continuum points to the room we have for improvement of our own communication skills. Because we can all think of those instances in which we have been in intensely enjoyable or rewarding interactions, we can assess to what extent our typical, everyday interactions fall short of the ideal end of the continuum. This textbook does not promise to make you an ideal communicator in terms of this continuum. It does, however, offer you some insights and some tools for moving you closer to this end of the continuum. What you do with this information depends in part upon your willingness to learn and the degree to which you can accept the fact that you have room to improve.

In this text we will consider the topic of interpersonal communication. We will provide information that will help you understand and analyze interpersonal communication and activities that will help you synthesize your understanding and allow you to practice and develop interpersonal communication skills. We will consider the components of interpersonal communication in chapters 4 through 11. In these chapters we will analyze the basic building blocks of effective interpersonal communication that appear to be generalized across many contexts. In chapters 12 through 15, we will consider specific contexts in which interpersonal communication occurs. We will examine the conversation among strangers, acquaintances, and friends, intimate communication, and family communication. In these chapters we will discuss some of the unique features of communication that occur in each of the contexts.

In order to understand the material in later chapters, we need to establish some basic definitions and parameters for interpersonal communication. This introductory material is provided in chapters 1 and 2. In chapter 2 we will consider interpersonal relationships. In this chapter, we will examine the nature of interpersonal communication and offer a definition of it. We will further delineate this definition by adding unique characteristics of interpersonal communication and we will focus on the systemic nature of interpersonal communication. We will offer a section on the improvement of interpersonal communication, which, of course, is the focus of this text. Let us begin with a consideration of the nature of interpersonal communication.

The Nature of Interpersonal Communication

Definition of Interpersonal Communication

Broadly defined, *interpersonal communication is the process of transaction between people from which meaning is mutually derived.* We will further delineate this broad definition later in this chapter when we consider some of the distinguishing characteristics of interpersonal communication. Let us examine each of the terms in this definition now through a dialogue.

Morgan and Paige are college roommates who have lived together for over a year. They were randomly assigned as roommates during their first year at college and became very close friends. They elected to share a room for their second year of school. However, the relationship between the two young women appears to have altered during the intervening summer. The conversation that follows occurred in October of their sophomore year.

Morgan: You never talk to me anymore.

Paige: What's on your mind?

Morgan: It's not what's on *my* mind; it's that I never know what's on *your* mind.

Paige: Well, what do you want to know?

Morgan: Everything!

Paige: That doesn't make any sense.

Morgan: Well, tell me how you're feeling, what you're thinking, what's been going on with you for the past month.

Paige: I think we talk *too much*.

Morgan: You never talk to me.

Paige: Well, maybe you talk too much.

Morgan: About what?

Paige: About everything and anything!

Morgan: One of us has to talk.

Paige: You talk, but you don't seem to say anything.

Morgan: That doesn't make any sense.

Paige: You're right, it doesn't!

Morgan: Maybe we should find other roommates.

Morgan and Paige appear to be experiencing a change in their relationship. Formerly close friends, they now seldom communicate with each other. When they do communicate, their conversations are marked by conflict, disagreement, and turmoil. In this particular conversation, the two appear to have discrepant notions about how much of themselves they should share with each other. Paige appears to be moving away from Morgan while Morgan appears to desire the closeness that the two once shared. The two may eventually resolve their differences or they may, as Morgan suggests, find new roommates.

Interpersonal communication is a *process* characterized by change and action. The process cannot be stopped, and it has no beginning and no end. The dialogue between Morgan and Paige clarifies this notion. Although the conversation itself is started arbitrarily with a statement by Morgan, this is not the actual beginning of their dialogue. Did it begin when they entered the room, when they began discussion of the topic this conversation revolves around, when they first conceived of the issues they were to discuss and went through imaginary dialogues in their minds, in previous discussions on this topic area, with the first words spoken in this conversation, or the first glance in each other's direction? An argument could be made that the conversation began at any of these points. But to do so is to oversimplify the communication *process* at work. The conversation, in many ways, started at *all* these points—and at none of them.

In a process, so many of the elements that comprise the process interact in such reciprocal and mutually influencing ways that everything affects everything else. Thus, to point to a beginning is to ignore all the other things influencing the process up to that point. Similarly, when does it end? Does this conversation end with Morgan's parting words, with a physical exit of the scene, when both or either of them stop thinking about the exchange, when they stop talking about the issues altogether in their relationship, or when the relationship itself comes to an end? And what if they decide at a later point to get back in touch with one another? You can see the process notion of interpersonal communication as we examine this dialogue.

Interpersonal communication is a transaction, a reciprocal giving and receiving. The conversation between Morgan and Paige goes back and forth, almost like a tennis game. The reciprocal nature of interpersonal communication allows a comment by one person to be followed by a comment by the other person. Morgan's statement, "You never talk to me," is a response to Paige's assertion, "I think we talk too much," and is followed by Paige's "Well, maybe you talk too much," to which Morgan inquires, "About what?" The comments have a clear connection and are reciprocally enacted. Nonverbal communication can be similarly performed, although we cannot examine nonverbal behavior from a printed dialogue. When exchange does not occur— when one person talks and the other person does not respond verbally or nonverbally—interpersonal communication is not occurring.

Meaning is mutually influenced by the participants in interpersonal communication. It is easy to think of meaning as being "exchanged" in interaction, and people commonly think of communication as successful if they believe they have somehow gained "possession" of the meaning the other participant "possessed" in his or her mind. This is intuitive, but oversimplifies the notion of meaning, and makes it sound as if true exchange of meanings is possible. In fact, it seems extremely unlikely, if not truly impossible, that you can ever have the exact same meaning for a message that someone else has, or intends.

We each have our own personal experiences that color our perception of the meaning of symbols and messages. Thus, when we interact with another, it is inappropriate to say that we exchange meanings, in the same way we might exchange baseball cards so that you would have the card I previously had and I would have the one you previously had. Instead, it is more appropriate to say that meaning is mutually influenced through interaction. The meaning that you derive from a conversation in this sense is a mutual product of both or all participants involved. If the other participants have no effect on the meanings you would have attributed to the situation by yourself, then *interpersonal* communication cannot be said to have occurred. Furthermore, the more influence participants have upon one another, the more similar— not identical, but similar—meanings are likely to become. It is in this sense that meaning is mutually influenced and, to some extent, shared. Creating more agreed-upon meanings among communicators is at least one mark of improvement in interpersonal communication.

Communicators may agree upon meanings that are mutually derived, but still disagree. For example, suppose you are trying to cash a check and you tell the check-cashing clerk that your complete address, phone number, and driver's license number is printed on the front of the check. She responds by turning the check over, stamps it, and asks you to fill in your address, phone number, and driver's license number. You again explain that all of this information is on the front of the check. She answers that she heard you, but all of the information must be on the *back* of the check in order to be read by a computer. You then explain that you have cashed checks here many times before and have never filled out the back of the check with the information that is already on the front. She replies that you must either fill in the required information or she will not cash your check. In this instance, each of you had a different opinion about what was to occur. Meaning was influenced, but you remained in disagreement throughout the conversation. In the conversation between Morgan and Paige, however, communication was shallow at the beginning. The two had different goals and did not have a common understanding of their situation. As they continued to converse, they began to see their mutually exclusive goals and decided to terminate the conversation, if not the relationship.

Characteristics of Interpersonal Communication

Beyond the broad definition of interpersonal communication just offered, we can further delineate this form of communication by identifying six unique characteristics of interpersonal communication. These six characteristics are explained with relevant examples from the preceding dialogue and the next interaction.

Interpersonal communication begins with self.   All of our perceptions of communication—observations, understanding based on our senses, or insight—are tied to ourselves; our particular communication interactions are limited by who we are and what we have experienced. The language we use, the attitudes we express, and the ideas we share reflect our own particular background and experiences.

In order to clarify this characteristic of interpersonal communication, let us consider another dialogue. In this conversation, a supervisor is talking to one of her employees on Monday morning. The woman has held her current position for about six months and the man has been in his position for nearly two years.

Martha: Hi, Tom. What did you want to see me about?

Tom: Well Martha, I was wondering if I would be able to take Friday off. My wife and I thought about taking off and going to the lake for three days with our kids.

Martha: That sounds great. Let me see if I can arrange it. If Dave will cover for you during the morning and we can postpone some of your less urgent business until Monday, there's no reason you can't go.

Tom: Thanks, I'll talk to you on Thursday to make sure everything is set.

Martha: Good, I'll see you then.

Three days pass and Tom checks in with Martha on Thursday afternoon.

Tom: Hi Martha. Do you have a minute?

Martha: Sure Tom, come on in.

Tom: Did you talk to Dave?

Martha: I'm sorry, Tom, about what?

Tom: About covering for me tomorrow morning so I can take the day off.

Martha: I'm really sorry, Tom, I completely forgot all about it. Just after you came in the other day, *my* supervisor called me about an important matter and then we had a staff meeting and I spent the rest of the week working on the quarterly report. I just forgot.

Tom: That's great. I plan on a long weekend and you just forget.

Martha: I am sorry.

Tom: Tell it to my wife and kids!

How does interpersonal communication begin with self in this dialogue? Martha is a single businesswoman who places her work above her personal needs. She is highly task-oriented and while she appreciates the personal needs of her employees, she could demonstrate more sensitivity to them. Tom, on the other hand, is a family man who frequently puts the needs of his family ahead of his job. Unlike Martha, who has received three promotions in two years, he has been at the same job for that length of time. Martha is secure and able to admit her mistakes; Tom is somewhat insecure about his working relationships, especially with a female supervisor. The differences in their backgrounds and experiences affect this dialogue.

Barnlund suggested the personal nature of interpersonal communication in his discussion of the "six people" involved in every two-person communication situation.[2] The six perspectives that emerged, according to Barnlund, include:

1. how you view yourself
2. how you view the other person
3. how you believe the other person views you
4. how the other person views himself or herself
5. how the other person views you
6. how the other person believes you view him or her

Barnlund suggests that we "construct" both ourselves and others through the relationships that we have, those that we wish to have, and those that we believe we do have.

In the conversation between Morgan and Paige, a difference in how each viewed herself and how she viewed the other person was evident in the beginning. Morgan wants increased interaction similar to that which she knew in the preceding academic year. Paige clearly does not have this goal. Paige states that she believes that Morgan talks too much and says too little. Morgan does not appear to share this perception of herself. In interpersonal communication we need to keep in mind the various perspectives that are involved and that we often fall back, instead, on the centrality of self in communication. In other words, we view a conversation from our own perspective and forget to consider other ways of viewing the same interaction.

Interpersonal communication is transactional.   Closely related to the many perspectives by which persons can view interpersonal communication is the idea that interpersonal communication is transactional. Before we define this term, we need to consider some basic definitions. All communication is based on our use of *codes*—systematic arrangements or comprehensive collections of symbols, letters, or words that have an arbitrary meaning. The process of communication consists of persons encoding and decoding messages. We *encode* when we put a message or thought into a verbal and nonverbal code and we *decode* when we assign meaning to a particular message. Three views of communication have evolved that are distinctive and that make certain assumptions about the encoding/decoding process. The first view, which is deeply rooted in the historical beginnings of the communication discipline, suggests that communication is an *action* that one person performs. One communicator sends a message (encoding) to another person who receives that message (decoding). Communication as action is similar to a game of catch in which only one person throws the ball and another catches it. If only Morgan or Paige and if only Martha or Tom expressed a message that was completely understood by the other person, we might conclude that communication as action was exemplified. However, this was not the case in either conversation.

The second perspective that evolved portrays communication as an *interaction* that occurs between two or more people. In this view, one person sends a message (encoding) to another person who receives that message (decoding). The receiver responds by sending another message (encoding) to the originator of the first message who then receives the message (decoding). This point of view would suggest a game of catch that included a single ball tossed from one person to another. Only one person could catch the ball and only one person could throw the ball at any particular time. The print medium distorts the conversations between the two couples in the previous dialogues and their conversations may appear to be interactions. However, even when we examine the verbal messages, we notice that each message is not directly related to the entire previous message. For instance, when Morgan tells Paige that she wants to know how Paige is feeling, thinking, and what has been happening recently in her life, Paige responds by stating that she thinks the two talk too much.

The third point of view states that communication is a *transaction*. This perspective suggests that the communicators simultaneously encode and decode messages. The two activities can occur at the same time in the same person and may both be occurring among all of the communicators in an interpersonal transaction. We observe the abundance of verbal and nonverbal cues in our communication environment at the same time that we are offering verbal and nonverbal cues to other people. We do not take turns encoding and decoding messages in this view. The transactional perspective could be likened to a game of catch in which all of the players had several balls that they would be both throwing to others and receiving from them as well as balls that they would be juggling to represent the thoughts that were being encoded and decoded within themselves. The term that is used for the juggling balls, or communication within the individual, is *intrapersonal communication*. You can see how the transactional perspective of communication accommodates Barnlund's notion of at least six perspectives being available in any two-person interaction (see fig. 1.1).

The analogy may appear complex and confusing, but it is far less complex than the transactional interpersonal communication situation it is alleged to represent. A variety of thoughts probably entered Morgan's and Paige's minds as they talked. They may have been considering alternative ways to relate to each other or alternative people with whom to relate. They may have reminisced over past experiences or contemplated a future without the other person. All of these thoughts may have been occurring simultaneously with their conversation and may have affected it. In addition, we are unaware of the extent to which they interrupted each other or began new thoughts when the other person was completing an earlier statement.

Interpersonal communication includes both content and relationship aspects. Interpersonal communication, to a greater extent than other communication situations, includes both content and relationship aspects. For instance, if a

Figure 1.1   The transactional perspective of communication.

public speaker informs us of the importance of wearing a seat belt when we are driving an automobile, we are more interested in the facts and figures that the speaker can supply to support his or her case than we are concerned about the relationship that exists between ourselves and the speaker. We might note that the speaker is an "expert" in the area, a local consumer advocate, or a neighbor, and this credibility may influence us to some degree, but not to the same extent that the content of the message does. On the other hand, if your dad tells you that unless you wear a seat belt, you will be unable to have access to the family car, the facts and figures of automobile safety take a back seat. The relationship that exists between your parent and yourself, including an understanding of the extent to which he will carry out his threat, is as persuasive in this case as was the logical evidence presented by the speaker in the public speaking example.

The abundance of nonverbal cues that exist in the interpersonal situation frequently clarify the relationship among communicators. For instance, you may choose the same words, "Sit down," when talking to your younger brother or sister who is rambunctiously running through a room as you do in offering a chair to your aging grandparent. The tone of your voice, the volume you select, your pitch and intonation all vary between the two situations and serve to suggest a far different relationship between the communicators. In the first instance you are commanding your younger sibling and implying a position of power or authority over his or her behavior; in the second case, you are showing deference and offering assistance. Although the content of the message is the same, the relationship that is suggested is different, but essential.

Interpersonal communication requires that all communicators share immediacy and salience of feedback.   In distinguishing interpersonal communication from other forms of communication, it is important to consider a concept commonly known as "feedback." Feedback can be likened to the "messages" that a computer is constantly monitoring about the gasoline mixture in modern fuel-injected automobiles or the "messages" that temperature variations cause in a thermostat sensor. *Feedback* is any response from other participants that influences the behavior of the communicator. Just as the computer monitors and thermostat sensors pick up changes in their environments that trigger changes in their own processes, the communicator "senses" his or her own environment to regulate his or her own behavior accordingly.

It was not long ago that communicators had to be *proximal*—that is, physically close to one another—for feedback to be fully communicative. "Interaction" by letters for example, simply is not the same as face-to-face interaction, primarily because the feedback is so restricted. You cannot continually adjust your behavior in accordance with what you read in the letter that, in turn, affect the writer of the letter, and so on. However, proximity itself is no longer a requirement for feedback to be fully functional. The advent of teleconferencing, videoconferencing, and videophones will revolutionize the way we think about and behave toward "long-distance" communication.

What features of feedback actually make interpersonal communication distinct? Immediacy and salience. *Immediacy* refers to the quickness with which feedback is received. The difficulty with letters is that responses take so long to reach their destination that they no longer have simultaneous influence on the interaction. It is the immediacy of feedback that allows behavior in interpersonal interaction to reciprocally, instantly, and simultaneously affect the behavior and meanings of all participants involved.

In addition to immediacy, however, the salience of feedback is important as well. *Salience* refers to the intensity, richness, and completeness of feedback. The reason that videophones are so much more communicative than telephones is the salience of their feedback. Suddenly, all the nonverbal information of the face is added to the vocal characteristics and content of the verbal messages. Suddenly, the message is received with a vividness and completeness that was missing before. Suddenly, you are able to interact with someone a thousand miles away in a manner very similar to face-to-face interaction. Clearly, this mode of interaction is not as salient as face-to-face, since mutual movement is not very feasible, and the senses of smell and touch are obviously limited. Still, the salience of the medium allows the feedback to be much more important in the interaction and to approximate face-to-face interaction. While few of us have been exposed to interactive video technologies, their innovation has forced us to reexamine the nature of the communication process and the characteristics that make interpersonal communication unique.

Interpersonal communication consists of communicators who are interdependent.   In intrapersonal communication, the communicator is totally independent of other people. In public speaking, the speaker is dependent upon an audience to serve as his or her listeners, and the audience is dependent upon the speaker for a particular message or address. The communicators in the interpersonal situation are neither totally dependent nor independent. Instead, their relationship is one of interdependence, or mutual dependence, among all of the communicators. The linear dependence that occurs in public communication is replaced with a circular interdependence. Morgan could not control Paige's responses, nor could Paige control Morgan's. Morgan could not force Paige to open up and share her feelings nor could Paige encourage Morgan to put more distance in their relationship. The two are clearly interdependent upon the other for their needs in this relationship. Tom could not gain a day off from work without assistance from Martha and Martha could not have her apology accepted without Tom's consent.

Another way of thinking about this is to consider the goals that Morgan and Paige had in this interaction. Both had certain goals they wished to achieve. At the core of the interaction, they wanted each other to believe their own versions of reality. Thus, Morgan "saw" their relationship reality in one way, while Paige "saw" a different reality. Since their relationship was important to both of them, they both minimally had the goal to convince the other of the correctness of their own perspective. Given this goal, it is easy to see that they are interdependent upon each other. Since Morgan cannot make the relationship into what she wants it to be unless Paige sees things the way she does, and Paige cannot have the relationship the way she desires unless Morgan accepts her view of things, they are dependent upon each other for their goal achievement.

Virtually all conversations you find yourself in are guided by goals of some sort, even though you may barely be aware of them. To the extent that the other persons in the conversation are instrumental to your goal achievement, you are dependent upon them. To the extent that you are in some way important to their goals, they are dependent upon you. To the extent that all parties to a conversation are dependent upon each other, they may be said to be interdependent. Sometimes this interdependence is as simple and basic as wanting someone with whom to "shoot the breeze." Even in this sense, you are clearly dependent upon the other person to maintain the conversation of which you are only a part.

Interpersonal communication is irreversible and unrepeatable.   Intrapersonal communication has the advantage of being reversible. We can support one candidate for the presidency one day and reverse ourselves and support an entirely different person at another time. Sometimes we have the good fortune of forgetting our previous commitment and believe that we are highly consistent. Intrapersonal communication has no public record; we can change our thoughts as frequently as we wish.

Public speeches have an advantage of being generally repeatable. No public speech is identical to another earlier speech, but politicians have demonstrated that a large number of public addresses can be very similar to each other. Stock speeches that deal with the economy, the price of oil, and poverty have been created and given, with minimal change, to a variety of different audiences.

Interpersonal communication is neither reversible nor repeatable. Think about the last argument you had with someone for whom you cared. You may have made statements that you later regretted. You may even have told the other person that you did not mean what you had said or that you wanted to "take it back." Unfortunately, we cannot treat interpersonal communication in the same way that we treat an undesired tape-recorded segment—by reversing the tape and erasing the message. We can forgive others and ourselves for the mistakes we make in interpersonal communication, but we cannot erase them.

Paige may never tell Morgan that the reason she shared so little of herself with Morgan was because of a personal problem about which she was embarrassed. Morgan cannot deny that she made a real attempt, in this instance, to reestablish their relationship. If the two decided, after this conversation, that they wanted to work on their relationship, they could not erase their differing perspectives at this point in time. If Tom later apologized to Martha for losing his temper, both would still recall that it occurred. Martha cannot pretend that she did not make a mistake and Tom cannot deny that he reacted strongly to her forgetfulness. We may interpret our conversations differently, but we cannot reverse them.

Similarly, we cannot repeat interpersonal communication. An interpersonal communicator may rehearse a particular message he or she wants to deliver to a friend, but beyond the initial statement, little of the preplanned message will be realized. The intervening factor in interpersonal communication is, of course, the communication from the other person. In responding to your initial message, the other communicator may dramatically change the topic, tone, or purpose of the conversation. We can no more repeat a conversation than we can repeat a pleasant evening with someone we love. Too many factors that are not under our control can intervene and alter the entire situation.

In describing interpersonal communication as irreversible and unrepeatable, communication can be viewed in much the same way as a river is conceived in the saying, "You can never step in the same river twice." The meaning is that the water in a stream is constantly flowing onward, always progressing forward, subtly shifting and altering the sandy foundation that contains its fluid. In much the same way, communication is constantly affecting the relationships that contain the communication. Thus, the relationship is never exactly the same at any two points in time. Communication is always molding, defining, shaping, and altering the relationship of which it is a part. You cannot repeat a message because the relationship is not exactly the same as it was when the message was first provided. Indeed, the first message altered the relationship itself, and therefore by definition, the relationship that contextualizes the next message cannot provide exactly the same meaning for the message as the first message received. In the same way, the first message cannot be reversed, since the original relationship cannot be "recaptured" in its original state and recreated exactly as it was. The past is gone, and the river will never be exactly like it was.

Systemic Nature of Interpersonal Communication

Interpersonal communication never occurs in a vacuum. It occurs within a group of people and within a large social system. The characteristics of a society impinge upon interpersonal communication, and interpersonal communication, by the same token, interacts with the society in which it occurs. The interdependence of the two implies mutual dependence. If we alter features in the society, the changes will affect every component in interpersonal communication. Changes in a feature of interpersonal communication will result in alterations in all aspects of society.

Identifying the Characteristics
of Interpersonal Communication

Tape-record or transcribe a conversation in which you are involved. Explain how each of the characteristics of interpersonal communication is involved in the conversation. What conclusions can you draw?

Interpersonal communication occurs within a group of people and within a larger social group.

Three global features of society have emerged in recent times that have direct impact on interpersonal communication. First, *our society has become increasingly large.* Our population has increased in size, and government, business, the military, law enforcement agencies, and schools have accordingly increased in size and scope. Multinational corporate structures have replaced the family farm. The increasing number of people and the increasing size of institutions may result in an individual feeling that he or she has less control or less importance than in earlier times. The individual and the family unit no longer hold center stage in the scheme of things.

As a result of the large size and scope of our society, individuals may feel unimportant or out of control. People seek importance and they seek control of their world. In order to meet these needs, individuals need to feel as though they are *fully participating* in their society. Our participation is important in interpersonal relationships, in our jobs, in our neighborhoods and communities, and in other institutions and organizations in our society.

When we no longer feel like we are a part of our society, our interpersonal relationships, and our communities, we begin to experience what is known as alienation and anomie. *Alienation* is the feeling that we no longer matter in society. Society seems too big, too unwielding, too distant, and too unresponsive to our needs. *Anomie* is the more personal experience of aloneness and separation from others. It is similar to the feeling of loneliness. Both these feelings are painful and destructive to both psychological health and the fabric of society itself. Communication is one of the only ways we come to feel integrated and part of the many networks that comprise our society. Communication takes on tremendous importance in this regard, as it becomes one of the primary means through which we maintain society and the many varied and complex human interrelationships that comprise it.

Second, *our society has become increasingly complex.* In addition to the overpopulation problem, we are now faced with an increasingly complicated set of interrelationships of a seemingly endless variety of subcultures. Individuals in our culture may develop in a variety of ways. Each person's destiny is no longer predictable. The greater number of options may be a mixed alteration in life: on the one hand, it is a luxury that we have not observed in earlier cultures; on the other, this complexity is difficult for persons to deal with psychologically. The increased choices may add confusion.

The complexity of our culture affects interpersonal communication because the manner in which we interact with others can take a variety of forms. The number of different relationships that we establish and the form that those relationships take can be confusing. We are called upon to play a variety of roles each day. In order for us to cope with our changing, numerous selves, we need to feel *centered.* Each of us needs to feel as though we have a core that defines a particular self. We need to feel as though we have a set of unique characteristics that we maintain as we relate to others.

A third alteration in our society is the speed with which changes occur. Change is part of a dynamic society, but the speed at which changes are now occurring is a new feature. The use of videotape recorders provides an example of a rapid change. Ten years ago, few (if any) homes had them; now more than half the households with television sets also have a videotape recorder. Yet all changes are not positive and the rapidity of the current changes make them difficult to examine and assess. In addition, the amount of knowledge that is needed in order to examine current changes is enormous, and, in some cases, the speed with which changes occur does not allow sufficient time to gain necessary information.

This rapid change affects our interpersonal communication. Responses that were appropriate at one point in time become completely inappropriate at another time. Male insensitivity, for instance, an accepted response at one time, has become outdated. Female unassertiveness, once preferred, is now frequently viewed as dysfunctional. The speed of the changes in our culture call upon us to be *flexible and adaptable.* We must be able to change our communication behaviors, as well as other behaviors, to respond in appropriate, functional ways.

As early as 1968, Warren Bennis and Philip Slater characterized our "temporary society" as one in which technology, mobility, and rapid cultural change was leading inexorably to a society comprised of short-lived and unstable systems. Slater notes that "social change is occurring so rapidly that every few years individuals at a given stage in the life cycle are experiencing a somewhat different social environment. . . ."[3] They argue that when the only constant in a society is change, then numerous changes must also occur in the social fabric and dynamics of that society. Among the conditions these writers predict are widespread alienation, anomie, disillusionment, greater strain on primary relationships such as marriage, and increasing uniformity and conformity in identities.

In one of their more intriguing and thought-provoking statements, Slater indicates that "contemporary transformations in social relationships largely take the form of converting spatial patterns into temporal ones."[4] In other words, our relationships used to be influenced primarily by proximity, by who we lived and worked near. But given the rate of social change and the high level of social mobility, we are altering our expectations about the very nature of our social relationships. One consequence the authors predict is greater "serial monogamy," in which people will have several spouses but stay married to only one at a time. The very concept of marriage "until death do us part" may be changing because of, or as a reflection of, the rapid changes in our society.

In addition to these global changes in our society, we can examine specific alterations that have occurred, or are currently occurring in our culture, largely as a result of the larger global changes. Five specific changes that we can identify and that affect interpersonal communication are the increasingly media-constructed culture, changes in the family structure or unit, the increasing number of older people in our population, the greater mobility of individuals, and the changes in the labor force.

Media-constructed culture.   The media, to an increasing extent, persuade people that they should look, feel, smell, or behave in certain prescribed ways. Advertising no longer limits women to the roles of homemaker or bathroom cleaner; instead, women are shown as "bringing home the bacon," but, of course, only if they cook it. Men are depicted as uncaring, unfeeling beings who are ruled by their hormones in a number of the popular evening adventure programs. Children, it appears, may be controlling the family as their consumer demands for sugar-sweetened cereals and readily breakable toys are fostered by the ads they see on TV. Beyond these stereotypical representations of people in the media, we need only consider the most recent presidential election to understand the effect of the media on the decision-making that occurs in our society.

Our media-constructed world influences our communication with others. Appropriate and inappropriate ways of behaving and communicating are clearly delineated on television. Television soap operas suggest that premarital and extramarital love affairs are commonplace. Situation comedies suggest that men and women often live together without marriage. Employment opportunities appear to be readily available when we view dramatic presentations of individuals aspiring to be physicians, lawyers, private investigators, or business executives in one program and we find that the person has achieved that goal in the next program. Television shows, commercials, billboards, magazines, and virtually the entire advertising market has developed an image of the perfect human body. Models are almost invariably tall, slender, perfectly complected, and sporting well-toned muscles and skin. Beauty is the norm on television. While there are notable exceptions, perhaps more today than ever before, television is still perpetuating standards of behavior, values, and appearances that are increasingly difficult to fully adhere to.

To the extent that our own feelings do not correspond to our television alter-egos, we feel disoriented, incomplete, or deviant. These negative feelings may interfere with our communication with others or we may try to behave in ways that are inconsistent with our feelings or our own reality. We need to establish our own identity separate from the media-created selves we view. We need to learn communication strategies that will assist us in achieving our goals without becoming a victim of a media-created system. In chapter 4 we will consider how clichés, euphemisms, and other distortions of reality, through language, interfere with our clear conception of who we are and what we want. In chapter 6 we will examine the role of self-disclosure in interpersonal communication and we will determine how an awareness of our self and an expression of that self through disclosure will assist us in this regard.

It is important to note here that we are not condemning television or the media in general. Indeed, television undoubtedly provides many valuable services to society at large. Media can inform, educate, and influence for noble causes and it can even serve to comfort and entertain those who are depressed, lonely, or outcast. The key is that it should not become our only source of reality or our primary means of contact with society and its standards. When that occurs, we fall victim to something that is always to some extent a fabrication.

The influence of media.   A few years back, the last episode of *Dallas* for the season ended with a mystery character shooting one of the main characters, J. R. It seemed that the nation was gripped by a sudden fascination with this cliff-hanger ending. Comedians laid blame on who shot J. R. Bumper stickers and T-shirts were sold entitling the bearer to the dubious yet self-proclaimed confession of "I shot J. R." Even many who never watched or followed such prime time soap operas were eager to discover the next season who really shot J. R. The influence of soap operas and the media in general on our lives is well-documented and apparent to most of us.

Identify some of the effects that media has had on you and on your communication behavior. What magazines do you read? What television programs do you regularly watch? What kind of music do you listen to? What books do you read? Identify some of the values that are expressed in these mediated sources. For instance, soap operas may support a more traditional lifestyle with women portrayed as wives and mothers or in traditionally female occupations such as nursing. Some of the current popular music suggests that sex is a natural outcome when you have established a positive relationship with another person—no matter how brief. News magazines may have a liberal or a conservative slant. Are your values similar to those that are suggested or incorporated in the media to which you regularly attend? How are they different? How are they similar? To what extent did the media affect your values? How does this affect your communication with others?

Changes in the family structure.   The family structure is changing in our culture. Some writers have suggested that the family, which has been a viable unit for centuries, may be disintegrating. Jane Howard, author of *Families*, disagrees. She writes:

> *They're saying that families are dying, and soon. They're saying it loud, but we'll see that they're wrong. Families aren't dying. The trouble we take to arrange ourselves in some semblance or other of families is one of the most imperishable habits of the human race. What families are doing, in flamboyant and dumbfounding ways, is changing their size and their shape and their purpose. Only 16.3 percent of this country's 56 million families are conventionally "nuclear," with breadwinning fathers, homemaking mothers, and resident children. That leaves 83.7 to find other arrangements, which are often so noisy that the clamor resulting is easily mistaken for a death rattle.[5]*

One of the primary reasons why the family structure has changed is that its core, the institution of marriage, has also changed dramatically. An extensive analysis of demographic trends has revealed that:

> *In recent years there have been considerable shifts in the decisions made by American adults regarding family formation and dissolution, and these shifts are consistent with the view that marriage is weakening as a social institution. Beginning in 1960 or earlier and continuing through 1980, there has been an increasing tendency to postpone marriage and perhaps to avoid it altogether; the probability that a marriage will end in divorce has risen steadily and even accelerated during the 1970s; and the rates of remarriage following divorce have either leveled off or continued to decline.[6]*

While marriage is far from a vanishing species, it is clear that the organism is evolving over time.

One of the causes for increased divorce may lie in the fact that people have not felt free *not* to marry. Gail Sheehy, author of *Passages: Predictable Crises of Adult Life,* supports this conclusion. She relates two interviews:

> *"I made a head decision," explained a writer. "This was the time. I didn't really have any deep desire to get married, but I thought I should. Doris expected it." He is now middle-aged and divorced.*

A lawyer admitting to the same automatic response was uncomfortable about parting with his romantic illusions; he is only 30. "Within six months before or after our graduation from law school, all but one of my friends got married. I don't think it could be that everybody met the right girl by coincidence. There must have been an element of it being the right time. Not to take away from Jeanie. . . ."[7]

Patterns of sexual activity affect interpersonal relationships. Improved birth control methods, the discovery of drugs to cure or curb venereal disease, and a new morality have all contributed to different patterns of sexual activity. Children are maturing far earlier today than in previous centuries. For example, a recent *Newsweek* article reports, "In the past century, the age of menarche, or first menstruation, has dropped from about 17 years to 12.5."[8] The earlier maturity may cause young people to feel obligated to experiment with sex in the same way that their parents felt obligated to marry by a certain age. Peer pressure encourages earlier sex. One interviewer writes:

Mary, a 15-year-old sophomore from Newton, Mass., recalls how she was swept up into the brave, sometimes bewildering, new world of adolescent hedonism. "I wasn't able to handle the pressure," she says. "I was part of a group in junior high that was into partying, hanging out and drinking. I started to have sex with my boyfriend and it was a real downer. It was totally against what I was, but it was important to be part of a group. Everybody was having sex."[9]

More recently, the fear of AIDS has altered sexual activity again.

Single parents now raise children. Just a few years ago it was relatively uncommon for a woman who became pregnant, but was not married, to have her child and raise it alone. In 1970 nearly one out of every eight children was living with a single parent, but by 1982 almost one-fourth of all children were in a single-parent family.[10] Abortion, too, was a seldom selected alternative. As a consequence, an unmarried woman who became pregnant twenty or thirty years ago had little choice but to give her child up for adoption. Today, with a number of alternatives available, women who surrender their children to adoption agencies often express regret. People today make choices about whether their interpersonal relationships will include children based on career choices, economic conditions, and concerns about who will provide the "primary parenting" of the child or children. At least one author has suggested that families might better be labeled "affinity groups"[11] because they are held together by mutual needs rather than by traditional blood ties.

The changing nature of the family affects our interpersonal communication. A family is a social system, a microstructure of the larger society. Any change in the family is reflected in changes in the entire family unit. The loss of any member—as a result of death, divorce, or a move caused by a change in employment—affects all of the other individuals in the family. Coping in a family that is significantly different from a family in which we were raised causes strain and need for adaptation. We need to maintain our freedom as well as allow closeness and intimacy in our family groupings. We may need to learn communication skills that will allow us to be open, honest, responsive, and fair to other family members. In chapter 14 we will consider the context of family communication in more detail. Chapters 8 and 9 will identify specific skills related to active listening and empathic understanding that are basic to the family setting.

Increasing older population.   The aging of America has been discussed by a number of authors. At the current time, between four thousand and five thousand people turn 65 each day. The median age of individuals, 27.9 in 1970, will approach 40 within the next two decades. And by 1999, instead of the present 22 million persons who are 65 or older, our country will include well over 30 million in this age group.

The increasing number of older people also affects our communication. We must learn how to cross the subcultural barrier of age. We must recognize the richness that variety among people allows. Communicating with persons older than ourselves may call for new strategies and increasing sensitivity to differences. Successful communication with elderly people may serve as its own reward. Consider your own interactions with persons who are 65 and older. You may have already experienced special communication problems with older people and you may have made attempts at overcoming these problems. Chapters 4 and 5, which consider differences in verbal and nonverbal cues as a result of age differences, among other factors, may provide some assistance to you. Also chapter 12, which focuses on conversations among strangers, acquaintances, and friends, might provide you with some ideas for communicating more effectively with older persons.

Increased mobility.   Americans appear to have movable roots from the increased mobility that is apparent in our culture. A massive migration appears to have occurred in the past ten years from the Snowbelt to the Sunbelt. States in the Northeast and North Central areas appear to be losing the largest populations. Pennsylvania, for instance, has lost approximately 400,000 residents in the past decade. Relocation may be a function of preferred climate or of employment advancement. Family units regularly move away from other relatives, and individuals within families may have a different residence than their "family" on a temporary or permanent basis. In a one-year span between 1984 and 1985, one-fifth of the American population (46.5 million) moved to new residences.[12]

The increased mobility affects our communication with others. We need to be able to initiate conversations with strangers, to overcome shyness, and to be able to relate in new ways. We need to establish relationships quickly with others and to be able to end relationships successfully. Our communication skills must include the abilities to maintain short-term, as well as long-term, relationships, We need to be able to make friends in new places and in new situations and we need to be open to others who have similar needs. Chapter 2, which considers interpersonal relationships, and chapter 12, which considers the conversations that occur among strangers, acquaintances, and friends, are both relevant to successfully dealing with increased mobility.

It is difficult to overemphasize the potential importance of these trends. As discussed earlier regarding the rapidity of change in our society, it seems that our mobility may be changing the way in which we make relationships and the expectations we have for the stability and durability of our relationships. If, for example, the average person moves every three years, it follows that persons need the skills necessary to initiate, establish, maintain, and, of course, end relationships in a satisfactory manner in a relatively brief period of time. How many relationships can you think of in your own life, other than those with your immediate family, that have lasted much longer than three years? How frequently do you interact with these people over time? How satisfying are these long-term relationships? As people move around more and more, the time span for relationships may become compressed. It is in this way that Bennis and Slater implied that time is replacing proximity as the primary dimension along which relationships occur.

Other, more subtle changes may be resulting from social mobility as well. For example, it is conceivable that people are developing more diverse repertoires of conversational topics, as they come in contact with more diverse people and social contexts. It may even be that people are incorporating more communicative flexibility and adaptability as they find themselves in new and different social environments. Those who do not adapt and incorporate such skills are likely to experience loneliness and alienation as they find themselves unable to establish satisfying relationships in their new environments.

Changes in the labor force.   Developments in the labor force are also in a state of flux. Current unemployment is expected to change. By 1990, the U.S. Department of Labor's Bureau of Labor Statistics has estimated that the U.S. labor force will expand by 15 percent. The desirability of this expansion will be dependent upon our level of unemployment at that time. Another contemporary development in the labor force is the large number of persons who are *misemployed*—hired to do work for which they have little interest, background, or ability. This problem is partly a result of the fact that the number of individuals who have college degrees is increasing at a far greater rate than are the professional-administrative positions to which they aspire and the fact that a large number of women have successfully entered the labor force.

Another striking development is the rapid movement of married women into the work force. Over half of all married women are employed outside the home, and, as of 1982, 49 percent of married mothers of preschool children held jobs outside the home.[13]

The alterations in the labor force are also of importance in our interpersonal communication. Each of us needs to be able to find employment that is appropriate for us. We must be able to sensitively determine the work environment that is suitable for our needs. We need communication skills that allow us to be clear in our statement of needs in the employment interview. We must demonstrate understanding to subordinates and superiors. Chapter 7, which considers the role of assertiveness in interpersonal communication may assist you in stating your needs to others; chapters 8 and 9 are especially useful in demonstrating your understanding of your coworkers as well as your superiors and subordinates; finally, chapter 15 offers specific advice on the interviewing context in interpersonal communication.

Relating Societal Changes to Interpersonal Communication

Interpersonal communication can be examined in terms of the larger social system in which we live. Society impinges upon our interpersonal communication, and, in turn, the communication that occurs among people affects the society. Similarly, interpersonal communication can be examined in terms of the smaller units in which it occurs. Interpersonal communication occurs in family units, in intimate settings, in the interview, and with acquaintances, strangers, and friends. Examine the brief interactions below and attempt to determine if conflict or misunderstanding occurred as a result of (1) a media-constructed reality, (2) changing nature of the family, (3) increasing number of older people, (4) increased mobility, or (5) alterations in the labor force.

_____ 1.   **Man:**   What do you mean you're leaving? I thought we had a good relationship. I've got a good job and I provided well for you. Didn't I buy you this house? Don't I work hard?

Woman: I want more than a house. I want someone who listens to me and cares about what I think. All I am to you is the mother of your children—I'm tired of being home with them all day. I guess I want to find out who I am.

Man: This all started because you enrolled in that psychology of women course. Women's libbers are destroying families.

Woman: No, I felt this way before I took that class.

_____ 2.   **Man:**   Hi, I noticed you across the room when I first came in.

Woman: Yes, I noticed you, too.

Man: Where are you from?

Woman: I go to school at the State University.

Man: Me, too. Hey, there's a bar across the street from the College of Communication. Why don't we go there and become better acquainted?

Woman: I don't think so—I hardly know you.

Man: (walking away disgustedly): What are you—some kind of tease?

Relating Societal Changes to Interpersonal Communication continued

_____ 3.   **Woman:**   I'm interested in applying for the position that you advertised.

             Man: I'm sorry, but that position has already been filled. Anyway, we were looking for someone much younger.

_____ 4.   **Woman:**   I've been experiencing a lot of headaches.

      Physician: Have you experienced any changes in your routine?

         Woman: Well, I'm working at two part-time jobs now.

      Physician: And you also have a family?

         Woman: Yes, I have a husband and three children.

      Physician: Is it possible that you're trying to do too much?

         Woman: I don't know—other people seem to manage all right. I spend about fifty hours away from home on my two jobs and going back and forth. And I'm also enrolled in a night class two nights a week.

      Physician: How much sleep are you getting?

         Woman: About five or six hours each night.

      Physician: I think you'd better try to slow down.

         Woman: I can't quit. Everybody calls me "Wonder Woman" and I'm not about to disappoint them.

_____ 5.   **Man:**   I understand that you're hiring nurses.

         Woman: Yes.

           Man: I'd like to apply.

         Woman: (laughing): You want to be a nurse?

           Man: Yes, I have experience and I have just moved here. My wife is a high-school teacher and we moved because she got a new position at Central High.

         Woman: I don't know where you came from, but we've never had a man apply for our nursing jobs before.

           Man: Are you going to give me an application form?

After you have identified the cause for the conflict or misunderstanding, rewrite each dialogue in order to resolve the problem. Have you had similar interactions in which another person misunderstood you because of one of these specific changes in our society? Explain how you handled it. What specific skills did you use? Would you have handled the situation differently if you were engaged in the interaction again? How?

The Improvement of Interpersonal Communication

Can we increase our interpersonal communication competence? At least two answers to this question have been offered. The older, historical answer is clearly "no." Interpersonal communication has not been systematically investigated nor taught until very recently. People apparently believed that competence in this mode of communication was a skill that people possessed or did not possess. Or, they felt that nearly everyone was already skilled in interpersonal communication and did not need further training. In either case, the response was that interpersonal communication competence could not be increased.

More recently, individuals in our culture have suggested that interpersonal communication skills can be easily taught. Best sellers including *Body Language, Be the Person You Were Meant to Be, I'm OK—You're OK, How to Read a Person Like a Book, When I Say No, I Feel Guilty,* and *I Ain't Much Baby— But I'm All I've Got* that gained popularity in the 1960s and 1970s suggest the self-help nature of interpersonal communication. Short courses on *est,* transcendental meditation, relaxation techniques, assertiveness training, and marital communication suggest that interpersonal communication can be learned in a few easy lessons. Some trainers, consultants, and gurus suggest that instant gratification is available through their workshops or programs. More often than not, such promises are ill-founded and many even border on fraudulent. While much serious work is being done in the areas of training and learning interpersonal skills, much of the "layperson's" market is littered with intuitive, poorly-researched, and sometimes patently false advice.[14]

Some communication researchers have rejected the earlier notion that interpersonal communication skills cannot be taught. We view interpersonal communication as a set of behaviors that can be systematically examined, learned, and taught. On the other hand, we recognize the limited value of "instant" interpersonal communication competence. Our culture has provided us with an abundance of "quick-and-easy" products and processes. We may find that some of these are acceptable and appropriate substitutes—instant coffee, instant oatmeal, instant banking, and instant car washes. A number of such innovations may be less satisfactory—"one-night-stands," 7-day diets, coffee makers that are designed to malfunction within a year, and paper plates that fall apart before you are through using them. Interpersonal relationships that are not designed to last beyond a weekend, communication skills that only assist us in learning a single behavior, or communication competence which considers our social selves to the exclusion of our task-related selves similarly leave us with feelings of frustration, loneliness, and limited success.

Barbara Gordon, an award-winning television producer, details her experiences when she quit taking Valium in her book, *I'm Dancing as Fast as I Can.* Gordon experienced a complete breakdown, lost the man with whom she lived, and lost her career. After she had recovered, Gordon wrote:

> *I think I know who I am now because of a new strength in myself, and the strength of the people who have been close to me. It is better to remember them than all the people who contributed to the illness along the way. No more scapegoats. And no happy ending either, no epiphany, no single moment of synthesis and complete understanding with flashing lights and the roar of drums. Long, laborious, painful, expensive, frustrating and time-consuming, living is. But living is preferable. As Woody Allen says, "I'm not afraid of death, I just don't like the hours."*[15]

Nonfiction books that were written longer ago might have ended with a fictional "happy ever after" message. Gordon's self-revelations are more realistic and reflect our current understanding that we have no "easy answers." We live in a very complicated, changing, difficult time. Our romantic longings for happiness, success, and lasting love that come in a moment and remain for a lifetime are only dreams.

Interpersonal communication competence can be increased; but we cannot become more successful in our interpersonal relationships in a few easy lessons or by simply reading a book on the subject. Becoming more successful in interpersonal communication requires a commitment to learning various communication skills, to understanding differences in communication situations, and to practicing those abilities. Finally, we recognize that our understanding of the theory and practice of effective interpersonal communication may not always result in desired outcomes. Interpersonal communication, by its nature, involves other people who may have conflicting goals or perspectives.

The Importance of Flexibility

The improvement of your interpersonal communication skills is highly dependent upon an underlying approach to human behavior. *Behavioral flexibility* is the ability to alter behavior in order to adapt to new situations and to relate in new ways when necessary. It provides the key to success in interpersonal communication situations. To the extent that we can identify and describe specific ways of behaving differently and to the extent that we can put our understanding into practice, we move toward effectiveness in interpersonal communication.

The importance of flexibility has been demonstrated in other areas of inquiry. Biologists, botanists, and other scientists have explained the extinction of certain animals and plants as a function of their inability to adapt to a

Behavioral flexibility, the ability to alter behavior in order to adapt to new situations and to relate in new ways when necessary, provides the key to success in interpersonal communication situations.

changing environment. Changes in the physical environment necessitate physical changes in order to survive. Plants and animals that did not adapt to major ecological changes are no longer present in our environment.

Similarly, psychologists and social scientists have shown interest in psychological flexibility. Most recently, researchers have demonstrated the superiority of *androgyny*—holding both masculine and feminine traits—over our past notion that men should be masculine and women should be feminine. Essentially, psychologists have shown that androgynous individuals are more flexible and therefore more successful in various kinds of situations.

Behavioral flexibility in interpersonal communication is also important. Changes in the physical environment require physiological changes in order to survive; changes in our society and our behavioral environment require behavioral changes if we are to survive sociologically and psychologically. To the extent that we refuse to adapt our behavior, we risk the extinction of personal and economic satisfaction. Our personal and professional goals can be achieved if we are willing to understand and practice behavioral flexibility.

Our society continues to change and we, as individuals, change. Our attitudes and values at eighteen may or may not reflect our feelings when we are thirty. For instance, have you considered how you would cope with the situation of losing your job after you have spent years training for it? You might not have thought about how you would handle a child with a serious congenital defect. If you marry a person who has a profession that requires a great deal of public relations work or entertaining, will you have the interpersonal communication skills to assist your spouse with his or her career? Rapid professional advancement may not be on your agenda, but it may occur. A death in your family may cause changes in your relationships. All of these changes and many more may occur in your life. Such changes require flexibility. Gail Sheehy, author of *Passages: Predictable Crises of Adult Life,* recommends that we acknowledge these changes and that we alter our behavior to respond to them appropriately.

> *We are not unlike a particularly hard crustacean. . . . With each passage from one stage of human growth to the next we, too, must shed a protective structure. We are left exposed and vulnerable—but also yeasty and embryonic again, capable of stretching in ways we hadn't known before. . . . Coming out of each passage, though, we enter a longer and more stable period in which we can expect relative tranquility and a sense of equilibrium regained. . . . A developmental stage, however, is not defined in terms of marker events; it is defined by changes that begin within. . . . We must be willing to change chairs if we want to grow. There is no permanent compatibility between a chair and a person. And there is no one right chair. What is right at one stage may be restricting at another or too soft.*[16]

Becoming a Competent Communicator

This text is designed to assist people in becoming more competent in their interpersonal communication skills. This competency-based approach involves the identification of the characteristics, abilities, and qualities that distinguish effective interpersonal communicators from those who are ineffective. It proceeds by assisting people to acquire those skills that are necessary in gaining control of their environment.

The word *control,* in this context, does not refer to gaining a superior position over another person or group of people, but rather to the successful and satisfying ability to achieve intended outcomes by the communicator in ways that are appropriate to the interpersonal context. More specifically, *interpersonal competence* can be defined as the ability to engage in appropriate and effective interaction. Interaction is *effective* if it accomplishes the goals of the communicator, and it is *appropriate* if it avoids violating any valued rules, expectations, or norms of the relational context in which the behavior occurs.

Effectiveness in interpersonal communication requires that persons are able to understand, explain, and make predictions about interpersonal communication situations and that they are able to behave in a manner that is consistent with their understanding and their intentions. Appropriateness in interpersonal communication requires that persons attend to the others they are interacting with, show concern and interest in the values and standards of the others, and incorporate to some extent or another the interests of the others. Ultimately, the ideal or competent communicator is one who is capable in any given situation of attaining personal goals while simultaneously maintaining the integrity of the interpersonal relationship within which those goals are achieved. Competence is not demonstrated by persons who can theorize about interpersonal communication but are unable to act upon their knowledge. Nor is a person competent who accidentally achieves his or her goals in a particular interpersonal communication situation but cannot explain why he or she met success. Both understanding and behavior are necessary requisites for the competent interpersonal communicator. The material in this text will assist you in becoming more knowledgeable about interpersonal communication and will allow you to improve in your ability to explain and diagnose communication situations. The delineation of skills and the activities and exercises will help you become more effective in your interpersonal communication behavior. Together, the theory and the practice will allow you to become a more competent interpersonal communicator.

As you read this text, you should keep in mind the underlying notion of communication competence. You will read about the importance of various communication skills and you will be encouraged to experiment with the addition of these skills to your communication repertoire. Your effectiveness as an interpersonal communicator will depend upon your ability to adapt to new situations and to relate in new ways when necessary. You will be called upon to identify and describe specific behavioral choices in particular situations and to select the appropriate choice given all of the alternatives. None of the skills described in this book will individually assist you in becoming more effective, nor will the regular practice of any set of these skills be all that you will be required to know and implement. Instead, you will understand and be able to act upon your understanding in order that you can determine, given all of the situational and human variables, the appropriate behavioral choices for you, the competent interpersonal communicator.

Summary

You may view interpersonal communication as a topic that is relatively unimportant for you or you may see it as an area of study that is highly complex and difficult to understand. You may view it as something that anyone can master in a relatively short amount of time or as something that cannot be taught. You may view success in interpersonal communication to be largely an accident or a result of careful and deliberate choice. In this chapter we attempt to dispel some of these points of view about interpersonal communication.

Interpersonal communication is highly important when we consider the amount of time we devote to engaging in it. While it consists of interactions among complex human organisms, some generalizations can be made. We cannot master the skills involved in interpersonal communication in a few easy lessons, but we can become more competent in this area of human behavior. Success in interpersonal relationships is not a matter of chance but the result of an understanding of certain components and an application in specific contexts.

We define interpersonal communication, broadly, as the *process of transaction between people from which meaning is mutually derived* and further clarify the concept by stating that it begins with self, requires that all communicators share immediacy and salience of feedback, consists of communicators who are interdependent, is transactional, includes both content and relationship aspects, and is irreversible and unrepeatable. Interpersonal communication is systemic in nature, which means that it exists within larger systems and smaller subsystems. Global features of our society, including an increased size, an increased complexity, and an accelerated pace, all affect interpersonal communication. Similarly, specific features of our culture including the media-constructed reality, the changes in family structure, the increasing number of older people, the greater mobility of individuals, and the changes in the labor force similarly affect our interactions with others.

You can become a more competent interpersonal communicator. Interpersonal communication is a complex activity that cannot be improved in a few simple lessons, but a commitment to learning a number of communication skills, to understanding differences in communication situations, and to practicing those abilities can result in improvement. Our behavioral flexibility, or ability to alter our behavior in order to adapt to new situations and to relate in new ways when necessary, is important to success in interpersonal communication. Becoming more competent in interpersonal communication will allow you to gain control of your environment.

Notes

1. Charles T. Brown and Charles Van Riper, *Speech and Man* (Englewood Cliffs, N.J.: Prentice Hall, 1966), pp. 1–2.
2. Dean C. Barnlund, "A Transactional Model of Communication," in *Foundations of Communication Theory,* ed. Kenneth K. Sereno and C. David Mortensen (New York: Harper & Row, Publishers, 1970), pp. 98–101. Another interesting exploration of these notions can be found in R. D. Laing, H. Phillipson, and A. R. Lee, *Interpersonal Perception* (New York: Harper & Row, 1966).

3. Warren G. Bennis and Philip E. Slater, *The Temporary Society* (New York: Harper & Row, 1968).

4. Bennis and Slater, p. 92.

5. Jane Howard, *Families* (New York: Simon & Schuster, 1978), p. 13.

6. T. D. Espenshade, "Marriage Trends in America: Estimates, Implications, and Underlying Causes," *Population and Development Review* 11 (1985): 193–245.

7. From *Passages* by Gail Sheehy, pp. 119–20. Copyright © 1974, 1976 by Gail Sheehy. Reprinted by permission of the publisher, E. P. Dutton, Inc.

8. "The Games Teen-Agers Play," *Newsweek,* September 1, 1980, p. 51.

9. "The Games Teen-Agers Play," *Newsweek,* September 1, 1980, p. 48. See also M. D. Newcomb, "Notches on the Bedpost: Generational Effects of Sexual Experience," *Psychology* 23 (1986): 37–46.

10. Espenshade, p. 213.

11. Harold G. Shane, "Forecast for the 80's," *Today's Education,* April–May, 1979, p. 62.

12. Associated Press, *Dallas Times Herald,* December 27, 1987.

13. Arland Thornton and Deborah Freedman, "The Changing American Family," *Population Bulletin* 38 (1988): 4.

14. See Kenneth Cinnamon and Dave Farson, *Cults and Cons: The Exploitation of the Emotional Growth Consumer* (Chicago: Nelson-Hall, 1979).

15. Barbara Gordon, *I'm Dancing as Fast as I Can* (New York: Harper & Row, 1979), p. 281.

16. From *Passages* by Gail Sheehy, pp. 24–25. Copyright © 1974, 1976 by Gail Sheehy. Reprinted by permission of the publisher, E. P. Dutton, Inc.

Additional Readings

Berger, Charles R. and Bradac, James J. *Language and Social Knowledge.* London: Edward Arnold, 1982.

Bostrom, Robert N., ed. *Competence in Communication: A Multidisciplinary Approach.* Beverly Hills, Calif.: Sage, 1984.

Dance, Frank E. X., ed. *Human Communication Theory.* New York: Harper & Row, 1982.

Fisher, B. A. *Interpersonal Communcation: Pragmatics of Human Relationships.* New York: Random House, 1988.

Glaser, Susan R. *Toward Communication Competency: Developing Interpersonal Skills.* New York: Holt, Rinehart & Winston, 1980.

Haslett, Beth. *Communication: Strategic Action in Context.* Hillsdale, N.J.: Lawrence Erlbaum Associates, 1987.

Knapp, Mark and Miller, Gerald eds. *Handbook of Interpersonal Communication.* Beverly Hills, Calif.: Sage, 1985.

Miller, Gerald R. and Steinberg, Mark. *Between People: A New Analysis of Interpersonal Communication.* Chicago: Science Research Associates, Inc., 1975.

Miller, Gerald R., ed. *Explorations in Interpersonal Communication.* Beverly Hills, Calif.: Sage, 1976.

Reardon, Kathleen K. *Interpersonal Communication: Where Minds Meet.* Belmont, Calif.: Wadsworth, 1987.

Roloff, Michael E. *Interpersonal Communication: The Social Exchange Approach.* Beverly Hills, Calif.: Sage, 1981.

Rubin, Rebecca B. and Nevins, Randi J. *The Road Trip: An Interpersonal Adventure.* Prospect Heights, Ill.: Waveland Press, 1988.

Spitzberg, Brian H. and Cupach, William R. *Interpersonal Communication Competence.* Beverly Hills, Calif.: Sage, 1984.

Wilmot, William W. *Dyadic Communication,* 3d ed. Westminster, Md., Random House, 1987.

An Introduction to Interpersonal Relationships

Charlie Brown may be expressing a common sentiment in this cartoon. The nature of interpersonal relationships, including love relationships, is difficult to explain and to discuss. In this chapter we will consider the nature of such relationships. We will note that interpersonal relationships are characterized by mutuality of definition, stages, multidimensionality, continuity, complexity, and changeableness. You probably are already aware of the importance of interpersonal relationships in your own life, but we will offer some specific ways in which interpersonal relationships are important. Finally, we will elaborate on stages that appear to occur in the development and deterioration of most interpersonal relationships.

Identifying Relationships

Each of us is involved in a number of relationships. Identify some of the relationships in which you are involved by completing this exercise. Fill in each blank with some of the names of persons who fit the description given. After you have filled in the first set of blanks, analyze the persons in each group and attempt to determine common characteristics or descriptors that exist.

	Names of persons	Common characteristics
Family members	_____	_____
	_____	_____
Casual friends	_____	_____
	_____	_____
Close friends	_____	_____
	_____	_____
Dating partners	_____	_____
	_____	_____
Work colleagues	_____	_____
	_____	_____

Are you surprised by the characteristics that identify most of your family members, friends, and others? What conclusions can you draw?

The Nature of Interpersonal Relationships

Definition of Relationships

Relationships may be defined as associations or connections, but they are actually far more complex than such a simple definition suggests. In the introduction to their book, *Theory of Relationships,* Silverman and Silverman explain:

> *Consider for a moment a passenger ship in New York harbor, whose destination is Southampton. It is a "ship," of course, because we choose to call it "a ship," and an entity because we define it as one.*
>
> *It is also, among other things, engines, cabins, decks, and dinner-gongs—these are some of its parts or components. If we were to rearrange the components, or lay them out side by side, the entity would no longer be a ship, but perhaps look more like a junk-yard. The "parts," then, may be said to "make up" the whole, but the whole is defined by these parts in a particular relationship, each one not only to those attached to it, but also to the whole itself.*[1]

The point that Silverman and Silverman appear to be making is that the whole is greater than the sum of its parts when we are considering relationships. Because the parts of the ship are arranged in that particular way, the whole can be used for transport, recreation, sport, leisure, and the like on water. Were the parts arranged in any number of other patterns or relationships, then the whole would be an entirely different entity. In short, what makes the ship a ship is not its individual parts, but the particular relationship of these parts to one another. In this way, the whole becomes "more" than simply the contribution of all of its specific components. An understanding of this elusive notion is essential in dealing with the complexity of human relationships.

An *interpersonal relationship* is made up of two or more individuals in a developing and interdependent process of functioning, characterized by certain recurring patterns of interaction. Interpersonal relationships are different from the individuals involved. A married couple is not simply two individuals; a family is not simply a group of five people; and a business partnership is not simply three people. In each case, the relationship—marriage, family, or business relationship—is more than the sum of its parts. Behaviors and attitudes of an individual may change in the context of a relationship.

For instance, you may be a beer-drinking, fun-loving, liberal Democrat who believes in open communication, but who lacks an ability to empathize with others. You begin to date (have a relationship with) a person who is a teetotaler, a serious, conservative Republican who has difficulty in self-disclosing (revealing who he or she really is) but is a good listener. As your relationship develops, you begin to drink less beer, but you continue to enjoy good times. You find that serious conversations can be rewarding although you tend to dominate them with personal information. Your partner still does not drink, but he or she begins to acknowledge the enjoyment of parties. This person improves in the ability to provide feedback to your self-disclosures and demonstrates a great deal of empathy for you. The two of you change your behavior and attitudes as a result of the relationship. You may or may not exhibit your older behavior and attitudes in other relationships; however, you have adapted in this current relationship. To the extent that we are sensitive to the relationship and are able to demonstrate behavioral flexibility, relationships effect changes in the individuals involved. These changes produce unique entities in the relationship—distinct from that which would have existed without the individuals interacting together.

Consistent patterns of interaction are also involved in interpersonal relationships. These patterns of interaction may be described as rules governing the relationship. These rules may be generally understood across a variety of contexts or they may be unique to a particular relationship. For example, we normally greet someone whom we know with a relatively content-free message. We may say, "Hi, how are you doing?" "What's new?" "Great day, isn't it?" "I'm surprised to see you!" or simply "Hello." In each of these cases we are acknowledging both the presence, and our recognition of the other person, but we are exchanging very little information. This pattern is typical across a wide variety of relationships.

On the other hand, patterns of interaction may be highly specific to a particular relationship. For example, you might hug a family member whom you have not seen for some time, but you may rarely show affection to friends in this way. You might spend fifteen minutes to a half-hour talking to your spouse after you are in bed each night. You might talk to a close friend on the telephone for a long period of time three or four times a week. You may have a special term of endearment for your brother or sister. We will consider the general stages through which most relationships move later in this chapter. These stages are suggestive of certain patterns of interaction that have some consistency across most relationships. In chapters 12 through 15 we will consider some particular contexts which may include unique patterns of interaction, and the concept of rules will be examined specifically in chapter 10.

Characteristics of Interpersonal Relationships

Let us build on our general understanding of relationships by defining the characteristics of interpersonal relationships. We can identify seven specific characteristics. Interpersonal relationships (1) have a mutuality of definition, (2) have stages, (3) are multidimensional, (4) are complimentary, symmetrical, noncomplementary, or anticomplementary, (5) exist on a continuum, (6) are complex, and (7) are constantly in flux. Let us consider each of these in more detail.

Interpersonal relationships have a mutuality of definition.   Mutuality of definition is a key concept in understanding interpersonal relationships. Jay Haley explains this notion:

> When two people meet for the first time and begin to establish a relationship, a wide range of behavior is potentially possible between them. . . . As the two people define their relationship with each other, they work out together what sort of communicative behavior is to take place in this relationship. From all the possible messages they select certain kinds and reach agreement that these rather than others shall be included.[2]

In other words, we do not independently define our relationships; instead, we define them in conjunction with the other person or the other people involved.

Universal rules do not govern interpersonal relationships. Individuals involved in relationships create their own rules that are agreed upon for a particular relationship. The same individual may find himself or herself involved in a multitude of relationships—each with an entirely different set of rules. The definitions that are agreed upon in a particular relationship become a characteristic of that relationship rather than a characteristic of any of the individuals involved in the relationship.

The many varied types of human relationships, and the many unique ways in which rules are developed to define and regulate these relationships, help to explain why so many people are interested in understanding and observing relationships. Many of us are curious about marriages that include a "house-husband" and a working wife; a gay relationship that, except for the sex of the partners, appears to be a typical marriage; a business relationship in which the subordinates do not defer to the person in charge; and parent-child relationships that appear to be based on total equality. We are interested in alternative relationship styles and interpersonal relationships that are different from our own.

The love relationship is particularly interesting and offers a multitude of styles. People "in love" often behave in ways that others do not understand. For instance, you may find yourself staying up all night to talk to the person you love, even though you would be unwilling to spend the same amount of time preparing for a class. You might consider quitting a job, dropping out of school, or moving in order to accommodate your love relationship. You might begin to drink, go on a diet, or run five miles every day because of your partner. Sharp changes in your behavior and unusual new behaviors may result in surprise, or even disapproval, from others.

On a less positive side, it is important to recognize that the complete deterioration of a relationship happens when little or no mutuality of definition occurs. Disagreeing on one aspect of the relationship—who takes out the garbage, how the kitchen should be cleaned, who should initiate sexual intimacies, when people should talk to each other—may not result in the demise of a relationship, but disagreement on a variety of these matters, or extremely important matters, can signal major differences in relationship definition and may result in the end of the relationship.

Interpersonal relationships have recognizable stages.   A number of researchers and authors have suggested that interpersonal relationships develop following a fairly regular series of stages, or sequences. Later in this chapter, specific stages in the development and deterioration of relationships will be examined. At this point, we should merely be aware that interpersonal relationships frequently follow a similar sequence. When a relationship does not follow a predictable sequence, it may be upsetting to the individuals involved. If a person who has just met another asks the other to become sexually intimate, the second person will probably not respond positively. Similarly,

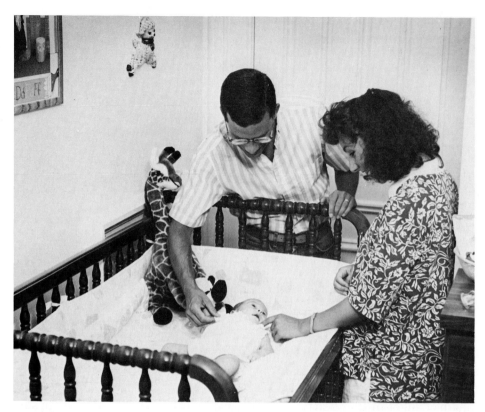

Interpersonal communication occurs in relationships that are complex and constantly in flux.

when the termination of a relationship happens without warning and without the preceding stages that suggest that the relationship is not healthy, shock and surprise may occur. Gail Sheehy, in *Passages: Predictable Crises of Adult Life,* writes about such an event:

> *An exceptionally alert and active woman of 60 had lived a long and comfortable married existence in the Fifth Avenue Hotel. Her husband died. She found herself, overnight, without the funds to carry on. She had no choice but to leave her home and all her friends of forty years. The only relative who could take her in was a disagreeable sister-in-law down South. Despite this abrupt and total dislocation, the widow went gracefully about closing up her New York life. At dinner the night before she was to leave, her minister and friends praised her remarkable strength of character. The next morning they came by to drive the widow to the airport; no one answered the door. They broke in and found her sprawled on the bathroom floor in her underclothes. No bump, no bruise*

explained it as a slip. She was simply unconscious. Baffled, her friends drove the widow to the hospital. The intern found nothing on prelimi- nary examination. . . . She began to alter even beyond the recogni- tion of her friends. She fumbled over simple questions, confused names and dates, and eventually lost her orientation altogether. Her minister and friends retreated in polite horror. Within a matter of hours she had disintegrated into a babbling old woman.[3]

The termination of this relationship and its attendant changes resulted in the woman's response. The lack of warning and the suddenness of the change probably contributed to the disintegration of psychological and physical health of this woman. It is easy to overlook the extent to which we depend on our relationships with others to order our world, structure our experience, and make basic predictions about the outcomes of our actions. When this wom- an's established relationship dissolved, an entire way of life (an entire "reality") ended. Things that were once understood and taken for granted became uncertain and difficult. One can only speculate that the woman's re- sponse would have been different if she had been prepared by the sequence of typical stages in the termination of a relationship.

Interpersonal relationships are multidimensional.   Individuals are not simple, one-dimensional animals. Each of us is composed of a variety of character- istics, sets of competing needs, a multitude of experiences, and different as- pirations. When we come into a relationship with another person, the large number of dimensions that identify us interact with a similarly large number of features that define the other. The relationship takes on a set of character- istics that include all of these dimensions but they are organized in ways that are unique to the particular relationship.

Relationship Development

In order to understand the pattern of development of interpersonal relation- ships, keep a journal in which you record your specific reactions to a particular relationship. First, record how you felt when you first met the other person. Who initiated the conversation? How did each of you respond? How much self- disclosure occurred? Next, record how you felt at subsequent meetings with this person. Did your initial feelings change? Did you engage in more disclosures of personal information? Did one of you determine how quickly the relationship grew? Did you attempt to speed up or slow down the relationship development process? Finally, if the relationship has now terminated, why did it end? Did one of you initiate the ending of the relationship? How did you feel when the rela- tionship was ending? What conclusions can you draw from this analysis of a spe- cific relationship? Do you believe that your conclusions are generalizable to other relationships in which you have been engaged? How is it similar or different?

One dimension of relationships that has been considered extensively is the amount of rigidity in a relationship. Some relationships are characterized by their predictability. Consider your parents' relationship when you were growing up. Did their daily routine follow a predictable pattern? When conflict occurred, was the pattern by which it was resolved fairly similar, time after time? Were certain remarks by your mother followed by a similar response from your father each time they occurred? Other relationships are characterized by their changing nature. When you ask your friend to join you for dinner, he or she may happily accept one evening, but appear to be angry that you even asked on another occasion.

Rigidity in a relationship may be a result of one individual's inability to respond in different ways. In the first chapter we discussed the importance of behavioral flexibility and we emphasize that concept here. The person who can only respond in one way severely limits himself or herself in a relationship. For instance, the person who is unassertive may find success in some relationships—as a customer, as an employee, or as a submissive spouse—but may discover that unassertiveness interferes in other relationships—as a customer with a legitimate complaint, as an employee who is being treated unfairly, or as a submissive spouse who is being treated without love.

To the extent that individuals and relationships have flexibility, their chances for success improve. The effective relationship adapts to changes in the individuals who are involved, the communication norms, the setting, and the larger society. Improvement in relationships requires change rather than self-defeating rigidity.

Communication researchers have identified a variety of dimensions of interpersonal relationships; however, two universal components have been identified. These two dimensions are *amount of control* and *emotional tone*. The importance of these two components in analyzing human interactions have been identified by researchers in psychology, sociology, and child development.[4] You may find them useful in analyzing your own interpersonal relationships.

The amount of control that a person exhibits in an interpersonal relationship refers to his or her attempts to direct and define the relationship. The Doonesbury cartoon (see p. 47) provides a particularly apt, although somewhat subtle, example of control in a relationship. Joanie's expression of her feelings, "I'm just a little depressed," are placed in a context of female needs by her male friend. The relevance of this exchange is not its content, but the relational statement. In effect, Joanie's friend is stating that he feels he has control of the relationship, is capable of explaining Joanie's feelings, and that Joanie's depression is a result of her need for others rather than a personal feeling. Her response, "Now I'm really depressed," also contains an important relational statement. Joanie may be stating that she rejects her friend's attempt to control the interpersonal situation, that she rejects control of her feelings by another person, or that she recognizes that a continued relationship with this person may include additional attempts at control.

The control dimension in interpersonal relationships has been viewed as a continuum with dominance at one end and submission at the other. The two extremes, dominance and submission, appear to have a reciprocal relationship in interactions. In other words, one person's attempt at controlling the interaction is followed by the other person's willingness to allow him or her to control it. Many lasting relationships are based on a pattern of one person's dominance and another person's submissiveness. Research in male/female communication and in communication patterns in organizations between superiors and subordinates have provided extensive support for the reciprocal nature of dominance and submission in interpersonal relationships.[5]

The emotional tone of the relationship can similarly be viewed as a continuum with affection at one end and hostility at the other. This dimension has also been called an affiliation-aggression or a loving-distrusting dimension. Relationships can exist at any point on this continuum. Affection and hostility appear to have a relationship of similarity to each other. If one person

Multidimensionality in Relationships

Interpersonal relationships are multidimensional, but you and the other person involved in the relationships might disagree about where, on a number of scales, your relationship falls. Examine the following conversation and complete the scales at the end. This dialogue occurred in a neighborhood bar on a Friday night.

Sarah: It's really late.

Clark: I sure enjoy unwinding at the end of the week.

Sarah: Do you know how late it is?

Clark: No, but I'm having a good time.

Sarah: Maybe we should start thinking about going home.

Clark: Hey, there's Sally and Bob.

Sarah: Clark, I have a lot to do tomorrow and I'm really tired.

Clark: Let's ask Sally and Bob over for a nightcap and then we'll call it a night.

Sarah: You know that one thing will lead to another and we won't go for another hour or two!

Clark: You know I work hard all week and I need one night to relax. All you ever do is complain. If you want to go home, take the keys and go. I'll find my own way.

Sarah: I'm not leaving without you.

Clark: Fine, fine, let's just go before I lose my temper.

Based on your reaction to this brief conversation, put an "X" on each of the scales where you believe Sarah sees this relationship and an "O" where Clark might place it. What is the significance of the difference in perspective that the two might have? Do you believe that, if this is a typical exchange, this couple has a good or poor chance of enjoying a long relationship? Why? Discuss this exercise with your classmates.

1. PREDICTABLE ——————————— UNPREDICTABLE
2. POSITIVE ——————————— NEGATIVE
3. ENJOYABLE ——————————— UNENJOYABLE
4. CONTROLLABLE ——————————— UNCONTROLLABLE
5. RELAXING ——————————— UNRELAXING
6. EXCITING ——————————— UNEXCITING
7. TOLERANT ——————————— INTOLERANT
8. CALM ——————————— AGITATED
9. EASY ——————————— DIFFICULT
10. OPEN ——————————— CLOSED

shows affection for another, the second person is most likely to respond with some amount of affection; if one person is hostile to another, he or she will probably be treated in kind. We are all aware of affectionate relationships that continue over time and we know of relationships that are filled with hostility that appear to last. Relationships in which one person is highly affectionate and the other is highly hostile are less likely. Affection from one person that is not matched by the other may mark the termination of a relationship.

Interpersonal relationships can be complementary, symmetrical, noncomplementary, or anticomplementary.   These concepts derive from the former discussion of the basic dimensions of interpersonal relationships. Each pattern involves a certain type of reciprocity (response pattern). Furthermore, the particular response pattern differs depending on which dimension is being considered. For example, given the dimensions of affective tone and amount of control, A and B have a *complementary relationship* if both tend to like each other, but one tends to be controlling while the other tends to be passive. In other words, control and affect complement each other in different ways. The underlying principle of complementarity is that two or more persons' interpersonal tendencies are compatible and facilitative together. Compatibility can also be seen at a more specific level, such as when an answer follows a question, an assertion is followed by agreement, and so on.

Whereas complementary relationships reveal a kind of "fit" in which the interpersonal system can be considered as a "cooperative" system, *symmetrical relationships* operate in a manner more akin to competition. Dominating behavior evokes dominant responses, whereas affiliative behavior is responded to by dislike and repulsion in symmetrical relationships. Episodes of "one-upsmanship," in which each person consciously or unconsciously attempts to match or "outdo" the other person, illustrate symmetry. At a more specific level, symmetry can be seen when an assertion or statement of opinion is followed by an assertion or a counterassertion.

Noncomplementary relationships are those that are complementary on one of these dimensions but not the other. One person might be friendly and submissive, while the other is hostile and dominant. This suggests that the dimensions "cancel" each other out to some extent. That is, noncomplementary relationships have both competitive and cooperative features.

Anticomplementary relationships are those in which both or all dimensions work in opposition. A relationship in which both participants are hostile *and* dominant is anticomplementary. The difference between anticomplementary and symmetrical relationships is the extent to which all aspects of the interpersonal system are competitive and incompatible. Interpersonal conflicts frequently reveal anticomplementary episodes, in which screaming, name-calling, and negative affect escalate in similar fashion and come to permeate the current state of the relationship.

Interpersonal relationships exist on a continuum.   Relationships are multidimensional and an individual relationship can be considered in light of these dimensions. For example, a relationship may be placed on a continuum that has dominance at one end and submission at the other, as we previously discussed. In a similar way, you may examine your relationships by considering other dimensions such as positive-negative, open-closed, weak-strong, etc. Placing bi-polar opposites at the ends of continuums and identifying where a particular relationship falls may be useful in analyzing your relationships. Keep in mind that relationships are neither good nor bad; instead, they fall on a continuum with such terms used as endpoints, or poles, by which we measure and describe our relationships with others. It is also important to note that relationships change over time; the placement of a relationship on a continuum at one time may not be the same as the placement of the relationship at another time.

Interpersonal relationships are complex.   We have already considered the notions that interpersonal relationships are multidimensional and that these dimensions can be placed at the endpoints of a number of continuums. The statement that interpersonal relationships are complex should come as no surprise. The complexity of interpersonal relationships is partly a result of the many dimensions and the varying states of each dimension. For instance, a relationship may be defined as open-closed, difficult-easy, serious-unserious, enjoyable-unenjoyable, changing-stagnant, etc. The relationship may be placed on these, and a variety of other continuums, for one point in time. At another time, the relationship may be defined differently in terms of each of these dimensions. Also, the two individuals who are involved may each define the relationship differently. Finally, the complexity of interpersonal relationships is increased because they exist within a society, they exist within a particular setting, they include individuals who have varying needs, and they include communicators who have certain assumptions about appropriate communication norms that are to be followed.

Interpersonal relationships occur within a larger relationship—society. In the first chapter we considered specific features of our society that affect interpersonal communication. In a similar manner, these features affect our relationships. For example, we may find that we have relationships of shorter duration, that we have to initiate a relationship with another person more quickly, or that we have to terminate relationships routinely in our highly mobile society. Societal mores may similarly alter the behaviors that will occur within a particular relationship. Laws that govern the behavior of "consenting adults" in matters of sexuality may interfere with your own choices.

Interpersonal relationships occur within a particular setting. You may not be able to express your anger toward your brother while you are sitting in church; you may not be able to deepen your relationship with a lover while you are at a family dinner; and you may not be able to end a relationship when the other person involved is deeply depressed over the death of a parent. The setting can alter relationship development and deterioration.

The communicator's specific needs affect interpersonal relationships. Marriages know many forms because of the divergent needs of the individuals who are involved in them. Some people marry in order to overcome loneliness, others marry for economic security, and others marry to fulfill their sexual needs. Other relationships, too, vary as a result of the different needs that individuals within the relationship hold.

Interpersonal relationships are affected by the communication norms that exist. If a communication norm in an office where you work is that personal matters are not discussed with the supervisor, the relationship between yourself and your supervisor is limited to a strictly business relationship. This might be advantageous because it eliminates unnecessary discussion and gossip; on the other hand, it may be disadvantageous because of the low *esprit de corps* that it engenders. Regardless of whether it is positive or detrimental, this communication norm affects the relationship.

In addition to these factors, relationships become increasingly complex as they endure over time. When you become acquainted with another person, you have a rather limited set of behaviors that are appropriate. You might smile, nod, or say something similar to "How do you do?" In the same way, we have a limited variety of ways to relate to others. At first, we have little common experience or past history on which to draw. As our relationship develops, we can communicate with greater variety in both the verbal and nonverbal realms. The possibilities of expression increase and the relationship itself becomes increasingly complex.

However, increased complexity does not necessarily imply decreased predictability. For example, when you talk to a family member or an intimate partner you take into account numerous features of relational history. You know not to say certain things and that other things are relatively safe to say because of previous experience with this person. Thus, the relationship is more complex because of the many variables you cope with and consider when dealing with this person. However, given your knowledge of these variables, you may be able to predict this person's responses much better than you could a stranger or acquaintance.

Interpersonal relationships are constantly in flux.   Interpersonal relationships are continually changing. The romantic notion of finding someone to love and to live with "happily ever after" is only a fairy tale. Relationships do not begin and then stabilize for eternity. They appear to follow stages similar to human growth—they are born, go through a period of adolescence, become adult, and eventually die. People and their relationships never stay "on hold"; instead, the people change, their relationships change, and the situation changes around them. Later in this chapter we will consider some of the stages that most relationships appear to go through as they develop and deteriorate.

In addition to developing and deteriorating, we may state that interpersonal relationships are constantly in flux in another way. Interpersonal relationships are irreversible and unrepeatable. This point is similar to that presented in chapter 1 stating that communication is irreversible and unrepeatable. We cannot reverse a relationship or negate it. When you consider a close relationship that you had with someone three years ago that ended because of a particular event, you may feel regret that the relationship ended over something so trivial. And yet, even when we try, we cannot go back and retrieve that lost relationship. Similarly, we often cannot take a relationship back to an early stage of acquaintance after we have developed a deep friendship with another person. Relationships change: they are not retroactive.

You also cannot repeat a relationship. The woman whose husband dies will never enter into another marriage that is the same as her earlier one. The friendship that you miss with a friend from high school will never again be found with the new friends that you make in college. The relationship with your parents will not be the same as the relationship that you establish with your own children. Relationships are unique and changes in individuals, time, or other factors result in changes in the relationships.

The Importance of Interpersonal Relationships

Interpersonal relationships are important to each of us. We enter into relationships with others for at least three reasons: (1) to learn about ourselves, (2) to control our environment and to cope with changes and alterations in that environment, and (3) to increase pleasure and positive experiences and/ or to decrease pain and negative experiences. Let us consider each of these reasons in more detail.

To Learn about Ourselves

We learn about ourselves and develop more positive feelings about ourselves through our relationships with others. Self-evaluation is less reliable when we do not substantiate it with the judgments of others. Our own judgments are strengthened when they are supported by others. We do not have the same perspective by which to view ourselves that other people have. As a consequence, we can learn about ourselves simply by listening to the information that others provide to us.

We also learn about ourselves as we view our interactions with others. For instance, you might think of yourself as outgoing and gregarious; however, you notice that when you are in a group of people, nearly everyone talks more than you do. Perhaps you believe that you are a good listener, but when you spend time in conversation with your spouse, you observe that well over half of the time, you are the one who is speaking. Your interactions provide you with valuable information about yourself.

Your positive feelings about yourself may increase as you enter into relationships with others. You may feel better because you are no longer lonely, because you are being intellectually or physically stimulated, or because of the attractiveness of the other person. You may also feel better about yourself because of the acceptance that an interpersonal relationship suggests. Someone cares about you. The bleakest day can be brightened by the addition of a friend. Ideally, our interpersonal relationships should not operate to make us feel egocentric and superior to others, but we should be aware of the strongly positive impact that relationships do have on individual members.

To Control Our Environment

We develop interpersonal relationships in order to cope with the changes in our environment and in order to manage our everyday existence. Single parents complain about the difficulties of serving as "both mother and father" to small children. People who live alone tell about the difficulties of having to cope with all of the household chores that must be done.

Communicators attempt to reduce their uncertainty about others through interaction. When we first come in contact with a relatively unknown other, much of our interaction with that person will consist of efforts to increase our understanding of the other person. Why? Because the better we know another person, the better we can predict their reactions to statements and events, and the better we can influence our relationship with that person. You may think of this as sounding "manipulative" and "scheming." However, it is clear that most of us prefer to know others because this knowledge allows us to control the outcomes of our interactions with them.

To Maximize Positive Experiences

Finally, each of us enters into interpersonal relationships in order to maximize positive experiences and to minimize negative experiences. Indeed, it has been suggested by more than one researcher that relationships will only continue if they provide more relative benefits than costs to the communicators.[6] Among the costs that accrue are time spent in the relationship, energy expended in order to help the relationship develop, psychological stress created by the relationship, and social discomfort. The benefits may include personal growth, increased feelings of positive worth, accomplishment of tasks that are difficult to accomplish alone, and general coping.

We determine whether to make alterations in our relationships based on a cost/benefit analysis. When the costs begin to outweigh the benefits, we find ourselves helping the relationship to deteriorate. For instance, if you find that a relationship that you have with another student, based on studying together for exams, becomes a situation in which you provide him or her with all of the assistance and receive no help in return, you may begin to be unavailable for study sessions. However when the benefits outweigh the costs, we may escalate moves to develop the relationship. For example, if a younger sister becomes increasingly interested in one of your hobbies and offers to help you with it and, simultaneously, becomes less argumentative about other matters, you may begin to spend a great deal of time with her.

Examining Your Personal Relationships

Make a list of some of the people with whom you have relationships—family members, friends, acquaintances, co-workers, service people, salespeople, members of organizations to which you belong, neighbors, persons in the same political party, pen pals, fellow students. After you have compiled an extensive list, attempt to determine *why* you have each relationship. Use the reasons listed in this section of the book as a starting point and try to determine additional reasons for having particular relationships. What conclusions can you draw? Have you learned new information about your relationships?

In addition to assessing the costs and benefits of our relationships, we are also conscious of the costs and benefits of our alternatives. If the intrinsic costs and benefits of current relationships were the only factors considered, there might be far more relational disengagements and divorces than there are currently. Instead, a person generally takes the value of alternative options into account when judging an ongoing relationship. This helps to explain why many people remain in abusive or dissatisfying relationships for so long. The relationship itself may not be satisfying, but the members may not perceive that there are any preferable alternatives. Females have often been known to stay in physically abusive and violent relationships because they believed that relationships were supposed to be that way, that they deserved the treatment, or that they would not be able to find a better relationship.

Our relationships with others are always in a state of flux; we may experience spurts of growth in one relationship while another begins to die; we may find ourselves involved in a number of different relationships that are all growing; or we may find that many relationships with others are deteriorating or dying within a short period of time. Relationships change either as a function of one or both partners or as a function of a force outside of the individuals involved. In the next section we will consider stages in interpersonal relationships that should assist you in becoming increasingly sensitive to development and deterioration in your interpersonal relationships. The information in that section will aid you in gaining control of your relationships, including fostering the development of some relationships and encouraging the termination of others.

Development, Stability, and Deterioration of Relationships

Earlier in this chapter we considered the notion that interpersonal relationships are always changing. They are never static; they do not remain the same from one point in time to another. Within any relationship, interaction occurs that causes the relationship to change. The components of interpersonal communication—expressiveness, composure, other-orientation, and interaction management—which are discussed in this text assist us in controlling those changes or in coping with them. In addition, we can categorize communication behaviors into those that contribute to the development or those that assist in the deterioration of an interpersonal relationship.

Recently, a number of authors have described stages in the development and deterioration of relationships.[7] In this chapter, we will first consider four stages unique to the development of an interpersonal relationship: attention, attraction, adaptation, and attachment; then we will discuss stability; and finally we will consider four stages unique to the deterioration of an interpersonal relationship: inattentiveness, disinterest, divergence, and detachment.

Development of Interpersonal Relationships

In general, we move through the stages of attending to others, being attracted by them, adapting to them, and finally, becoming attached to them. These developmental stages may be very short in duration or may span years. We may find ourselves moving backward, as well as forward, through these stages. Nonetheless, they appear to occur regularly in developing relationships. Let us consider each stage in the process.

Attention.   When we are with a group of others, we do not attend to each of them equally. We tend to focus on one or more people and ignore the others. Maureen Dean in her book, *"Mo": A Woman's View of Watergate,* related the first evening that she and her future husband, John Dean, met. She writes:

> *At last, John took over the conversation, and he directed it to me. We talked and talked and talked. We both seemed to realize there was a special magic and occasionally we found ourselves totally ignoring our host and his friend—who plainly was no longer a threat. We made studied efforts to launch four-way conversations, but managed to fool no one. Seeing what was happening to us, our companions smiled and told us to forget them. . . .*[8]

While we may disagree with Maureen Dean's romantic interpretation of this event, she clearly describes the stage of attending to another person that occurs early in the development of a relationship.

The attention stage may be brief and may simply involve the first few seconds that you observe or listen to someone. In a crowded room you select a person to study. You notice a member of the opposite sex standing on a street corner as you approach. You give an older man who is seated next to you on an airline flight special consideration. On the other hand, you may spend a great deal of time attending to the actions of another person. During this initial stage you decide if you wish to continue the relationship by assessing whether the person is attractive or unattractive to you. For example, Zunin and Zunin observed that the first four minutes of contact between people, whether relative strangers or intimates, reveals whether or not a successful relationship or episode is likely to ensue.[9] If you decide that the person is attractive, you move to the second stage in the developmental sequence; if you determine that he or she is unattractive, you may terminate the relationship by moving to the first stage in the deterioration of a relationship—showing inattentiveness. Suppose, in this instance, you find the person attractive; how will you indicate your attention? Nonverbally, you may move closer, you may stand or sit in a position that will allow you to observe the person and allow the person to observe you, you may look directly or gesture to the other person. Verbally, you may offer a greeting: "Hi," "Hello," "Nice evening, isn't it?" "Interesting party," or "It's really crowded in here, isn't it?" After these initial nonverbal and verbal cues, you may move to the second stage in the development of an interpersonal relationship.

Attraction.   Attraction to others is fairly easy to define, but difficult to explain. Research indicates that attraction to others can take at least three distinct forms: task, social, and physical.[10] *Task attraction* represents the extent to which a person is considered desirable to work with on a given problem. The *social attractiveness* of a person is the extent to which others want to spend time with the person, generally in informal settings. *Physical attractiveness* concerns the extent to which a person is viewed as having desirable bodily and appearance features. Clearly, we may find ourselves attracted to a person in one of these respects but not in others. In addition, these forms of attraction should not be confused with the concepts of liking and loving, which tend to develop after initial attraction and tend to involve more complex or intense emotional states.

The research findings on interpersonal attraction are clear in demonstrating that we find attractive people more likable than unattractive people. Similarly, a number of studies show that we attribute positive characteristics to people we find attractive and we relate negative characteristics to people we find unattractive. The difficulty with the research findings is that interpersonal attractiveness is not defined. Each of us appears to define this concept in different terms.

Interpersonal attractiveness has been described from a number of different perspectives. While each one explains the concept to some extent, the theories are sometimes in direct disagreement. Predictions about interpersonal attractiveness seem difficult at this point in our understanding of the phenomenon. Four of the more popular explanations are offered here.

Reinforcement suggests that we respond favorably to people who respond well to us. Reinforcement may be seen as a kind of reciprocity. In other words, we like people who like us and we dislike people who dislike us. People in our support systems—families, work groups, roommates—who praise our accomplishments and encourage our growth are rewarded as we view them as attractive. Persons with whom we interact who offer little encouragement or reinforcement are not granted the same reward.

Interpersonal attraction is based on a variety of factors.

Proximity refers to the idea that we find people who are close to us attractive and people who are far away from us unattractive. Proximity includes physical, psychological, attitudinal, behavioral, and other forms of distance. The cliché, "out of sight, out of mind," is consistent with this explanation. We date, fall in love with, and marry people who live in our neighborhood, who attend our university, or who work for the same hospital. We spend time with people who like the same spectator sports, participate in the same political party rallies, or attend the same religious services.

Similarity means that we are attracted to people who are just like us. How often have you seen a couple who has been married for years who shared the same physical appearance? If you spend an hour or two every day in physical exercise in order to keep your body trim and your heart healthy, you will prob-ably not be attracted to someone who is considerably overweight. You may be surprised to find that your bad mood in the morning is matched by your spouse's disposition at the same time.

Complementarity appears to be in direct contradiction to similarity as it suggests that people who are different from each other in major ways attract. The cliché, "opposites attract," and the children's poem, "Jack Sprat could eat no fat, his wife could eat no lean," both illustrate this principle. If you are quick to make decisions, but occasionally make poor decisions because of your haste, you may seek out a partner who carefully considers every detail before making any decision. If you are highly task-oriented, you may find a great deal of happiness with someone who is more concerned with relational matters. A dominant person usually has the most successful relationship with someone who is submissive.

The concepts of similarity and complementarity may not be contradictory. First, some people may simply prefer one or the other in their relational part-ners and friends. Second, it may be that we tend initially to be attracted to those who are similar to us, yet, as the relationship develops over time, find certain differences between self and other more sustaining. These differences may be in the form of complementary resources or behavioral role tenden-cies, rather than in values or personality. For example, there is some evidence, albeit somewhat dated, that men tend to be attracted to beauty in women, while women tend to be attracted to socioeconomic success.[11] Such a "money-for-beauty" arrangement, when it does occur, seems to illustrate a way in which attraction can be based upon complementary resources.

Another reason complementarity plays an important role in the attraction process. Berscheid has provided an elaborate theory of emotions in close re-lationships. This theory differentiates feelings from emotions.[12] Feelings are simply an evaluation of something as positive or negative. Emotions, on the other hand, involve physiological arousal. Thus, one may *perceive* them-selves to be strongly attracted to someone, but unless this perception is ac-companied by arousal, it is not an emotional state. The relevance of this to complementarity is that arousal is most likely to occur when there is an in-terruption or violation of expectancies. Couples who become "emotionally gutted" may simply find themselves too predictable. Without differences to provide some level of unpredictability, strong emotional attachments may ac-tually be diminished. The notion of the "romance" going out of a relationship seems related in part to the lack of spontaneity and excitement of not knowing entirely what to expect next.

These four representative principles that guide interpersonal attractiveness suggest the difficulty we have in providing clear predictions about this vari-able. Nonetheless, attraction is the second stage in the interpersonal devel-opmental process. If you have attended to another person and found him or her to be attractive, you will probably demonstrate your attraction in a variety of ways. Nonverbally, you will probably use positive facial expression such as smiling, you will probably move closer to him or her, and you will probably rely on an open body position and a forward lean. Verbally, you may reinforce your nonverbal message with specific statements about the attractiveness of the other person: "You've really got a good sense of humor," "You seem to put everyone at ease," "I wish I had your quick mind," "You have beautiful hair," or "I enjoy listening to you talk." At this point you may be ready to move to the next stage of adaptation.

Adaptation.   In the adaptation stage, we begin adjusting to the other person, we attempt to accommodate him or her, we may assimilate the other's behavior or personal style. At this point we have begun to make a commitment and are willing to demonstrate this commitment through our behavior. We may make relatively minor changes like the way we style our hair or more significant changes including our religious affiliation, our place of residence, or our membership in a particular political party.

Two students in the same college class developed a relationship during the course of a particular fall quarter. The young woman was invited to the home of her friend for the Thanksgiving holiday. During the previous few weeks, her friend quit attending the Lutheran Church and joined the Presbyterian Church in which she was a member. He also registered as a Democrat, even though his parents were staunch Republicans. The man's parents were upset by these changes in their son, but they did not say anything about his decisions. At the Thanksgiving Day meal, a younger sister offered the blessing for the meal which included, "And God, help Paul to live up to Mom and Dad's dreams and become a Lutheran Republican again." This accidental disclosure actually cleared the air and allowed the family members to discuss the changes in their family. The family was experiencing a deterioration in their relationship with their son while the two college students were experiencing a developing relationship with each other.

We may demonstrate our interest in developing the relationship further by verbal and nonverbal cues that would suggest our adaptation to the other person. We may gesture in the same way that the other person gestures, we may begin to take similar long strides when walking together, we may sit in the same way, or we may sleep in the same position. In addition to behaving similarly with our nonverbal cues, we may compliment the other person's nonverbal behavior. For instance, if others touch us, we may cuddle to their touch, when they reach out to us, we may respond; or when they stare at us, we may avert our eyes. Verbally, we demonstrate our adaptation in a variety of remarks: "Tell me what you'd like to do, I'm open to anything," "I'm in the mood for pizza tonight, but I'm interested in what you'd like," "I'm willing to visit your parents this weekend with you, but I'd like you to visit mine next weekend," or "Do you need someone to talk with tonight?" After we have adapted to another person, we may move to the next stage, attachment.

Attachment.   Attachment is the final stage in interpersonal development. When we attach ourselves to someone else, we form some bond, some link, or some method of joining together. Many people signal their attachment to another person by the exchange of material items—rings, pins, sweaters. Our culture provides a number of rituals that allow us to demonstrate our attachment to another—pinning ceremonies, engagement parties, and weddings.

Attachment may be less formal or less public than the traditional wedding complete with the exchange of rings. Someone may be introduced as "my old man," "my old lady," "my best friend," or "my partner" to suggest attachment. Others decide to share a room, an apartment, a house, or some other physical property. Attachment may be similarly shown by nonverbal possessiveness. Although people vary, they may stand or sit very close together in this stage. Intimacy normally signals a relationship that has reached the stage of attachment.

Other signs of attachment are likely to be revealed in the form of exclusivity, commitment, and interdependence. *Exclusivity* refers to the ways in which partners identify each other as occupying a unique relationship. Generally, intimates reach "an understanding" that they will not "see" other people. Statements that refer to a "best friend" or indicate that "I love only you" indicate this notion of exclusivity and uniqueness.

Commitment is displayed in a variety of ways. For example, everyday talk is likely to incorporate much more future orientation. That is, partners are more likely to discuss things they intend to do in the future. Plans are made for what will happen or what the persons want to happen, as opposed to less intimate relationships that exist more in the recent past, the present, and short-term or individual futures. Partners are also likely to reveal commitment through public displays of intimacy, whether through physical and romantic touching for lovers or open promises of eternal support for friends. "No matter what happens, I want you to know that I'll always be your friend," and statements of this sort illustrate the level of commitment to a relationship.

Interdependence is one of the hallmarks of relational development. In Chapter 1 we noted that interdependence is a necessary feature of any kind of interpersonal communication. Naturally, highly developed relationships are likely to display higher levels of interdependence. As relationships become closer, the members tend to share a variety of resources: property (e.g., books, records or CDs, clothes, etc.), activities (e.g., sports, parties, hobbies, etc.), time and space (e.g., living together, taking courses together, taking trips together, etc.), and services (e.g., taking notes for one another, providing a ride while the car is being repaired, taking care of a pet while the other is on vacation, etc.). Each of these resources involves a level of interdependence with the other person.

Intimate relationships tend to be filled with this sharing. The interdependence is both a result of, and a cause, of attachment. As you become more interdependent upon another person, the more your positive outcomes become associated with that person. Conversely, the more you like or love someone, the more you tend to naturally intermingle these resources. The display of exclusivity and commitment also facilitates the development of interdependence.

Stability in Interpersonal Relationships

Attachment is the final stage in the developmental process, but relationships do not simply stop or stagnate at this point. Too many of us grew up with the romantic notion that once you were married, you lived "happily ever after." Relationships, unfortunately or fortunately, are constantly in flux. Aspects of the relationship are continually changing regardless of the stability of the relationship. In the past few years, researchers have begun to investigate stable relationships. They have defined stable relationships as those in which a given level of intimacy is achieved and maintained. They agree that periods of stability within relationships do not mean that the relationships are not changing in any way, but that the basic patterns of exchange tend to be established and accepted by the persons involved. For instance, one writer suggests that stable relationships can be characterized by three features: "(1) relationships stabilize because the participants reach some minimal agreement (usually implicitly) on what they want from the relationship, (2) relationships can stabilize at differing levels of intimacy, and (3) a 'stabilized' relationship still has areas of change occurring in it."[13] Nonetheless, very little empirical data has been amassed to provide clear notions of communication patterns that occur in stable relationships. One recent study offers some promise and determines that persons who desire stability in their relationships appear to use avoidance, balance, and directness. People use avoidance as they ignore those behaviors in which the other person engages that might alter the relationship, and they avoid engaging in behavior themselves that might result in an alteration in the relationship. They use balance as they tend to keep emotional support levels and other features constant. Finally, they use directness as they engage in direct statements about their preference to maintain the relationship.[14] These behaviors may be useful to consider in those instances in which you wish to maintain a specific relationship.

Many relationships do not remain stable. You may find that after you have reached the stage of attachment, you find yourself experiencing activities and behaviors that are suggestive of another of the developmental stages. Or, you may find that you are experiencing stages in the deterioration of a relationship, even though you are attempting to maintain it. Let us turn our attention to the deterioration of interpersonal relationships.

Deterioration of Interpersonal Relationships

A great deal of research and theorizing has been done on the development of interpersonal relationships, which is contrasted with the relatively small amount on the deterioration of such relationships. Some writers have suggested that the dissolution process in a relationship mirrors the developmental stages, but simply occurs in reverse.[15] This "reversal hypothesis" has been questioned in recent research[16] and we may only conclude that research in this area is uncertain at the present time. At any rate, it provides an interesting avenue of thought. Let us consider four stages of deterioration: inattentiveness, disinterest, divergence, and detachment.

Inattentiveness.   In the same way that we begin the development of a relationship with attention, we begin relationship deterioration by a lack of attention. We are inattentive to people with whom we are beginning to terminate a relationship. We fail to consider the friend who once ate lunch with us each day, we show little respect for a once close business associate, and we visit less often in the period of time before a neighbor moves from town.

How do you signal inattentiveness to another person? Nonverbally, you may be focusing on a third individual, you may have physically turned away, or you may have put more distance between yourself and the other person. Verbally, you may simply offer no comment to the other person. Inattentiveness is differentiated from the next stage in the deterioration of a relationship as it may simply be a lack of regard or the failure to notice someone else whereas disinterest makes a more negative statement.

Generally speaking, inattentiveness is a relatively simple oversight of another person, whereas disinterest involves a more conscious and deliberate attempt to ignore or put down a person in situations calling for interaction. For instance, in a social setting, you may fail to notice a business colleague who is across the room or may determine that it is too difficult to squeeze through the crowd to say, "Hello." You have thus demonstrated inattentiveness. On the other hand, if that business colleague makes an attempt to move through the others to speak to you and you indicate that you are not interested, you have demonstrated disinterest.

Disinterest.   The second stage in the deterioration of a relationship is disinterest. We disregard children who are about to leave home, we become apathetic toward a marriage partner who threatens to leave, we remain neutral when someone who was previously close to us expresses strong emotion. Our apathy at this stage stands in strong contrast to expressions of concern, love, and understanding that we once demonstrated freely. Phil Donahue's relationship to his children during his first marriage seems marked by a lack of real concern. Donahue writes:

I had never been told that children needed to be cuddled, needed approval and attention, needed measured and thoughtful discipline. I honestly thought that being a father meant giving presents at Christmas and birthdays, occasionally changing diapers, occasionally spanking and occasionally baby-sitting for the "little woman's night out."[17]

Disinterest can be demonstrated through a number of verbal and nonverbal cues. We may not smile when the other person looks our way, we may not change our body position when someone comes upon us with the intent of talking in mind and we turn away, or we may continue to walk out of the room even though the other person makes it clear that he or she wants to speak to us. Verbally, we may tell the other person that we don't care about him or her, that we don't care what he or she does, or that we don't care what he or she thinks.

Divergence.   Inattentiveness and disinterest may be followed by the third stage in deterioration: divergence. At this point in the relationship, the two people return to their prior stage of being two separate entities. Divergence includes the departure from a norm or other deviation. It is marked by aloofness. Two people may be deeply involved in establishing relationships with alternative partners at this point.

How would you show another person that you no longer wanted to maintain a relationship at its current status and were ready to enter into this stage of divergence? Nonverbally, you might physically draw away. When the other person tried to touch you, you might move outside of his or her reach, when the person walked toward you, you might walk away, when he or she moved toward you, you might move so you were looking in another direction, and the other's smiles or positive facial expression might cause you to frown or to use negative expression. Verbally, you might state that you want a change in your relationship, that you want a "trial separation," want to date others, or want some new experiences. In addition, verbal communication could be expected to reveal less frequent usage of plural pronouns (e.g., "we," "us," "our," etc.) and more use of singular pronouns (e.g., "I," "me," "my," etc.), less reference to the future, and more scheduling of individual activities rather than shared activities. During this stage of the relationship, members may begin to integrate more into their own social networks, almost as if they are lining up new avenues of relational development and social support in anticipation of exiting their current relationship.

Detachment.   The final stage in the deterioration of a relationship is detachment. Detachment is the final act or process of totally disconnecting. At this point, both physical and psychological separation occur. People dissociate themselves from places, ideas, and perspectives that are associated with their previous relationship. We may become totally dissociated with the needs or concerns of the other person.

Detachment may be inevitable, but it is still painful. Detachment may occur because of the choice of one partner, because of the choice of both partners, or because of some outside force. Death, for instance, is generally not a choice

Stage	Depiction	Sample Nonverbal/Verbal Communication
Attention		*Listening or watching another person.* "Hi, how are you?"
Attraction	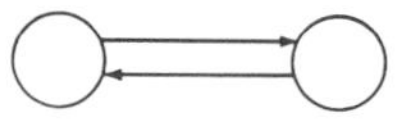	*Smiling, positive facial expression, eye contact, forward body lean.* "You've got a nice smile."
Adaptation	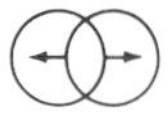	*Alterations in nonverbal communication.* "I didn't enjoy jogging before I met you—now I love it!"
Attachment		*Sitting, standing close together; increased touching.* "Let's get married."

Figure 2.1   Relationship development.

Stage	Depiction	Sample Nonverbal/Verbal Communication
Inattentiveness	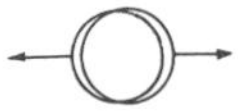	*Failing to listen or observe another person.* "I didn't hear you. Were you talking to me?"
Disinterest	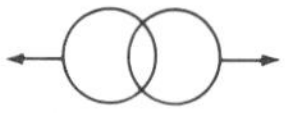	*No facial or bodily expressiveness.* "I really don't care what you do."
Divergence	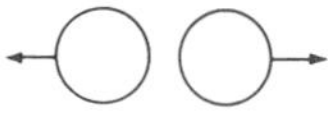	*No changes or alterations in facial or bodily movement regardless of the message sent by the other person, or else, a strikingly different set of nonverbal behaviors from the past.* "I'm not going to play the passive little lady anymore!"
Detachment	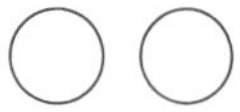	*No nonverbal communication; or negative facial expression, sitting and standing far apart, no touching.* "I'm leaving you—I've met someone else."

Figure 2.2   Relationship deterioration.

that is consciously made to end a relationship. The termination of a relationship may be a positive or negative experience. Sometimes one relationship must be terminated in order for others to develop. We find it necessary, to some extent, to terminate the relationship with our parents in order to develop closer relationships with a lover or a spouse. We leave a marital partner and a relationship that was harmful to both parties to enter into a marriage that allows growth and freedom. We move from one neighborhood into another in order to have sufficient room for our family. Detachment may be demonstrated through the lack of nonverbal or verbal communication or through final statements about the end of it. The end of a relationship, like its beginning, can have negative or positive consequences. The stages of relationship development and deterioration and examples of nonverbal and verbal communication in each stage are provided in figures 2.1 and 2.2. With this depiction of the stages of relationship development and deterioration we conclude our consideration of this introductory material on interpersonal relationships.

Summary

In this chapter you learned about interpersonal relationships. You considered the changing and increasingly complex nature of relationships. You can now define a relationship, identify the characteristics of interpersonal relationships, and suggest the dimensions on which interpersonal relationships may be gauged. You know that interpersonal relationships are important because they allow you to understand yourself better, they allow you to gain control of your environment, and they allow you to increase your positive experiences. You are probably engaged in a number of interpersonal relationships right now. You may wish to consider the recognizable stages through which relationships develop—attention, attraction, adaptation, and attachment—and the recognizable stages through which relationships deteriorate—inattentiveness, disinterest, divergence, and detachment—and determine where you would place some of your relationships. Stability in relationships appears to be marked by behaviors that include avoidance, balance, and directness.

Interpersonal communication always occurs within a relationship. Interpersonal relationships are characterized by having a mutuality of definition, stages, a multidimensional feature, being capable of being placed on a continuum, being complex in nature, and by constant change. In our consideration of interpersonal communication components, the next unit in this text, we need to keep the importance of relationships in mind. The components that we examine—clarity, confidence, and concern—are affected by the unique features of the interpersonal relationship in which they occur. Later in this text we will consider some specific relationships in which interpersonal communication occurs including conversations among strangers, acquaintances, and friends, intimate communication, family communication, and the interview.

Notes

1. Sanford L. Silverman and Martin G. Silverman, *Theory of Relationships* (New York: Philosophical Library, 1963), p. xi.
2. Jay Haley, "An Interactional Description of Schizophrenia," *Psychiatry* 22 (1959), 321–32.

3. From *Passages* by Gail Sheehy, p. 9. Copyright © 1974, 1976 by Gail Sheehy. Reprinted by permission of the publisher, E. P. Dutton, Inc.

4. M. P. Duke and S. Nowicki, Jr., "A Social Learning Theory Analysis of Interactional Theory Concepts and a Multidimensional Model of Human Interaction Constellations," in J. C. Anchin and D. J. Kiesler (eds.), *Handbook of Interpersonal Psychotherapy* (New York: Pergamon Press, pp. 78–94); M. B. Freedman, T. F. Leary, A. G. Ossorio, and H. S. Coffey, "The Interpersonal Dimension of Personality," *Journal of Personality* 20 (1951) 143–61; R. LaForge and R. F. Suczek, "The Interpersonal Dimension of Personality: III. An Interpersonal Checklist," *Journal of Personality* 24 (1955) 94–112; and J. S. Wiggins, "Circumplex Models of Interpersonal Behavior," in L. Wheeler (ed.), *Review of Personality and Social Psychology* Vol. 1 (Beverly Hills, Calif.: Sage, 1980), 265–94.

5. See, for instance, Phyllis Chesler, "Marriage and Psychotherapy," in the Radical Therapist Collective, eds., produced by Jerome Agel, *The Radical Therapist* (New York: Ballantine Books, 1971), pp. 175–80; Don H. Zimmerman and Candace West, "Sex Roles, Interruptions and Silences in Conversation," in *Language and Sex: Difference and Dominance,* ed. Barrie Thorne and Nancy Henley (Rowley, Mass.: Newbury House Publishers, 1975), pp. 105–29; and Barbara Eakins and Gene Eakins, "Verbal Turn-Taking and Exchanges in Faculty Dialogue," *Papers in Southwest English IV: Proceedings of the Conference on the Sociology of the Languages of American Women,* ed. Betty Lou Dubois and Isabel Crouch (San Antonio, Tex.: Trinity University, 1976), pp. 53–62.

6. See, for instance, J. W. Thibaut and H. H. Kelley, *The Social Psychology of Groups* (New York: Wiley, 1959), pp. 80–99; G. C. Homans, *Social Behavior: Its Elementary Forms* (New York: Harcourt Brace Jovanovich, 1961); and M. E. Roloff, *Interpersonal Communication: The Social Exchange Approach* (Beverly Hills, Calif.: Sage, 1981).

7. See, for instance, I. Altman, A. Vinsel, and B. B. Brown, "Dialectic Conceptions in Social Psychology: An Application to Social Penetration and Privacy Regulation," *Advances in Experimental Social Psychology* 14 (1981) 108–60; L. A. Baxter and W. Wilmot, "Interaction Characteristics of Disengaging, Stable, and Growing Relationships," in R. Gilmour and S. Duck (eds.), *The Emerging Field of Personal Relationships* (Hillsdale, N.J.: Lawrence Erlbaum Associates), pp. 145–59; S. Duck, "Social and Personal Relationships," in M. L. Knapp and G. R. Miller (eds.), *Handbook of Interpersonal Communication,* (Beverly Hills, Calif.: Sage, 1975) pp. 655–86; M. L. Knapp, *Interpersonal Communication and*

Human Relationships (Boston: Allyn & Bacon, 1984); D. A. Taylor and I. Altman, "Communication in Interpersonal Relationships: Social Penetration Processes," in M. E. Roloff and G. R. Miller (eds.), *Interpersonal Processes: New Directions in Communication Research* (Newbury Park, Calif.: Sage, 1987) 257–77; L. R. Wheeless, V. E. Wheeless, and R. Baus, "Sexual Communication, Communication Satisfaction, and Solidarity in the Developmental Stages of Intimate Relationships," *Western Journal of Speech Communication* 48 (1984) 217–30.

8. Maureen Dean with Hays Gorey, *"Mo": A Woman's View of Watergate* (New York: Simon & Schuster, 1975), pp. 23–24.

9. L. Zunin and N. Zunin, *Contact: The First Four Minutes* (New York: Ballantine Books, 1972).

10. J. C. McCroskey and T. A. McCain, "The Measurement of Interpersonal Attraction," *Speech Monographs* 41 (1974): 267–76.

11. S. S. Brehm, *Intimate Relationships* (New York: Random House, 1985), pp. 75–77.

12. E. Berscheid, "Emotion," in H. H. Kelley, et al. (eds.), *Close Relationships* (New York: W. H. Freeman, 1983), pp. 110–68.

13. William W. Wilmot, "Relationship Stages: Initiation and Stabilization," in *Contexts of Communication,* ed. Jean M. Civikly (New York: Holt, Rinehart & Winston, 1981), p. 99.

14. Joe Ayres, "Strategies to Maintain Relationships: Their Identification and Perceived Usage," *Communication Quarterly* 31 (1983), pp. 62–67. See also K. Dindia and L. A. Baxter, "Strategies for Maintaining and Repairing Marital Relationships," *Journal of Social and Personal Relationships* 4 (1987): 143–58; and B. C. Shea and J. C. Pearson, "The Effects of Relationship Type, Partner Intent, and Gender on the Selection of Relationship Maintenance Strategies," *Communication Monographs* 53 (1986): 352–64.

15. See, for example, I. Altman and D. A. Taylor, *Social Penetration.* (New York: Holt, Rinehart & Winston, 1973); and M. L. Knapp, *Interpersonal Communication and Human Relationships* (Boston: Allyn & Bacon, 1984).

16. See, for example, S. P. Banks, D. M. Altendorf, J. O. Greene, and M. J. Cody, "An Examination of Relationship Disengagement: Perceptions, Breakup Strategies and Outcomes," *Western Journal of Speech Communication* 51 (1987): 19–41; L. A. Baxter, "Strategies for Ending Relationships: Two Studies," *Western Journal of Speech Communication* 46 (1982): 223–41; L. A. Baxter, "Relational Disengagement: An Examination of the Reversal Hypothesis," *Western Journal of Speech Communication* 47 (1983): 85–98; L. A. Baxter, "Trajectories of Relationship

Disengagement," *Journal of Social and Personal Relationships* 1 (1984): 29–48; L. Lee, "Sequences in Separation: A Framework for Investigating Endings of the Personal (Romantic) Relationship," *Journal of Social and Personal Relationships* 1 (1984): 49–73; S. L. Ragan and R. Hopper, "Ways to Leave Your Lover: A Conversational Analysis of Literature," *Communication Quarterly* 32 (1984): 310–17; W. W. Wilmot, D. A. Carbaugh, and L. A. Baxter, "Communicative Strategies Used to Terminate Romantic Relationships," *Western Journal of Speech Communication* 49 (1985): 204–16.

17.   Phil Donahue & Co., *My Own Story: Donahue* (New York: Simon & Schuster, 1979), p. 74.

Additional Readings

Berger, Charles R. and Chaffee, Steven H. eds. *Handbook of Communication Science*. Newbury Park, Calif.: Sage, 1987.

Brehm, Sharon S. *Intimate Relationships*. New York: Random House, 1985.

Burgess, Robert L. and Huston, Ted L. *Social Exchange in Developing Relationships*. New York: Academic Press, 1979.

Cahn, Dudley D., Jr. *Letting Go: A Practical Theory of Relationship Disengagement and Reengagement*. SUNY Series in Human Communication Processes. Albany, N.Y.: State University of New York Press, 1987.

Cushman, Donald P. and Cahn, Dudley. *Communication in Interpersonal Relationships*. SUNY Series in Human Communication. Albany, N.Y.: State University of New York Press, 1985.

Duck, Steve. *Human Relationships*. Beverly Hills, Calif.: Sage, 1986.

Duck, Steve. *Relating to Others*. Chicago, Ill.: Dorsey, 1988.

Duck, Steve and Perlman, Daniel. *Understanding Personal Relationships: An Interdisciplinary Approach*. Beverly Hills, Calif.: Sage, 1985.

Jones, Warren H. and Perlman, Daniel, eds. *Personal Relationships*. Vol. 1. Greenwich, Conn.: JAI Press.

Kelley, Harold H. and Associates. *Close Relationships*. New York: W. H. Freeman, 1983.

Knapp, Mark L. *Interpersonal Communication and Human Relationships*. Boston, Mass.: Allyn & Bacon.

Millar, Frank E. and Rogers, L. Edna. *A Relational Approach to Interpersonal Communication*. Beverly Hills, Calif.: Sage, 1976.

Morton, T. L., Alexander, James F., and Altman, Irwin. "Communication and Relationship Definition." In *Explorations in Interpersonal Communication,* edited by Gerald R. Miller. Beverly Hills, Calif.: Sage, 1976, pp. 105–26.

Roloff, Michael E. "Communication Strategies, Relationships, and Relational Changes." In *Explorations in Interpersonal Communication,* edited by Gerald R. Miller. Beverly Hills, Calif.: Sage, 1976, pp. 173–96.

Watzlawick, Paul, Beavin, Janet H., and Jackson, Don D. *Pragmatics of Human Communication.* New York: Norton, 1976.

The Process of Perception

© 1980 Newspaper Enterprise Association, Inc. Reprinted by permission.

Differences in perception are not always as humorous as the cartoon illustrates. Sometimes such differences can lead to conflict and a lack of understanding. Perception is an underlying factor in interpersonal communication. Our knowledge of the role perception plays in the communication process may be essential to effective and appropriate interpersonal communication.

Differences in perception, in the way people see, hear, smell, taste, or feel a specific stimulus, are common. Whether we are describing an event (say, an automobile accident), an idea (how communication occurs), or something about ourselves (how we feel about our own bodies), we encounter differences in perception. Individual experiences are not identical. Neither are individual perceptions, even of the same event. Perceptions are personal constructs of the perceiver.

The Nature of Perception

Perception Is Related to Communication

Perception is related to communication in at least two ways. Our perceptions of ourself affect our communication. If we believe ourself to be shy, we may tend to avoid communicating. If we believe that we are aggressive, we may tend to dominate conversations and to be loud and boisterous. We sometimes draw inferences about other people's self-concepts from the way they speak.

Perception is also important because it is the process by which we come to understand others. We make judgments and draw conclusions about other people within a few seconds of meeting them.[1] We use the nonverbal cues available, including the person's facial expressions, vocal patterns, body language, clothes, and jewelry, as well as what the person says. Our perception of the other person, including the way the person looks, sounds, and smells, provides immediate information.

Our perceptions of ourselves affect our interactions with others.

The perceptions we have of others affect our communication with them. A number of minority group people—blacks, hispanics, and handicapped persons, for example—have related their experiences with others. Frequently, the early portion of a conversation focuses on their uniqueness—their race, their nationality, or their particular handicap. People who talk with them tend to be limited in their early perceptions. Often, the topic of conversation does not shift until these persons have known each other for some time.

Definition of Perception

Perception is the process by which we come to understand ourselves and others. In the past, people believed that perception was nothing more than sensing objects in the environment: people were merely tape recorders that recorded the events that occurred around them—*passive perception.* Sights, sounds, smells, and other stimuli were sent to them. A second implication was that people were objective. In other words, no one added or subtracted from the stimuli—*objective perception.* This point of view also implied *inherent meaning* in the object being perceived. No room for interpretation existed because the stimulus supposedly contained all of the meaning.

What occurs in perception is that our sensory receptors (eyes, ears, noses, tongues, and bodies) are stimulated by objects in our environment. The stimulus may be a spoken word, an unusual smell, a brush against our arm, the written word, or some unique taste. The sensory receptors capture the particular stimulus, and nerves transmit the sensation to the brain. The brain interprets the sensation and assigns meanings to it in order for us to gain an

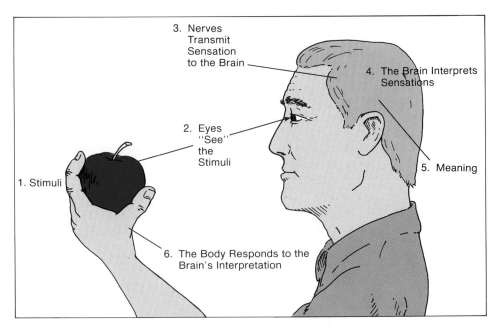

1. Stimuli

2. Eyes "See" the Stimuli

3. Nerves Transmit Sensation to the Brain

4. The Brain Interprets Sensations

5. Meaning

6. The Body Responds to the Brain's Interpretation

Perception is far more complex than merely sensing stimuli.   **Figure 3.1**

understanding of the stimulus. This cycle is depicted in figure 3.1. We will consider the processes that occur in perception later in this chapter. At this point, we simply note that perception is far more complex than merely sensing stimuli.

The contemporary view of perception is that it is *subjective, active, creative,* and *interpretive.* People add to, and subtract from, the stimuli to which they are exposed. They blend the external stimuli and their internal states. Recent research on the human brain demonstrates that individual brain development is highly variable. In addition, as we shall discover in the next section, factors other than physiological differences between people account for differences in perception.

Consider the last time you were driving in the country. As you drove between the fields on the two-lane highway, your attention shifted from one stimulus to another. You did not passively absorb all of the stimuli in the environment, but you actively chose to focus on the sports car that zoomed past you and to ignore the family sedan you followed for a number of miles. When a large van came into view in your rearview mirror, you did not objectively perceive the vehicle, but instead you began to think about your truck-driver friend, and you subjectively thought the truck as a means of income. When you looked at the fields planted with corn and barley, you did not identify an inherent meaning in the plants that others would easily share, but you recognized, in your creative way, that the plants were different from those with which you were familiar.

To understand how the contemporary view of perception affects communication, try to remember the last week of final exams. Perhaps, as you were rushing to an exam, you noticed one of your friends coming toward you. You singled out your friend from a number of other people on the sidewalk. When you noticed him, you did not drop your glance, but you maintained eye contact to signal you wanted to talk for a moment or two. As you began the conversation, you noticed it was beginning to rain and the rain was very cold. You began to feel uncomfortable and wondered why your friend continued to talk. Your thoughts shifted back to the exam. Your friend remarked that you seemed touchy. As he walked away, your friend told himself, "That's what happens when you lend people money—they try to ignore you!"

If you assumed that the older view of perception was accurate, this conversation would be difficult to interpret and understand. If you take into consideration that perception is active, subjective, and creative, your friend's misunderstanding can be explained.

Differences in Perception

We have just demonstrated a common phenomenon—different people perceiving the same event in different ways. Moreover, perception is subjective, active, and creative. Differences occur in perception because of physiological factors, different past experiences, and differences in present feelings and circumstances.

Physiological Factors

None of us is physiologically identical to anyone else. We vary in height, weight, body type, sex, and in our senses. People can be tall or short, have less than perfect vision, or suffer from impaired hearing. They can be particularly sensitive to smells or odors. Sensitivity to temperature similarly varies from one individual to another.

Biological sex may be an important physiological difference to be considered in perception. Some authors have suggested that hemispheric differences in the cerebral cortex of the brain are sex-linked. These differences are said to account for females' language facility and fine hand control and males' spatial and mathematical abilities, as well as their increased likelihood of suffering with dyslexia, stuttering, delayed speech, autism, and hyperactivity.[2] However, conclusive evidence has not been established for an anatomic difference between the brain structures of human females and males.

Past Experience

Just as our physiological features affect our perceptions, our past experiences similarly alter what we see or hear. Our past experiences lead us to expectations about the future. For instance, suppose you were given a reading assignment in one of your courses and, on the day your assigned reading was to have been completed, your instructor asked you to put away your books and to number from one to twenty-five on a sheet of paper. What would you assume? Most likely you would predict that you were about to have a quiz or exam on the required reading. This assumption about the current situation is based on your past experiences.

The idea that our past experiences create expectations about the future is basic to the theory of *perceptual constancy.* According to perceptual constancy, we rarely change our perceptions of something once we have established a particular image of it. We are able to "see" the objects in our bedroom, even when the light bulb burns out and the room is dark. If we move some items from a counter on which they have rested for a long time, we may still "see" the objects there even after they are gone. Similarly, amputees often report they still experience some "feeling" in the location of their missing appendage. All of us have a tendency to view things as stable and unchanging after we have formed our opinion.

Perceptual constancy operates on other levels as well. We frequently come to hold an attitude and then refuse to alter that attitude, even when we are provided with contrary evidence. This phenomenon is called an attitude-set or mind-set. The harmful effects of tobacco, caffeine, and alcohol have been revealed in the past few years. Many people held a previous attitude that these drugs were not hazardous to their health. Their past experience with these drugs and their mind-set do not allow them to perceive the new data as important or meaningful to them.

Differences in perception based on past experiences also occur because of the roles we play, the culture with which we are familiar, and the subculture of which we are a part. Our *roles,* for example, may include being a student, a worker, a son, or a daughter. These roles affect our perceptions of the events around us. We may play specific roles in particular communication contexts. For instance, you may always perceive yourself as a supportive conversationalist when you are talking to another person. To fulfill this role, you may listen carefully and provide many verbal and nonverbal responses to the other communicator. If you perceive yourself as a "clown" or "tension-releaser" in a small group setting, you might perceive any slip of the tongue as an opportunity for creating humor.

How does growing up in different cultures affect our perceptions? We learn how to perceive the people and events around us based on cultural values, attitudes, and beliefs. In chapters 4 and 5, we will observe that people's culture affects their communication. At this point, we recognize our culture affects our perceptions. Singer, an intercultural communication researcher, maintains that what we see, hear, taste, touch, and smell are conditioned by our cultures. He postulates that our perceptions are largely learned. Further, he observes that the greater the experiential differences among people, the greater the disparity in their perceptions. On the other hand, the more similar their experiential backgrounds, the more similarly they will perceive the world.[3]

Our cultural background affects our perceptions and our interactions with others.

Some examples may clarify the relationship of culture to perceptions. In Malaysia, exchanging gifts when you visit someone's home is expected behavior; in Canada, it would be viewed as unusual. In the Philippines, women and men are treated more equally than in India. The relative importance of communication and of silence changes, too, as we move from one culture to another. Americans generally hold a strong, positive feeling toward oral communication, but some other cultures do not share this perception. In many parts of the world, silence, rather than talk, is the preferred mode of behavior.

The attitudes, values, and beliefs of our culture affect our perception of ourselves as well as our perceptions of other people. For instance, if you grew up in a culture that treated children as unique and capable individuals, you might feel far differently about yourself than if you grew up in a culture that viewed children as property or that viewed children as an interference in achieving "the good life." Similarly, women who are taught to perceive their role as secondary to men are apt to perceive assertive women as impolite, improper, or inappropriately socialized.

Growing up in different subcultures encourages differences in perception, too. The crowding that occurs on a street in a large city is upsetting to a rural person. Similarly, country children are more likely to become apprehensive about communicating than are urban children.[4] Women and men learn to perceive the world around them in vastly different ways, which results in different modes of communicating. Pearson, in *Gender and Communication,* cites hundreds of sources that demonstrate the specific and unique ways that women and men perceive the world and communicate about it.[5] Similarly, individuals in the black community learn to perceive the world differently than do Americans of Mexican heritage.

One subcultural difference with which you are probably familiar is the so-called generation gap. The difference in age between yourself and your parents, instructors, or classmates may significantly affect your perception of them and, consequently, your communication with them. A difference in age can affect how you respond to music and perceive events, what you say about them, and the meanings that are evoked when they are mentioned in a conversation. Subcultural differences affect our perception and, thereby, our communication.

Present Feelings and Circumstances

Differences in perception also arise from different feelings and circumstances. A headache, backache, or toothache can cause you to perceive a critical comment when a friendly one is being offered. You sometimes may not see a stop sign if your thoughts are elsewhere. Your health may affect your ability to perceive sensory stimuli. Similarly, if you are tired, you may perceive stimuli differently than when you are well-rested. Other physiological needs like hunger or thirst may affect your perceptive skills.

Your daily, monthly, or yearly cycle may affect how you perceive stimuli. If you are an "evening person" you might not be able to discriminate among multiple choice answers on an exam at 8 A.M. as well as you could later in the day. If you are having a bad week, you might be offended by the humor of one of your friends; later in the month, you might find the same remark very humorous. Accordingly, you might perceive stimuli more acutely in the cooler months of winter than you do in the warmer summer months.

If you have ever spent a night alone in a large house, a deserted dormitory, or an unfamiliar residence, you probably understand that perceptions are altered by circumstances. Most people experience a remarkable change in their hearing at night when they are alone. Creaking, whining, scraping, cracking sounds are heard, although none was heard in the daytime. The lack of other stimuli—including light, other sounds, and other people with whom to talk—coupled with a slight feeling of anxiety, provide the circumstances that result in more acute hearing.

Similar circumstances may account, in part, for the mirages seen by lonely travelers. Commander Robert Peary encountered massive snowy pinnacles that appeared to rise thousands of feet above the plain of solid ice deep inside the Arctic Circle in 1906. Seven years later, Donald MacMillan, another explorer, verified his discovery. However, when MacMillan asked his Eskimo guide to choose a course toward the peaks, the guide explained that the spectacle was only *poo-jok* (mist). Meteorologists have explained the existence of such mirages but have hastened to add that they are "reported infrequently because people aren't looking for them."[6] The variance in the feelings and circumstances of the many explorers may account for the differences in sighting or not sighting specific illusions.

Activities during Perception

According to the most recent information, people engage in three separate activities during perception. None of us is aware of these separate processes because they occur quickly and almost simultaneously. Nonetheless, each activity is involved in our perceptions. The three activities include *selection* (we neglect some of the stimuli in our environment and focus on a few), *organization* (we group the stimuli in our environment into units or wholes), and *interpretation* (we give particular meanings to stimuli).

Selection

None of us perceives all the stimuli in our environment. For example, if you drove to school today, you were bombarded with sights, sounds, smells, and other sensations during your ride. At the time, you elected to perceive some of the stimuli, and you chose to disregard others. Now, you can recall some of the stimuli you perceived, but you have forgotten others. In the future, you will also expose yourself to some sensations and ignore others.

Our selectivity is of at least two types. First, we are selective in the stimuli to which we attend. *Selective attention* means we focus on certain cues and ignore others. On our way to school, we check our timing with the bank clock, but we fail to notice the couple walking in front of the bank. We may overhear someone gossiping about us in the next room but not hear what one of our parents is saying in the same room.

Second, we select the stimuli we will recall or remember. *Selective retention* means we categorize, store, and retrieve certain information, but discard other information. If you played the car radio on your way to school, try to remember one of the songs you heard, or one of the commercials, or one of the public-service announcements. Although your attention may have been drawn to a particular song or message this morning, you may find that you cannot remember anything you heard. Your mind has discarded the sounds

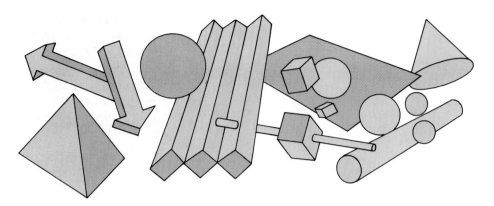

The unorganized figure.   Figure 3.2

you heard from your radio. You may recall a criticism your date offered last night but have forgotten your mother made a similar comment two days ago.

The relationship between selection and communication can be clarified by the concept of stereotyping. *Stereotyping* is the process of placing people and things into established categories, or of basing judgments about people or things upon the categories into which they fit, rather than on their individual characteristics. Stereotyping has a negative connotation because we sometimes exhibit "hardening of the categories," placing items in inappropriate categories, or else we do not recognize that others categorize differently than we do. All of us stereotype to a certain extent, but particular stereotypes vary from person to person. Stereotyping involves selective attention and selective retention.

A specific example will illustrate the relationship among these concepts. Suppose you perceive women to be emotional and men to be logical. To maintain this stereotype, you selectively attend to women who behave emotionally and ignore those who are unemotional. Similarly, you selectively attend to men who are logical, rather than to those who seem unpredictable. When you try to recall the significant men and women in your life, you find the women were either moderately or extremely emotional and the men were fairly rational. You have selectively retained the memory of those who fit your stereotype. Selectivity in perception affects stereotyping, and stereotyping is a process by which we categorize so we can communicate with others.

Organization

All of us have a tendency to organize the stimuli in our environment. The unorganized figure 3.2 is difficult to describe if we only glance at it for a minute. When we attempt to describe it, we do so by organizing the lines we see. We

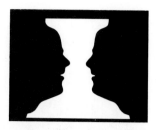

Figure 3.3   An example of figure and ground: A vase or twins?

Figure 4.9f from *Fundamentals of Child Development,* Second Edition, by Harry Munsinger, copyright © 1975 by Holt, Rinehart and Winston, Inc., reprinted by permission of the publisher.

Figure 3.4   An example of figure and ground: Ink blobs or a bearded man?

might say it consists of straight and squiggly lines, or it has a rectangle, a triangle, and a square, or we may categorize the stimuli in some other way. The important point is we attempt to organize the figure as we describe it.

We organize stimuli in a number of ways. One method of organizing is to distinguish between *figure* and *ground.* In figure 3.3, some people perceive a vase or a candlestick, while others perceive twins facing each other. People who see a vase identify the center of the drawing as the figure and the area on the right and left as the ground, or background. Conversely, people who see twins facing each other see the center as the background and the area on the right and left as the figure.

Figure 3.4 is another illustration of the principle of figure and ground. As we first glance at the drawing, we perceive nothing but ink blobs—nothing is clearly distinguishable as either the figure or the background. If we continue to look at the drawing, however, we perceive the face of Christ or a bearded man at the top center of the picture. When we see the face, it becomes the figure; the rest of the drawing becomes the ground.

Just as we use figure and ground to organize visual stimuli, we also use it to organize the messages that people offer us. For example, traditional values in the American culture placed the husband as the head of the household while the wife was viewed as less important. Symbolically, wives, rather than husbands, have changed their names to become part of a newly established family. Recently, a grandmother was curious about her granddaughter's reluctance to change her last name to her spouse's name upon marriage. Speaking to the couple, but focusing on the granddaughter, the grandmother asked, "And why didn't you change your name?" The husband replied, "I already had my career established and I thought it would confuse my clients."

An example of closure: Ink blobs or a cat?   **Figure 3.5**

An example of closure: A triangle or straight lines?   **Figure 3.6**

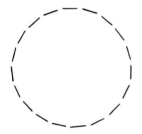

An example of closure: A circle or straight lines?   **Figure 3.7**

The actress Ina Claire, who was an early star in "talking pictures," married John Gilbert, who was a romantic hero of silent movies. Shortly after their marriage took place, a reporter asked her how it felt being married to a celebrity. Ina Claire replied, "Why don't you ask my husband?"[7]

In both of these examples, the humor or surprise occurs because the communicators have a different notion of figure and ground. In the first example, the grandmother perceives the husband as the figure and the wife as the ground while the husband articulates the opposite assumption. In the second case, the actress suggests to the reporter that she, rather than her husband, is the celebrity.

Another way of organizing stimuli is described as *closure*. We engage in closure every time we fill in things that do not exist. If someone showed us figure 3.5 and asked us what we perceived, we would probably say that it was a picture of a cat. But, as we can clearly see, the figure is incomplete. We can see a cat only if we are willing to fill in the blank areas. Additional examples of closure are given in figures 3.6 and 3.7. Most of us would identify figure 3.6 as a triangle and figure 3.7 as a circle, rather than claiming that both are simply short lines.

Figure 3.8   An example of proximity: Three groups of lines or
                 nine separate lines?

Closure is used in our interactions with others. When we fill in a word or a phrase for another person, we are using closure. When we have a long-term relationship with another person, we can frequently communicate with them without speaking at all. Alfred Hitchcock, the producer of such movies as "Psycho" and "The Birds," was able to create such thrillers without the advantage of having an audience observe the work as it was being created. In fact, Hitchcock never sat among his audiences when they viewed his completed films. A reporter asked him if he missed hearing them scream. "No," he replied, "I can hear them when I'm making the picture."[8] His successful film career may have occurred, in part, because he was able to "fill in" the audience response to his work.

We also organize stimuli according to their *proximity.* The principle of proximity or nearness operates whenever we group two or more things that simply happen to be close to each other. When we group according to proximity, our assumption is "birds of a feather flock together," even though we know this is not always true. In figure 3.8 we tend to perceive three groups of lines with three lines in each group, rather than nine separate lines, because of the principle of proximity or nearness.

We use proximity in our interactions with others as well. For example, we use people's occupations to make assessments of their behaviors. We may assume that if a person is a writer, he or she would be fluent with language, or if a person is a mathematician, he or she would be able to consider the symbolic nature of things. A politician used such an assessment boldly. At an embassy reception, he approached Ann Landers, newspaper columnist, and drawled, "So you're Ann Landers. Why don't you say something funny?" Without missing a beat, Landers replied, "Well, you're a politician. Tell me a lie."[9]

Similarity also helps us to organize stimuli. We sometimes group elements together because they resemble each other in size, color, shape, or other attributes. For example, we tend to believe that people who like the music we do also enjoy the same movies we do. We assume that a suit that looks like one of our own is probably within the same price range. In figure 3.9, we perceive squares and circles, rather than a group of geometric shapes, because of the principle of similarity.

Similarity is useful as we organize messages others send to us. Reporters frequently asked former President Jimmy Carter about his stance on moral issues since he was a devout Southern Baptist. They probably reasoned that since he had a strong religious background, he would similarly hold clear moral values. Carter was able to use this situation to a humorous advantage

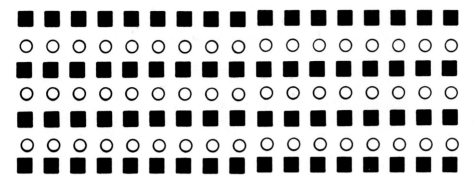

An example of similarity: Squares and circles or a group of geo-   Figure 3.9
metric figures?

on one occasion. A reporter asked him, "Mr. President, how would you feel
if you were told that your daughter was having an affair?" "Shocked and over-
whelmed," replied Carter, adding, "but then, she's only seven years old."[10]
The reporter may have expected Carter's initial response, on the basis of similarity, but was surprised by the rationale offered in the second part of the
answer.

To understand the relationship between the organizing of stimuli and communication, let us consider a typical party. When you arrive at a party, you
immediately begin to organize the stimuli—the people there—into groups.
You focus first on your friends and acquaintances, who serve as *figure,* and
largely ignore the strangers present, who serve as *ground.* Those friends who
are standing closest to you will talk with you first because of their *proximity.*
The people with whom you will spend the most time are those who you perceive to be *similar* to you. Finally, you notice two married friends, separated
for a number of months and considering divorce, arrive together. As the evening progresses, they tend to stand together and to talk in an intimate way.
You achieve *closure* by assuming they have reconciled their differences. When
you approach them, your mood is light and your conversation is spirited. This
example illustrates how organizing stimuli—one activity of perception—affects communication. It helps to determine with whom we speak, how we
speak, what we speak about, how long we speak, and the tone of voice we
use.

Interpretation

Each of us interprets the stimuli we perceive. The more ambiguous the
stimuli, the more room we have for interpretation. The basis of the well-known
inkblot test lies in the principle of interpretation of stimuli. Figure 3.10 shows
three inkblots a psychologist might ask you to interpret. The ambiguity of the
figures is typical.

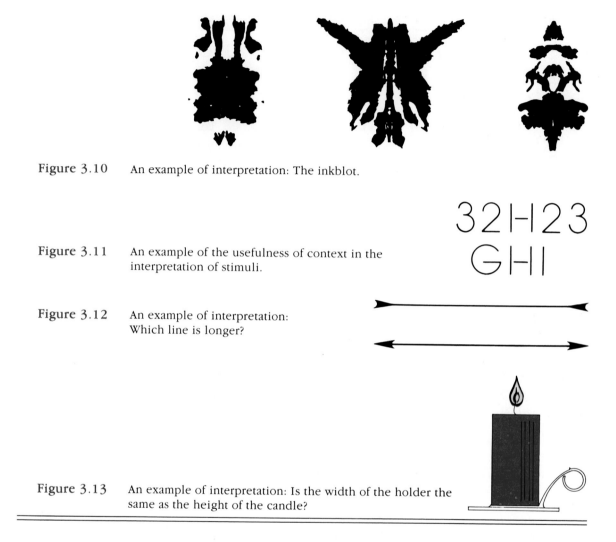

Figure 3.10   An example of interpretation: The inkblot.

Figure 3.11   An example of the usefulness of context in the
interpretation of stimuli.

Figure 3.12   An example of interpretation:
Which line is longer?

Figure 3.13   An example of interpretation: Is the width of the holder the
same as the height of the candle?

In our interpretation of stimuli, we frequently rely on the *context* in which
we perceive the stimuli, or we *compare* the stimuli to others. Sometimes, there
are helpful clues. For example, in figure 3.11, the letters and numbers are
useful to us as we attempt to interpret the middle figure. The contexts indicate
that, in the top diagram, the middle figure is two number ones with a dash
between them, while in the bottom diagram, the middle figure is an H.

Nonetheless, comparisons and the use of context can be confusing. All of
us are familiar with figures like 3.12 and 3.13. In these figures, we perceive
differences in the lengths of the lines, and in the height of the candle and the
width of the candle holder, although no differences exist.

Differences in Perception

Jack can see he sees
what he can see Jill can't see,
and he can see
that Jill can't see that she can't see,
but he can't see WHY
Jill can't see that Jill can't see. . . .
Jill can see Jack can't see
and can't see he can't see.
Jill can see WHY
Jack can't see,
but Jill cannot see WHY
Jack can't see he can't see. . . .
Jack can't see he can't see
and can't see
Jill can't see Jill can't see it,
and vice versa.

R. D. Laing includes this poem in his collection *Knots.* The poem captures the complexity of perception and the difficulty of establishing common perceptions.

Discuss an experience in which you and another person attempted to reach an agreement but could not. Identify the differences in perception, suggest reasons for those differences, and enumerate the methods you attempted to use to validate your perceptions.

From R. D. Laing, ''Differences in Perception'' in *Knots.* Copyright © 1970 Pantheon Books, Division of Random House, Inc., New York, NY.

John Gilbert, an early film actor, provides a humorous example of failing to use the context in interpreting a verbal response. Gilbert was especially anxious to speak with a particular actress at rehearsals one day and he asked a stagehand where she was. The stagehand replied, ''She's round behind.'' Gilbert quickly replied, ''Yes, I know that, but where is she?''[11]

The relationship between the interpretation of stimuli and communication can be demonstrated in a situation that may be familiar to you. Women who work in large businesses or corporations may more frequently serve in secretarial or clerical positions than in executive or managerial jobs. As a result, a person who is unfamiliar with a particular office may mistakenly request a cup of coffee from the lawyer instead of her secretary. The stereotype leads the visitor to an inaccurate assumption and an incorrect interpretation, which, in turn, leads to difficulty in communication.

Interpretation is important in our interactions with others. Sigmund Freud, the founder of modern psychoanalysis, relied upon interpretation in his analytic work. Freud is remembered for a number of theories, many of which remain controversial. He is also remembered through anecdotes. Perhaps one of the most well known concerns cigar smoking. Freud was a habital cigar smoker and on one occasion, as he was puffing on a long cigar, one of his students asked him about the habit. The student noted that cigar smoking is often thought of as a symbolic activity and that the cigar is frequently interpreted as a phallic symbol or as an emblem of masculinity. The student asked Freud if cigar smoking carried any particular symbolic weight for him. Freud puffed reflectively for a few moments, and then replied, "Sometimes a cigar is just a cigar."[12] The humor is derived from Freud's unwillingness to interpret the act.

Summary

In this chapter we examined the role of perception. Perception is the process by which we come to understand ourselves and others, and understanding is an activity basic to interpersonal communication. The older view of perception suggested it was passive and objective, and that meaning was inherent in the stimuli perceived. The contemporary view of perception is that it is a subjective, active, and creative process.

Differences in perceptions arise among people. Physiological features of the individual, including height, weight, body type, gender, and differences in our senses, contribute toward those differences in perceptions. Past experiences, including those dependent on our cultures and subcultures, also affect our perceptions. Finally, our current circumstances and our present feelings affect our perceptions.

What occurs in perception? While we are unaware of the separate processes that occur, we engage in selection, organization, and interpretation. Each of these was examined in detail in this chapter.

Notes

1.   See, for example, C. R. Berger and R. J. Calabrese, "Some Explorations in Initial Interaction and Beyond: Toward a Developmental Theory of Interpersonal Communication," *Human Communication Research* 1 (1975): 99–112.

2.   Richard Restak, *The Brain* (New York: Bantam Books, 1984), p. 244.

3.   Marshall R. Singer, "Culture: A Perceptual Approach." In *Intercultural Communication: A Reader,* 4th ed., edited by Larry A. Samovar and Richard E. Porter (Belmont, Calif.: Wadsworth, 1985), p. 63.

4.   V. P. Richmond and D. Robertson, "Communication Apprehension as a Function of Being Raised in an Urban or Rural Environment" (Monograph, West Virginia Northern Community College, 1976).

5. Judy C. Pearson, *Gender and Communication* (Dubuque, Iowa: Wm. C. Brown Publishers, 1985).

6. Alistair B. Fraser, "Fata Morgana—The Grand Illusion," *Psychology Today* 9 (January 1976): 22.

7. Clifton Fadiman, *The Little, Brown Book of Anecdotes* (Boston: Little, Brown & Company, 1985), p. 105.

8. Fadiman, *The Little, Brown Book of Anecdotes,* p. 281.

9. Fadiman, *The Little, Brown Book of Anecdotes,* p. 341.

10. Fadiman, *The Little, Brown Book of Anecdotes,* p. 127.

11. Fadiman, *The Little, Brown Book of Anecdotes,* p. 242.

12. Fadiman, *The Little, Brown Book of Anecdotes,* p. 223.

Additional Readings

Broadbent, Donald E. *Perception and Communication.* New York: Oxford University Press, 1987.

Heider, Fritz. *The Psychology of Interpersonal Relations.* New York: Wiley, 1958.

Higgins, E. Tory and Bargh, John A. "Social Cognition and Social Perception." *Annual Review of Psychology* 38(1987): 369–425.

Lewicki, Pawel. *Nonconscious Social Information Processing.* Orlando, Fla.: Academic Press, 1986.

Mackie, Fiona. *The Status of Everyday Life: A Sociological Excavation of the Prevailing Framework of Perception.* International Library of Sociology. New York: Routledge, Chapman & Hall, 1985.

Nisbett, Richard and Ross, Lee. *Human Inference: Strategies and Shortcomings of Social Judgment.* Englewood Cliffs, N.J.: Prentice Hall, 1980.

Pryor, J. B. and Day, J. D., eds. *The Development of Social Cognition.* New York: Springer-Verlag, 1985.

Tagiuri, Renato and Petrullo, Luigi, eds. *Person Perception and Interpersonal Behavior.* Stanford, Calif.: Stanford University Press, 1958.

Welker, R. L. *Integrative Activities of the Brain: Determinants of Organized Perception Behavior.* Neurobiology Series. New York: Wiley, 1986.

Wyer, Robert S. & Srull, Thomas K. "Human Cognition in Its Social Context." *Psychological Review* 93(1986): 322–59.

Components

Over the next eight chapters, we will examine the skills that can enhance your communicative competence. This brief overview is intended to assist you in both comprehending their nature and their relevance to communicative competence. The particular skills selected for this textbook will be best understood in the context of a general model of communicative competence.

Consider what makes for an excellent acting performance. Generally speaking, *motivation* is important for an actor to give a good performance. Actors who lack confidence or simply see little value to their performance are likely to be viewed as nervous or simply uninvolved in their role. However, an actor who is motivated may still give a poor performance if he or she lacks *knowledge* of the script, role, audience, author's intentions, props, and context. You can imagine the chaos if several actors were trying to perform a play in which only some of them knew their lines at separate places in the script. However, even actors who are motivated to perform well and are well-versed in the script may give a poor performance if they simply lack the acting *skills* to perform with motivation and knowledge.

In short, to give a good performance an actor is likely to need to be motivated to perform well, knowledgeable about how to perform well, and skilled in enacting the specific behaviors that comprise the performance. Your everyday interpersonal transactions are not much different from the demands of the actor. Across most conversations you will encounter, the more motivated you are to communicate well, the more knowledgeable you are about conversation, and the more skilled you are in your behavior, the more likely you are to be competent in your communication.

The particular skills that comprise competent interpersonal transaction are covered under four general areas: expressiveness, composure, other-orientation, and conversational coordination. *Expressiveness* concerns the ways in which we use behavior to express ideas and meanings.

Composure concerns confidence in our manner and assertion of our rights. *Other-orientation* means that you show interest and concern for the other person in the conversation. *Conversational coordination* involves the processes of turn-taking and topic management. Whereas composure promotes the self, other-orientation promotes the other person. And while expressiveness projects one's own intentions and meanings, conversational coordination helps assure that these meanings are enacted in a manner specifically adapted to the rules and norms of the other person. Thus, these skills represent both the importance of the self and the importance of the other.

You will benefit most from this textbook in general, and these chapters on skill in particular, if you are genuinely motivated to become a better communicator, if you devote yourself to understanding and knowing more about communication, and if you practice what you want and know to refine your skills. The chapters that follow should assist you in this endeavor.

Verbal Expressiveness

The "Bizarro" cartoon by Dan Piraro is reprinted by permission of Chronicle Features, San Francisco, CA.

In the cartoon, Bradley's notion of interesting conversation appears somewhat different from his wife's. His wife, furthermore, seems somewhat oblivious to the source of Bradley's complete boredom. She obviously takes a while before she notices his total lack of interest. Bradley apparently finds her topic and style of conversation less than scintillating. Her conversational style is simply not very expressive. In the next two chapters we will examine some of the characteristics that make conversations more or less expressive. This chapter will consider verbal characteristics, and nonverbal components of expressiveness will be the topic of chapter 5.

In this chapter we will describe the nature of verbal communication by defining the term and by considering the notions that words are symbolic and arbitrary. We will consider some of the unconventional ways that we use language; we will discuss the inconsistency in the rules of our language; we will focus on ambiguity, vagueness, and inappropriate categorization that occurs in our usage; we will identify ways in which we deliberately distort meaning through our language choices; and we will consider the role of differences in perception on communication. After consideration of some of the problems in verbal expressiveness, we will suggest specific methods of improving our verbal effectiveness in interpersonal communication.

The Nature of Verbal Communication

Definition of Verbal Communication

Before you were a year old, before you could walk, and before you could put thoughts together, you began using language. The first "da da," "ma ma," or "wa wa" was richly rewarded by your parents and by significant other people. Slowly you learned to put words together to form phrases, sentences, and longer units of meaning. We have used verbal communication for virtually our entire lives, but rarely do we consider its significance, its nature, or even its definition. *Verbal* literally pertains to, or is associated with, words. The word *verbal* focuses on the words rather than on the ideas they represent. *Communication* is the process of mutually deriving meaning. *Verbal communication,* then, is defined as the process of mutually deriving meaning through the use of words.

Words are symbolic.   Words may represent an object, a concept, an event, a person, or an idea. However, they merely represent these other things, through association, resemblance, or convention. In the same way that a diamond ring worn by a woman symbolizes an upcoming wedding, a Phi Beta Kappa key represents scholastic excellence, or a uniform designates that a person is a member of a military officers' training program, words symbolize other things or concepts.

Words are arbitrary.   Words represent other objects, events, ideas, people, or concepts because a group of people have agreed to use them in those particular ways. When groups of individuals—subcultures like young people, black Americans, or women—decide to use a word in a particular way, they are free to do so upon agreement by the members of that specific group of people. We have no "natural" or "real" reasons to refer to one thing by one word and another thing by another word. The Dutch word *seeples* is every bit as "correct" as is the English word *onions* and what is "groovy" yesterday may be "gross" tomorrow.

While it may seem ridiculous to think about it, there is no legitimate reason we ended up referring to the seating devices in your classroom as "chairs." They might just as well have been named "fish" or "zwigthackers." At some point in the development of our symbolic system of communication, enough people accepted the term "chair" to represent a certain type of seating device. The symbol possesses no necessary, inherent relationship to the thing to which it refers.

Words accrue meaning from their context.   There are many ways in which words, as symbols, generate meaning based upon the context in which they occur. One influence is from the verbal context. The term "proposition," for example, may mean a statement or assertion, a logical statement as in a theorem, a proposal, or an "invitation" to engage in some form of future relationship behavior (e.g., a sexual proposition). Which one of these meanings is intended depends in large part on how the term is placed in the context of other words. The word obviously takes on different meanings in the statement, "Selling advanced weapon systems to Middle Eastern countries is a risky proposition," than it does in the statement, "He made a lewd proposition to her at the party." The difference in meanings depends on the words that contextualize the term in question.

Another influence of context is the nonverbal behavior surrounding the word. The word "love" is highly ambiguous in our culture. At times our nonverbal contextualization of the term assists in making its meaning more clear. It is likely to receive different inflection patterns and be combined with different behaviors when referring to a brother or sister than it is when referring to a romantic intimate. At some point in the development of a romantic relationship, someone says the phrase, "I love you." The next move is probably very important to the trajectory of the relationship. If the response is, "I like you, too," there are apparent discrepancies in the meanings. However, even when both responses use the same terms, the *way* in which the phrase, "I love you," is said can result in meanings similar to, "I like you." Sarcasm usually works because of a discrepancy between the verbal and nonverbal levels of meaning. The statement, "I guess we're havin' some fun now, huh?" could be an accurate reflection of the speaker's feelings, or if said in a very restrained, almost bored manner, could mean just the opposite. A somewhat less obvious difference in meanings can be due to written versus oral nonverbal contexts. The phrase, "They razed the building to the ground," sounds contradictory when spoken, because the term "razed" sounds like "raised." When spelled out, it is far less confusing, given the obvious difference in words.

Finally, words take on different meanings based upon the physical and social context in which they are spoken. Bill Cosby used to do a routine in which, while being worked on by a doctor, overhears the physician say, "Oops!" Cosby notes that when he uses the term, he knows what "oops" means, but he is terrified of what it may mean when a doctor uses the phrase in the middle of performing a procedure on a patient. Research has suggested that one of the reasons that interpersonal violence is so common in dating relationships is that many males actually seem to think that "no" is more likely to mean "yes" during a date, despite it meaning "no" in all other contexts.[1] Words obviously are attributed with different meanings depending upon the type of context in which they are used.

Words Can Obstruct Communication

The symbolic, arbitrary nature of words causes language to be a vehicle of confusion as often as it is a means of clarity among persons. Each person learns a set of words that can be slightly, or significantly, different from the set of words that another person may learn. Our personal language is affected by our country and culture, our nationality and neighborhood, our vocation and values, and our attitudes and abilities.

We are not very likely to share all of these variations with even one other person; nonetheless, we are expected to communicate clearly with all others. What can we do given this situation? Clearly, we cannot become another person and totally gain control of his or her language, but we can become aware of common problems that obstruct clarity in our interpersonal communication. We can identify five reasons for lack of clarity in verbal communication. First, people use language in unconventional or unusual ways. Second, our language is inconsistent in its rules. Third, people sometimes speak ambiguously, vaguely, or they do not categorize appropriately or sufficiently. Fourth, individuals occasionally deliberately distort meaning through their language choices. Finally, persons may make incorrect word choices as a result of different perspectives. Let us examine each of these reasons in more detail.

People use language in unconventional ways.   Clarity in communication is dependent upon using words as people have agreed to use them or as convention dictates. Unfortunately, people do not always follow convention, or they may follow agreements made with a smaller group of individuals, or perhaps an agreement with themselves in determining what words will mean. We use words in an unconventional way when we make grammatical, structural, or other errors, and when we use colloquialisms, clichés, euphemisms, slang, jargon, and regionalisms.

Some substitutions of incorrect words cause confusion, even though they seem almost commonplace. For example, the sentence, "There is a suspicious-looking person walking on both sides of the street," may confuse the listener. Did the speaker mean that two suspicious-looking people existed and one was walking on one side of the street and one was walking on the other, or did the speaker mean that a single suspicious-looking person was walking on one side of the street and then on the other? "There is a suspicious-looking person on each side of the street" might communicate the intended meaning clearly and accurately. If someone asks if he or she is to turn left, and your response is "right," what should the other person conclude? He or she may assume that it is correct to turn left or might guess that it is correct to turn right. The correct interpretation may be drawn, but a great deal of room for confusion exists.

Incorrect pronunciation can also lead to confusion. Each of us has had the experience of reading a word but not pronouncing it in oral communication. We read the word *chimera* and understand its general meaning from the context, but we are unsure of its pronunciation. It could be "shim-mer-A" or "ky-MEER-a." Nonetheless, we may attempt to use it in a conversation. While a friend may clearly understand the word *chimera,* he or she may be very confused by the word *shim-mer-A* which we have interjected.

William Safire had the experience of interviewing former Governor Jerry Brown of California when Brown mispronounced the word *synecdoche.* Instead of "sin-EK-doe-key," Brown said "SY-neck-dosh." Safire caught the mispronunciation, but was unsure of how he should respond. On the one hand, he did not want to correct a governor; on the other, he did not want Brown to continue making the error. Finally, he used the word himself, correctly, later in the interview. Brown appreciatively interrupted, "Is that how you pronounce it? I'd seen the word in print, but I never heard anybody pronounce it before."[2] In this case, little harm was done (unless Safire's report of the incident hurt Brown's credibility), but the effect of mispronunciations can lead to confusion or strained feelings between the communicators.

Finally, we sometimes put words together in an incorrect way which may distort our intended meaning. *Syntax*—the arrangement of word forms to show their mutual relations in sentences—must also be taken into consideration if we wish to communicate clearly. A common error that occurs involves the use of a misplaced prepositional phrase. For instance, "Mary enjoys having dinner in her robe" suggests that Mary's food is spread out in her robe and that she eats from the garment, while "Dressed in her robe, Mary enjoys having dinner" probably conveys the intended meaning. Correct word choice, pronunciation, and syntax are all essential to clarity in interpersonal communication.

Colloquialisms are words or phrases that are used in informal conversation, but not in more formal communication. Colloquial words and phrases are sometimes meaningless, ambiguous, or outdated. Examples of colloquialisms are "Have a good day now," "See you later," "I'm fixin' to . . . ," "Great," "Super," "Have a happy," "Take care," "I'm telling you," "You're telling me," "Snackies," and "Din-din." Colloquialisms may confuse listeners or may merely annoy them.

Clichés are words or phrases that are overused and that have lost their effectiveness because of overuse. Clichés are often little more than fillers in conversations. Examples of clichés include "to go hog wild," "skeleton in the closet," "to be in the same boat," "you can't take it with you," "a bird in the hand is worth two in the bush," "you made your bed, now you can lie in it," and "you can't teach an old dog new tricks." Clichés are, by definition, overused. They do not provide fresh insight or a unique way of viewing reality; rather they reduce ideas to a pedestrian level of staleness or flatness.

Euphemisms are mild or inoffensive words that are substituted for harsh or offensive words. Most euphemisms are substitutes for short, abrupt words; the names of physical functions; or the terms for social unpleasantness. For instance, the manufacturer of cigarettes may state that his customers experience "premature terminal health difficulties," and a parent whose child is cohabiting with another young adult may refer to the partner as a "close friend." Other popular euphemisms in current usage are "terminated" for being fired, "writing a book" for being unemployed, "sanitary engineer" for garbage collector, "housing units" for homes, "fresh input" for information, "meaningful relationships" for love affairs, and "feelings of hostility" for hatred. You may recall the variety of terms, including "Reaganomics," which are euphemistic substitutions for discussing the Reagan administration's budget proposals and tax cuts.

Informal conversation may include colloquialisms, cliches, and other unconventional language usage.

Euphemisms have the advantage of being more polite language, but they frequently distort reality. "Unemployed" may be more accurate than "writing a book," and "no intention of getting a job" may be more to the point than wordy phrases about necessary job conditions, requirements concerning the working environment, and other prerequisite employment situations. Euphemisms only provide the comfort that delusion offers. Reality becomes more palatable, but it also becomes less authentic. Interpersonal communication based on delusion is unsatisfying and possibly confusing to the communicators. The disadvantages of using euphemistic language usually outweigh the advantages.

Slang is the term by which we refer to the specialized language of a group of people who share a common interest or belong to the same subculture. Slang may include words and phrases that are highly colloquial and are generally not used in formal English. Slang frequently consists of new words or of current words employed in some special sense. Some people use the term, "the pits," to represent a negative situation while others refer to more desirable situations as "really rad." To "go straight" may mean to behave in a conventional or reputable manner while "rubbing someone the wrong way" may mean to impress them in a negative manner.

Back Door Last rig in convoy

Breaker 21 CB cut-in signal

Chicken Coop Weighing station for trucks

County Mounty Local police

Double Nickels 55 mph (the national speed limit)

Ears CB radio

Eighteen-Wheeler A five-axle truck

Flip Side Return trip

Four-Wheeler Passenger car

Front Door Lead rig in convoy

Green Stamp Money or toll road

Pavement Princess A hooker who works truck stops

Plain Wrapper Unmarked police car

Put The Hammer Down Floor the accelerator pedal

Rocking Chair Middle rigs in a truck convoy

Seat Covers Girls in cars

Shakytown Los Angeles, because of its earthquakes

Smokey Bear Highway patrol, also simply "smokey" or "bear"

Smokey Taking Pictures State trooper with radar

Ten-Four OK

Tijuana Taxi Police car with flashing lights

We Gone Transmission completed

An example of subculture slang.   Figure 4.1

Slang is temporary in nature. The 1950s terms "scuzz" and "zilch" were forgotten in the 1960s when slang terms like "pig," "groovy," and "uptight" were used, only to be replaced with another set of slang in the 1970s which included such terms as "turkey," "gross," and "queer."

The short life that slang terms enjoy contributes to a great deal of confusion in communication. Does *bad* mean *good* or truly *bad?* Not so long ago people received invitations for "gay affairs." How would you respond to such an invitation today? One of the purposes of slang is to make a group of persons distinct and unique from other groups and from the "mainstream" of people. One subculture that has created a distinct language is the "CB" (citizens' band radio) culture, used most often by interstate truckers (listed in figure 4.1).[3]

The combination of the temporary nature of slang and the use of slang by special subgroups to separate them from others contributes to a lack of clarity in communication across groups that relies on the use of slang. Persons may respond to slang words in terms of historical meaning or in light of an incorrect subgroup reference. Or, the term may have no meaning at all for the listener. Slang is thus generally discouraged as a means to clarity in interpersonal communication. It is likely to only be effective with group members or peers who are familiar with the slang or who are likely to adopt the terms.

Jargon refers to meaningless talk, language that is not understood, or to the language of a special group or profession. While we think of slang as being associated with subcultural groups like teenagers, blacks, women, members of the drug culture, and CB radio owners, jargon is associated with physicians,

B.C.   **by johnny hart**

By permission of Johnny Hart and Creators Syndicate, Inc.

educators, electricians, economists, and sports afficianados. Words like "pulmonary edema," "dyad," "consensual validation," "gridder," and "tackle" are jargon. Jargon, like slang, can lead to a lack of clarity in interpersonal communication that may be accompanied by a negative feeling between the communicators. Of course, when used in the context of a particular subculture or network of relationships such terms may make communication more efficient and clear. Scientists in every discipline develop jargon or argot to refer to specific concepts unique to their areas of study. Generally, the persons in the particular discipline use the terms to communicate with each other, even though few outsiders would comprehend the terms in the same way, if at all.

Regionalisms are words or phrases that are unique to a particular region of a country. Ivy, in John Steinbeck's *The Grapes of Wrath,* was aware of regionalism when she said,

> *Everybody says words different. Arkansas folks say 'em different, and Oklahomy folks says 'em different. And we seen a lady from Massachusetts, an' she said 'em differentest of all. Couldn't hardly make out what she was sayin'.*[4]

Vocabulary, pronunciation, and grammar vary from one part of the country to another. In the east, a "soda" is a soft drink; in the midwest, it consists of ice cream, flavoring, and soda water. Lunch is served at noon in New York City, but at 3 P.M. in Iowa. Dinner occurs at noon in Minnesota, but at 7 P.M. in Virginia. Some people "wahsh," others "warsh," and still others "woysh." You may "take" the bus to school or "bring" the bus to school. A friend may ask you to "come with" or to "come with me."

Regionalisms, like slang and jargon, tend to bind a group of people together. However, negative effects can result from the use of regionalisms. First of all, people from other regions of the country are often stereotyped or prejudged. A person may be thought to be quaint or naive, suave or stupid, or cultivated or conceited as a result of his or her distinctive regional language.

In addition, confusion in communication can occur. The lack of clarity may be no more serious than receiving ice cream when you only wanted a soft drink, but you could gain an economically impoverished child ("poor boy") when you simply wanted a sandwich! Regionalisms generally do not increase your competence as a clear interpersonal communicator.

Our language is inconsistent in its rules.   Speakers of English are plagued by inconsistencies as the characters in the "B.C." cartoon suggest. Structural rules that are generally true have exceptions; spelling rules cannot be generalized to all cases; and rules of grammar change from case to case. Some special problems bother the oral communicator. *Homonyms*—words that sound the same, but have a different spelling and meaning—can confuse the listener in interpersonal communication settings. For example, a young female stating, "I can't wait for my prints to come," could just as easily be interpreted as her eagerness for a "white knight" than her waiting photographs to return from the developer. Communicators sometimes lack the necessary context or background to understand the particular usage that the speaker intends.

Editorialists and others attempt to rectify our inconsistencies. Theodore M. Bernstein regularly writes about language difficulties in his column. The following is typical of Bernstein's essays:

> *Bi bi, confusion. Thousands and thousands of people are puzzled by some words beginning with bi-. Their dictionaries say, for instance, that bi-yearly means once every two years, and in the next breath says it means twice a year. . . . Bimonthly is no problem; it almost always means every two months. Biweekly, however, usually means every two weeks, but sometimes means twice a week. Biannual means twice a year, but biennial means every two years. So the puzzlement persists. But there are signs that it will abate within the next semicentennial period. The cure is simple: Get everyone to reserve bi—to mean two and use semi— to mean half. Not a semibad idea, is it?*[5]

The denotative and connotative meanings of words can also confuse listeners. Every word has a *denotative meaning*—dictionary definition agreed upon by most people—and a *connotative meaning*—subjective, individualized, emotional meaning. When you use the word *teacher,* for instance, you may have the denotative meaning of a person who instructs students in a particular subject or in a particular grade level. A listener may connotatively think of a teacher as someone who is helpful, understanding, and warm while another listener may think of a teacher as someone who is strict, hateful, and cold. Connotative meanings are only similar to the extent that experiences are similar.

People speak ambiguously, abstractly, or do not categorize appropriately or sufficiently.   Ambiguity or vagueness can create problems in interpersonal communication. Physicians frequently complain about patients who lack

Unconventional Usage

Write down at least ten words or phrases that provide examples of unconventional usage. For instance, include errors that you have heard others make, colloquialisms that are used by your peers, clichés that you have heard from relatives, euphemisms that an older person has used, slang from a younger sibling, jargon from someone in a different occupation or with a different background, and a regionalism from someone who has recently moved to your area. After you have identified at least ten examples, share your list with other classmates and determine if they can explain the intended meaning of the word or term. Discuss how verbal clarity is affected by the use of these and similar terms.

specificity in describing their symptoms. Patients may simply say, "I hurt," "I don't feel well," or "I haven't felt like myself lately," in explaining what is wrong. Similarly, communicators may offer each other too little specific information in conversations.

Figurative language may be used to clarify an idea, but can result in confusion. The abstract nature of figurative language may provide the misunderstanding. For instance, if someone tells you that another person is "as high as a kite," you understand that the person is not literally above the ground, but may be happy because of some good news, drunk on alcoholic beverages, or may have taken a drug.

In a similar way, insufficient categorization can lead to confusion in interpersonal communication. For example, if you ask a friend if "Baby" is invited, too, when she invites you to her house for dinner, what or whom will your friend assume about your question? Is "Baby" a three-month-old infant, a four-year-old child, or a cat or dog? The categorization or groupings that we make are sometimes significantly different from those made by other people or they are insufficient to adequately describe that which we are attempting to communicate.

Three types of inappropriate or insufficient categorization can be identified: indiscrimination, polarization, and frozen evaluation. *Indiscrimination* refers to the neglect of differences and the overemphasis of similarities. When we meet a new person on campus, we are eager to know his or her major, class standing, and if he or she lives on or off campus. We use stereotypes to draw conclusions about the attitudes, beliefs, and values of others. The language that we use encourages the practice of indiscrimination. We have a relatively small number of words to discuss a relatively large number of concepts. For instance, if a new acquaintance discloses that she is a home economics major, we may tell someone else that she is "traditional." Or, if someone shares that he is a member of the Democratic Party, we may conclude that he is "liberal." The labels "traditional" and "liberal" may each cover a wide variety of perspectives, but our vocabularies may be limited to these and few other terms to differentiate between persons of varying persuasions.

Polarization is the error of mistaking contraries (two phenomena between which there is "middle ground") for contradictories (two phenomena which are authentic dichotomies). For instance, people polarize by stating that everyone is either against them or with them when others may agree with some of their behaviors, but disagree with their values. Hitler made the error of polarization when he said, "Everyone in Germany is a National Socialist—the few outside the party are either lunatics or idiots."[6]

Frozen evaluation is spreading an evaluation over the past or the future without regard for changes. When you plan on attending a ten-year class reunion and tell your spouse about the "class beauty" he is about to meet, you make the error of frozen evaluation and may find that she is no longer the most attractive woman in the group. Your spouse may then wonder about how you define "attractive." Future references to attractive people may be met with confusion.

People deliberately distort meaning through their word choices.   Politicians and advertisers are well known for their practice of deliberately distorting meaning. They carefully word their promises in order that they are not liable for failure. As interpersonal communicators, we occasionally attempt the same practice. We may speak in wordy, meaningless phrases in order to fool others or we may attempt to fool ourselves through our choice of words. For instance, your friend may try to impress you with his knowledge by stating that he is "attempting to reconceptualize the history of epistemology" in an assigned philosophy paper when he simply means that he is not plagiarizing his primary sources. Or, you may defensively argue that all you had for lunch was a salad since you are on a diet, and neglect to mention the three buttered rolls that accompanied the salad. As listeners we practice selective perception and hear only part of a message, thus distorting the speaker's intentions or we interpret the message in our own unique way to satisfy our personal desires. If our friends tell us that they won't mind watering our house plants while we are away on a break, as long as we are willing to return the favor, we may only hear that they are willing to water *our* plants and make no plans to return the favor.

People make incorrect word choices as a result of different perspectives.   Our native tongue affects perception. Edward Sapir and Benjamin Lee Whorf proposed a hypothesis stating that our perception of reality is determined by our thought processes and that our thought processes are limited by our language; therefore, our perception of reality is dependent upon our language.[7] The Sapir-Whorf Hypothesis explains why Eskimos, with their many words for snow, can perceive many variations in the white substance while Hawaiians can distinguish between various kinds of surf. This short dialogue illustrates the confusion that can occur when we use words differently as a result of differences in perception.

Alex: (looking at an expensive foreign automobile): Boy, that's really some lady—I wonder how she performs.

Ann: (glancing at an adult female walking on the street): I'm really surprised by the way you talk. We've been together for six months and we've talked about sexism and treating women as sexual objects before. Why do you do this?

Alex: Boy, you're really going too far now.

Ann: I'm going too far? You talk about other women and how they "perform," and I'm the one who's going too far. And, by the way, if you haven't noticed, I'm not a boy!

Alex: Boy, I'll never understand women.

Wordland

We have considered five reasons for words obstructing clear communication. Read the following dialogue from *Alice's Adventures in Wonderland* and suggest why the conversation is so confused. Rewrite the dialogue in a manner that results in clear communication between Alice and the Cat.

"Would you tell me, please, which way I ought to go from here?"
"That depends a good deal on where you want to get to," said the Cat.
"I don't care much where" said Alice.
"Then it doesn't matter which way you go," said the Cat.
"—So long as I get somewhere," Alice added as an explanation.
"Oh, you're sure to do that," said the Cat, "if you only walk long enough."
Alice felt that this could not be denied, so she tried another question, "What sort of people live around here?"
"In that direction," the Cat said, waving its right paw round, "lives a Hatter, and in that direction," waving the other paw, "lives a March Hare. Visit either you like: They're both mad."
"But I don't like to go among mad people," Alice remarked.
"Oh, you can't help that," said the Cat. "We're all mad here. I'm going mad, you're mad."
"How do you know I'm mad?" said Alice.
"You must be," said the Cat, "or you wouldn't have come here."
Alice didn't think that proved it at all; however she went on: "And how do you know that you are mad?"
"To begin with," said the Cat, "a dog's not mad. You grant that?"
"I suppose so," said Alice.
"Well, then," the Cat went on, "you see a dog growls when it's angry, and wags its tail when it's pleased. No, I growl when I'm pleased, and wag my tail when I'm angry. Therefore I'm mad."
"I call it purring not growling," said Alice.
"Call it what you like," said the Cat.[8]

Competence in Verbal Expressiveness

The March Hare and Alice had a disagreement in *Through the Looking Glass:*

"You should say what you mean," the March Hare went on.
"I do," Alice hastily replied, "at least—at least I mean what I say—that's the same thing you know."
"Not the same thing a bit!" said the Hatter.
"Why you might just as well say that 'I see what I eat' is the same as 'I eat what I see'!"[9]

Many of us feel that we communicate clearly. We are astounded when people seem to misunderstand that which we tell them. After all, we "say what we mean" and "mean what we say." Our verbal skills can be improved, however, in order that we become increasingly clear in our interpersonal communication. The following skills will assist you in gaining increased clarity.

1. *Use language in conventional, or agreed-upon, ways.* Attempt to use appropriate structure and grammar in your conversations. Using the correct verb form, recommended pronunciation, and proper word choices will not confuse listeners nor will they result in a loss of credibility. Your understanding of correct English usage is important in oral communication just as it is important to effective writing.

    Of course, this rule of thumb should not be applied without care to adapt one's language to the intended listeners. If your listeners are known to be expecting informal usage, or if you are aware of the types of word choices the listeners already understand, then obviously conventional usage is less important. This simply means that when the audience or listener is not well known, and in more formal contexts, conventional usage is likely to be the most adaptive choice initially. When the listener is known to be likely to comprehend and expect unconventional usage, and in more informal contexts, use of unconventional forms of language is more reasonable.

    The formality of your conversation should be appropriate for your partner. Asking, "What's up, fuzz?" is clearly less appropriate than, "What's the trouble, Officer?" to a highway patrol officer who has stopped you while driving your car. Colloquialisms, clichés, euphemisms, slang, jargon, and regionalisms should be used with care. Try to be sensitive to those phrases or words that you regularly use and consider the different meanings that they might hold for someone from a different part of the country, for someone from a different subculture, for someone of a different age, for someone with a different area of interest, or for someone who is

Confusion from Unconventional Usage

Examine the following excerpts from conversations. Explain the unconventional usage that occurs. Rewrite the initial comments in order to avoid the confusion.

_____ 1.   Jim: Tom's a turkey!

        Grandma: Why Jim, what do you mean? I've never heard your brother gobble.

Unconventional Usage: _____

Jim: _____

Grandma: _____

_____ 2. Employer: These procedures were conducted with an overall view of the conclusions that were to have been reached through implementation.

        Employee: I don't understand.

Unconventional Usage: _____

Employer: _____

Employee: _____

_____ 3. Physician: I'm afraid you have aldosteronism.

        Patient: Is that serious?

Unconventional Usage: _____

Physician: _____

Patient: _____

_____ 4.   Bob: Want a pop?

            Ann: I have a dad.

Unconventional Usage: _____

Bob: _____

Ann: _____

_____ 5.   Jay: You're a dummy!

            Dee: Why do you say that?

Unconventional Usage: _____

Jay: _____

Dee: _____

Recall one recent incident in which you, or someone with whom you were speaking, used language in an unconventional way. What was the result? How could the situation have been altered?

different from you in other ways. The informal level of colloquialisms, clichés, etc., may be inappropriate for the situation as well.

2. *Clarify inconsistencies in usage.* If you are using a word or phrase in an unusual way, explain your usage. When you choose to use a word that has more than one meaning, define the term appropriately. Keep in mind that every word has a denotative meaning and a connotative meaning. Listeners may draw upon a connotative meaning of a word that is far different from your intended meaning. When you use words that you suspect may have strong connotative meanings for your listeners, try to emphasize the denotative meaning or your own particular relationship to the word.

3. *Keep your message simple and direct.* A number of practices can assist you in keeping your message simple and direct. Using specific words and phrases will be useful. The word that refers to the smallest number of objects is more specific than the word that refers to a large number of objects. For example, *collie* is more specific than *dog, green* is less specific than *olive green.* *Concreteness* is the practice of being specific and precise; using specific statements. A simplified vocabulary assists in concreteness. Avoid ambiguous, vague words that have a high level of abstraction. Do not use complex words and phrases that cannot be easily understood by the listener. Substance can be given to abstract terms by relating them to people, places, and events. Accurate, specific, and informative words should be used. Instead of using "thing" or "gadget," use "lever" or "valve." The lack of specificity in this dialogue leads to confusion.

Joe: What did we do in class yesterday? I skipped it.

Jan: Which class?

Joe: Psych.

Jan: Nothing.

Joe: Didn't we have class?

Jan: Yes, but we didn't do anything.

Joe: I'm sure you just sat around doing nothing.

Jan: Well, you know what I mean. Nothing important.

Joe: But what did we cover in class?

Jan: Oh, stuff about conditioning. Here are my notes, you can copy them.

Do not overburden your listener with unnecessary, irrelevant information. Keep your message to the point, embellishing as necessary, but without unimportant sidetrips. Rambling about unrelated events will confuse the listeners and may lose their attention. Provide essential information that is relevant to your purpose. Avoid verbosity, excessive details, and extra words. Brevity and conciseness add clarity and strength to your interpersonal messages. The lack of precision and directness is demonstrated in the first dialogue. Notice the improvement in the second dialogue when both communicators are specific and to the point.

Driver: Could you tell me where I'd find that ice cream parlor that is known for having 31 flavors?

Pedestrian: 31 flavors? Yes, you know where that oak tree is? Well, I'm pretty sure there is a signal there, too. Turn left at the tree—that would probably be going south. Well, go in that direction a little ways and you'll see it on the passenger's side.

Driver: I don't have a passenger.

Driver: Could you tell me how to get to Baskin Robbins?

Pedestrian: Yes, go to the first signal, turn left, and it's two blocks down on your right. You can't miss it.

4.   *Practice descriptiveness.* When we describe observable behavior or the properties of an object without offering an evaluation or judgment, we are practicing *descriptiveness.* This skill stresses relying on a person's senses rather than on his or her emotions. Sensory detailing clarifies messages. Descriptive detail helps you by linking your ideas to previous or current observations of the other person. Notice how the lack of descriptiveness causes confusion in this dialogue.

Conversation	Analysis
Charlie: Hand me that paper. **Fred:** Where is it at?	*Clarity is decreased as Charlie uses few words and ambiguous words. Clarity could be increased by use of more descriptive words.*
Charlie: That paper. **Fred:** This paper? **Charlie:** No, the one that you have in your hand.	*Charlie offers more description by suggesting the location of the paper, but he still does not say which paper. Fred has a number of papers in his hand.*

Fred:	I've got three papers in my hand. Which one do you mean?	*Clarity is increased as more descriptiveness and less ambiguity is used.*
Charlie:	The bacteriology paper.	
Fred:	The lab manual or the class outline?	*All of the confusion about the paper could*
Charlie:	The lab manual with the experiment outlined on it.	*have been avoided by the use of more descriptive words.*

Advertisers must be descriptive in order to attract the attention of the buyer. They urge us to use our senses and imagination, as in these examples:

The glowing shades of sun-warmed stone, of heather freshly gathered from wild country fields. Estee Lauder captures it all as only she can for your eyes, lips, cheeks, fingertips.

Extraneous, evaluative words may distract the listener. He or she may focus on the emotional word you have added rather than on your central message. Evaluative language may add no additional meaning to the thoughts you are attempting to express. An example of this is contained in *Stuart Little:*

Suart said, "I'm looking for a bird named Margalo. You haven't sighted her, have you?"
"Can't say I have," said the storekeeper. "What does she look like?"
"Perfectly beautiful," replied Stuart, wiping the sarsaparilla off his lips with the corner of his sleeve.
"She's a remarkable bird. Anybody would notice her. She comes from a place where there are thistles."[10]

The storekeeper in *Stuart Little* had little descriptive information upon which to draw a conclusion. Similarly, the witness in the first interrogation that follows offers evaluation rather than description. Contrast the first response to the officer's questioning with that of the second witness.

Police Officer:	How would you describe the robber?
Witness:	He was moving awfully fast, but from what I saw, he was carrying a helmet, was wearing dark glasses, and blue jeans. He looked like one of those motorcycle freaks, you know how they dress. They're really taking over the whole country.
Police Officer:	You mentioned that the man was carrying a helmet. Did he escape on a motorcycle?
Witness:	Well, I did see a couple of them parked down the street so I suppose he did.

Police Officer:	How would you describe the robber?
Witness:	He was about six feet tall, weighed around 190 pounds, had brown eyes and hair, and had really large feet. He wore blue jeans, a brown leather jacket, and heavy boots.
Police Officer:	Could you pick him out of a line-up if one was arranged?
Witness:	Well, I think so.

Making statements based on assumptions and inferences as though they are facts does not represent logical thinking. Using judgmental words, phrases, or sentences can antagonize or confuse the listener. In this conversation, Reba's emotional response to her chemistry test confuses her roommate and creates conflict between the two.

Reba:	I just flunked my chemistry test.
Carolyn:	Really? That's too bad, but are you sure you flunked it?
Reba:	Well, I probably got a "C," but no better.
Carolyn:	Well, that's not really so bad.
Reba:	Not too bad! I studied all night for that test!
Carolyn:	I'm sorry. I just thought that a "C" sounded good compared to flunking it.
Reba:	Oh, you don't even care anyway. Besides, it's not your problem!

5. *Clarify your ideas through definitions, examples, and comparison and contrast.* Definitions may be used to clarify words or concepts that are unfamiliar, obscure, or different from the other person's typical associations for the words or concepts. One method of definition is putting the item you are discussing into a class of objects with which the listener is already familiar.

Examples assist in clarifying concepts. Both real and hypothetical examples are helpful. You will generally want to use examples after you have stated the concept; occasionally you may suggest exemplary information before you explain your ideas. You may recommend to a dinner partner, "Let's have a dry white wine tonight—for example, a Sauterne would be nice."

When you use comparison and contrast, you use familiar concepts to point out similarities and differences with the unfamiliar concept you are introducing. Relationships can be established and general principles can be drawn by comparing similar or contrasting different phenomena. In this conversation, the confusion that exists at the beginning of the conversation is somewhat dissipated as comparison, contrast, and other methods of clarification are used.

Conversation	Analysis
Robert: I want you to meet me at the old gas station tonight at 8.	*Robert is jumping to the conclusion that Doug knows where the old gas station is. He is not considering his listener's point of view.*
Doug: Tell me where it is.	
Robert: You dummy, you don't know where the gas station is? All the kids know that! You go down Benson Avenue until you hit the park.	*When Robert insults Doug by calling him a "dummy," he does not really mean it.*
Doug: Which park? The one with the baseball fields or the picnic tables?	*Robert fails to identify which park he means. His ambiguous statement needs more description.*
Robert: You turn right at the ball park and keep going until you hit an old house, the one that looks like a barn. Then turn left on the dirt road and keep going.	*Robert clarifies which park he is referring by using description, comparison, and contrast to describe the house. Robert fails to tell how far to go down the dirt road.*
Doug: Keep going! How far is "keep going"?	
Robert: The old gas station is just beyond the shaky, wooden bridge. The one with several of its planks missing. Got me?	*Robert singles out the bridge by describing it in detail and putting emphasis on it.*
Doug: Yeah, I think so.	*Doug understands most of the message, but he is still somewhat uncertain.*

6. *Use repetition and paraphrasing.* Repeating your message to the listener in the same words is known as *repetition;* repeating your message in different words is known as *paraphrasing.* Both techniques are useful to increase clarity. Paraphrasing is used in this dialogue by both the speaker and the listener to increase clarity.

    Two students, Ann and Beth, are talking on the telephone. Ann is attempting to explain a homework problem to Beth.

Beth: Explain the problem to me.

Ann: All right, let's try. First of all the problem involves two springs, one mass, and a dashpot.

Beth: Got it.

Ann: Now draw an x-y coordinate system. The x surface provides the normal force for the mass.

Beth: Come again.

Ann: The mass rests on a horizontal surface.

Beth: Okay.

Ann: One of the springs and the dashpot are connected from the mass, to the y axis, which is an immovable wall. At the opposite end of the mass is the other spring which is supplied with a forcing displacement. Got that?

Beth: Yeah, I think so.

Ann: Read it back to me then.

Beth: We have a mass resting on a horizontal surface, with a driven spring on one side and a spring and a dashpot on the other end connected to a wall.

Ann: Right!

7. *Index your ideas.* Communication is always framed by some form of context. The context provides useful information regarding how symbols are to be interpreted. However, competent use of language can also help to clarify the context, and, in so doing, the entire interaction episode. Indexing a message simply means to infuse its form and content with information regarding the particular episode being encountered.

   A message needs to be indexed, or "qualified,"[11] on at least four levels: *content, actor, coactor* (or listener), and *context.* The content we have already discussed. *Content is indexed* to the extent that the semantic content of the message is clear. *Actor indexing* means that the person encoding a message has made the message reflect his or her own meaning. *Coactor indexing* refers to adapting the message to the other person in the conversation. Finally, the message can be *indexed* in terms of the *particular context* in which it occurs. Philip's remark in the cartoon seems general because it provides minimal information regarding the specific topic, self, audience, or situation. In fact, it is so abstract and "detached" from the particular conversation that such a remark could be made in virtually any episode in which any town is mentioned. Messages will tend to be more clear when they imply a sense of place, time, self, and audience.

8. *Use organizational devices in your conversation.* When you introduce a new topic, offer some explanatory information. Organize your thoughts into some understood pattern— chronological, cause-effect, general to specific, or spatial order, for instance. Do not use extensive flashbacks or backtracking. Do not

Philip takes pride in being a generalist.

Reprinted with special permission of Cowles Syndicate, Inc.

include random, unrelated thoughts. Group similar ideas into recognized categories. Do not separate connected thoughts. Use transitions or some kind of connection between different ideas. Show the relationship among your ideas by numbering them or using other appropriate introductory clauses or phrases ("In addition . . ." "Another factor which . . ." "More important than . . ."). Use parallel construction when attempting to communicate the same or similar ideas. Summarize long or complex interpersonal messages.

9.   *Use accurate language.* We need to avoid intentional distortion in our conversations with others. Do not deliberately set out to confuse your listener. As you have probably already noted, clarity in communication is difficult to achieve. When communicators deliberately set out to confuse, the result can be disastrous. Avoid shortcuts and acronyms—words formed by using the first letters of a number of words (ROTC for Reserve Officers' Training Corps; TCA for tele-communicative arts; OEO for Office of Economic Opportunity); do not make false starts ("I guess I'll go to the— John, do you want to go to the party?"); and avoid the kind of egocentrism which ignores the listener. As you communicate interpersonally, try to continually think about those language choices which will make your message as clear as it can be.

Marital Conflict

Conflict at work and at home can occur as a result of our language usage. The following dialogue took place in one home at about 6 P.M. Conversations like this are familiar to persons who are married as well as to persons who are not. Identify the specific problems that occur in the language that is chosen. Then, rewrite the dialogue in a manner which would be more satisfying for the couple.

Husband: What a day!

Wife: It couldn't have been any worse than mine.

Husband: Every time I walk in the door this place is a mess—there are clothes strewn everywhere.

Wife: I don't get any help from anyone. Everybody throws their coats and books all over.

Husband: I work all day—I can't come home and clean house, too.

Wife: You could at least hang up your own coat.

Husband: Where are the kids?

Wife: I don't know why they can't clean up their own rooms.

Husband: Why isn't dinner ready?

Wife: I was waiting for the hamburger.

Husband: What hamburger?

Wife: Didn't you bring it?

Husband: What hamburger?

Wife: I told you two days ago that I was using the last pound of hamburger from the freezer.

Husband: You didn't say you wanted me to buy any.

Wife: Why do you think I told you I was out of it?

Husband: You women are all alike—you expect someone to read your minds!

Wife: Oh yeah, you try to hold down a job and do all the work around here.

Husband: Well, you know what you can do with that!

Summary

In this chapter you discovered the various elements and characteristics of verbal expressiveness. You are able to define verbal communication and distinguish its characteristics. Verbal communication consists of words which are symbolic and arbitrary in their relationship to referents.

You also learned that common, yet unconventional, forms of verbal expression, such as clichés, slang, and jargon, often impair communication competence if not used in the appropriate contexts. There are several other practices, including word choices, ambiguous word usage, and deliberate distortion, that further diminish communicative competence. Clarity and effective communication of meaning is likely to come about from increasing conventional usage, clarifying inconsistencies, referencing the here-and-now of the conversation, and from using direct, descriptive, organized, and illustrated messages.

Many conflicts and problems can result when we do not say what we mean and when what we mean is not interpreted accurately by others because our messages are not adapted competently to the other person. Although behavioral flexibility is essential in adapting verbal communication to one's particular communicative context, several general principles of message formulation can be learned and practiced. In general, verbal messages are considered to be more under conscious control than nonverbal messages. Thus, learning the principles of verbal expressiveness are especially amenable to your personal development and improvement. The next chapter examines the process and nature of nonverbal expressiveness.

Notes

1.   R. L. Shotland and L. Goodstein, "Just Because She Doesn't Want to Doesn't Mean It's Rape: An Experimentally Based Causal Model of the Perception of Rape in a Dating Situation," *Social Psychology Quarterly* 46 (1983): 220–32.

2.   William Safire, "What's that you Say, Guv?" *Des Moines Register,* March 31, 1979, p. 20.

3.   "Pavement Patois" from *Newsweek* (January 26, 1976). Copyright © 1976 by Newsweek, Inc. All Rights Reserved. Reprinted by permission.

4.   John Steinbeck, *The Grapes of Wrath* (New York: Heritage Press, 1940), p. 184.

5. Theodore M. Bernstein, "Bi-bi, Confusion," *Des Moines Register,* January 17, 1979, p. 45.

6. Adolf Hitler in William V. Haney, *Communication: Patterns and Incidents* (Homewood, Ill.: R. D. Irwin, 1960), p. 125.

7. Benjamin Lee Whorf, "Science and Linguistics," in *Language, Thought and Reality,* ed. John B. Carroll (Cambridge, Mass.: M.I.T. Press, 1956), pp. 207–219.

8. Lewis Carroll, *Alice's Adventures in Wonderland.* (Macmillan, 1865).

9. Lewis Carroll, *Through the Looking Glass and What Alice Found There.* (Macmillan, 1872).

10. E. B. White, *Stuart Little* (New York: Harper & Row, 1945), pp. 95–96.

11. See J. B. Bavelas, "Situations that Lead to Disqualification," *Human Communication Research* 9(1983): 130–45; J. B. Bavelas and B. J. Smith, "A Method for Scaling Verbal Disqualification," *Human Communication Research* 8(1982): 214–27.

Additional Readings

Brandes, Paul D. and Brewer, Jeutonne. *Dialect Clash in America: Issues and Answers.* Metuchen, N.J.: The Scarecrow Press, Inc., 1977.

Brown, Roger. "How Shall the Thing Be Called?" *Psychological Review.* 65(1958): 15–20.

Dillard, J. L. *Lexicon of Black English.* New York: The Seabury Press, 1977.

Ellis, Andrew and Beattie, Geoffrey. *The Psychology of Language and Communication.* New York: Guilford Press, 1985.

Ellis, Donald G. and Donohue, William A., eds. *Contemporary Issues in Language and Discourse Processes.* Communication Series. Hillsdale, N.J.: Lawrence Erlbaum Associates, 1986.

Escholz, Paul, et al. *Language Awareness.* New York: St. Martin's Press, 1978.

Goodman, Gerald and Esterly, Glenn. *The Talk Book: The Intimate Science of Communicating in Close Relationships.* Emmaus, Penn.: Rodale Press, 1988.

Lazarus, Sy. *Loud and Clear: A Guide to Effective Communication.* New York: AMACOM, 1975.

Partridge, Eric. *Slang: Today and Yesterday.* New York: Barnes & Noble, Inc., 1970.

Salomon, Louis B. *Semantics and Common Sense.* New York: Holt, Rinehart & Winston, Inc., 1966.

Sperber, Dan and Wilson, Deirdre. *Relevance: Communication and Cognition.* Cambridge, Mass.: Harvard University Press, 1986.

Thorne, Barrie and Henley, Nancy, eds. *Language and Sex: Difference and Dominance,* 2d ed. Rowley, Mass.: Newbury House, 1982.

Verschueren, Jeff. *What People Say They Do with Words—Prolegomena to an Empirical-Conceptual Approach to Linguistics Action.* Vol. 14, Advances in Applied Developmental Psychology. Norwood, N.J.: Ablex, 1985.

Vocate, Donna R. *The Theory of A. L. Luria: Functions of Spoken Language in the Development of Higher Mental Processes.* Hillsdale, N.J.: Lawrence Erlbaum Associates, 1986.

Nonverbal Expressiveness

BLOOM COUNTY   by Berke Breathed

BLOOM COUNTY by Berke Breathed. © 1982, Washington Post Writers Group. Reprinted with permission.

In the last chapter, you learned about expressiveness through verbal discourse. Generally speaking, the more expressive verbal communication is, the more competent it is perceived to be. Of course, verbal expression is only one of the primary modes through which we communicate. Nonverbal expression is the other primary mode.

Steve Dallas might prefer to think otherwise, but nonverbal cues provide a great amount of meaning to others. The students draw intense impressions on the basis of his nonverbal behavior, regardless of the actual accuracy of those impressions. This chapter on expressiveness explores the means of nonverbal communication.

The Nature of Nonverbal Communication

Definition of Nonverbal Communication

Communication was defined in chapter 1 as *the process of mutually deriving meaning.* In chapter 4 we used that definition to create a definition of *verbal communication,* which we stated was *the process of mutually deriving meaning through the use of words.* In this chapter we will begin with our basic definition of communication and go on to define *nonverbal communication* as *the process of mutually deriving meaning through all interpersonal means that are not verbal.* Nonverbal communication includes our bodily movements, our facial expression, our use of space, our touching behavior, our vocal cues, and our clothing and other artifacts.

Some authors have defined nonverbal communication as those events in which words are neither spoken nor written.[1] The importance of this emphasis is that it stresses that *nonverbal* refers to that which is not words rather than that which is *not oral.* The term nonverbal should not be confused with the word *nonoral. Nonoral* refers to *phenomena that are not oral*—bodily movement, the use of space, and our clothing would be examples. The written word—such as an English composition, a novel, and this textbook—is similarly nonoral. *Nonverbal* includes *those phenomena that are not verbal* such as bodily movement, facial expression, and our use of space. Vocal features such as the pitch, loudness, and inflection of our voices would also be included as nonverbal. Nonoral can include written words; nonverbal cannot. Conversely, nonverbal includes the oral and vocal features of speaking; nonoral does not.

How do verbal and nonverbal cues differ? Nonverbal cues appear to be *continuous* while verbal cues are *discrete.* That is, gestures and other nonverbal movements do not appear to have a beginning and an end in the way that we can identify when a verbal message begins and when it ends. Nonverbal communication appears to be learned very *early* in life while verbal communication appears to follow at a *later* time and at a slower pace. Nonverbal communication may consist of both *signs and symbols* while verbal communication is entirely *symbolic.* In other words, nonverbal actions may carry their own meaning while words are always arbitrary symbols that only represent something else. Nonverbal communication may be viewed to exist more in the world of the *emotional* while verbal communication may be seen to thrive in the world of the *intellectual.* Finally, because of some of the characteristics that have already been cited, nonverbal communication may be viewed to be more *"natural"* or *closer* to persons while verbal communication may be seen to be *"created"* and more *distant* from them.

How do verbal and nonverbal messages interact? Nonverbal cues may be used to clarify a message through *emphasis.* We demonstrate how angry we are by the intensity with which we state the words. Nonverbal cues may *repeat* the verbal message. We tell a friend that we don't understand something and, at the same time, shake our head to indicate a lack of understanding. Nonverbal cues may be *substituted* for verbal cues. Instead of replying ''Yes,'' or ''No,'' we simply shake our head in one direction or the other. Or, nonverbal cues may *complement* the verbal message. In other words, the nonverbal cues add other information not included in the verbal message. When you describe the ''big one that got away,'' after a fishing expedition, you will probably complement your story with an exaggerated illustration of the size of the fish. We should note, however, that nonverbal cues can also add confusion to the verbal message. Later in this chapter we will consider more specific explanations as to why this confusion is caused. At this point we will merely point out that nonverbal cues can *contradict* the verbal cues that are offered. We tell someone that we are starved and then we pick at the food that is prepared.

Categories of Nonverbal Communication

Whenever we categorize communication behavior, we risk the error of oversimplification and creating artificial boundaries. Nonetheless, we cannot understand or explain a phenomenon as complex as interpersonal communication without analyzing it into smaller components. The categories of nonverbal communication that are presented here have been identified as the most useful way of viewing nonverbal communication by scholars and researchers of communication. These categories include (1) facial expression and bodily movement, (2) space and touching, (3) vocal cues, and (4) clothing and other artifacts.

Facial expression and bodily movement.   The term *kinesics* has been coined by nonverbal researchers to refer to the study of people's facial expression and bodily movements. Our faces and bodies communicate a wide variety of emotions. Socrates maintained that ''Nobility and dignity, self-abasement and servility, prudence and understanding, insolence and vulgarity, are reflected in the face and in the attitudes of the body whether still or in motion.''[2]

Other researchers have determined that our faces express *how* we feel while our bodies express the *intensity* of our emotion.[3] A great deal of variability exists among persons and the amount of facial expression they use. Indeed,

Paul Ekman has estimated that the human face is capable of displaying seven thousand different appearances, based upon possible variations in facial musculature.[4] Two primary factors that appear to account for these differences are sex and personality. In general, women use far more facial expression than men, they show their emotions more through their face than do men, and they smile more than do their male counterparts.[5] In addition, persons who are highly adept at observing and interpreting the nonverbal cues of others appear to be poor at offering clear nonverbal cues. An inverse relationship exists between skill in sending and receiving nonverbal cues.[6] Finally, a study has demonstrated that people can be categorized into "internalizers," those who have feelings but do not express them and "externalizers," those who express their feelings through facial expression and other means.[7]

What are the implications of these studies for you? To what extent do you show your feelings through facial expression? Do you avoid smiling, frowning, or other facial cues? Do you overuse these cues so others are unclear what the meaning behind them is? One study, for instance, demonstrated that children did not respond in the same way to women's smiles as they did to men's. The children's more neutral reaction to female smiles suggests that they were more accustomed to observing women smile and thus the smile did not communicate the same intensity of joy or happiness that the more rare male smile held.[8]

Have a classmate or friend specifically observe your facial expression and offer his or her observations about your use of facial expression. If you tend to be an "internalizer," experiment with more facial expression; if you are an "externalizer," or a person with a ready smile or an abundance of facial cues, consider the confusion that might be caused by your overuse of facial expression.

Gestures and posture are part of bodily movement. Gestures include the movement of parts of the body while posture involves the continual, consistent adjustment of the entire body. Gestures are less likely to be controlled consciously than are some of our other nonverbal cues and thus they often comprise more accurate statements of our feelings about the communication situation and the people involved in it. For instance, we may "dress for success" to impress others when we go to a job interview, but we may show our nervousness by twisting a ring, playing with our hair, or wringing our hands.

Eye contact is one type of gestural communication. The eyes have been identified as the most important single part of the body in transmitting information nonverbally. The length of gaze, the dilation of the pupils, the opening of the eyelids, and other alterations can convey the most subtle messages. For instance, did you know that your pupils dilate when you feel affectionate toward another person and they tend to close when you feel anger, hostility, or coldness?[9] Men and women have been shown to be different in their use of eye contact. Women tend to watch others more, especially when they are speaking, but to avert their gaze or look away when no one is speaking. Men, on the other hand, tend to stare at other people, but be less attentive when another person is speaking to them.[10] Women communicate politeness or submissiveness through their eye contact while men communicate rudeness, status, or dominance.

Ekman and Friesen categorized hand movements, another type of gestural communication, as emblems, illustrators, and adaptors.[11] *Emblems* represent a direct verbal translation of one or two words that are universally understood or are understood by a particular group of people.[12] For instance, the raised thumb of a pedestrian indicates that the person is hitchhiking, a clenched fist by a member of a feminist women's group suggests a call for power, while other hand and finger gestures may communicate insults, vulgarities, or obscenities. *Illustrators* may augment the verbal content of a message or may contradict it. *Adaptors* are movements that are learned in childhood in order to satisfy personal needs and are adapted to adulthood to deal with stress-producing situations. Playing with a pen or another small object, twisting your hair, scratching your head, or rubbing your nose are common adaptors.

Posture is the final category of kinesics that we will consider. Scheflen analyzed posture into three distinct groups. He used the terms *inclusiveness-*

In a face-to-face argument, vocal objections are reinforced by posture, parallel body orientation, and gestures.

noninclusiveness to refer to the manner by which members of one group include or exclude others by turning their bodies inward or outward. If three friends are conversing and are standing in a tight circle, their posture discourages others from joining them. If four students are waiting in the hallway for a class to begin and two of them are standing with their bodies in an outward position from the others, fellow students will probably feel free to join them and initiate conversation.

Vis-à-vis (face-to-face) or *parallel body orientation* refers to the manner in which two people can relate to each other—by posturing themselves in a face-to-face position or by establishing a parallel position. A face-to-face position is common when people are conversing; the parallel body orientation occurs when people view television, a movie, or a sports event together. Combinations of vis-à-vis and parallel body position are also possible and occur when two couples talk while sitting on love seats that flank a fireplace or when three or more people share a meal at a booth.

Congruence-incongruence describes the ability of group members to imitate each other. In a congruent situation, the body positions will be copies of each other and a shift by one person will result in a shift by the others. Scheflen found that people who had common attitudes on a particular subject would posture themselves congruently while people who had dissimilar beliefs would assume an incongruent posture.[13]

Kinesic Sensitivity

Jean Paul Sartre, writing of his experiences with the Nazi regime, asserted:

Because the Nazi venom worked its way even into our thoughts, every accurate thought was a conquest; because an all-powerful police sought to force us into silence, every word became as precious as a declaration of principle; because we were persecuted, each of our gestures carried the weight of a commitment.[14]

The experience of the holocaust of the 1930s and 1940s appears to be overwhelming to those who recall events of that time. The importance of communication is emphasized in this passage from Sartre. In less intense experiences, gestures and other nonverbal cues sometimes carry a commitment as well. Spend fifteen to thirty minutes observing and recording the kinesic behavior of people in a public area on your campus. After you have recorded the facial expression, gestures, and posture of a number of people, try to draw conclusions about relationships among the people, whether they agree or disagree about the topic under discussion, their mood, and what they are attempting to communicate to others through kinesics. Discuss your observations and conclusions in class.

Space and touching. Space and touching are sometimes treated as separate areas of nonverbal communication. However, as you shall see, touching is an extension of the closeness that can be established through the use of space. *Proxemics,* the human use of space, was introduced in 1966 by Edward T. Hall in his book *The Hidden Dimension.* In 1969 Robert Sommer analyzed the topic further in *Personal Space: The Behavioral Basis of Design.*

In order to understand the role of space in human communication, we need to consider both territoriality and personal space. We define *territoriality* as the need to create and to retain specific areas as our own. Animal researchers have studied this phenomenon in animals and psychologists have researched territoriality as a human need. Individuals establish their territory in many ways. While you go to get more coffee, you leave your plate and tray on the table. When you go to the beach, you often look for an optimally unoccupied space among the crowd, and then stake out a defensible territory by laying out the towels, a radio, ice chest, suntan lotion, etc. When you search the stacks in the library, you leave your notebook and pen on the table. You might place personal items in your room, on your desk, or on your bed. Items like fences, "no trespassing" signs, and engagement rings symbolize territoriality. Similarly, signs that warn, "Do not disturb," "Private," "Employees only," "Keep out," and "If you can read this, you're too close," are attempts to maintain a certain area as one's own. Territoriality refers to areas that are not easily movable or are immovable; it suggests a space that is separate from an individual (see fig. 5.1).

Personal space, on the other hand, moves with a person and, in fact, is the area surrounding him or her. Each individual determines how much physical distance he or she feels should be maintained with others. We seldom reflect on personal space; however, when someone invades our personal space we may feel defensive or may experience stress.

Personal space varies as a function of individual characteristics, the relationship between people, the physical setting, and the cultural background of persons. We find, for instance, that size and sex are two characteristics of individuals that affect personal space. People who are smaller require a smaller amount of personal space[15] and women appear to show little discomfort in smaller amounts of space.[16] Our relationships with others also affect personal space: we stand farther away from enemies, strangers, authority figures, people of higher status, physically handicapped persons, and individuals from different racial groups.[17] The physical setting can alter our personal space as people tend to stand closer together in large rooms and farther apart in small rooms.[18] Finally, the cultural backgrounds of the individuals involved in communication can affect personal space. Persons from the Middle East and Latin America tend to stand far closer than do Americans or Europeans when they converse.[19]

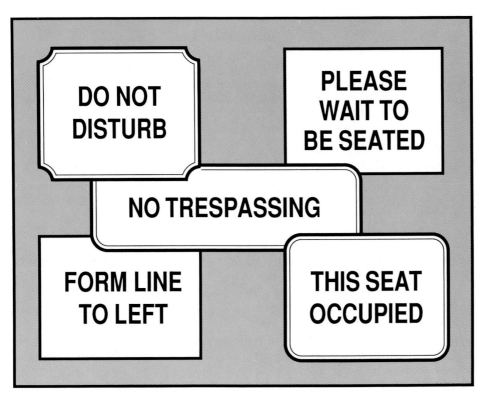

Signs of territoriality.

Figure 5.1

BLOOM COUNTY by Berke Breathed. © 1988, Washington Post Writers Group. Reprinted with permission.

Body Talk

The popular song whose lyrics include the line, "Let me hear your body talk" suggests the importance of touch in communicating with others. During the next three days, experiment with the use of touch to demonstrate your feelings of acceptance for others. When you are introduced to a new person, reach out and shake his or her hand. If you have a personal discussion with a close friend, put your arm around him or her to show your concern. If a friend stops to chat, touch his or her arm or shoulder as you converse. After you have experimented with touch for three days, recall your experiences. Did your touching behavior encourage reciprocal touching? Did the other person appear to be uncomfortable? Did you feel uncomfortable? Will you continue to use more touch in your interpersonal communication with others?

Hall categorized the four most commonly used personal distances into public distance, social distance, personal distance, and intimate distance. *Public distance* ranges from twelve feet onward. It is generally used by teachers in classrooms and speakers in public speaking situations, rather than by communicators in an interpersonal setting. *Social distance* ranges from about four to twelve feet. Interpersonal communication among acquaintances, persons who work together, and between salespeople and customers generally occurs in this distance. *Personal distance* exists between eighteen inches and four feet. Interpersonal communication among close friends and lovers in public occurs in this range. *Intimate distance* ranges from skin contact to about eighteen inches. This distance is used for communication among persons who are emotionally close and is typically used in a private setting.[20]

Touching, as we see, is at one end of the range of intimate distance. Many researchers of nonverbal communication agree that touch is an extremely powerful way of communicating with other people. As early as infancy, most people begin associating touch as a pleasurable experience. The positive association with touch remains for most of us. The specific meaning of a touch is dependent upon the relationship of the two people who are involved, the specific situation, the type of touch, and where a person is touched. In most cultures, touch is associated with positive attitudes while a lack of touch is associated with negative ones. Touch may be one of the clearest indications that we appreciate, are affectionate toward, or have acceptance of others. Communication scholars refer to touching as *tactile communication.*

Vocal cues.   Vocal elements are considered nonverbal communication because they, too, are *not* verbal. At the beginning of this chapter we distinguished between verbal and oral. You may wish to review that discussion if you find that including vocal cues in a chapter on nonverbal communication seems confusing. *Paralinguistics,* literally, "that which accompanies language," is the term that is used for vocal cues.

Vocal cues may be considered to fall into the following categories: (1) rate—the rapidity or slowness with which an individual speaks, (2) volume—the loudness or softness that a person uses, (3) pitch—the highness or lowness of a person's voice, (4) inflection—the changes or lack of changes in pitch, (5) enunciation—an individual's articulation and pronunciation, and (6) quality—the pleasantness or unpleasantness of a person's voice, which might include nasality or raspiness, among other characteristics.

Clarity in interpersonal communication is greatly dependent upon accurate and recognizable paralinguistic features. For instance, persons who speak very quickly all the time may appear nervous or high in energy; people who regularly speak slowly may seem to be bored, tired, or careful thinkers. Speaking loudly suggests dominance while speaking softly suggests submissiveness. A high pitch may cause us to believe that the other person is high strung or effeminate; a low pitch is associated with masculinity. We generally associate upward inflection at the end of a sentence as a signal that the other person is asking a question. If someone speaks in a monotone when requesting information, we might misunderstand and not respond. On the other hand, the continual use of upward inflections at the end of all sentences may cause us to offer unnecessary and unwanted replies. Incorrect articulation or pronunciation may result in confusion or a belief that the other person is poorly educated. Unpleasant voice qualities can interfere with the message the speaker is attempting to relay. Appropriate pitch, rate, inflection, volume, enunciation, and pleasant voice quality are all essential to clear communication. Similarly an overuse of vocal fillers—"ah," "mm," "uh," or "um," silence, or laughter will confuse or irritate others.

Clothing and other artifacts.   The study of clothing and other artifacts for communication purposes is known as *artifactual language* or *object language.* Included in artifactual language are clothing, hairstyles, cosmetics, jewelry, and other items with which we decorate our bodies. These artifacts communicate a great deal to others about us including our sex, age, role, socioeconomic class, status, group memberships or affiliations, personality, and our relationships to individuals of the opposite sex. Persons with high status or power tend to dress more casually than their subordinates. Baseball players wear uniforms that identify the team to which they belong. A certain amount of affluence is suggested by designer jeans with the name of the designer on the back pocket. Three-piece conservative business suits suggest particular occupations including banking, government, law, or medicine.

Artifacts also indicate the time in history, the time of day, and the climate. It has become acceptable in some groups for men to have their ears pierced and wear earrings. Recently, some attention has been given to a handful of men in our country who have begun to wear skirts. Skirts were worn at earlier times in the history of some cultures but are rather rare for men today. At various points in our history, women wore long dresses; today, they sometimes wear them for formal or evening occasions, but they probably would not wear them if they were going to spend a day outdoors in 90-degree weather. You may have a "summer wardrobe" and a "winter wardrobe" that reflects changes in weather between the two seasons.

Clothing and artifacts provide physical and psychological protection, are used for sexual attraction, and are an indication of our self-concept. Hunters wear a particular color in order that other hunters do not shoot at them. Deep-sea divers wear wet suits. Clothing similarly keeps us warm in cold weather; but long sleeves, high necks, and fairly long skirts on women may be worn to dissuade others from perceiving them as sexual objects. Persons with high self-concepts may dress in brief clothing because they are proud of their bodies or they may dress more conservatively, feeling that they possess far more than a physical body. It is difficult to accurately interpret the intent of all clothing and artifactual choices because the same cue may provide different meanings.

Clothing and other artifactual cues can assist us in reinforcing a message or can confuse others by contradicting our verbal messages and our other nonverbal signals. For example, people will probably believe that the diamond pinky ring or the Lincoln Continental are more indicative of relative wealth than are the statements of "having a difficult time meeting the high cost of living." Statements about personal confidence and high self-esteem might be questioned if the speaker regularly dresses in somber colors and in dowdy styles. If a woman wears styles that are appropriate for preteen-agers and wears her hair in pigtails, we might question her if she complains of not being treated as an adult. Consistency in verbal and nonverbal messages are essential if we are to clearly communicate with others.

Clothing Communicates

Have you thought of the many ways that clothing and other artifacts affect your communication? In order to clarify how your artifactual language affects your communication, try this: For three days, record the clothing, jewelry, cologne, and other artifacts that you wear. Try to analyze what they may be communicating to others. Are they appropriate for your age, sex, status, role, socioeconomic class, group memberships, personality, and your relationship to the opposite sex as you perceive them? Are they indicative of the current styles, the time of day, and the climate? Do they allow sexual attraction or disallow this kind of attractiveness? Do they properly indicate your self-concept? After you have analyzed your thoughts in a short paper, ask two or three friends to similarly analyze your clothing. Discuss differences and similarities in your perception and that of your friends. Try to explain how your clothing confuses or clarifies your interpersonal communication with others.

Nonverbal Expressiveness in Interpersonal Communication

What you say is less important than *how* you say it! Many researchers have investigated the relative contribution of verbal and nonverbal elements to communication. The most conservative estimates have suggested that 35 percent of the social meaning in a situation is transmitted verbally and that 65 percent is transmitted nonverbally,[21] while the most liberal estimates have stated that only 7 percent of the emotional meaning is transmitted verbally with the remaining 93 percent relying on the nonverbal.[22]

In an analysis and review of the research on this question, Burgoon suggests that the conservative estimate is generally more accurate, although the author is quick to point out that to separate two channels of meaning that are so intertwined is a hazardous and error-prone endeavor.[23] Although the figures vary, all of the studies of this kind have supported the finding that well over half of the message is contributed by nonverbal elements. The importance of nonverbal communication is considerable.

Perhaps you have read one or more of the books that are listed under "Additional Readings" at the end of this chapter or other books on nonverbal communication. You may have concluded that nonverbal clarity is actually a simple matter. In other words, you learn a few nonverbal cues and you are able to accurately and completely understand another person's intent. Nonverbal clarity is really not that simple. The meaning of another person's nonverbal cues may vary as a function of other characteristics of that person, as a function of characteristics of the observer, or as a function of the characteristics of the environment.

Influences on Interpreting Nonverbal Behavior

The other person's personality, background, and other influences may alter his or her nonverbal behavior. You may generally conclude that persons who stand or sit very close to you have positive feelings for you. The person you are dating sits close to you, your parents stand closer to you than do mere acquaintances, and you find that people who agree with you tend to place themselves close to you. An individual from a Latin American country will probably stand and sit close to you regardless of his or her feeling for you. Persons from this culture learn to have a far smaller personal "bubble" and consequently interact with others in closer proximity.

The characteristics of the observer may affect an accurate and complete assessment of the meaning in another person's nonverbal communication. The place where you are sitting or standing necessarily limits the amount of information you can receive from the other person's movement. Clearly, if you cannot see a person's face, you will have difficulty interpreting his or her nonverbal cues; but, similarly, not seeing his or her hands, legs, or a portion of his or her body may distort the meaning in the movement. In addition to physical limitations, our own personalities, expectations, attitudes, beliefs, and values all affect our observations of others and inferences that we draw.

The environment may similarly affect the accurate reading of nonverbal cues. While you might normally be able to conclude that persons who regularly cross their arms and sit in a closed position are trying to signal to others that they are not approachable, the unusually cold temperature in a room may cause the same bodily orientation. A person with a grimace on her face may be reacting to an unpleasant odor rather than expressing her feelings. The bizarre clothing of an individual may indicate that he is on his way to a costume party rather than attempting to draw attention to himself.

Problems in Interpreting Nonverbal Behavior

The complete and accurate assessment of another person's nonverbal communication is complicated. Some generalizations can be drawn, but these must be understood and applied as only generally true. Individual persons and particular circumstances limit the universality of these cues to all people and to all situations. In addition, three specific problems unique to nonverbal communication confuse the interpretation of particular cues: (1) the same cue can be used to communicate a number of different meanings, (2) different cues can be used to communicate the same, or similar, meanings, and (3) conflicting verbal and nonverbal cues are sometimes present in the same message.

We sometimes use identical cues to express different feelings. For instance, you might laugh in an uncontrolled manner when something strikes you as hysterically funny but you might laugh in the same uncontrolled way when facing a number of minor crises in a row. Most of us have probably encountered an instance in which we were uncertain whether someone we hear or see is laughing or crying, despite the usual difference between the underlying emotions. A brisk pace may indicate excitement or it may express anger. A raised hand may suggest that you are taking an oath, demonstrating for a cause, indicating that you would like to answer a question, or demonstrating that you have a question that you would like to ask. It may also indicate that a physician is examining your right side, that you want a taxi to stop for you, that you are trying to stop a blow to the head, or that you are applying deodorant.

Occasionally, we use different cues when we are trying to communicate the same feeling. Perhaps no emotion has as many different cues associated with it as does the feeling of love or affection that we have for another person. We might sit and stand more closely to the person we love; we might talk

BLOOM COUNTY   by Berke Breathed

BLOOM COUNTY by Berke Breathed. © 1982, Washington Post Writers Group. Reprinted with permission.

more softly or use a different vocal intonation. The facial expression we use, the gestures we choose, and the posture we assume may all be different when we are in the presence of someone we love. Many people dress differently if they are going to be in the exclusive company of the person they love. Children have even more ways of expressing affection than do adults. They may tease the other person, they may try to kiss that person, or they may even resort to fighting as an expression of their feelings.

Finally, verbal and nonverbal cues may conflict. Earlier, we used the example of the person who sports an expensive ring or drives a luxury automobile and yet complains about the "cost of living." In this case, the person is presenting us with a situation in which the verbal and the nonverbal cues conflict: the artifacts have one message and the words have another. This situation falls into a category known as the "double bind."[24] A double bind occurs whenever conflicting verbal, conflicting nonverbal, or conflicting verbal and nonverbal cues are present. The conflict between the two contradictory messages creates a difficult situation for the observer: he or she is not clear about which cue or set of cues to follow. Consider the double binds that you may create for others. Do you ever tell friends to stop by to chat and then appear distracted when they do? Have you ever told a person that you cared for him but then made no effort to demonstrate your concern? Have you ever told an instructor how much you enjoy her class and then neglect doing the reading assignments? Have you ever had a parent punishing you yet saying that it "hurts me more than it hurts you"? In the middle of a heated argument, have you heard or spoken the phrase "I love you" in such a way that it sounds like "damnit!" should follow the statement? Double binds are created when verbal and nonverbal cues are in conflict.

Competence in Nonverbal Expressiveness

In the last few paragraphs we have considered some difficulties that we will encounter as we attempt nonverbally to communicate clearly. We stated that the meaning of another person's nonverbal cues may vary as a function of the other person, as a function of the observer, or as a function of the environment. In addition, we discussed three specific problems that may occur: (1) we may use the same cue to indicate a variety of feelings, (2) we may use a variety of cues to suggest the same feeling, and (3) we may use conflicting verbal and nonverbal cues.[25] With these considerations in mind, the following nonverbal skills are presented to assist you in becoming increasingly clear in your interpersonal communication.

1. *Use nonverbal cues; use nonverbal cues that are appropriate for the other person; use nonverbal cues that are appropriate for the situation and environment; and use nonverbal cues that are appropriate for you.* These four general guidelines are keys to all nonverbal clarity. When we observe an absence, or minimal use, of nonverbal cues, we experience difficulty in interpreting another person's message. The use of nonverbal cues can assist others in understanding our feelings, our mood, our attitudes, and our current perceptions. Consider how you can add clarity to your interpersonal messages by adding nonverbal cues including facial expression, vocal cues, bodily movement, gestures, eye contact, and other indicators.

    Our nonverbal cues should be appropriate for the other person. Subcultural differences must be taken into consideration. The clenched fist of a black activist may elicit a different meaning from a Minnesota labor leader than that which was intended. Consider the nuances and subtleties of different interpretations by various subcultures. The same factors that affect verbal communication—region of the country, subcultural differences, particular professions—are similarly called into play in the interpretation of nonverbal cues.

    The situation and the environment may include relevant characteristics that should be considered in the use of nonverbal cues. Dressing in sheer clothing and high heels is as inappropriate for a football game in November as is showing your distaste for your mother-in-law's "special recipe" through your facial expression. Are certain gestures "taboo" because of the place in which you find yourself? Are you limited to particular body positions and postures? Observe the behavior of others to gain some notion of the appropriate norms of nonverbal behavior in new or unique situations.

    Nonverbal cues should also be appropriate for you. If you have a conservative background, you may feel awkward wearing provocative clothing; if you suffer from a hearing loss, you may not

Illustrator gestures, such as pointing or the suggestion of size, have universal meaning in our culture. Use them appropriately to augment, rather than to contradict, your verbal message.

be able to turn away or stand very far from the other person and still hear what is being said. Recognize that you have unique characteristics that may cause you to behave differently than others. If you believe that this will result in confusion for others, explain the circumstances or rationale for your behavior. Individuals will better understand the person who "sits too close" if it is explained that he or she has a hearing loss than if they are left to their own interpretations.

2. *Develop consistency in your use of nonverbal cues, select different cues to communicate different meanings, and avoid the use of conflicting verbal and nonverbal cues.* Try to use similar cues to express similar feelings. If you show your need for affection by withdrawing in one situation, pouting in another, being assertive in a third, and by crying in a fourth, you will probably confuse the other person. Attempt to develop some consistency in your cues so others have some opportunity to understand your feelings and ideas through the cues that you offer.

As much as possible, select different cues to communicate different meanings. Vary your nonverbal cues in order to differentiate between ideas. If you always respond verbally the same way, for instance, responding that you "don't care" to all suggestions, people become confused. Similarly, when you use the same set of nonverbal cues in all situations, others have difficulty accurately interpreting your meaning. Experiment with different ways of responding. Develop a larger repertoire of cues from which to choose.

Avoid the use of conflicting verbal and nonverbal cues. When you offer conflicting sets of cues, you create double binds for others. Rather than conveying differing cues, attempt to use nonverbal cues that reinforce or complement the verbal message that you offer.

3. *Use bodily movement and facial expression to increase understanding of your message.* Bodily movement and facial expression are valuable resources for the interpersonal communicator. Do not add unnecessary movements or distracting mannerisms, but try to determine nonverbal methods of increasing clarity through these nonverbal means of expression. Shift your posture and position to punctuate your thoughts. Do not be afraid to move around and to show through your entire body how you feel. Smile, frown, look confused if you are, and use other facial expressiveness that will increase the likelihood that the other person will understand you. The feedback that you can supply to others is invaluable in clear communication.

4. *Use emblem gestures, illustrator gestures, and adaptor gestures appropriately.* Use emblem gestures that are universally understood or that are understood by the person with whom you are communicating. Appropriate emblem gestures create the precision of communication; inappropriate emblem gestures confuse and offend the other person. Use illustrator gestures to augment the content of your verbal message. Do not be afraid to point, to suggest size, or to demonstrate your verbal message with other illustrators. Avoid the use of adaptor gestures when they may contradict your verbal message. If you verbally state how confident you feel as you nervously play with your ring, you may confuse the other person.

5. *Use an outward or open body position when you want to include others; use an inward or closed body position when you want to exclude others.* Consider what your body is communicating to others. Are you expressing a willingness to communicate when that is not your intent? Are you closing yourself off to others through your body position? Subtle messages are sent through the way we choose to sit or stand.

6. *Adopt a congruent body position when you share beliefs, feelings, attitudes, and values with others; adopt an incongruent body position when you do not.* As others move around you, respond with similar or dissimilar movement. Again, consider how your body position may affect the messages that you are inadvertently sending to others.

7. *Establish eye contact and maintain it when you wish to communicate; stare into space, allow your eyes to wander around the room, and use no eye contact when you do not wish to communicate with the other person.* You may be able to send clear messages to others about your willingness or unwillingness to communicate simply through your eye contact, or lack of eye contact, with them. Experiment with eye contact and recognize that averting the gaze, staring, watching attentively, and looking elsewhere when someone talks to you all have clear communicative meaning.

8. *Establish clear territorial lines that are congruent with your needs and use a comfortable distance when you are conversing with others.* Territoriality appears to be an important need of people as well as animals. Display personal objects in your territory to clarify your feelings about these areas. Similarly, stand or sit at appropriate, comfortable distances when you are conversing with others. Stand or sit at a greater distance when you do not wish to communicate and reduce the space between you and others when you wish to talk. Use less space when you want to discuss personal or intimate matters, use more distance when the conversation is less personal.

9. *Use touch appropriately to demonstrate warmth, concern, affection, or openness to other people.* Touch can have strong communicative meaning. Use it appropriately to show your positive and negative feelings to others. Consider the variety of ways that you can touch others. Do not be afraid to experiment with this mode of communication.

10. *Change pitch, rate, inflection, and volume as appropriate to indicate your intent and to complement your verbal message and avoid vocal fillers like "mm," "ah," "uh," and "you know."* Alterations in vocal cues are invaluable in suggesting meaning to others. Lack of change, on the other hand, not only confuses, but it may bore others. Vocal fillers, similarly, are distracting, boring, and add nothing to your message. Have a friend listen to determine if your voice is monotonous—free from change—or if you rely on unnecessary fillers.

11. *Use appropriate rate, projection, quality, articulation, and pronunciation.* Use a moderate speaking rate. Do not speak so quickly that others cannot understand you or speak so slowly that they lose interest before you have completed your thought. Use adequate vocal projection. Normally, volume is no problem in interpersonal communication; however, a few people speak so softly that they cannot be heard at even close range. Establish a quality of voice that is free from nasality, raspiness, whininess, and other unpleasant qualities. If you are unsure if your voice has unpleasant qualities, ask a close friend how he or she responds to

your voice. Articulate clearly. Speak distinctly in order that one word is not confused with another. Pronounce words correctly. Norm Crosby may be able to amass wealth by his comedic routines based on mispronunciations but interpersonal communicators seldom benefit. If you are unsure of the pronunciation of a word, check a dictionary or a pronunciation gazetteer or ask someone who might know.

12. *Wear appropriate clothing and use appropriate artifacts.* Wear clothing and use artifacts that are appropriate for your own particular characteristics, the other people involved in your communication, and the environment. Dress in a manner that is attractive rather than outlandish. Consider your own body type and figure when you select clothing. Consider how others will respond if you show up in an outdated outfit or in clothing that is strikingly dissimilar from their own. Allow yourself to dress informally on some occasions, but do not exclude a more formal appearance for other situations. Use artifactual communication to reinforce or strengthen your verbal message; avoid the wearing of distracting or confusing clothing and artifacts. Consider how others may interpret a specific article of clothing or view a particular piece of jewelry. Is this the message you want to communicate? If not, consider some alternatives.

13. *Avoid extreme levels of behavior.* Most forms of behavior can be said to be curvilinear to impressions of communicator competence. Curvilinearity in this sense simply means that too much of a bad thing (or too little of a bad thing) can actually diminish people's impression of you. For example, normally we might think that as a person demonstrates higher levels of nonverbal expressiveness, that others' impression of this person will improve. However, we can imagine a person who is simply *too* expressive. When a person's gestures, facial expressions, and vocal variety are exaggerated, they seem artificial or inappropriate in most contexts. Thus, generally speaking, moderately high levels of expressiveness are better than either low or extremely high levels.

14. *Seek to adapt your nonverbal communication to the expectations of the context.* More will be said of this in chapters 12 through 15. In general, however, we can anticipate what kinds of behavior are expected in given contexts. We know that we are likely to behave differently during job interviews than at parties with our friends. We are likely to behave differently at a Thanksgiving dinner with our family than when chatting with a good friend over coffee. The key is not to simply know that these differences exist, but to understand what it is about these contexts that leads us to behave differently. The first context example in the previous comparisons (i.e., job interview, holiday dinner) is more formal than the latter (i.e., party, chat). Thus, try to ascertain what nonverbal behaviors

are generally allowed and disallowed in formal contexts, in comparison to informal contexts. These examples indicate that many of our adaptations of behavior to context follow systematic rules of context. If you can figure out the rules that apply, then you can better adapt your behavior to the context.

Communicating Nonverbally for Clarity

The following dialogue is comprised of ambiguous verbal phrases. We are unable to discern the message that is intended by reading it. In order to practice your nonverbal skills, select one of the following pairs of individuals and try to communicate in the way that they would communicate nonverbally. Do not forget any of the nonverbal codes—use appropriate eye contact, gestures, movement, space, touch, vocal cues, and artifacts. Have someone else attempt to guess the role that you are playing and what the situation suggests.

Situation 1:   Two people who are on their first blind date.

Situation 2:   At a bus stop, a person unexpectedly meets a former steady date with whom he or she has broken up.

Situation 3:   A person sees his or her parent in a nursing home.

Situation 4:   Two friends meet who have had a misunderstanding and have not spoken for the past few days.

Situation 5:   A parent and a child meet who have not seen each other for three months.

Situation 6:   Two acquaintances meet, neither of whom can identify how he or she knows the other person.

Situation 7:   A businessperson who has sued another person meets that individual at a party at the home of a common friend.

Situation 8:   Two persons who are attempting to reconcile their differences meet for the first time in a few months.

Situation 9:   A former employer with whom you had a very positive relationship comes upon you in a park where you are playing with your children.

Situation 10:   A coworker whom you dislike sits next to you in a physician's waiting room.

Dialogue:

Person 1:   Well, hello . . .

Person 2:   Uh, hello . . .

Person 1:   I, um . . .

Person 2:   You what?

Person 1:   I am surprised to see you.

Person 2:   Yes, me too.

Person 1:   How are you?

Person 2:   Fine.

Communicating Nonverbally for Clarity continued

Person 1:	How is everything?
Person 2:	About the same as usual.
Person 1:	Are you busy right now?
Person 2:	Well, not really.
Person 1:	Would you care to talk?
Person 2:	Do you want to?
Person 1:	Well, we could.
Person 2:	Yes, we could.
Person 1:	Okay.
Person 2:	Fine.

Discuss the role of paralinguistics, touching, kinesics, proxemics, and artifactual communication. How is meaning added to words through the nonverbal codes? Which cues helped you the most in understanding the role you or another person played?

Summary

In this chapter, you learned how to define and identify nonverbal communication and its major forms and characteristics. Nonverbal communication was found to include facial and body movements, the use of space, vocal cues, clothing, and artifacts. Problems and principles of interpreting nonverbal communication indicate that we typically trust nonverbal communication more than verbal communication in the judgment of meaning. While nonverbal messages are highly contextual and need to be adapted to the specific conversational encounter (just like verbal messages), there are several general skills and principles that can enhance one's communicative competence. Basically, a person needs to use nonverbal communication that is congruent with situational expectations and the verbal content of the message and provide some variability both within and across episodes of transaction with others.

Communicative competence usually requires that persons be able to express themselves. Since there are only two primary modes of expression, verbal and nonverbal, it is clear that development of communicative competence will depend greatly on one's ability to master these modes of communication. For the most part, these modes of communication are the basic building blocks of all the other skills to follow in chapters 6–11. Pay attention toward the end of each of these chapters, in which the verbal and nonverbal components of the other skills are explained.

Notes

1. See, for instance, R. Harrison, "Nonverbal Communication: An Approach to Human Communication," in *Approaches to Human Communication,* R. Budd and B. Ruben, eds. (New York: Spartan Books, 1972), pp. 253–68; and Mark Knapp, *Nonverbal Communication in Human Interaction,* 2d ed. (New York: Holt, Rinehart & Winston, 1978).

2. Socrates, Xenophon, *Memorabilia III* in *Nonverbal Communication: Readings with Commentary,* ed. Shirley Weitz (New York: Oxford University Press, 1974), p. vii.

3. Paul Ekman and Wallace V. Friesen, "Head and Body Cues in the Judgment of Emotion: A Reformulation," *Perceptual and Motor Skills* 24 (1967): 711–24.

4. D. Goleman, "The 7,000 faces of Dr. Ekman," *Psychology Today,* February 1981, pp. 43–49.

5. See, for example, "Women's Faces Show Emotions: Men Hide Theirs," *Phoenix Gazette,* 13 December 1974; Jeanette Silveira, "Thoughts on the Politics of Touch," *Women's Press* 1 (Eugene, Ore.: February 1973), p. 13; and Nancy Henley, *Body Politics: Power, Sex, and Nonverbal Communication* (Englewood Cliffs, N.J.: Prentice Hall, 1977), pp. 163–66.

6. J. T. Lanzetta and R. E. Kleck, "Encoding and Decoding of Nonverbal Affect in Humans," *Journal of Personality and Social Psychology,* 16(1970): 12–19.

7. R. W. Buck, V. J. Savin, R. E. Miller, and W. F. Caul, "Communication of Affect Through Facial Expressions in Humans," *Journal of Personality and Social Psychology* 23(1972): 362–71.

8. Daphne Bugenthal, J. W. Kaswan, L. R. Love, and M. N. Fox, "Child versus Adult Perception of Evaluation Messages in Verbal, Vocal, and Visual Channels," *Developmental Psychology* 2(1970): 367–75.

9. For a review of research concerning eye and visual behavior, see chapter five in R. G. Harper, A. L. Wiens, J. D. Matarazzo, *Nonverbal Communication: The State of the Art.* (New York: Wiley & Sons, 1970); and C. L. Kleinke, "Gaze and Eye Contact: A Research Review," *Psychological Bulletin* 100 (1986): 78–100.

10. See, for instance, Ralph Exline, David Gray, and Dorothy Schuette, "Visual Behavior in a Dyad as Affected by Interview, Content, and Sex of Respondent," *Journal of Personality and Social Psychology* 1(1965): 201–9; William Libby, "Eye Contact and Direction of Looking as Stable Individual Differences," *Journal of Experimental Research in Personality* 4(1970): 303–12; and Michael Argyle, *The Psychology of Interpersonal Behavior* (Baltimore: Penguin, 1967), p. 115.

11. Paul Ekman and Wallace V. Friesen, "The Repertoire of Nonverbal Behavior: Categories, Origins, Usage and Coding." *Semiotica* 1(1969), 49–98.

12. For an examination of the meaning of emblems across cultures, see D. Morris, P. Collett, P. Marsh, and M. O'Shaughnessy, *Gestures: Their Origins and Distribution* (New York: Stein and Day, 1979).

13. A. E. Scheflen, "Quasi-Courtship Behavior in Psychotherapy," *Psychiatry,* 28(1965): 245–56.

14. Jean Paul Sartre in John Bartlett, *Familiar Quotations,* ed. Emily Morison Beck, 14th ed. (Boston: Little, Brown, 1968), p. 1058.

15. Michael Argyle and Janet Dean, "Eye-Contact, Distance, and Affiliation," *Sociometry* 28(1965): 289–304.

16. B. R. Addis, "The Relationship of Physical Interpersonal Distance to Sex, Race, and Age" (Masters thesis, University of Oklahoma, 1966).

17. Carol J. Guardo, "Personal Space in Children," *Child Development* 40(1969): 143–51.

18. Robert Sommer, "The Distance for Comfortable Conversation: A Further Study," *Sociometry* 25(1962): 111–16.

19. Edward T. Hall, "Proxemics—The Study of Man's Spatial Relations and Boundaries," *Man's Image in Medicine and Anthropology* (New York: International Universities Press, 1963).

20. Edward T. Hall, *The Silent Language* (Greenwich, Conn.: Fawcett Publications, Inc., 1959).

21. Ray L. Birdwhistell, *Kinesics and Context* (Philadelphia: University of Pennsylvania Press, 1970), pp. 128–43.

22. Albert Mehrabian and Susan R. Kerris, "Inference of Attitude from Nonverbal Communication in Two Channels," *Journal of Consulting Psychology* 31(1967): 248–52.

23. See Judee Burgoon, "Nonverbal Signals," in *Handbook of Interpersonal Communication,* Mark Knapp and Gerald R. Miller, eds. (Beverly Hills, Calif.: Sage, 1985), pp. 344–90.

24. Gregory Bateson, D. D. Jackson, J. Haley, and J. H. Weakland, "Toward a Theory of Schizophrenia," *Behavioral Science* 1(1956): 251–64.

25. For an analysis of individual differences and skills in nonverbal communication, see *Skill in Nonverbal Communication: Individual Differences,* R. Rosenthal, ed. (Cambridge, Mass. Oelgeschlager, Gunn & Hain, 1979).

Additional Readings

Ashcraft, Norman and Scheflen, Albert E. *People Space: The Making and Breaking of Human Boundaries.* Garden City, N.Y.: Anchor Press/Doubleday, 1976.

Birdwhistell, Ray L. *Kinesics and Context: Essays on Body Motion Communication.* Philadelphia: University of Pennsylvania Press, 1970.

Burgoon, Judee, Buller, David B., and Woodall, W. Gill. *Nonverbal Communication: The Unspoken Dialogue.* New York: Harper & Row, 1988.

Davis, Martha. *Understanding Body Movement.* New York: Arno Press, 1971.

Druckman, Daniel, Rozelle, Richard M., and Baxter, James C. *Nonverbal Communication: Survey, Theory, and Research.* Beverly Hills, Calif.: Sage, 1982.

Ekman, Paul, Friesen, W. V., and Ellsworth, P. *Emotion in the Human Face.* New York: Pergamon Press, 1972.

Harper, Robert G., Wiens, Arthur N., and Matarazzo, Joseph D. *Nonverbal Communication: The State of the Art.* New York: Wiley, 1978.

Leathers, Dale G. *Successful Nonverbal Communication: Principles and Applications.* New York: Macmillan, 1986.

Mehrabian, Albert. *Nonverbal Communication.* Chicago: Aldine-Atherton, Inc., 1972.

Patterson, Miles L. *Nonverbal Behavior: A Functional Perspective.* New York: Springer-Verlag, 1983.

Richmond, Virginia, McCroskey, James, and Payne, Steven. *Non-verbal Behavior in Interpersonal Relations.* Englewood Cliffs, N.J.: Prentice Hall, 1987.

Rosenfeld, Lawrence B. and Civikly, Jean M. *With Words Unspoken: The Nonverbal Experience.* New York: Holt, Rinehart & Winston, Inc., 1976.

Rosenthal, Robert, ed. *Skill in Nonverbal Communication: Individual Differences.* Cambridge, Mass.: Oelgeschlager, Gunn & Hain, 1979.

Scheflen, Albert E. *Body Language and Social Order.* Englewood Cliffs, N.J.: Prentice Hall, 1973.

Siegman, Aron W. and Feldstein, Stanley, eds. *Multichannel Integrations of Nonverbal Behavior.* Hillsdale, N.J.: Lawrence Erlbaum Associates, 1985.

Szasz, Suzanne. *The Body Language of Children.* New York: Norton, 1978.

Wiemann, John, M. and Harrison, Randall P. eds. *Nonverbal Interaction.* Beverly Hills, Calif.: Sage, 1983.

Self-Disclosure

BLOOM COUNTY by Berke Breathed. © 1983, Washington Post Writers Group. Reprinted with permission.

Cutter John and Bobbi are discovering that even when we try to achieve genuine, open, and meaningful disclosure, the process is a difficult one to negotiate. Their attempt to "try to get to know each other" is not greatly facilitated by the information that is then disclosed. In addition, their attempt to get beyond small talk so early in the relationship makes the type of disclosure that then occurs seem rather odd and out-of-place. Self-disclosure is generally a more complicated process than we assume.

This section is about maintaining composure in relationships. *Composure* means not only the avoidance of anxiety and apprehension, but the presence of confidence and self-control in expressing oneself. Two of the most important aspects of composure will receive extended review: the process of self-disclosure and the process of assertion and conflict management. Both processes involve the skills of revealing oneself and handling anxiety-provoking issues. A better understanding of these processes begins with an examination of the nature of self-disclosure.

The Nature of Self-Disclosure

Definition of Self-Disclosure

Sometimes you choose to make yourself the topic of a conversation. We refer to this kind of interpersonal communication behavior as self-disclosure. *Self-disclosure* is defined as communication in which a person voluntarily and intentionally tells another person accurate information about himself or herself that the other person is unlikely to know or to find out from another source. Self-disclosure includes low-risk statements like "I hate cauliflower," or "I like the new styles for men," to high-risk statements such as "I can't marry you," or "I want a deeper relationship with you." Self-disclosure may include nonverbal messages as well as verbal messages. Examples of nonverbal self-disclosure are when you smile broadly when someone asks you if you were selected for a job for which you interviewed, when you use a sarcastic tone of voice in describing your "happy home life," and when you affectionately hug someone you love.

Self-disclosure is voluntary.   If you feel coerced into telling another person details about yourself, it is not considered self-disclosure. For instance, if your parents insist upon knowing the hour you arrived home from a date, the information that you give them is not self-disclosure. On the other hand, if you angrily offer the comment that you did not get home until 3 A.M. because you were seeing someone of whom your parents disapprove, this information might be considered self-disclosure. Similarly, if an instructor demands that you explain your absences from class or an employer requires that you provide information about yourself in an employment interview, you are not engaging in self-disclosure. Self-disclosure includes any information that you voluntarily determine that you will share with others.

Self-disclosure is intentional.   It is not accidental. Each of us has experienced the situation in which we said more than we intended. You begin to tell your boyfriend that you would like to go to a different restaurant for dinner and you end up in an argument in which you attack his ability to be sensitive to your needs. You tell your mother that you regret not visiting home over the weekend as she requested, and you end up agreeing that you believe it would be best if you stayed with her for the entire summer. After a few drinks, you tell your boss how you really feel about your job even though you did not intend on "talking shop." These accidental disclosures are not within the parameters of our definition.

Self-disclosure includes intentional statements that we choose to make to others. When you decide to tell the person you have been dating for some time of your love; when you plan on sharing your feelings about certain working conditions with your supervisor and then share those perceptions; or when you tell a friend about a disappointment you have experienced, recognizing that he or she will understand your depression, you are engaging in the intentional communication that is called self-disclosure.

Self-disclosure is accurate information.   We do not present ourselves in the same way in all situations. We emphasize different aspects of our personality and other characteristics. For instance, to some people you may call yourself "an interesting person," to others, "a college student with a good future," and to still others, "a 'B' student." In each of these cases, you are emphasizing a slightly different aspect of who you are. All of these self-references provide accurate information about the person you know as yourself.

Occasionally people distort the information about themselves that they share with others. For instance, the college professor who introduces herself as "Dr. Johnson," when she has not completed all of the requirements for the Ph.D., the senior professor who maintains that he has written many books when he has not even signed his first contract, and the job applicant who asserts that he has "extensive experience" when he has never held a full-time position, all err in their information. Distortion, lying, concealment, or other forms of dishonest information are not included within the definition of self-disclosure. Self-disclosure includes accurate information.

Relationship of Self-Acceptance to Self-Disclosure

Understanding and accepting who we are assists us in the self-disclosure process. Our *self-concept* is the awareness of our total and unique being. It includes our *self-image,* or the sort of person we believe we are, and our *self-esteem,* the way we feel about who we are. If you identify yourself as an inner-city college student, you are referring to your self-image; if you state that your life is filled with conflict or that you are struggling because of all of the roles that you are playing, you are alluding to your self-esteem.

Our self-concept is largely based upon our interactions with others. As an infant and child growing up, we learn about "who" we should and should not be through the positive and negative messages of those around us. As George Herbert Mead theorized, a child begins to develop a sense of self as others see the child.[1] In order to understand this process, two distinctions need to be made. First, self-concept can be based upon both objective and subjective accomplishments. Objective accomplishments include such things as mastering a task or problem. You know when you get a basketball through a hoop, and you get a grade for how well you conjugate a verb for a classroom assignment. Subjective accomplishments refer to those actions, the meaning of which must be interpreted, that produce responses in others. You attempt to say something funny, and other's laughter seems somewhat forced. You look to others' visual reaction to your outfit. You try to argue a point with someone and end the argument without a clear winner. All of these instances involve ambiguous situations in which the value of your behavior is gauged by how others respond.

Clearly, most of the qualities that we consider important about ourselves in life belong in the subjective category. Even such seemingly objective accomplishments as obtaining a political office, making a good salary, or losing twenty pounds while on a diet achieve most of their value from how others

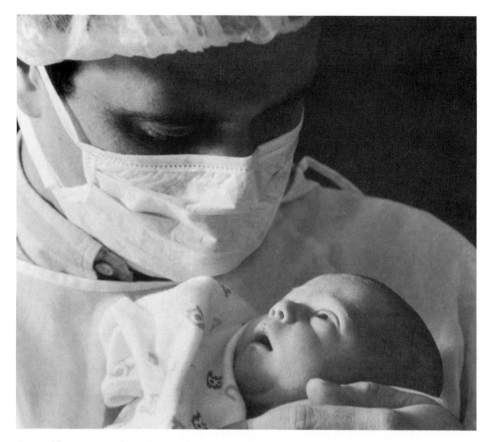

Our self-concept is based upon how others see us from the time of birth.

respond. The status of a political office is determined by society, much of the value of a high salary is in the status symbols it purchases, and the result of losing twenty pounds is often interpreted in terms of other people's standards of attractiveness and their comments about how much better we look having lost the weight. Our self-worth is powerfully influenced by the responses of others.

Our self-concept is not a static entity. We are not given a self-concept when we are young that does not change. On the contrary, our self-concept is always in process, always changing. Further, our self-concept is not the same with all people, in all situations, and at all times. The way you see yourself vis-à-vis your mother may be far different than the way you see yourself in terms of your spouse. You may feel a great deal of acceptance from one member of your family, but very little from another member.

The second process involved in the development of self-concept is learning to view self as a *reflected self*. A reflected self is one's view of oneself as others might view self. A child at first learns to engage in certain behaviors, and avoid engaging in others, based upon relatively simple reinforcement by primary caretakers. Eventually, however, the child begins to generalize rules for appropriate conduct by considering what the caretakers would think *if* the child engages in a certain behavior. For example, the child may receive punishment when caught lying to his or her parents. At some point in the future, the child may have to turn in an assignment late to a teacher. In considering how to excuse his or her irresponsibility, the child may consider lying to the teacher. In considering this, the child also wonders, "What would my parents think of me if I were to lie to my teacher?" This process of viewing self from the viewpoint of others involves the development of a reflected self. Over time, this reflected self evolves from the viewpoint of a particular "other," into what Mead calls a *generalized other*. The generalized other represents an idealized collection of societal standards and evaluations of conduct. The more a person can live up to or surpass the standards of this generalized other, the higher this person's self-concept will tend to be.

Dimensions of Self-Disclosure

Researchers have found that self-disclosure has a number of different dimensions.[2] Among the aspects of self-disclosure that can be identified are (1) the amount of disclosure, (2) the positive/negative nature of self-disclosure, (3) the depth of disclosure, (4) the timing of disclosure, and (5) the target person involved in self-disclosure. These dimensions are important to understand as they clarify the complex nature of self-disclosure and as they suggest guidelines for your self-disclosure behavior. Let us consider each of the dimensions.

Amount.   Self-disclosure may be examined in terms of total amount. Everyone does not disclose the same amount of information about themselves. You may know people who seem to say relatively nothing about themselves and others who tell you everything about their past experiences, present situations, and future goals. You may wish that some of your friends would open up more to you and you may find that you feel very uncomfortable with your acquaintances who "tell all."

The literature on self-disclosure does not supply a prescriptive answer to a desirable amount of self-disclosure; instead, the research suggests that self-disclosure should be reciprocal. If you are conversing with someone who self-discloses a great deal, you may feel free to similarly disclose; conversely, if your conversational partner is reluctant to share personal information, you should exercise more caution. In general, as the disclosure of one person increases, so does the self-disclosure of the other person.[3] When individuals fail to reciprocate, they are viewed as incompetent.[4] Patterns of reciprocity appear to be stable and may be established within the first five minutes of interaction.[5]

Positive/negative nature.   Disclosive statements may be positive in tone or negative in tone regarding what they imply about yourself. Disclosing that you have a communicable disease clearly will be interpreted negatively by most people, while the disclosure of having devoted two years of your life to the Peace Corps is likely to be evaluated positively. People who disclose uniformly negative or positive information during a first encounter or date are likely to sabotage the relationship. Too much negative information is likely to make the person appear too flawed, whereas excessive positive information may well imply egotism, or even narcissism.

Normative information regarding the positive or negative dimension of self-disclosure appears to be related to the level of intimacy or nonintimacy of the information that is disclosed. For example, when individuals disclose information that may be considered to be nonintimate, they frequently self-disclose positive information first, followed by neutral statements, and ending with negative information. If you were going to talk about your academic career, then, you might talk first about your high grades, then about transferring from one university to another, and finally, you might disclose that you were on academic probation for one term. The pattern for intimate self-disclosure suggests that persons first disclose negative information, then positive, and finally, neutral statements.[6] In a conversation with an opposite-sex friend, you might first disclose that you have recently broken up with a person whom you loved, then you might share that you have almost forgotten this other person because of your relationship with the person with whom you are talking, and conclude with a generalization about your intimate relationships.

Depth.   Self-disclosure may be deep or shallow. Communication about aspects of yourself that are unique and cause you to be vulnerable, including your specific goals and your intimate life, are considered to be deep. Shallow disclosures include those statements about yourself that are superficial and nonintimate. Statements about foods you like are fairly shallow disclosures and statements about your sexual preferences are generally considered fairly deep. Again, the literature offers little prescription for individuals who are concerned with appropriate depth of self-disclosure. You may wish to keep in mind the normative information on the relationship between positive/negative disclosure and intimacy of disclosure that was previously discussed.

Timing.   Self-disclosure also can be examined in terms of the time in which it occurs in a relationship. A number of studies have demonstrated that a great deal of self-disclosure tends to occur with strangers and in the initial stages of a relationship, less occurs during the middle stages of a relationship, and

Intimate Self-Disclosure

The following dialogue occurred after a class at a coeducational university. Read the dialogue and then answer the questions at the end.

Dorene: I don't understand why there's so much prejudice on this campus! There are people from all over the world here, but I feel a lot of discrimination.

Sue: I know what you mean. Dorene, do you mind if I ask you a question?

Dorene: I guess not.

Sue: What country are you from?

Dorene: Korea.

Sue: How long have you lived in the United States?

Dorene: Since I was ten months old. I was adopted from Korea by an American family.

Sue: Do you know anything about your background?

Dorene: No, all I know is that I'm Korean-American. I was told that my father was probably an American serviceman and that my mother was a Korean woman. My mother couldn't take care of me so she abandoned me at a local city hall. Someone found me and brought me to the orphanage. Shortly after I was taken to the orphanage, I was adopted. First I got the measles and the adoption had to be delayed for two months. Then, on the trip to the United States the plane got fogged down in Alaska. Well, I finally made it. I'm really thankful that I was adopted, but I really wonder about some things.

Sue: What do you mean?

Dorene: Oh, nothing really, I guess sometimes I wonder about my real parents. I wonder if I have any brothers and sisters, and which parent I look most like. I guess stuff like that.

Sue: That's really interesting. I hope you don't mind the questions.

Dorene: No, I don't mind. Why were you interested?

Sue: Because I know what it's like to feel prejudice. I have been dating a guy from Iran for the past semester.

Dorene: I see.

Consider the following questions:

1. Do you think the amount of self-disclosure in which Dorene engaged was appropriate? Under what circumstances would it be appropriate? What circumstances would render it inappropriate?
2. Does Sue's explanation for why she is interested in Dorene's self-disclosure alter the situation?
3. Do you think the amount of self-disclosure in which Sue engaged was appropriate? If you were Sue in this situation would you have disclosed differently?
4. How long do you think Sue and Dorene have known each other?
5. Is Dorene's self-disclosure negative or positive?

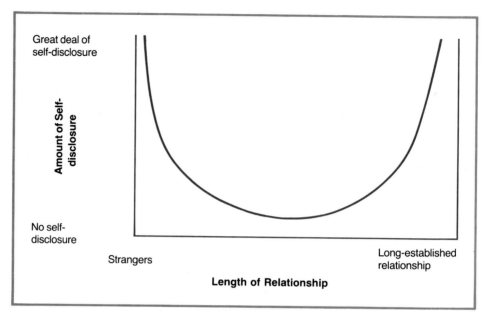

Figure 6.1   Self-disclosure in relationships.

self-disclosure increases as the relationship time increases.[7] This pattern is illustrated in Figure 6.1. Self-disclosure can occur early or late in the development of a conversation or the development of a relationship.

The phenomenon of self-disclosing to strangers is particularly interesting. This is often referred to as the "stranger on the plane" (or train or bus) phenomenon. We might conclude that people will self-disclose to a stranger because he or she offers them the safety of anonymity. The stranger does not know who you are and cannot identify you to others. In addition, the stranger cannot reveal the information to people whom you know. Airline travel provides many opportunities for self-disclosure to strangers. The editorialist Ellen Goodman humorously described these "Confessions at 35,000 Feet":

There probably is an urge for soul-baring and protectiveness in most people. These two urges come together at 35,000 feet. Here at last is intimacy with anonymity, confiding without revealing. It is an encounter session that ends at the baggage counter. Air travel is, at times, a verbal one-night stand.[8]

The duration of the relationship affects the amount of self-disclosure and the kind of self-disclosure that appears appropriate. As we previously discussed, persons generally begin with nonintimate information that is positive, followed by neutral, and concluded by negative; they offer intimate information beginning with negative information, followed by positive, and then neutral. Timing is an important dimension of self-disclosure that should be taken into account when you choose to disclose information about yourself to others.

Target person.   The target person in self-disclosure is the person to whom you disclose. You may regularly self-disclose to your mother, but you rarely share the same information about yourself to your father. This pattern has been established in the research on self-disclosure.[9] You may self-disclose to your marital partner if you are married, to the person you are dating, or to a same-sex friend. The person to whom you self-disclose is significant and is a final dimension of self-disclosure that should not be overlooked.

The target person may fall into one of at least four categories. He or she may be a very close friend who is deeply concerned about you and involved with you. The person may be someone who is less involved with you, but for whom the disclosure is appropriate because of the ongoing relationship, task, or topic under discussion. For example, you disclose information to physicians and counselors that you are unlikely to disclose to others because disclosure is "licensed" in such relationships by nature of the task. Or, the listener may be rather uninvolved and disclosure occurs because the two of you are becoming acquainted. Finally, the other person may be quite uninvolved with you and may be receiving a disclosure for which no solicitation was made. In general, self-disclosure becomes increasingly less appropriate as we move through these four categories.

With the exception of strangers whom we do not expect to see again, the research suggests that we disclose most to people to whom we feel close or toward whom we feel affectionate.[10] A great deal of risk is involved in self-disclosing to people we do not know well. The literature suggests that people demonstrate a preference for strangers who self-disclose little rather than a great deal[11] and that individuals who self-disclose a great deal to relative strangers are viewed by others as maladjusted or inappropriately socialized.[12]

Appropriate Timing of Self-Disclosure

The following dialogue occurred on a commercial airline flight from Des Moines, Iowa, to Chicago, Illinois. If you were Passenger #2, how would you continue in this conversation? Some people might pretend to take a nap, others would read, while still others might seek additional information. Would you offer reciprocal self-disclosure? How would you feel if Passenger #1 gave you her or his name? Would it make any difference if the other passenger was male or female? Would the age of the other passenger alter your reaction to her or him?

Passenger #1:   Hi, how are you?

Passenger #2:   Hi, just fine, thanks.

Passenger #1:   How far are you going?

Passenger #2:   To Chicago and then on to Baltimore.

Passenger #1:   I see you're in the service.

Passenger #2:   Yes, I've been in the Navy for almost a year.

Passenger #1:   Are you heading to your ship?

Passenger #2:   Right, the U.S.S. *Coronado.*

Passenger #1:   I'm on my way home to Pittsburgh. I was in Rochester, Minnesota, at the Mayo Clinic. You see, I have a problem with my back. I think it must be hereditary—my father had a bad back, too.

Passenger #2:   Minnesota is a long way from Pennsylvania.

Passenger #1:   Yes, but it's worth it. None of the doctors in Pennsylvania could help me. The doctor who was seeing me had his license removed because he was a drug addict. I guess he had a pretty hectic life and the pills were easy for him to get.

Passenger #2:   That's too bad.

Passenger #1:   You know I can really understand it. I have to take pretty strong medicine for my back. I think I might be addicted to it.

Passenger #2:   I'm sure that could happen.

Passenger #1:   But I think I really have a drug problem. What do you think I should do about it?

Passenger #2:   Well, I don't know . . .

Passenger #1:   Have you ever been addicted to anything?

Theories About Self-Disclosure

In discussing the various dimensions of self-disclosure, we have stated that each of us does not exhibit the same self-disclosing behavior. Some people self-disclose a great deal of intimate information early in relationship development while others self-disclose very little information, very shallow information, and self-disclose very late in a long-established relationship. A number of theories have been advanced that have offered to explain why self-disclosure occurs. We turn to a consideration of those theories that suggests factors that appear to motivate people to self-disclose.

Exchange theory.   The exchange theory states that people feel an obligation to exchange comparable behaviors in order to maintain equity in their relationships. Equity is achieved when one person self-discloses and the other person reciprocates. An interesting example of the reciprocal nature of self-disclosure is found in Brando and Stein's book, *Brando for Breakfast:*

> *One evening Marlon broke his seclusion and submitted to the widely quoted interview by Truman Capote published in* The New Yorker. *To ensnare his quarry, Capote resorted to the only psychological finesse that could succeed: "I made up stories about what lushes my family were,"* he admitted, *"and, believe me, I made them lurid, until he began to feel sorry for me and told me his to make me feel better. Fair exchange."*[13]

An unequal situation is created when one person discloses and the other does not. This unequal situation normally has a negative effect on the development of the relationship. In addition, the unequal self-disclosure creates tension, which motivates the nondiscloser to reveal information. An equitable situation may thus finally occur.

Attraction theory.   The attraction theory is based on the idea that we self-disclose most to those people to whom we are attracted. Self-disclosure is viewed as a positive outcome and we reward people who are attractive to us with information about ourselves. When we reveal ourselves to our friends, we are indicating our attraction to them. The listener feels that he or she is respected and trusted. Reciprocal liking and disclosure often follow.

Information theory.   This theory stresses the importance of the information in self-disclosure, or the information that the act of self-disclosing provides. It holds that the person who discloses first indicates to the other person that disclosure is appropriate. In other words, the first self-disclosure provides information regarding the appropriateness of self-disclosure. To the extent that the second person is sensitive to this cue, he or she will reciprocate. Situational demands, rather than a felt obligation (exchange theory) or a feeling of attraction for the other person (attraction theory), motivates the second person to self-disclose.

Self-Disclosure Situational Inventory

Ten situations are listed below. Imagine yourself in each of the situations and rate each from "1" to "5," using the following scale:

1 = I would discuss a very limited number of topics and would only discuss them on a very superficial level.

2 = I would discuss a few topics and generally would discuss them superficially.

3 = I would discuss most topics and would discuss some of them in some depth and detail.

4 = I would discuss almost any topic and would discuss all of them in depth and detail.

5 = I would discuss any topic, including personal information about myself, in the most complete detail.

_____ 1.   You are in a classroom, waiting for a new class to begin, and a person you have never met before sits down next to you and begins a conversation.

_____ 2.   You are at home having the evening meal with your family.

_____ 3.   You are applying for a job at a local franchise-owned restaurant.

_____ 4.   You are sitting next to a stranger on a bus.

_____ 5.   You are alone with your boyfriend or girlfriend at your home.

_____ 6.   You are having dinner with friends in a restaurant.

_____ 7.   You are in a discussion group on open marriage.

_____ 8.   You are introduced to a group of strangers at a cocktail or beer party.

_____ 9.   You and your parents are driving to a vacation spot.

_____ 10.   You are a member of an interpersonal communication class.

After you have answered each of these ten questions, consider your responses. To whom do you self-disclose most? In what situations do you self-disclose? Does your mood affect your self-disclosure? Do you self-disclose to same-sex or opposite-sex people most frequently? Are you satisfied that your self-disclosure is appropriate for the other person or people involved, the situation, the topic, and yourself?

The Importance of Self-Disclosure

We have explored the nature of self-disclosure; let us consider now the role that self-disclosure can play in our interpersonal communication and in our lives. At least three direct benefits can be derived from the ability to self-disclose: (1) we can develop a greater understanding and acceptance of ourselves, (2) we can develop a greater understanding and acceptance of others, and (3) we can develop deeper, more meaningful relationships.

Greater Understanding and Acceptance of Ourselves

This benefit of self-disclosure is perhaps the most obvious. Simply talking about a topic often helps us to more clearly understand it. Have you ever been confused about a decision you had to make and asked a friend for advice? You may have found that by clearly and carefully explaining the situation to your friend, you resolved the conflict for yourself. Oftentimes we use another person as a "sounding board." We are not really seeking assistance, we merely need to clearly articulate the problem and the solution emerges. The same situation arises with self-disclosure. As we share ourselves with another person, we must put complex thoughts into language that can be understood by another person. As we do so, we often make discoveries about our own motivations, needs, and goals. Relationships among events, experiences, and behaviors may emerge.

Understanding, of course, is the first step to acceptance. As we unravel the intricate webbing of our personalities and gain an understanding of ourselves, we move toward an appreciation of ourselves. Both positive and negative self-disclosures assist in the process of accepting ourselves. When we self-disclose positive information—successes, victories, accomplishments—we reinforce our own positive feelings. The praise or congratulations that others offer is also encouraging.

Finally, negative self-disclosure often serves a cathartic purpose—it allows us an opportunity to "get something off our chest." The weight of negative information is often too heavy to carry alone.

Self-disclosure of negative information can actually result in positive outcomes. It may allow us to understand and accept ourselves and it may encourage closer relationships with others.

Greater Understanding and Acceptance of Others

In the first chapter we considered the transactional nature of interpersonal communication. We discussed the notion that people are not exactly the same from one situation to another or when they are with different people. We create and re-create images of other people that are consistent with their behaviors. The communication behavior of others is largely used in this "creation process." Self-disclosure, in this case, serves the function of clarification. For example, Joe tells you that he grew up without a father. You make assumptions about how this loss may have affected Joe and try to understand Joe's behavior in light of this information. When Joe is angry about all of Fred's opportunities, when he shows cynicism about his own masculinity, and when he shows difficulty in making a decision to marry and have children, you may feel that you have some explanation for his behavior. As others share information about themselves, we gain a greater understanding and acceptance for them and the behaviors they exhibit. When we do not know people well, when they have not self-disclosed to us, when we have little understanding of them, we often conclude that they are relatively shallow or uninteresting. Self-disclosure allows us to understand and appreciate the complexity of others.

Better Relationships through Self-Disclosure

When we fail to engage in self-disclosure, our relationships become limited and shallow. We assume there is little more to the other person than "meets the eye." Conversely, we may draw incorrect inferences about others when we know little about them. Self-disclosure allows us to develop deeper relationships and to understand and accept others. This dialogue provides an example:

Husband: You know, I feel a little funny bringing this up, but there's something that's been bothering me for a while.

Wife: What is it?

Husband: Well, I guess I feel jealous of your relationship with Dave.

Wife: I didn't know you had any feelings about it.

Husband: Well, I do.

Wife: Why don't you tell me how you feel?

Husband: I know that you knew Dave before you knew me and I guess I have had the feeling for a while that the two of you were pretty close. I guess I wonder if you still feel pretty close to him.

Wife: We did date for a while before I met you, but when I met you, I never went out with him again.

Husband: Do you ever think about dating him now?

Wife: No, I really haven't. I've felt so close to you that the thought of being with anyone else seems excessive.

Husband: Do you really feel close to me?

Wife: Of course I do.

Husband: Could we talk more about our lives before we met each other?

Wife: I think it might be helpful.

If you were the wife in this dialogue, how would you have responded to the husband's questions? Do you believe that people should tell each other about relationships that occurred before they met? Do you think the husband was justified in asking the questions he did? If you had the concerns expressed by the husband, would you have handled the situation in the way that he did? Do you think that most married couples talk to each other this way? Do you know of marriages that have dissolved as a result of little or limited self-disclosure? Do you know of marriages that have dissolved as a result of too much self-disclosure? What conclusions have you drawn about self-disclosure in intimate relationships such as marriages? Do you believe this dialogue is generalizable to most intimate situations, regardless of the marital status of the two people involved? Have you had similar conversations? What personal experiences allow you to understand self-disclosure in intimate settings?

Deeper, More Meaningful Relationships

When we fail to self-disclose, we leave our relationships open to chance. We use limited information and draw extended inferences. Communication occurs to the degree that people establish some degree of common understanding. The most superficial exchanges can occur with anyone, but deep levels of communication rarely occur with anyone but a very close friend. The more information another person shares, the more we understand him or her. Similarly, the more we self-disclose, the more the other person understands us. Each of you has experienced the kind of relationship that was so close that the other person had only to mention a word or phrase to have you recall an event or experience. Perhaps you have even been able to elicit laughter from a friend by stating the "number" of a joke you have previously shared. To the extent that common information is held by two people, common understanding can occur and relationships are allowed to develop and deepen.

Research seems to support the role of self-disclosure in promoting satisfying relationships. For example, satisfaction in both social[14] and marital[15] relationships is related to the amount of disclosure in those relationships. Furthermore, self-disclosure functions as a primary means by which relationships are formed and developed. In a cross-national study, Won-Doornink found strong evidence that self-disclosure functions differently at different stages of relationship intimacy.[16] Generally speaking, the disclosure and reciprocity of nonintimate information decreases steadily as opposite-sex relationships increase in intimacy. However, comparing the "early," "middle," and "advanced" stages of relationship intimacy, it was found that highly intimate information is both disclosed and reciprocated most in the middle stages of relational intimacy, somewhat less so in advanced stages, and least in the early stages of relationship development. It seems that middle stages of relationships are particularly fertile times for relationship advancement and that interactants use self-disclosure to advance the relationship during this stage. During latter stages the relationship is established to the point that neither immediate reciprocity nor continuous intimate disclosure is necessary to sustain a satisfying relationship.

Sidney Jourard's statement serves as an appropriate conclusion to this section on the importance of self-disclosure:

> *A self-alienated person, who does not disclose himself truthfully and fully, can never love another person nor can he be loved by the other person. . . . Effective loving calls for knowledge of the object. . . . How can I love a person whom I do not know? How can the other person love me if he does not know me?*[17]

What are some of the implications of failing to self-disclose? Do you know anyone who appears unable or unwilling to self-disclose? Does this person appear to be well-adjusted? Would you be surprised if he or she committed a violent act of some kind? Why do we fail to notice individuals who do not self-disclose? To what extent do you self-disclose to others? Are you satisfied with the amount of self-disclosure in which you engage?

Competence in Self-Disclosure

Self-disclosure is an important ability for the competent interpersonal communicator. Self-disclosure, like the other skill areas discussed in this text, should not be practiced at all times and in all situations. The situation, the other person, and your intent must all be taken into consideration when you decide to self-disclose information. Keeping these variables in mind, let us consider some of the specific verbal and nonverbal skills of self-disclosure.

Verbal Skills of Self-Disclosure

Self-disclosure is evident in a number of different verbal skills. Listed here are some of the verbal skills that demonstrate self-disclosive behavior. You may wish to incorporate some of these skills into your interpersonal communication if you are not already practicing them. These skills also assist in self-assertion and are cross-listed in chapter 7.

1. *Make "I" statements to others and use owning statements.* These verbal skills are the most basic to self-disclosure. Tell others about your feelings, needs, attitudes, beliefs, and thoughts by using the basic "I" statement: "I think . . . ," "I feel . . . ," "I believe . . . ," and "I need. . . ." Owning your feelings and thoughts involves the acknowledgment and acceptance of your own feelings and thoughts. When you use owning statements, you admit that what you believe or feel is a function of your own perceptions, rather than a universally held truth. Instead of saying, "Everybody who knows anything about higher education chooses a large Eastern university to attend," state, "I prefer to attend college in the East at a large university."

2. *Use clear, specific language.* Do not hide your feelings behind ambiguous statements. Avoid telling others about yourself by relying on ambiguities, euphemisms, slang, or other vacuous language. Use specific and concrete terms to describe your past and express your present feelings. Instead of saying, "I guess the

president is doing okay,'' explain, ''My political beliefs are most closely aligned with the Republican Party: I voted for Bush and I still support his economic practices and his handling of foreign affairs.''

While some qualifiers strengthen and clarify your ideas, you will want to avoid meaningless qualifying words and phrases. Vivid adjectives can more accurately portray your past experiences, but weak and meaningless qualifiers only serve to dilute your message. Avoid qualifiers like ''sort of,'' ''kind of,'' ''about,'' ''rather,'' ''somewhat,'' and ''generally.''

3. *Use direct statements.* Do not avoid disclosure by using indirect statements. Rather than saying, ''I sometimes wonder if people who grow up in homes that have no fathers have difficulty with their sexual identity,'' state clearly, ''I have felt some confusion about my sexual identity.''

    Similarly, you will want to avoid words and phrases that negate your self-disclosure. Do not begin an explanation of some event in your life with the phrase, ''Well, my experience wasn't very interesting, but . . . ,'' ''My feelings are not very strong, however . . . ,'' ''I guess my childhood doesn't seem as exciting or interesting as yours, but . . . ,'' or ''I don't really have much to tell.'' Instead use ''My experience may be interesting . . . ,'' ''My feelings are moderately strong . . . ,'' ''An experience from my childhood is similar . . . ,'' and ''I have something to add. . . .''

4. *Use complete sentences and express complete thoughts.* Self-disclosure can be avoided by using unfinished sentences. You might begin by stating, ''My feelings about abortion are . . .'' and then trail off with vocalized pauses, ''um, you know, well.'' Complete your feelings and ideas when others ask you about them. Provide sufficient information so your perspective is clear to others.

Nonverbal Skills of Self-Disclosure

Verbal self-disclosure is complemented by nonverbal skills. The following nonverbal skills assist in self-disclosure. Have a friend observe your nonverbal behavior when you are self-disclosing to determine if you are practicing these skills.

1. *Use a direct body orientation and establish an open body position.* Sitting away from the other person and angling your shoulders and body away from him or her indicates to the other communicator

that you do not wish to self-disclose or it creates a "double bind" for the other person. Instead, sit or stand facing that person directly. Similarly, closing your body off from your listener by folding your arms in front of your chest or by crossing your legs or ankles may indicate an unwillingness to self-disclose. Assume an open position as you self-disclose to others.

2. *Use spontaneous, appropriate gestures.* Do not add gestures to your self-disclosure unless they add meaning to your message. An abundance of gestures suggests nervousness and may interfere with self-disclosure.

3. *Establish and maintain frequent direct eye contact.* Looking away from your listener may suggest embarrassment or uneasiness with the situation. The listener may believe that you do not want to self-disclose about the particular topic under discussion, that you may not want to self-disclose to that person, or that you do not wish to self-disclose at all.

4. *Use positive, responsive facial expression.* Facial gestures can add a great deal of meaning to your self-disclosure. Your smiles, frowns, and looks of bewilderment assist the listener in understanding your self-disclosure.

5. *Use touch appropriately.* Self-disclosure touches people in a figurative sense. Do not be hesitant to strengthen your message by literally touching others as well. Touch is a powerful means of communication that complements self-disclosure.

6. *Avoid vocalized pauses.* Do not allow yourself the habit of using vocalized pauses like "um," "ah," "well," and "mm." These vocal fillers may suggest a hesitancy on your part to open up to your fellow communicator. They allow hesitancy that may be understood to be retreating behavior.

7. *Project your voice in order to be heard.* Speakers who use a very quiet voice when disclosing are often thought to be reticent about self-disclosure. The unstated message appears to be that they really are not inclined to disclose.

8. *Articulate clearly.* Mumbling, like monotonous rate and rhythm, suggests that you do not want to self-disclose. Speaking distinctly aids in the clarity of your message and it demonstrates your willingness to self-disclose.

Self-disclosure occurs through these verbal and nonverbal skills. In the exercise that follows, you will have an opportunity to determine if you can apply the use of these skills in a dialogue.

Classroom Interaction

In the following dialogue the complex nature of self-disclosure is demonstrated. The conversation occurs in a classroom, just before class begins. Eric is a very confident person who self-discloses freely and encourages Kathy to do the same in the beginning of the dialogue. Kathy is somewhat reticent and hesitates to self-disclose at first. During the course of the conversation, the situation changes and Eric appears to lose some of his confidence as Kathy takes the initiative.

Dialogue	Explanation
Eric: (smiling, speaking loudly and clearly) Hi, Kathy. How are things going for you?	*Kathy is sitting in the back of the classroom. When Eric sits down next to her, she appears to be nervous. She looks away, fidgets, frowns, and appears not to wish to communicate. Eric's voice is strong, clear, and projects well. His body is open and unrestrained. He has erect posture and he smiles.*
Kathy: (weak voice, weak smile, and no eye contact) Uh, hi.	*Kathy relies on a vocalized pause and appears hesitant to even engage in any communication.*
Eric: Did you get much studying done for that math quiz? I studied a lot, but I know I killed it.	*"I" statement and ownership of the problem demonstrate self-disclosure. Nonverbal cues of open body, expressive face, and spontaneous gestures complement the verbal message.*
Kathy: I don't know how I did.	*Ambiguity coupled with a monotone voice suggests that Kathy does not want to disclose.*
Eric: I wonder if you had any problem with the integrals. I don't think they were covered adequately in class. I didn't think it was fair that they were included on the test. I particularly thought that number six was tricky.	*Eric invites Kathy to disclose. He uses specific information, "I" statements and models self-disclosure for Kathy.*
Kathy: (frowning and shrugging) I, well, I'm not, uh, sure if I got those or not. I guess I just want, uh, to, you know, to pass the course.	*Kathy's facial expression and the shrugging of her shoulders suggests that she does not want to communicate. She relies on vocalized pauses, qualifiers, and ambiguous language. She appears to be unsure of her goals in the math class.*
Eric: I like the class, but I can understand how you feel. I'd be happy to study with you before the next quiz, if you would like.	*Eric smiles and shows openness in his body position. He relies on "I" statements and acknowledges Kathy's feelings while clearly stating his own.*
Kathy: I don't know, maybe that would help. I guess I don't know if I have the time to spend on that class.	*Kathy qualifies her response. She negates her message and uses extraneous filler material. She again appears to be uncertain of her feelings and unable to convey her honest thoughts.*

Classroom Interaction continued

Eric:	How do you spend your weekends? Do you usually go home or stay on campus?	*Eric changes the topic since Kathy appears to show some reluctance in discussing the class.*
Kathy:	Um, well, I sometimes go home and at other times I stay on campus.	*Kathy appears even less willing to disclose than before. She shows discomfort nonverbally as she squirms, looks away, and frowns.*
Eric:	What are you doing this Friday night?	*Eric is direct in his question and again demonstrates nonverbal confidence.*
Kathy:	Um, well, I guess I'll be here at school.	*Kathy answers, but does so in ambiguous terms.*
Eric:	Would you like to see the movie at the campus theater?	*Eric again uses specific information to encourage Kathy to disclose.*
Kathy:	Well, I guess that would be fine.	*Kathy agrees, but not without qualifiers and fillers. She also hesitates between words.*
Eric:	I heard the show is terrific. My roommate saw it last night and he's still laughing.	*Eric adds more of the particulars. He attempts to assure Kathy that she has made the right decision.*
Kathy:	Do you have a car?	*Kathy turns the tables at this point by asking Eric to disclose more information about himself.*
Eric:	Well no, no, I don't. I thought we could walk.	*Eric frowns, looks away, and closes his body by crossing his arms. He pauses between his words and appears hesitant to respond.*
Kathy:	I usually don't mind walking, but I sprained my ankle in an intramural basketball game two days ago and it's difficult to walk very far on it. I wouldn't mind walking if we allowed enough time to go slowly and stop now and then.	*Kathy offers specific information which explains why she asked the question. She looks directly at Eric, has assumed an open body position, and uses spontaneous gestures as she points toward her bandaged foot.*
Eric:	I can borrow my roommate's car. Under the circumstances, I know he won't mind. I'll pick you up at 8:30.	*Eric resumes his confidence. He offers a specific suggestion and uses nonverbal cues that strengthen his message.*

Do you think this dialogue is typical? Have you engaged in similar conversations? Rewrite the dialogue so that Kathy is confident from the beginning and discloses more readily early in the conversation. Similarly, have Eric self-disclose and demonstrate more confidence throughout the dialogue, including the middle and end of the conversation. When you have finished rewriting the dialogue, consider how typical it is. Which dialogue would you prefer as a script if you were to be engaged in a similar conversation? Why? Recall or record a conversation with an opposite-sex acquaintance. Analyze the conversation. Were you satisfied with this interaction? How might it have been improved? Be as specific as possible in your analysis and suggestions for improvement.

Summary

You have considered the role of self-disclosure in this chapter. You can now define the concept, identify the dimensions, and explain three theories that have been advanced concerning self-disclosure. You know the relationship of self-acceptance to self-disclosure and you understand that appropriate self-disclosure is appropriate in terms of amount of self-disclosure, in terms of its positive or negative dimension, in terms of level of intimacy or depth, in terms of when it is offered, and with regard to the target person, or the person to whom you are self-disclosing. The complex nature of self-disclosure is clarified in this chapter.

A number of verbal and nonverbal skills demonstrate self-disclosure behavior. If we want to self-disclose to others, we use "I" statements and other owning statements, we use clear, specific language, we use direct statements, and we use complete sentences and express complete thoughts. Nonverbally, we use a direct body orientation and establish an open body position, we use spontaneous, appropriate gestures, we establish and maintain frequent, direct eye contact, we use positive, responsive facial expression, we use touch appropriately, we avoid vocalized pauses, we project our voices in order to be heard, and we articulate clearly.

Self-disclosure is one element of demonstrating confidence in interpersonal communication. The other element, self-assertion, is the topic of the next chapter. After you have mastered the material in this chapter and are able to demonstrate the skills that are included, you are prepared for the material on assertiveness. These two chapters assist you in becoming more confident as a communicator and allow you to demonstrate that confidence to others. You may not always wish to demonstrate confidence to others in your interpersonal communication, but when you do desire this outcome, you will have the necessary skills at your disposal. Your behavioral repertoire now includes self-disclosure skills. It is up to you, as an interpersonal communicator, to implement these skills when appropriate.

Notes

1.   George Herbert Mead, *Mind, Self and Society* (Chicago: University of Chicago Press, 1934).

2.   See, for instance, Shirley J. Gilbert, "The Communication of Self-Disclosure: Level Versus Valence," *Human Communication Research* 1(1975): 316–21; Shirley J. Gilbert and Gale G. Whiteneck, "Toward a Multidimensional Approach to the Study of Self-Disclosure," *Human Communication Research* 2(1976): 347–55; George A. Gitter and Harvey Black, "Is Self-Disclosure Revealing?" *Journal of Counseling Psychology* 23(1976): 327–32; and Lawrence R. Wheeless and Janis Grotz, "Conceptualization and Measurement of Reported Self-Disclosure," *Human Communication Research* 2(1976): 338–46.

3. See, for example, P. C. Cozby, "Self-Disclosure, Reciprocity, and Liking," *Sociometry* 35(1972): 151–60; P. C. Cozby, "Self-Disclosure: A Literature Review," *Psychological Bulletin* 79(1973): 73–91; and W. Morton Feigenbaum, "Reciprocity in Self-Disclosure Within the Psychological Interview," *Psychological Reports* 40(1977): 15–26.

4. Lawrence A. Hosman and Charles H. Tardy, "Self-Disclosure and Reciprocity in Short and Long-Term Relationships: An Experimental Study of Evaluational and Attributional Consequences," *Communication Quarterly* 28(1980): 20–29.

5. J. A. Kohen, "The Development of Reciprocal Self-Disclosure in Opposite Sex Interaction," *Journal of Counseling Psychology* 22(1975): 404–10.

6. Gilbert and Whiteneck, 347–55.

7. See, for example, P. T. Quinn, "Self-Disclosure as a Function of Degree of Acquaintance and Potential Power," (Master's thesis, Ohio State University, 1965); Dalmas I. Taylor, "Some Aspects of the Development of Interpersonal Relationships: Social Penetration Process," *Technical Report No. 1* (Center for Research on Social Behavior, University of Delaware, 1965); Dalmas I. Taylor and Irwin Altman, "Intimacy-Scaled Stimuli to Use in Studies of Interpersonal Relations," *Psychological Reports* 19(1966): 729–30; and Charles R. Berger, Royce R. Gardner, Glenn W. Clatterbuck, and Linda S. Schulman, "Perceptions of Information Sequencing in Relationship Development," *Human Communication Research* 3(1976): 29–46.

8. Ellen Goodman, "Confessions at 35,000 Feet," *Des Moines Register,* April 13, 1979, p. 16.

9. See, for example, R. M. Ryckman, M. F. Sherman, and G. D. Burgess, "Locus of Control and Self-Disclosure of Public and Private Information by College Men and Women: Brief Note," *Journal of Psychology* 84(1973): 317–18; R. P. Littlefield, "Self-Disclosure among Negro, White and Mexican-American Adolescents," *Journal of Counseling Psychology* 21(1974): 133–36.

10. Sidney Jourard, "Self-Disclosure and Other-Cathexis," *Journal of Abnormal and Social Psychology* 59(1959): 428–31; W. Worthy, A. Gary, and G. M. Kahn, "Self-Disclosure as an Exchange Process," *Journal of Personality and Social Psychology* 13(1969): 59–63.

11. See, for instance, S. A. Culbert, "Trainer Self-Disclosure and Member Growth in Two T-Groups," *Journal of Applied Behavioral Science* 4(1968): 47–73.

12. C. A. Kiesler, S. Kiesler, and M. Pallack, "The Effects of Commitment on Future Interaction on Reactions to Norm Violations," *Journal of Personality* 35(1967): 585–99.

13.   Anna Kashfi Brando and E. P. Stein, *Brando for Breakfast* (New York: Berkley Book, 1980), p. 87.

14.   J. P. Lombardo and R. D. Wood, "Satisfaction with Interpersonal Relations as a Function of Level of Self-Disclosure," *Journal of Psychology* 102(1979): 21–26.

15.   G. J. Chelune, E. M. Waring, B. N. Vosk, F. E. Sultan, and J. K. Ogden, "Self-Disclosure and Its Relationship to Marital Intimacy," *Journal of Clinical Psychology* 40(1984): 216–19.

16.   M. J. Won-Doornink, "Self-Disclosure and Reciprocity in Conversation: A Cross-National Study," *Social Psychology Quarterly* 48(1985): 97–107.

17.   Sidney M. Jourard, *The Transparent Self* (New York: Van Nostrand Reinhold Co., 1971), p. 32.

Additional Readings

Chelune, G. J. "Nature and Assessment of Self-Disclosing Behavior." In *Advances in Psychological Assessment,* vol. 4, edited by P. W. McReynolds. San Francisco: Jossey-Bass, 1978.

Derlega, V. J., and Berg, J. H., eds. *Self-Disclosure: Theory, Research, and Therapy.* Perspectives in Social Psychology Series. New York: Plenum, 1987.

Egan, Gerard. *Interpersonal Living: A Skills-Contract Approach to Human Relations Training in Groups.* Belmont, Calif.: Brooks/Cole Publishing Co., 1976.

Gibb, Jack R. *Trust: A New View of Personal and Organizational Development.* Los Angeles: Guild of Tutors, 1978.

Gilbert, Shirley J. "Empirical and Theoretical Extensions of Self-Disclosure." In *Explorations in Interpersonal Communication,* edited by Gerald R. Miller. Beverly Hills, Calif.: Sage, 1976.

Goffman, Erving. *The Presentation of Self in Everyday Life.* Garden City, N.Y.: Doubleday & Co., 1959.

Gordon, Chad, and Gergen, Kenneth J. *The Self in Social Interactions.* New York: John Wiley & Sons, Inc., 1968.

Jourard, Sidney M. *Disclosing Man to Himself.* New York: Van Nostrand Reinhold, 1968.

Jourard, Sidney. *Self-Disclosure: An Experimental Analysis of the Transparent Self.* New York: John Wiley & Sons, Inc., 1971.

Jourard, Sidney M. *The Transparent Self,* revised ed. New York: Van Nostrand Reinhold, 1971.

Luft, Joseph. *Of Human Interaction: The Johari Model.* Palo Alto, Calif.: Mayfield, 1969.

Moss, Carolyn. *Bibliographic Guide to Self-Disclosure Literature: 1956–1976.* Troy, N.Y.: Whitson, 1977.

Pearce, W. Barnett and Sharp, Stewart M. "Self-Disclosing Communication," *Journal of Communication* 23 (1973): 409–25.

Rogers, Carl R. *On Becoming a Person.* Boston: Houghton Mifflin Co., 1961.

Self-Assertion

Reprinted with special permission of King Features Syndicate, Inc.

This father's disclosure to his son illustrates a couple of fundamental lessons about communication: A lack of communication is not always the cause of conflicts among people. Further, there is more than just the obvious difference between "voicing" your feelings and striking someone with a saucepan. Hitting someone implies a total disregard for anyone else's rights and interests other than one's own. This chapter is about ways in which people handle their differences through interaction. Consider the following situations which may be familiar to you.

One of your friends calls you and talks on and on about an event that has occurred. The friend does not inquire if this is a good time for you to talk. You are in a hurry—you are already late for a class. What do you say?

A person with whom you work offered to give you a ride while your car was in the garage. You waited for nearly forty-five minutes and finally walked to work. When you arrive, your fellow worker is already at her job. What do you say to her?

Your roommate is socially active. He frequently gets in an hour or two after you are asleep. He turns on the overhead light when he arrives and makes a great deal of noise before settling down to sleep. You will be living with this person for at least another eight months. What will you say or do?

Each of these situations presents a potential conflict. In each case, you may respond assertively, aggressively, or nonassertively. Responding with anger or indifference may be viewed as aggression and allowing the other person to continue the same behavior may be viewed as nonassertion. But what is the assertive response? How can we deal with situations like these in a manner that will allow us to stand up for our own rights without abusing the rights of the other person? In this chapter you will discover the components of assertive communication behavior.

You will learn that assertiveness is a fairly new concept and that, originally, assertiveness training was provided primarily for women. You will be able to define assertiveness and be able to differentiate it from aggressiveness and nonassertiveness. You will be able to explain why assertiveness is important in interpersonal interactions. Finally, you will be able to identify the specific verbal and nonverbal skills that demonstrate assertiveness. Assertiveness, one element in the interpersonal component of confidence, provides an important addition to your behavioral repertoire.

The Nature of Assertiveness

History of Assertiveness

Andrew Salter is recognized as the originator of assertiveness training. Over thirty years ago, he wrote a book entitled *Conditioned Reflex Therapy*[1] in which he differentiated between the nonassertive and the assertive person. Largely as a result of Salter's seminal work, behavior therapists began assertiveness training. In the late 1960s, assertiveness gained in importance outside of the clinical setting. Feminists encouraged women to learn assertiveness skills. The popularity of assertiveness increased in the 1970s as was evidenced by the large number of best-selling books, the increased number of assertiveness training groups, and the greater emphasis on assertiveness in research. Today, both men and women recognize the relevance of assertiveness in their communication behavior.

Definition of Assertiveness

The sudden popularity of assertiveness has resulted in some confusion about the meaning of the term. In a general sense, assertiveness means standing up for your own rights without violating the rights of others. In the context of interpersonal communication, *assertiveness* is defined as the ability to communicate your own feelings, beliefs, and desires honestly and directly while allowing others to communicate their own feelings, beliefs, and desires.[2] The goal of assertiveness is self-respect and respect for others as demonstrated through communication behavior.

Some authors have viewed assertiveness as consisting of a bill of rights. These rights define the broad outline of legitimate assertive behavior. Consider, for example, to what extent you believe that you have the right (and possibly the obligation) to:

I.   be the judge of your own thoughts, feelings, and behaviors;
II. take responsibility for the initiation and consequences of your actions;
III. choose whether or not to offer justifications or excuses for your actions;
IV. decide whether you should have any role in solving other people's problems;
V.   change your mind when reason dictates;
VI. make mistakes and assume responsibility for their consequences;
VII. respond "I don't know";
VIII. be independent of the "good will" and advice of others in matters of exclusively personal concern;
IX. respond "I don't understand";
X.   say "no," and only "no," when others make requests or demands of your voluntary behavior.

You may begin to see just how many communication problems occur among people because they do not defend their most basic rights through communication. Obviously, however, these rights are not meant to be taken to extremes, relied upon exclusively, or performed with anger or ill-will. How do you know if you are performing such behaviors appropriately? One thing to consider is the extent to which the message you intend will be assertive, aggressive, or nonassertive.

Assertiveness Differentiated from Nonassertiveness and Aggression

Popular writers and textbook authors offer differing definitions of assertiveness, but nearly all of them agree that assertiveness falls on a continuum between nonassertiveness and aggressiveness. A characterization of the nonassertive person and the aggressive person clarifies assertiveness and the character of the assertive person.

Nonassertiveness involves the failure of standing up for your own rights or standing up for yourself in a dysfunctional manner. A nonassertive person denies himself or herself, does not accept his or her personal rights, and is inhibited from expressing his or her feelings, beliefs, or desires. The goal of many nonassertive people is to appease others. Appeasement of others may occur, but personal satisfaction rarely does. The nonassertive person is often hurt and anxious and rarely achieves his or her own goals. Other people may feel sympathy for the nonassertive person or may feel guilt or anger because they perceive that they are achieving their own goals at the expense of the nonassertive person.[3] For each of the situations that are offered at the beginning of this chapter, suggest a response that would be labeled as ''nonassertive.''

Aggressiveness involves standing up for your own rights and completely disregarding the rights of others. The aggressive person expresses his or her own feelings, but often hurts the feelings of others. When others interact with an aggressive person, they often feel defensive or humiliated. The goal of aggression is generally to win, but the aggressive person may know only temporary victory as others become filled with frustration, and even vengeance. Aggressive behaviors will often take the form of attempting coercive forms of power, such as threats or punishments.[4] For each of the situations in the introduction to this chapter, offer one response that would be clearly identified as ''aggressive.''

Assertiveness falls between these two extremes. The assertive person stands up for his or her own rights, but not at the expense of others. Assertive people respect themselves and others. They do not deny themselves, they accept their personal rights, and they are not inhibited from self-expression. They trust their own responses and they create a communication climate of honesty and openness. Others respond to the assertive person in a symmetrical assertive manner. In most cases, persons who respond assertively to each other find that they can each reach their own goals, unless their goals are mutually exclusive. For each of the three situations in the opening of this chapter, offer at least one response that would be assertive.

There are actually several specific types of assertive messages, each of which tends to be evaluated differently by others. *Refusal* assertion is one of the forms that most often comes to mind when people think about assertion. It consists of refusing to comply with a request or demand of some sort. However, assertions can also be *commendatory* in nature. You are being assertive when you express your thoughts or feelings when they are positive and complimentary.

Aggressive behaviors do not take the other person into consideration.

I want statements simply articulate your needs or preferences, without any particular elaboration or justification (e.g., "I prefer that you not be late for our dates from now on"). *I feel* statements express your emotional state, as in "Your arriving late makes me feel like you don't respect me." *Confrontive assertion* statements describe in relatively precise and objective terms what is objectionable and what is preferred (e.g., "You were very late tonight, and you didn't call to let me know. From now on, I would prefer that you call me if you think you are going to be late"). Finally, *empathic assertion* statements acknowledge another person's perspective or rights in the process of expressing your own (e.g., "I know you probably felt rushed to get off work and battle traffic to get here tonight, but I was worried about you when you didn't get here on time").

Assertive behaviors, on the other hand, do take the other person into consideration.

Of course, these types of statements can be creatively combined to make more comprehensive messages. For example, extending the previous example, an action-feeling-reason-preference form can effectively combine assertion forms in the following statement: "When you are late and do not call me to let me know (action), I feel rejected and unimportant (feeling), because it seems that either you aren't thinking of me or that I am less important than your work (reason). From now on, if you think you are going to be late, I really would prefer that you call me and let me know (preference)."

Although the research is often contradictory, generally it indicates that people respond differently to different forms of assertion. Straightforward assertions, especially *refusal* and *I want* types of statements, are viewed as more competent and skillful, but also as more unpleasant and unlikable. Positive assertions, such as *commendatory* assertions and *empathic* assertions appear to mitigate much of this effect, and are viewed as both competent and attractive.[5]

An Employment Opportunity

To determine if you understand the distinction among assertiveness, nonassertiveness, and aggressiveness, and to determine your own style of behavior, consider the following situation and identify which alternative you would choose; then label each of the three alternatives as assertive, aggressive, or nonassertive.
Situation and Setting:

You have been selected as a finalist for an excellent employment opportunity. You plan for your interview, arrive before the appointed time, and sit down in an outer office to wait to be called. Another person arrives about fifteen minutes later, apparently as a candidate for the same position. The secretary calls your name, but before you can respond, the late arrival jumps up, explains that he is in a hurry, and walks past the secretary for a meeting with the personnel manager. How do you respond?
Solutions:

1. You loudly tell the secretary that you have waited long enough, and that if this is how the firm operates, you do not want the job. Then, you storm out the door.

2. You state that you have waited for fifteen minutes, that the time for your interview has arrived, and that you believe that you, rather than the other person, should be allowed to discuss the position with the personnel manager.

3. You sit down, say nothing, and wait for the secretary to call you again.

The Importance of Assertiveness

Assertiveness training has been shown to have a positive influence on many people. Teachers, coaches, counselors, and employers can benefit from assertive behavior. Many employers have found that the corporation or company benefits when employees are sent to assertiveness training programs. The president of one company commented on why managers fail: "Managers fail because they lack self-confidence, desire, and determination to succeed despite obstacles, competition, and momentary setbacks." He described the assertiveness training program in which his employees were involved, "It builds maturity, character, confidence, the will to succeed and have an addiction to excellence."

Assertiveness training has also been shown to improve marital relationships. Communication problems are often at the root of the difficulties that marital partners encounter. Two contemporary authors explain that in many cases, the marital problem is caused as a result of one of the partners being dominant and showing aggressive behavior or as a result of both partners behaving in a nonassertive manner and not fully understanding the feelings of the other partner.[6]

Current research on assertiveness demonstrates relationships between this concept and other constructs. These studies help us understand the importance of assertive behavior in the contexts we have discussed. Assertiveness is positively related to a positive self-concept, communication skills, and satisfactory interpersonal relationships; it is negatively related to anger and anxiety.

Positive self-concept.   A recent study examined the relationships among sex-role stereotyping, self-concept, and assertiveness. The results of this study indicated that "assertiveness is positively related to self-acceptance in both sexes."[7] In chapter 6, we discussed the importance of a positive self-concept. Studies similar to the one cited suggest that assertiveness and a positive self-concept are related.

Satisfactory interpersonal relationships.   Marital relationships, which were mentioned earlier, provide only one kind of example of the relationship between assertiveness and satisfactory interpersonal relationships.[8] In addition, studies that have considered the role of assertion have suggested that assertive training helped to reduce self-reported anxiety and led to greater assertiveness in interpersonal settings.[9] Anxiety about interpersonal relationships resulted in a lack of assertiveness, and the inability to respond in an assertive manner showed itself in anxiousness about interpersonal communication situations.

Anxiety.   A number of studies have examined the relationship between assertiveness and anxiety. These studies have drawn the general conclusion that assertiveness is incompatible with anxiety, as was previously mentioned. Among the specific findings is the inverse relationship between assertiveness and neuroticism, trait anxiety, interpersonal anxiety,[10] and communication apprehension.[11] Persons who score high on assertiveness are generally not neurotic; they are not characterized by the personality trait of anxiety, they do not feel anxiety about interpersonal relations, nor are they generally apprehensive about public speaking experiences. In summary, assertiveness is important to a variety of persons because it relates to a positive self-concept, various communication skills, more satisfactory interpersonal relationships, and reduced anxiety in a number of settings.

Communication skills.   The research is extensive on the relationship between certain communication behaviors and perceptions of assertion. However, only a few verbal and nonverbal behaviors are consistently related to assertiveness: verbal intensity, talkativeness, vocal volume, speech affect (i.e., vocal emotion), inflection, statements about feelings, the content of compliance statements, and requests for specific change. Surprisingly, speech fluency, compliments, eye contact, smiles, and posture do not appear to be related to assertiveness in any consistent way.[12]

Are you an assertive communicator? Examine your interactions with others to determine if you typically communicate your feelings, thoughts, and desires while taking into consideration the feelings, thoughts, and desires of others.

Competence in Assertiveness

In order to determine your own assertiveness in interpersonal communication, you can simply listen to yourself as you honestly describe your relationships with others. Examine your interactions with parents, peers, coworkers, classmates, spouse, children, and superiors. Who is dominant in these relationships? Do you allow any of these people to take advantage of you? Do you express your feelings and ideas openly to each person with whom you interact? Do you take advantage of other people? Self-awareness is an important first step in becoming more assertive in interpersonal communication.

Identifying specific verbal and nonverbal skills that demonstrate assertiveness is an essential second step. Before we outline some of these skills, we need to keep in mind that assertive behavior is not universal. In other words, behaviors that may appear to be assertive in one situation may be viewed as aggressive in another and nonassertive in still a third. Behavior, response, intent, and context must all be taken into consideration. As you study and practice the verbal and nonverbal skills that are presented on the next pages, remember that these behaviors are generally viewed as representing assertiveness; in some contexts, in particular situations, and with specific people, they may be viewed as nonassertive or aggressive.

Verbal Skills of Assertiveness

Self-assertion may take many forms in our verbal usage. The following list contains some of the verbal skills that you can incorporate into your interpersonal communication in order to become more verbally assertive. You may find that you are already practicing some of these skills, while you need to work at developing some of the others. As you consider the verbal skills that demonstrate your competence in self-assertion, you might keep in mind an anonymous quotation: "If you say nothing, nobody will repeat it."[13] When we are assertive in our verbal behavior, others may disagree with us but we do not have the kind of invisibility that the nonassertive person possesses. You will recall that some of these skills are useful in self-disclosure and are cross-referenced in chapter 6.

1. *Make "I" statements to others and use owning statements.* Tell other people about your feelings, needs, and desires in the most direct form, by stating, "I think . . . ," "I feel . . . ," "I need . . . ," and "I want. . . ." Acknowledge that what you feel is a result of your own perceptions and that others need not prescribe to the same perspective.

2. *Use cooperative language.* Demonstrate that you are willing to share experiences, ideas, and thoughts with others through your language of cooperation. Examples of cooperative language include, "Can we . . . ," "Shall we . . . ," "How about if we . . . ," and "Let us. . . ."

3. *Use empathic inquiries.* Show the other person that you value his or her opinions, feelings, and thoughts. For instance, you might ask, "Do you think . . . ," "What do you wish . . . ," "Do you feel . . . ," or "What do you need?"

   When we are empathic, we avoid threats, put-downs, and evaluative comments to others. Aggressive communication is demonstrated through the use of threatening remarks. Common threats include, "If you don't . . . ," "You had better look out or . . . ," and "I'm warning you. . . ." Put-downs may also be classified as aggressive. Some examples of typical put-downs are, "Come on now," "You don't really mean what you say," "No one feels that way," and "You are obviously exaggerating." Evaluative statements like, "You should not . . . ," "This is ugly," and "You should try . . ." exhibit aggressive communication behavior. In addition, sexist terms, racist terms, and unfair stereotyping are aggressive in interpersonal communication.

4. *Use clear, specific language.* The avoidance of ambiguity and vague terms demonstrates assertiveness. Rather than stating, "Sometimes I tend to feel warm when others do not mind the temperature in a closed room," you might try, "Would you open a window?" Excessive qualifiers weaken a statement and may cause the user of the qualifier to appear nonassertive. Words and phrases that appear to be particularly nonassertive in tone are "Maybe," "I guess," "Sort of," "Kind of," "Only," "Just," and "Perhaps."

5. *Use direct statements and address other people directly.* Instead of stating something in a circumvented way, you can attempt to be as direct as possible. You should be direct particularly when asked to offer a straight answer. You should not respond abstractly to questions that begin, "Tell me honestly, what do you think about . . . ," "I really want to know your opinion on this . . . ," "Don't beat around the bush, what do you think . . . ," and "I want a straight answer." Sometimes we appear to be nonassertive when we minimize or negate our needs. You might find some of these words and phrases regularly creeping into your conversation: "It's not really important, but . . . ," "I don't really care," "It's not that I want to disagree, but . . . ," "Don't worry about me," and "I don't really need. . . ."

    Addressing another person directly means that rather than telling another friend how you feel about Mary or rather than not saying anything at all, you would talk directly to Mary, the person for whom the message is relevant. Similarly, if you wish to have some specific action taken, tell the person who is capable of taking the action rather than everyone else. Complaints and criticisms that are misdirected can be labeled as aggressive rather than as assertive.

6. *Use complete sentences and express complete thoughts.* Allowing your sentences to be half-finished indicates a lack of assertiveness. Others are only too quick to complete your thoughts from their own perspective. They are able to determine your feelings and thoughts for you. Offer sufficient information to others so they can understand your perspective.

7. *Use repetition.* Repeating a point you are attempting to make in a calm, clear manner demonstrates your ability to be assertive. Sometimes people fail to understand your point when you briefly allude to it on one occasion; repetition adds clarity. On other occasions, repeating your point demonstrates the strength of your convictions.

8. *Accept and encourage criticism.* Perhaps you have had the experience of being on the receiving end of criticism about you or some action you are about to take. Two methods of accepting that criticism will show others your ability to communicate in an

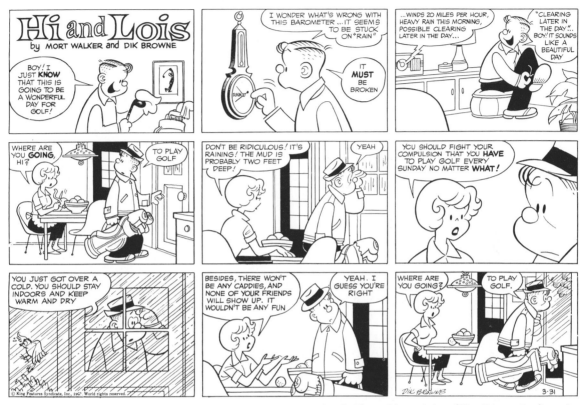

assertive manner. The first technique is to acknowledge the possibility or probability of truth in some part of the other person's remark. For example, if someone tells you that you are slow and lazy, you might respond by agreeing that you occasionally find that you are not as quick as others.

The second method of dealing with criticism assertively is to accept your faults by strongly and empathically agreeing with the entire criticism of your negative qualities and characteristics. For instance, you might comment to the person who has suggested you are slow and lazy that it must be difficult for someone who is as quick and ambitious as she is to deal with a person who has your temperament.

Occasionally you might wish to go further than acknowledging criticism and you may wish to actually encourage another person to criticize you. The two possible advantages of encouraging criticism are that it exhausts the other person's long list of complaints if that person is attempting to manipulate your behavior, and it may provide you with useful, instructive

Saying "No"

The following situations are probably familiar to you. For each of the statements, assume that you do not wish to purchase the product, have the service, or agree with the communicator. Suggest how you would assertively say "no," by writing a specific response to the question or statement.

1. **Salesperson**: I know you'll be interested in the magazines that I am selling.

   Response: _____

2. **Friend**: Let's go out for dinner and then see the new movie at the State Theatre.

   Response: _____

3. **Eight-Year-Old Child**: I'm selling cookies to go to camp—they're a dollar a box.

   Response: _____

4. **Clerk in a Cheese Store**: Try some of our new smoked sausage—it's only $2.99 a pound.

   Response: _____

5. **Opposite-Sex Friend**: Why don't we share an apartment next term?

   Response: _____

6. **Supervisor**: I assume you can stay an hour or two late tonight.

   Response: _____

7. **Parent**: We've planned a wonderful vacation for summer—the whole family will be together.

   Response: _____

information about yourself that can lead to self-improvement when it is offered in a constructive manner. Regardless of the motive, encouraging criticism can be one approach to assertiveness.

9. *Say "no."* One of the most common problems that individuals requesting assertiveness training mention is their inability to refuse requests. The word "no" is a useful addition to a person's assertive repertoire.

10. *Use silence appropriately.* Expressing assertiveness verbally is important; nonetheless, assertiveness can occasionally be shown by saying nothing. When other people are attempting to manipulate your behavior or your attitudes, it is sometimes effective to say nothing. The manipulator fails to achieve the satisfaction of altering your behavior or attitudes.

Nonverbal Skills of Assertiveness

We can demonstrate our assertiveness in interpersonal communication in nonverbal, as well as verbal, ways. The first six of the following skills are related to bodily movement and facial expression; the seventh relates to space and touching; and the last four are paralinguistic features. You might wish to review chapter 5 in order to reacquaint yourself with these categories of nonverbal behavior.

1. *Use a direct body orientation and establish an open body position.* Rather than sitting away from the other person, with your shoulders and body angled away from him or her, you demonstrate assertiveness by sitting with your body parallel to your partner's body. Angling away from the other person can be interpreted as nonassertive or aggressive. Similarly, closing your body off from others by folding your arms in front of your chest or crossing your legs or ankles may indicate an unwillingness to communicate your feelings and thoughts.

2. *Demonstrate a relaxed but attentive posture and, when standing, stand squarely but comfortably on two feet.* Your clear but relaxed mood can be shown in your posture. Others may interpret rigid posture as aggressive or as nonassertive. A steady, even stance demonstrates assertiveness. Standing first on one foot and then on the other may cause you to appear to be nervous and unassertive.

3. *Use spontaneous, appropriate gestures.* Using gestures in an artificial manner at inappropriate times does not lead other persons to feel that you are communicating assertively.

4. *Establish and maintain continual, but not constant, direct eye contact.* When you avert your gaze, that is, when you tend to look at the other person and then quickly look away, you appear to be nonassertive to others. When you fail to establish eye contact with the other person you similarly appear to be in a submissive role. Staring, on the other hand, can indicate aggression on the part of the person doing the staring. Continual, direct eye contact clarifies your role as an assertive communicator.

5. *Use responsive facial expression.* Smiling, frowning, and other expressiveness is shown on the face of the assertive communicator. A person who does not vary his or her facial expression may appear to be devious and aggressive or, conversely, afraid of his or her own responses.

6. *Avoid consenting, constant nodding behavior.* The habit of continually nodding approval to the speaker in an interpersonal setting may indicate nonassertion. Try to develop a sensitivity for your nodding behavior and eliminate this behavior when it occurs in response to manipulation or when you do not, in fact, agree with the speaker.

A Cancelled Date

In the following dialogue, Sally demonstrates an inability to communicate assertively with Fred. The notes in the right-hand column suggest Sally's difficulties. Try to determine how this dialogue could be improved to the mutual satisfaction of both people and in order that Sally would be communicating in an assertive way.

Dialogue	Analysis
Sally: Gosh, this might sound silly, but do you mind if we cancel our date for tonight?	*Sally uses qualifying words, phrases that negate her message; she speaks indirectly.*
Fred: Why?	
Sally: Well, it's just that, I don't know, I thought maybe we could see the movie tomorrow night.	*Again, the use of qualifying words and phrases that negate her message demonstrates a lack of assertion. She circumvents her message by adding new information.*
Fred: We could, but why don't we go tonight?	*Fred correctly accepts her suggestion, but persists in knowing her feelings.*
Sally: Um, it's just that, well, my mom said I had to babysit for my little brother.	*Sally finally states her reason, but adds vocalized pauses, qualifying words and phrases, and states the situation as though she has no choice in determining her plans for the evening.*
Fred: Why didn't you say so? Of course, we can go tomorrow night just as easily.	

Sally failed to use "I" statements and appeared to be unsure of Fred's reaction. Most likely, Fred would have responded more favorably if Sally had first clearly and directly stated that she was choosing to babysit for her brother at her mother's request. Rewrite this dialogue in two ways: (1) Sally behaves assertively and Fred responds favorably, and (2) Sally behaves nonassertively and Fred responds aggressively. Label the verbal skills or lack of assertive verbal skills for each comment. Compare your responses with those of your classmates.

7. *Use touch appropriately.* Touch is a very powerful method of communicating with others. Excessive touch may demonstrate aggression; too little touch may suggest nonassertion. Consider the situations in which you are willing to touch others and try to determine the interpretation others may give to your touching behavior.

8. *Avoid vocalized pauses.* Using vocalized pauses like "ah," "uh," "mmh," "eh," "like," and "you know" are habitual for some speakers. Have a friend or acquaintance listen to your communication with others to determine if you regularly use such patterns in your speech.

Airline Clerk and Customer Conflict

Assertiveness is demonstrated through a composite of the verbal and nonverbal skills that were outlined earlier. In the following dialogue, both persons are communicating assertively. Identify the verbal skills that are apparent.

Communicator	Dialogue	Verbal Skill
Airline clerk:	I'll check your skis for you, too.	_____
Passenger:	No, thank you. I'll keep my skis with me on the plane.	_____
Airline clerk:	You cannot board the plane with them, sir.	_____
Passenger:	I do not wish to check them. I will be happy to place them in the closet on board.	_____
Airline clerk:	If the skis are not checked, you will not be allowed to board the plane.	_____
Passenger:	Well, I don't know . . .	_____
Airline clerk:	The FAA regulation which covers personal items such as skis was created for your protection and the protection of the other passengers.	_____
Passenger:	Well, all right.	_____

9. *Change rate, rhythm, and inflection of your voice to punctuate your ideas and to indicate intent, but use a calm, steady voice.* A monotonous rate or rhythm is not only boring and tiresome for listeners, it also suggests a nonassertive speaker. Fluctuate your rate and rhythm in order to communicate more effectively. Nervousness or flightiness in your voice can be interpreted as an indication of lack of clarity about your ideas and about yourself. Attempt to speak in well-modulated, even tones.

10. *Project your voice so that it is loud enough to be heard easily.* You can err by speaking too softly—an indication of nonassertion—or too loudly—a suggestion of aggression. Speak in a volume so you can be easily heard by others, but not so loudly that you give the impression that you are attempting to dominate the conversation.

11. *Articulate clearly and pronounce words correctly.* Speaking indistinctly or mumbling may cause you to be viewed as nonassertive. Similarly, inappropriate pronunciation confuses listeners, and it does not characterize the speaker as a clear, assertive communicator.

These ten verbal skills and eleven nonverbal skills may be useful in your interpersonal interactions. In the next two exercises, you will have an opportunity to determine if you can apply these skills to specific dialogues.

Summary

In this chapter you have discovered the importance of self-assertion in interpersonal communication. You can now define the term, differentiate it from nonassertion and aggression, and can cite a brief history of the construct. You recognize the importance of self-assertion and know that it is positively related to a positive self-concept, communication skills, and satisfactory interpersonal relationships. Assertiveness is negatively related to anger and anxiety. Among the verbal skills that demonstrate assertiveness are "I" statements and owning statements, cooperative language, empathic inquiries, clear and specific language, direct statements, complete sentences, repetition, accepting and encouraging criticism, saying "no," and using silence appropriately. Nonverbal skills include a direct body orientation, an open body position, a relaxed, but attentive posture, spontaneous gestures, direct eye contact, responsive facial expression, the avoidance of consenting nodding behavior, using touch appropriately, avoiding vocalized pauses, changing rate, rhythm, and inflection in your voice, projecting your voice adequately, and articulating clearly. You have now completed the material on the component of confidence that is essential to the interpersonal communicator. Let us turn, next, to the component of other-orientation, that includes the increments of active listening and empathic understanding, the subjects of chapters 8 and 9.

Notes

1. Andrew Salter, *Conditioned Reflex Therapy* (New York: Creative Age Press, 1949).
2. See P. Jakubowski and A. J. Lange, *The Assertive Option* (Champaign, Ill.: Research Press, 1978) for a similar definition.
3. Robert Alberti and Michael L. Emmons, *Stand Up, Speak Out, Talk Back!: The Key to Self-Assertive Behavior* (New York: Simon & Schuster, 1975), p. 39.
4. See B. L. Hedlund and C. U. Lindquist, "The Development of an Inventory for Distinguishing Among Passive, Aggressive, and Assertive Behavior," *Behavioral Assessment* 6(1984): 379–90; J. G. Hollandsworth, Jr., "Differentiating Assertion and Aggression: Some Behavioral Guidelines," *Behavior Therapy* 8(1977): 347–52. See also an excellent review of related literature by J. P. Galassi, M. D. Galassi, and K. Fulkerson, "Assertion Training in Theory and

Practice: An Update," in *New Developments in Behavior Therapy: From Research to Clinical Application*, C. M. Franks (ed.) (New York: Haworth, 1984), pp. 319–75.

5. See R. J. Delamater and J. R. McNamara, "The Social Impact of Assertiveness: Research Findings and Clinical Implications," *Behavior Modification* 10(1986): 139–58; J. Gormally, "Evaluation of Assertiveness: Effects of Gender, Rater Involvement, and Level of Assertiveness," *Behavior Therapy* 13(1982): 219–25; D. B. Hull and H. E. Schroeder, "Some Interpersonal Effects of Assertion, Nonassertion, and Aggression," *Behavior Therapy* 10(1979): 20–28; J. S. St. Lawrence, D. J. Hansen, T. F. Cutts, D. A. Tisdelle, and J. D. Irish, "Situational Context: Effects on Perceptions of Assertive and Unassertive Behavior," *Behavior Therapy* 16(1985): 51–62; R. B. Levin and A. M. Gross, "Reactions to Assertive Versus Nonassertive Behavior: Females in Commendatory and Refusal Situations," *Behavior Modification* 8(1984): 581–92; P. N. Lewis and C. Gallois, "Disagreements, Refusals, or Negative Feelings: Perception of Negatively Assertive Messages from Friends and Strangers," *Behavior Therapy* 15(1984): 353–68; N. J. Warren and F. H. Gilner, "Measurement of Positive Assertive Behaviors: The Behavioral Test of Tenderness Expression," *Behavior Therapy* 9(1978): 178–84; B. G. Wildman and B. Clementz, "Assertive, Empathic Assertive, and Conversational Behavior: Perception of Likability, Effectiveness, and Sex Role," *Behavior Modification* 10(1986): 315–31.

6. Robert E. Alberti and Michael L. Emmons, *Your Perfect Right,* 3d ed. (San Luis Obispo, Calif.: Impact, 1978), pp. 147–51.

7. E. F. Currant and others, "Sex Role Stereotyping and Assertive Behavior," *Journal of Psychology* 101(1979): 223–28.

8. See R. C. Smolen, D. A. Spiegel, M. K. Bakker-Rabdau, C. B. Bakker, and C. Martin, "A Situational Analysis of the Relationship Between Spouse-specific Assertiveness and Marital Adjustment," *Journal of Psychopathology and Behavioral Assessment* 7(1985): 397–410.

9. See, for instance, William Lyman Ferrell, "A Comparison of Assertive Training and Programmed Human Relations Training in a Treatment Program for Problem Drinkers," unpublished Ph.D. dissertation, The University of North Carolina at Chapel Hill, 1977; James Frederick Warren, "The Effects of Assertion Training on Self-Acceptance and Social Evaluative Anxiety of University Students," unpublished Ph.D. dissertation, The University of Florida, 1977; and Joseph Wolpe and Arnold A. Lazarus, *Behavior Therapy Techniques* (New York: Pergamon Press, 1966).

10. H. Orenstein, E. Orenstein, and J. E. Carr, "Assertiveness and Anxiety: A Correlational Study," *Journal of Behavior Therapy and Experimental Psychiatry* 6(1975): 203–7; W. G. Morgan, "The Relationship Between Expressed Social Fears and Assertiveness and Its Treatment Implications," *Behaviour Research and Therapy* 3(1965): 45–53; L. P. Percell, P. T. Berwick, and A. Beigel, "The Effects of Assertive Training on Self-Concept and Anxiety," *Archives of General Psychiatry* 31(1974): 502–4; and M. L. Gay, J. H. Hollandsworth, Jr., and J. P. Galassi, "An Assertiveness Inventory for Adults," *Journal of Counseling Psychology* 22(1975): 340–44. See also M. J. Beatty, T. G. Plax, and P. Kearney, "Communication Apprehension and the Rathus Assertiveness Schedule," *Communication Research Reports* 1(1984): 130–33.

11. Judy C. Pearson, "A Factor Analytic Study of the Items in the Rathus Assertiveness Schedule and the Personal Report of Communication Apprehension," *Psychological Reports* 45(1979): 491–97.

12. See A. S. Bellack, M. Hersen, and S. M. Turner, "Relationships of Role Playing and Knowledge of Appropriate Behavior to Assertion in the Natural Environment," *Journal of Consulting and Clinical Psychology* 47(1979): 670–78; M. C. Bordewick and P. H. Bornstein, "Examination of Multiple Cognitive Response Dimensions Among Differentially Assertive Individuals," *Behavior Therapy* 11(1980): 440–48; R. M. Eisler, M. Hersen, P. M. Miller, and E. B. Blanchard, "Situational Determinants of Assertive Behaviors," *Journal of Consulting and Clinical Psychology* 43(1975): 330–40; R. M. Eisler, P. M. Miller, and M. Hersen, "Components of Assertive Behavior," *Journal of Clinical Psychology* 29(1973): 295–99; J. P. Galassi, J. G. Hollandsworth, Jr., J. C. Radeki, M. L. Gay, M. R. Howe, and C. L. Evans, "Behavioral Performance in the Validation of an Assertiveness Scale," *Behavioral Therapy* 7(1976): 447–52; R. G. Heimberg, D. F. Harrison, L. S. Goldberg, S. Desmarais, and S. Blue, "The Relationship of Self-report and Behavioral Assertion in an Offender Population," *Journal of Behavior Therapy and Experimental Psychiatry* 10(1979): 283–86; J. A. Kelly, J. S. St. Lawrence, A. S. Bradlyn, W. G. Himadi, K. A. Graves, and T. M. Keane, "Interpersonal Reactions to Assertive and Unassertive Styles When Handling Social Conflict Situations," *Journal of Behavior Therapy and Experimental Psychiatry* 13(1982): 33–40; R. A. Kolotkin, R. M. Wielkiewicz, B. Judd, and S. Weiser, "Behavioral Components of Assertion: Comparison of Univariate and Multivariate Assessment Strategies," *Behavioral Assessment* 6(1983): 59–70; J. S. Pachman and D. W. Foy, "A Correlational Investigation of Anxiety, Self-esteem, and Depression: New Findings with Behavioral Measures of Assertiveness," *Journal of*

Behavior Therapy and Experimental Psychiatry 9(1978): 91–101;
J. Rose and W. W. Tryon, "Judgments of Assertive Behavior as a
Function of Speech Loudness, Latency, Content, Gestures,
Inflection, and Sex," *Behavior Modification* 3(1979): 112–23.

13. Anonymous, *Putnam's Complete Book of Quotations, Proverbs,
and Household Words,* W. Gurney Benham (ed.) (New York:
G. P. Putnam's Sons, 1926), p. 790b.

Additional Readings

Adler, Ronald B. *Confidence in Communication: A Guide to Assertive and Social Skills.* New York: Holt, Rinehart & Winston, Inc., 1979.

Alberti, Robert E. and Emmons, Michael L. *Stand up, Speak out, Talk back!: The Key to Self-Assertive Behavior.* New York: Simon & Schuster, 1975.

Alberti, Robert E. and Emmons, Michael L. *Your Perfect Right: A Guide to Assertive Behavior,* 3d ed. San Luis Obispo, Calif.: Impact, 1978.

Baer, Jean. *How to Be an Assertive (Not Aggressive) Woman in Life, in Love, and on The Job.* New York: Rawson Associates Publishers, Inc., 1976.

Bower, Gordon and Bower, Sharon. *Asserting Yourself: A Practical Guide for Positive Change.* Reading, Mass.: Addison-Wesley, 1976.

Fensterheim, Herbert and Baer, Jean. *Don't Say Yes When You Want to Say No.* New York: Dell Publishing Co., 1975.

Gambrill, Eileen D. and Richey, Cheryl A. *It's up to You: Developing Assertive Social Skills.* Millbrae, Calif.: Les Femmes Publishing, 1976.

Jakubowski, Patricia and Lange, Arthur J. *The Aggressive Option: Your Rights and Responsibilities.* Champaign, Ill.: Research Press, 1978.

Lange, Arthur J. and Jakubowski, Patricia. *Responsible Assertive Behavior: Cognitive/ Behavioral Procedures for Trainers.* Champaign, Ill.: Research Press, 1976.

Linehan, Marsha and Egan, Kelly. *Asserting Yourself.* New York: Facts on File, 1986.

McFarland, Rhoda. *Coping through Assertiveness.* Coping with Assertiveness Series. New York: Rosen Group, 1986.

Phelps, Stanlee and Austin, Nancy. *The Assertive Woman.* San Luis Obispo, Calif.: Impact, 1975.

Smith, Manuel J. *When I Say No, I Feel Guilty.* New York: Bantam Books, 1975.

Sundel, Sandra Stone and Sundel, Martin. *Be Assertive: A Practical Guide for Human Service Workers.* Beverly Hills, Calif.: Sage, 1980.

Virkler, Henry. *Assertiveness.* Berkley, Calif.: University of California—Institute of Governmental Studies, 1988.

Whiteley, John M. and Flowers, John V. *Approaches to Assertion Training.* Monterey, Calif.: Brooks/Cole, 1978.

Active Listening

Lucy is incredulous that Schroeder intends to do nothing with his new album but listen to it. Her point of view may be shared by many people who see listening as a passive activity that can be accompanied by dancing, marching, whistling, or singing at the same time. Many of us "listen" to the radio or television while we study or work. If we were asked to identify one song we heard or one commercial announcement, however, we would probably find difficulty in doing so. In a similar way, we frequently "listen" to another person in an interpersonal communication situation while planning a shopping list, reminiscing about a pleasant evening, or worrying about an upcoming exam. Listening is active, not passive. It requires a great deal of energy and focus. Our inability to listen actively to others can cause serious communication problems.

In this chapter the role of active listening in interpersonal communication will be considered. You will discover that listening is different from hearing, that active listening is not the same as passive listening, and that feedback demonstrates active listening to those persons with whom we communicate. Many barriers interfere with your ability to listen to others. You may be unable to listen actively to another person because your focus is on yourself, because you have a preconceived perception of the other person, because his or her message actually interferes with listening, or because the environment provides distractions. Active listening is an important element in the communication process. We gain information, decrease conflict, achieve goals, and are able to enjoy deeper relationships with others when we are able to listen. How do we demonstrate active listening? Through verbal skills such as asking questions, providing clear verbal responses, the paraphrasing of others' messages, and through nonverbal skills such as bodily responsiveness, direct eye contact, and supportive comments. We will discuss all of this information in this chapter, but let us begin by considering the nature of active listening.

The Nature of Active Listening

Distinguishing Listening from Hearing

Many people assume that hearing and listening are the same phenomenon. However, the two are distinct activities. Hearing is simply the act of perceiving sound. It is a natural physiological act. As you may know from anatomy classes, sound waves produce vibrations within the ear that are transferred via mechanical connections to nerve ends that are stimulated by movement. An electrochemical charge is produced that is sent to a specific location of the brain and decoded into "sounds." Unless we suffer from physiological damage or some form of cerebral dysfunction, we cannot help hearing sounds of a certain intensity. Hearing is involuntary and simply refers to the reception of aural stimuli.

Listening, on the other hand, is a selective activity that involves the reception and the interpretation of aural stimuli. Listening is the decoding of sound into meaning; it bridges the gap between hearing and understanding. Hearing and listening appear to represent two phases. Hearing is the first phase and consists of the perception of sound. Listening, the second phase, involves an attachment of meaning to the aural symbols that are perceived. Hearing does not necessarily imply intention or application while listening always does. Listening is voluntary and requires thought.

The Components of Listening Ability

Listening is obviously a critical aspect of our interpersonal communication. Yes, despite its central role in interaction, it has not received much scholarly attention until only recently. Early research on listening virtually equated the entire process with lecture comprehension. Subjects would listen to a lecture and then be asked a series of questions about the content of the lecture. Later models provided an apparently more appropriate picture of the process. For example, Barker identified four components of listening: *attention, hearing, comprehension,* and *retention.*[1]

Attention is largely a motivational tendency. A listener must focus attention on a message in order to retain the message. The focus of attention is dependent, in large part, on the desire to acquire the information the message has to offer. *Hearing* is the physiological reception of the audible portion of the message. Once the message is attended to and heard, it must be *comprehended* as meaningful. This decoding process interprets the message. Finally, *retention* is the process of storing the message or its meanings in memory.

One problem with this model of listening is that it contains several factors that seem unrelated to *skills.* Attention is a motivational phenomenon. Hearing is a physiological phenomenon. Comprehension and retention clearly have skillful aspects to them, but they are too general to be of much use for skill development.

In response to these problems, Bostrom has developed a new model of listening. *Listening* is viewed as a form of "information processing" in which auditory signals are transformed in a series of stages into retained interpretations. Bostrom's model has three basic components: *sensory storage, short-term memory,* and *long-term memory.*[2] Sensory storage involves the sending of signals picked up by the sense organs to the brain. Usually, whether visual or auditory in nature, this "information" is stored for only milliseconds to a few seconds. This process would be considered the same as the traditional "hearing" component.

When this sense data is perceived as patterned in some way (i.e., something other than just random or meaningless "noise"), it is transferred to short-term memory. It is in short-term memory that the person begins acting on the message. It is used to formulate immediate response, rehearsed for slightly delayed use, or rehearsed for more permanent storage in long-term memory. Short-term memory lasts from milliseconds to about forty seconds, as decisions are made regarding the usefulness of the information. The process of rehearsal, the mental repeating of message elements, is used to retain the message for some use. For example, you have probably used rehearsal to dial a phone number you have gotten from the operator when you have nothing with which to write. Or you may have used rehearsal to try to remember a person's name whom you have just met at a party. To the extent that you successfully recall the name much later at the party, or even a week afterwards, you have moved the message to long-term memory.

If the message or its meaning is rehearsed enough, considered important enough, or salient enough, it will be moved into long-term memory. Long-term memory is what we commonly take to represent our listening skill. Information is retained for long periods of time after the communication event has occurred.

One of the distinctions of this model of listening is that it follows the path of the actual communicated message. That is, a statement is translated into sensory information, which is then acted upon by the mind to determine the retention of the information. A second distinction is that the model is clearly message-oriented, rather than strictly concerned with motivation or physiology. A person can consciously work to improve the skills of sensory storage (as when a blind person learns to read braille by developing a keener sense of touch distinction), short-term memory (as when you rehearse things you want to retain momentarily), and long-term memory (as when you use mnemonic devices to help you remember items for an exam, such as anagrams or associating concepts with familiar things).

While the Bostrom model seems to do a good job of identifying the *internal* aspects of listening skill, it does little to deal with the *external* features of listening. The external features concern those observable skills that facilitate listening or demonstrate an orientation to interpersonal communication that values listening. Later in this chapter we will examine a number of external listening skills that can be consciously monitored, practiced, and learned.

Distinguishing Active Listening from Passive Listening

We listen for a variety of purposes and with varying degrees of attention. Researchers have suggested a number of different category systems by which we can distinguish between various kinds of listening. Perhaps the most useful distinction, in a text on interpersonal communication, is that between active and passive listening. Barbara distinguished between the two kinds of listening:

> *In the former [active], the individual listens with more or less his total self—including his special senses, attitudes, beliefs, feelings and intuitions. In the latter [passive], the listener becomes mainly an organ for the passive reception of sound, with little self-perception, personal involvement, gestalt discrimination, or alive curiosity.*[3]

Passive listening is little more than hearing. It occurs when the potential receiver of the message has little motivation to listen carefully. We sometimes engage in passive listening for entertainment, amusement, escape, or just for fun. Examples of passive listening include listening to music, story telling, poetry reading, dramatic presentations, or television programs.

Active listening involves listening with a purpose. The purpose for listening may be to gain information, to obtain directions, to determine how another person feels, to acquire data, to understand others, to solve problems, to share interests, or to show support for others. Active listening requires constancy; it does not have the "hop, skip, and jump" pattern that characterizes passive listening. In active listening, you seek to understand both the background of the speaker and the central idea of the message. Nonverbal and verbal cues offered by the originating communicator are carefully considered for understanding. The listener attends to the words and to the feelings expressed by the other person. Active listening requires that the receiver hears the sender's various messages, attempts to understand the meaning of those messages, and then verifies his or her understanding by offering the sender appropriate feedback. Physically and psychologically, listening takes the same amount or more energy than does speaking.

Feedback Demonstrates Active Listening

Generally, Norbert Weiner is credited with originating concern about the notion of feedback.[4] The purpose of feedback is to change and alter messages so the intention of the original communicator is understood by the second communicator. Feedback includes verbal and nonverbal responses to another person's message. Later in this chapter we will identify specific verbal and nonverbal skills of active listening that may all be subsumed under the general topic of feedback.

Feedback may be distinguished on the dimensions of positive or negative, immediate or delayed, and verbal or nonverbal. Feedback is positive when we grant the other person reinforcement or encouragement; it is negative when we offer criticism or state a need for correction. If you smile at your instructors' jokes, you are offering positive feedback, and your instructors will probably be encouraged to engage in more attempts at humor. If you frown and only respond in monosyllables when your spouse or special friend arrives late, you are offering negative feedback, and if the person is sensitive, he or she will understand that you disapprove of tardiness.

Second, feedback may be immediate or delayed. It may occur immediately at the time of the original message or it may occur much later. Have you ever been hurt by a careless remark from a close friend or member of your family? If the comment was made with a number of other people, you may have pretended that it did not bother you or that you did not hear it. Later, in the privacy of the other person's company, you may have expressed your hurt, anger, or frustration. Such feedback is known as delayed. Delayed feedback is not always negative, as in this example, but it does always occur after a longer time span.

Third, feedback may be verbal or nonverbal. You should understand the difference between verbal and nonverbal communication as a result of your reading of chapters 4 and 5. We respond verbally when we say, "I see," or "I don't understand." We respond nonverbally when we nod our head, frown, or vocalize "hmm." Specific verbal and nonverbal feedback skills are offered at the end of this chapter.

Carl Rogers determined that feedback generally fell into one of five main categories: evaluative, interpretive, supportive, probing, and understanding. *Evaluative feedback,* which occurs most frequently in conversations, includes those responses that make a judgment about the worth, goodness, or appropriateness of the other person's statement. *Interpretive feedback,* which

Feedback, which demonstrates active listening, may be verbal or nonverbal, positive or negative, immediate or delayed.

occurs with the next most frequency, includes responses in which we attempt to explain to the other person what his or her statements actually mean. When we offer *supportive feedback* we are attempting to assist or bolster the other communicator. *Probing feedback* includes those responses in which we attempt to gain additional information, to continue the discussion, or to clarify a point that has been made. Finally, *understanding feedback,* which occurs least frequently in everyday conversations, has the purpose of attempting to discover completely what the other communicator means by his or her statements.

It may be interesting for you to note that the frequency of these kinds of responses probably occurs in an inverse order of appropriateness for length of relationship and usefulness to the communicators. For example, evaluative feedback occurs most frequently, and yet few individuals can accept evaluation from others until they have experienced a relationship of some duration and have come to trust the other person. Similarly, supportive, probing, and understanding responses, which are encouraged at the end of this chapter in the recommended verbal and nonverbal skills, are less frequently relied upon by interpersonal communicators. None of these response styles are inherently incorrect; we must examine the situation, the relationship with the other person, and other variables in order to determine an appropriate response.

Response Styles

In order to determine if you understand the various response styles that were determined by Rogers, complete the following exercise. For each of the statements, provide the kind of response that is requested. After you have provided the specified response, indicate which response you would probably use and which response would probably result in the most satisfactory communication for both persons.

1. "I can't believe the job market this year. I've never had a problem getting a summer job before and I have references from three different places. I spent all day looking for something that begins in June and so far I've had absolutely no luck!"

    Evaluative Feedback: _____

    _____

    Interpretive Feedback: _____

    _____

    Probing Feedback: _____

    _____

2. "My mom just called me and said that she and my dad were thinking about separating for a while. I can't believe it—they don't fight like my friends' parents and they have been married for over twenty years."

    Interpretive Feedback: _____

    _____

    Supportive Feedback: _____

    _____

    Understanding Feedback: _____

    _____

3. "I have had it with Bill. We've gone together for almost two years and he has never even said that he cares about me. I thought that by now we'd be engaged. If he wants to play around, I can too!"

    Evaluative Feedback: _____

    _____

    Supportive Feedback: _____

    _____

    Probing Feedback: _____

    _____

Response Styles continued

4. "I've been living with Donna for almost two years and I really thought that I knew her, but last night she told me that she was homosexual. I really didn't know what to say to her and I feel strange living with her now."

Supportive Feedback: _____

_____

Probing Feedback: _____

_____

Understanding Feedback: _____

_____

5. "I just got my grade report for this term. I knew I wasn't doing very well, but I never expected to find myself on academic probation."

Evaluative Feedback: _____

_____

Interpretive Feedback: _____

_____

Supportive Feedback: _____

_____

Barriers to Active Listening

With our common understanding of active listening in mind, let us consider why we do not actively listen to others. A number of factors appear to interfere with our skill in this area.[5] We can subdivide these barriers into four groups: those that deal with ourselves, those that deal with our perception of the other person, those that deal with the message, and those that deal with the environment. Let us consider each of these barriers in turn.

Ourselves.   A number of editorialists and authors have suggested that the 1970s were the "Me Decade" as demonstrated by such best-selling books as *How to Pull Your Own Strings, Looking Out for Number One, Be the Person You Were Meant to Be,* and *I Ain't Much Baby, But I'm All I've Got.* The same writers predicted that the 1980s would become the "We Decade" and persons would begin to see themselves relative to others rather than as separate individuals. Such a change might assist us in overcoming the barrier that self-focus provides in active listening.

While there are signs of seeing our futures as interconnected (e.g., the greenhouse effect, Food-Aid, Farm Aid, and *glasnost*), there are also signs of remaining in the "me" mode of thought (e.g., the divorce rate and the continuing pursuit of personal wealth and material possessions). Of course, we are still too close to the decade of the eighties to see what we have become.

Focusing on ourselves rather than the other person in a conversation can lead to confusion and conflict. Nonetheless, most of us engage in self-focus rather than other-focus from time to time. Indeed, Derber has persuasively argued that most talk is oriented toward gaining attention in some form, which implies a sense of focusing on self rather than others.[6] A number of factors account for this tendency. *Defensiveness* may be one cause. When we feel that someone is attacking one of our pet causes—the importance of eating natural foods, daily exercise, abstinence from liquor, or the smoking of marijuana— we tend to feel defensive and tune the other person out. While they are speaking, we begin to identify arguments that we will use to show them the inadequacy of their thinking. Rather than listen to the other person, we focus on our own ideas. Persons who devote a great deal of their time to specific causes may be particularly ready to respond to any provocation. Others may have a general tendency to dismiss views different from theirs and concentrate on their own position. Our tendency to be poor listeners as a result of defensiveness was explained by Stuart Chase: "It is reasonable that every time an incoming message collides with an active prejudice, it is distorted."[7]

Another reason that we focus on ourselves may be called *experiential superiority.* When people have experienced a variety of situations and circumstances that others have not, they may develop a feeling of superiority. For example, your grandfather may feel that he knows more about farming than a recent college graduate who majored in agriculture; your mother may feel that she knows more about male-female relationships than you do; and an instructor may feel that she knows more about the study habits of college students than does the average college sophomore. When people have such an experiential advantage, they sometimes dismiss another person's perspective as unimportant or without sufficient experiential base. The grandfather interrupts the agriculture student to tell him how "it was done"; your mother questions the depth of your feelings for your lover; and an instructor maintains that poor grades are simply a matter of not studying properly.

A final reason for self-focus is *egocentrism.* People who view themselves as the center of any activity or exchange are called egocentric. The final scene in the movie *Kramer vs. Kramer* depicts the mother who has just won custody of her small son going to tell the boy that she is not going to take him from his father. Her question to her ex-husband, just before the elevator doors shut, is "How do I look?" The comment may be interpreted as egocentric while her behavior of relinquishing custody of the child was not.

The following telephone dialogue provides an example of self-focus as a result of egocentrism. In this conversation, Laura has called Nancy to find out about her, but instead of following up on her intent, Laura rambles on about herself.

Nancy: Hello?

Laura: Hi Nance, how are you?

Nancy: Just great, Laura. I haven't heard from you in a long time. What's new?

Laura: Well, I've been pretty busy with my new job and night classes, too. You wouldn't believe how it curbs my nightlife!

Nancy: I know, I've been having the same problem, I . . .

Laura: Have you? I don't see how anyone could be busier than me . . . you should see my house. How do you manage to keep yours clean?

Nancy: Well, I just make out a schedule like . . .

Laura: A schedule? I wouldn't have time to make out a schedule. Did you read about Farrah Fawcett's daily schedule? Have you ever seen anyone look so healthy on five hours of sleep?

Nancy: I've wondered how much sleep is really necessary.

Laura: Yeah, I wonder if she has time for any social life. Well, you sound like you're pretty busy. I'd better let you go now.

Nancy: Well, I guess so.

Laura: Someone's at the door. I'll catch up on more of your news later.

Nancy: Goodbye.

Egocentric people may appear to talk to many other people. They frequently need the attention that other people provide. However, their listening skills are not highly developed.

Our perception of the other person.   Our perception of the person speaking also affects our ability to listen actively. For instance, on an immediate level, if we believe that the communicator is talking too fast, is not fluent, does not articulate clearly, or regularly mispronounces words, we may dismiss that person. If we believe that speakers are deliberately standing too far away from us to be heard easily or are purposely out of our line of vision, we may decide to tune them out.

Our preconceived attitudes, including status and stereotypes, may also affect our ability to listen. The other person's "image," personality, or role may create a barrier to active listening. We tend to listen uncritically to persons who have high status and we tend to dismiss the ideas of those people who are seen to be low in status. People of low status are often ignored. We sometimes trivialize a situation or the remarks of others to demonstrate to them that we feel that they have low status.

Our stereotypes also affect listening skills. People who belong to respected groups or to groups that are similar to those to which we belong receive our attention, although we may not listen critically to them. Persons who have group memberships in opposing or different organizations are generally not the recipients of our time or attention. The effect of stereotypes on active listening is demonstrated in this dialogue that occurred before class when a guest lecturer was scheduled in a required course.

Brian: This lecture is really going to be boring. I don't know why I bothered getting up for it. The kids from last quarter said it was a waste of their time.

Joan: But you don't know if he changed his format and perhaps added something that will be of interest to you.

Brian: No, I trust the other kids. This is going to be worthless.

Joan: I don't understand how you can judge the value of the lecture before it has even begun.

Brian: I've got my reasons. Didn't you hear that his topic is "Blacks in America"? I already know all I want and need to on that subject.

Joan: I wish you would try to be more open to new views. You may learn something contradictory to your stereotypic viewpoint.

Brian's stereotypes extended to the speaker and the speaker's announced subject matter. He prematurely dismissed the speaker because of the reports of fellow students during another quarter. In addition, he appears to be defensive in his reactions to the topic. Similar reactions on our part interfere with our active listening skills.

The message.   Surprisingly enough, the message itself can interfere with our listening. The widely quoted, "I know you believe you understand what you think I said, but I am not sure you realize that what you heard is not what I meant," offers this insight. *Factual distractions* occur when we focus on the facts rather than ideas. No institutions can be held as culpable as can our educational institutions for encouraging persons to develop this tendency. Examinations, reviews, and questions in the classroom often focus on specific facts rather than large ideas. We learn early to isolate the parts of a phenomenon rather than to develop an understanding of the entire process. Listening for the facts may be rewarded in the classroom, but it seldom is rewarded in interpersonal communication. A friend who tells you about her abortion is less likely to be appreciative if you remember the name of her physician but forget her emotional conflict than if you demonstrate that you have heard and understood her verbal and nonverbal messages about the situation. Similarly, a fellow discussant will be more satisfied if you recall the research he provided on a particular topic than if you can recall one of the statistics that he stated.

Semantic distractions occur when you use a word or phrase differently than a fellow communicator uses it or when you use an emotionally laden word. For instance, if man-linked words such as "chairman," "postman," or "fireman" bother you because they appear to limit the behavioral options of women, you may focus on these words and not hear the intent of the message. Or, if the word "gay" is used by a grandparent who is referring to the high spirits of another and you assume he or she is describing someone's sexual affectional orientation, you may be distracted and surprised by your grandparent's open-mindedness.

Mental distractions occur largely as a result of the difference between the speed with which we speak—about 125 words per minute—and the rate at which we can listen—about 800 words per minute. *Mental distractions* refer to the mental side trips on which we embark while we are waiting for the speaker's words to catch up with our thinking. The problem with mental side trips is that they frequently take a longer period of time than that needed for the speaker to provide us with new information to consider. Rather than admit that we did not hear all of the other person's message, we listen carefully for a moment, and then go on another excursion. As a consequence, our understanding of the speaker is minimized. Daydreams, recollections, and counter-arguments should not fill our thinking time; instead, we should attempt to clarify and consider the speaker's perspective during this time.

Another way in which the message can distort our listening has to do with the natural "logic" of speech. Language and the way in which we use language is highly narrative in nature. That is, statements cannot tell us everything about the things referred to. In relaying a description of an event, certain understandings on the part of the listener are taken for granted. Thus, as listeners we tend to "fill in the gaps" of messages. We weave a sensible story or picture of what the message implies. For example, consider the following sentences: The frog is on the lily pad. The lily pad is in the pond. The cabin is by the pond. The man is in the cabin. Many who listen to these declarative statements in sequence believe that the following statement is among those that they heard: The man sees the frog. This statement "makes sense" in terms of the story, despite the fact that there was no real story implied, and the statement was not made.[8]

The environment.   The physical environment can also interfere with active listening. Any stimulus that you can sense provides a potential distraction. Physical distractions include sights such as bright lights, loud designs on a drape, an attractive person, or an unusual sight. In the following conversation at a party, Jo Ann was clearly distracted by a couple that was dancing on the floor. Louise did not know that the couple consisted of Jo Ann's boyfriend and her roommate.

Distractions in Listening

In the next twenty-four-hour period, try to be very sensitive to those interactions in which someone tells another person (including you) that he or she was not heard correctly or that the second person was not listening. Record each of these experiences and attempt to determine the cause for the distraction in listening. Was the listener focusing on herself or himself rather than on the speaker? Was the listener distracted because of his or her preconceived ideas about the speaker? Did the message interfere with clear understanding? Were environmental factors responsible for the breakdown in listening? Do you listen very well? What most frequently accounts for the difficulties that you encounter in listening? With whom do you listen most carefully? With whom do you experience the most problems in listening?

Louise: Jo Ann, how are you?

Jo Ann: What? Oh Louise, hello. I was just watching that couple dancing.

Louise: How are you?

Jo Ann: Fine . . .

Louise: Did you hear what happened to me? Jo Ann! Did you hear what happened to me?

Jo Ann: Yeah.

Louise: Well, what do you have to say about it?

Jo Ann: About what?

Louise: About me getting elected.

Jo Ann: Elected for what?

Louise: Forget it!

A party atmosphere provides many distractions. In this situation, Louise probably should not have persisted when she recognized that Jo Ann was not giving her her full attention. On the other hand, Jo Ann might have clarified that she was distracted. Physical distractions can occur with any of the senses. An unusual odor—burning rubber, rotten eggs, garbage, smelly feet; an unusual sound—screeching tires, the wail of an emergency vehicle, a hissing sound, noise in the walls; or any other sensation may result in a distraction.

The Importance of Active Listening

When you recall a conversation that you have had with a friend, you probably focus on what each of you said. When you remember an argument with your roommate, you consider the words you each chose. When a friend asks you about a small group discussion in which you were involved, you generally recite the development of ideas that occurred. In other words, when we think about or discuss communication, we generally focus on the speaking aspects rather than the listening components. Researchers, too, demonstrate a bias in favor of communication skills other than listening: In a survey on research dealing with communication, only fourteen studies dealt with listening, while 2,500 were devoted to speaking, reading, and writing.[9] Our focus on speaking may be natural given the self-centered nature of communication that was discussed in chapter 1.

Nonetheless, we spend more time engaged in listening each day than we spend engaged in other communication activities. Listening occupies an average of about 29.7 percent of the average waking day. Students devote an even larger percentage of their time listening: The average student spends about 57.5 percent of his or her time listening.[10] One study found that we listen three times as much as we read, five times as much as we write, and one-and-one-half times as much as we speak.[11] Other studies have demonstrated that in interpersonal communication listening occupies between 42 and 66 percent of the communicator's time.[12]

One collection of scholars and executives estimated that ineffective listening annually costs American businesses billions of dollars. "Because of poor listening, letters have to be retyped; appointments have to be rescheduled; shipments have to be reshipped; individuals and organizations are unable to understand and respond to customers' and clients' real needs; employees feel ignored, disgruntled, and ultimately alienated from management; ideas are distorted by as much as 80 percent as they travel through communication channels; unnecessary conflicts disrupt operations and decrease production; and entire organizations are manipulated by propaganda techniques."[13]

For example, one study asked training executives employed by *Fortune* "500" companies to rate the communication skills of the managers in their organizations. The study found that these top-level managers were rated, as a whole, slightly below "fair" in their listening skills. In all, over 67 percent were considered to "lack training in good listening techniques."[14] These are just some of the implications of poor listening in the organizational context. We have all experienced the many problems and embarrassing predicaments in our social and intimate relationships as well. More competent listening enhances our quality of life in at least five ways: increased information, decreased misunderstanding, increased goal achievement, increased reciprocal listening, and deepening relationships.

Poor listening habits cost this country's businesses billions of dollars a year.

Increased information.   One sage wrote: "A good listener is not only popular everywhere, but after a while he knows something."[15] It has been suggested that 85 percent of all we know comes from listening. The information or knowledge that we gain from listening should not be minimized as a direct benefit.

Decreased misunderstandings.   Many misunderstandings and conflicts occur because people simply do not listen to each other. The argument between Alice and Humpty Dumpty in the excerpt from *Through the Looking Glass* occurs because of poor listening skills.

> *"How old did you say you were?"*
> *Alice made a short calculation, and said, "Seven years and six months."*
> *"Wrong!" Humpty Dumpty exclaimed triumphantly. "You never said a word like it!"*
> *"I thought you meant 'How old are you?' " Alice explained.*
> *"If I'd meant that, I'd have said it," said Humpty Dumpty.[16]*

Active listening reduces verbal conflict and helps us avoid arguments over meaningless questions.

Increased goal achievement.   We can increase the opportunity for achieving our goals in two ways through active listening. First, we sometimes can gain a desired end if we simply hear another person out. For instance, you may assume your parents will be angry about your end-of-term grades. When they begin to talk to you about them, you respond defensively and attempt to justify the situation, as in this dialogue:

Dad: Ann, I'd like to talk to you about the grade report we received for last term.

Ann: Look, I can explain everything—I took too many classes and they weren't easy.

Dad: I know that you had a heavy load. . . .

Ann: Heavy? It was more than heavy. It was unrealistic. You know when Mary went to college she didn't have to take as many credits as I did. No wonder she got high grades—who couldn't do well with so few credits!

Dad: I am not sure that Mary's record is relevant here.

Ann: Of course not, she's your favorite.

Dad: I just meant that . . .

If Ann had listened carefully and completely to her parent's response, she may have found out that he wanted to offer compassion and concern as well as initial disappointment, as in this example.

Dad: Ann, I'd like to talk to you about the grade report we received for last term.

Ann: Okay.

Dad: Mom and I were disappointed by the grades, but we know that you were taking an unusually heavy load.

Ann: Yes, I was.

Dad: We really respect the fact that you are trying to complete your undergraduate degree in three years instead of four years like your older sister did.

Ann: Thanks, Dad.

Dad: We've concluded that it's not possible to maintain high grades, finish in three years, and also hold down a part-time job.

Ann: It doesn't seem to be possible for me, Dad.

Dad: Well, we just want you to know that we respect your decision and your motivation. We'll try not to make comparisons with your older sister's grades and look at your record in light of the pressure you have placed on yourself.

Ann: Thanks, I really appreciate it.

Her parent's understanding was probably a desirable outcome for Ann. She was able to elicit this response because she listened patiently rather than interrupting or responding defensively.

A second way that we can achieve our goals is that active listening raises our credibility and we become more effective persuaders. Most speakers feel flattered when someone listens to them and they respond positively to the listener. The greater respect felt by the speaker allows the listener's ideas to take on increased importance. Dean Rusk recognized the persuasive effect of active listening when he wrote, "One of the best ways to persuade others is with your ears—by listening to them."[17]

Reciprocal listening.   A reciprocal listening arrangement generally occurs when one person practices active listening. By listening to another person you are modeling appropriate communication behavior to him or her. Others learn from your model. More cynically, this phenomenon may be explained by the idea that we listen to others only because we know they will then listen to us. In other words, we are waiting for our turn! Regardless of the cause, active listening to others will probably result in their active listening to you.

Deepening relationships.   A final outcome of active listening is deepening relationships. Relationships can become deeper because of the increased positive feelings that the communicators can develop for each other. The flattery that is often felt by the speaker, that was discussed earlier, contributes to this positive feeling. The distressing situation that occurs when people do not listen to each other is well documented. Countless individuals complain to marriage counselors that their partners simply do not listen to them. Shallow relationships or relationships that know an early death result when people do not listen to each other. Erma Bombeck offers her humorous observations about such a situation in her marriage. After discussing her husband's interest in football games and her feeble attempts at talking with him, she concluded:

I looked at my husband. He hadn't heard a word I said. Oh well, I just witnessed another record for a shut-out. . . eight months and four days.[18]

Our relationships with one another can only deepen to the extent that we truly listen to all of the verbal and nonverbal messages that the other person is attempting to communicate to us.

Although it may seem strange, we can demonstrate our active listening through verbal cues, such as questions, comments, and responses.

Competence in Active Listening

Active listening is an important communication skill. Our ability to listen actively can have both direct and indirect benefits. However, most of us are not very successful active listeners. A number of studies demonstrate that we do not listen very well.[19] Studies completed at the University of Minnesota found that people remember only about half of what they heard, even when tested immediately after a message. When they were tested two months later, they only remembered 25 percent of what they heard.[20]

Active listening, like the other skills discussed in this text, is not always advised in all situations with all people. Allowing verbally aggressive people to dominate conversations completely while you practice active listening skills would be clearly inappropriate. You probably will spend about half your time in interpersonal communication listening to another person. In order to maximize your listening ability you may wish to practice some of these verbal and nonverbal skills.

Verbal Skills of Active Listening

The notion of verbal components in listening may seem strange to you. You may reason that if you are engaged in listening, you cannot also be speaking. As you will recall from chapter 1, however, people encode and decode simultaneously and you can make verbal responses while you are deeply involved in listening. The verbal components of active listening are identified in the following list. In order to determine your current competence in this area, consider those skills that you regularly practice. Some of these skills are useful in demonstrating empathic understanding and are cross-referenced in chapter 9.

1. *Invite additional comments.* Suggest that the speaker add more details or give additional information. Phrases like "Go on," "What else?", "How did you feel about that?", and "Did anything else occur?" encourage the other person to say more and to continue to share ideas and information.

2. *Ask questions.* One method of inviting the other person to continue is to ask direct questions. The questions you ask may request more in-depth details, definitions, or clarification.

3. *Identify areas of agreement or common experience.* Briefly relate similar past experiences, or, in a few words, explain a similar point of view that you hold. Sharing common ideas, attitudes, values, and beliefs are the basis of communication. In addition, such comments demonstrate your understanding.

4. *Vary verbal responses.* Use a variety of responses such as "Yes," "I see," "Go on," and "Right" instead of relying upon one standard unaltering response such as "Yes," "Yes," "Yes."

5. *Provide clear verbal responses.* Use specific and unambiguous words and phrases in your feedback to the speaker. Misunderstanding can occur if you do not provide easily understood responses. In the example that follows, the farmer's ambiguous responses to his wife's questions confuse the issue. The student who supplied this dialogue stated that it provides a typical example of his parents' communication behavior.

Mom: What time do you want dinner?

Dad: Well, I have to grind feed and do chores up north and vaccinate a sick steer.

Mom: The meat loaf and potatoes will take about an hour to bake.

Dad: What time will Dan be home? Do you think he will have time to help me when he gets home?

Mom: I don't know if Dan can help you, but I would like to know what time you want to eat.

Dad: It will just have to be when I get all my work done.

Mom: I guess I will have to figure it out for myself.

The father in the preceding dialogue offered vague, general answers to the mother's questions. In the following dialogue, two roommates are discussing the end of a relationship, but the listener offers little clear feedback. The overused and ambiguous words are too general to supply the speaker with satisfaction.

Charlie: I've just broken up with my girlfriend.

Fred: Oh.

Charlie: We've gone together for the past three-and-a-half years and she just cut it off.

Fred: That's something.

In both dialogues, the listeners fail to supply clear responses to the other communicator. If the father in the first dialogue had answered his wife's questions directly and if Fred had offered more specific comments, these conversations would have been greatly improved and active listening would have been demonstrated.

6. *Use descriptive, nonevaluative responses.* Use responses like, "Yes," "I understand your explanation," "Your perspective is clear," and "I agree," rather than judgmental or negative statements including, "No," "That's not what I think," "I don't agree," or "I don't think so." Trivializing or joking about serious disclosures will suggest a negative evaluation of the speaker. Similarly, derogatory remarks or put-downs will be seen as offensive. Attempting to be superior to the speaker by stating that you believe that you have a more advanced understanding will suggest an evaluative tone. The conversation between Charlie and Fred that was begun earlier became worse as it continued. Not only did Fred respond with ambiguous comments, he also appeared to act superior to Charlie. The dialogue continues:

Charlie: Hasn't this ever happened to you?

Fred: No.

Charlie: I thought you broke up with Jane.

Fred: Yes, but that was different. You see, I broke it up, not her!

Charlie probably felt defensive because of Fred's act of superiority and demonstrated his frustration with the somewhat aggressive question about one of Fred's earlier relationships.

7. *Provide affirmative and affirming statements.* Comments like
    "Yes," "I see," "I understand," and "I know" provide affirmation.
    Offering praise and specific positive statements demonstrate
    concern.

8. *Avoid complete silence.* The lack of any response suggests that you
    are not listening to the speaker. The "silent treatment" induced by
    sleepiness or lack of concern may result in defensiveness or anger
    on the part of the speaker. Appropriate verbal feedback
    demonstrates your active listening.

9. *Allow the other person the opportunity of a complete hearing.*
    When you discuss common feelings or experiences, avoid
    dominating the conversation. Allow the other person to go into
    depth and detail; allow the other person the option of changing
    the topic under discussion; allow the other person to talk without
    being interrupted. Silence is frequently appropriate when the other
    person is talking. One woman reported the following conversation
    that she had had with her roommate's brother. She stated that she
    felt very frustrated because she was unable to complete any of her
    thoughts and that Jerry had not listened to her.

Jerry: So you and Maggie are going to move out of the house?

Char: Yeah, we're thinking about . . .

Jerry: Well, I think it's wrong. Have you talked with your folks about
        it?

Char: Yes, I talked to . . .

Jerry: Is it what they want?

Char: Yes . . .

Jerry: How do you know?

Char: Well, my mom said . . .

Jerry: What?

Char: (Hesitating because of the continuing frustration she is
        feeling): That it was up to me to make my own decisions about
        where I live.

Jerry: Well, that's not what she wants at all. She's just saying that
        because she knows that you are so headstrong and won't do
        what she wants anyway.

Char: I can't talk to you anymore about this now. I'll see you later.

Verbal Demonstrations of Active Listening

In each of the examples in the following lists, one person is making an assertion or asking a question. For each comment, provide the requested response. After you have completed the exercise, identify the response that you would probably offer. Would your response differ depending upon the other speaker? Would the age or sex of the other speaker alter your response? Offer examples of how your response would differ depending upon personality characteristics of the other communicator or circumstances within the environment.

1. "Would you close the door?"

    Ask Question: _____

    Provide Affirmative Statement: _____

    Restate Content: _____

2. "Jerry and I are breaking up—after five years."

    Invite Additional Comments: _____

    _____

    Ask Questions: _____

    Use Descriptive, Nonevaluative Response: _____

    _____

Char said that she felt a great deal of frustration in this conversation and that the net effect was to lower her concern for Jerry. After a number of similar conversations, she began to avoid him completely.

10. *Restate the content of the speaker's message.* Use repetition of key words, phrases, and ideas to demonstrate your understanding of the conversation. Such restatements should be brief.

11. *Paraphrase the content of the speaker's message.* Restate the speaker's message in your own words to determine if you understand the content of the message. Your goal in paraphrasing should be to completely understand the other person rather than to disagree or to state your own point of view.

12. *Paraphrase the intent of the speaker's message.* People generally have a reason for making statements or disclosing information. Demonstrate your understanding of the speaker's intention by attempting to state it in your own words. Paraphrases of content and intent should be concise.

Verbal Demonstrations of Active Listening continued

3. "Anorexia nervosa is a special problem for young women between the ages of 13 and 19 who are high achievers."

    Provide Clear Verbal Responses: _____

    _____

    Allow the Other Person the Opportunity of a Complete Hearing:

    _____

    Paraphrase Intent: _____

    _____

4. "I understood from your newspaper ad that you had blazers on sale—where are they?"

    Ask Questions: _____

    Provide Clear Verbal Responses: _____

    _____

    Paraphrase Content: _____

    _____

5. "You don't care what I think!"

    Invite Additional Comments: _____

    _____

    Identify Areas of Agreement: _____

    _____

    Use Descriptive, Nonevaluative Responses: _____

    _____

Nonverbal Skills of Active Listening

While we demonstrate active listening through the verbal skills previously listed, the majority of our active listening ability is shown through nonverbal communication. The following nonverbal components are essential in our ability to demonstrate active listening. Have a friend observe your nonverbal behavior as you listen to another person to determine if you are practicing these skills.

1. *Demonstrate bodily responsiveness.* Use movement and gestures to show your awareness of the speaker's message. Shaking your head in disbelief, checking the measurements of an object by indicating the size with your hands, and moving toward a person who is disclosing negative information would demonstrate appropriate bodily responsiveness. Large or exaggerated movements such as walking around the room and sweeping arm gestures are generally inappropriate.

2. *Lean forward.* By leaning toward the speaker, a good listener will demonstrate his or her interest in the speaker. A forward lean suggests responsiveness as well as interest. In addition, it places you in a physical state of readiness to listen to the speaker.

3. *Use direct body orientation.* Do not angle yourself away from the speaker; instead sit or stand so you are directly facing him or her. Parallel body position allows the greatest possibility for observing and listening to the speaker's verbal and nonverbal messages. When you stand or sit at an angle to the speaker, you may be creating the impression that you are attempting to get away or that you are moving away from the speaker. It also blocks your vision and allows you to be distracted by other stimuli in the environment.

4. *Use relaxed, but alert posture.* Your posture should not be tense or "proper," but neither should it be so relaxed that you appear to be resting. Slouching suggests unresponsiveness, a tense body position suggests nervousness or discomfort, and a relaxed position that is accompanied by crossed arms and legs, a backward lean in a chair, and a confident facial expression suggest arrogance. Your posture should suggest to other persons that you are interested and that you are comfortable talking with them.

5. *Establish an open body position.* Sit or stand with your body open to the other person. Crossing your arms or legs may be more comfortable for you because of habit, but it frequently suggests that you are closed off psychologically as well as physically. In order to maximize your nonverbal message to the other person that you are "open" to him or her, you will want to sit or stand without crossing your arms or legs.

6. *Use positive, responsive facial expression and head movement.* Your face and head will be the primary focus of the speaker. He or she will be observing you and the expression of your face and the movement of your head will be the key. You can demonstrate your concern by nodding your head to show interest or agreement. You can use positive and responsive facial expression such as smiling and raising your eyebrows.

7. *Establish direct eye contact.* The other person will be watching your eyes for interest. One of the first signs of a lack of interest is

the listener's tendency to be distracted by other stimuli in the environment. Examples include the instructor who continually glances out of the door of her office, the parent who looks at a pot that is boiling on the stove, the roommate who glances at the television program that is playing, or the business executive who regularly looks at her watch. Try to focus and direct your gaze at the speaker. When you begin to look around the room you may find any number of other stimuli to distract your attention from the speaker and from his or her message.

A football player at a "Big Eight" university reported this conversation in which poor eye contact contributed to his feeling that the coach was not interested in him. Interestingly, the reason he was quitting the team was because he had not felt that anyone on the coaching staff had taken interest in him.

Player: Coach, got a minute?

Coach: (Absorbed in paperwork): Yeah, sure, what do you want? Have a seat.

Player: I want to talk about the team.

Coach: (Not looking up): Go on, kid.

Player: I'm going to turn in my gear.

Coach: (Turning around to his filing cabinet): Go on.

Player: I just don't feel . . .

Coach: (Interrupting): Lewis, I want to see you after you are dressed.

Player: . . . feel like I'm of value around here.

Coach: (With his back to the player, digging through the filing cabinet): Uh-huh, go on.

Player: My gear is in my locker, goodbye, Coach.

The player stated that if the coach had finished his work and then devoted his full attention to him, the conversation would have been quite different. Eye contact could have made a great deal of difference in this case.

8. *Sit or stand close to the speaker.* Establishing proximity to the speaker has two benefits. First, you put yourself in a position that allows you to hear the other person and minimizes the distracting noises, sights, and other stimuli. Second, you demonstrate your concern or your positive feelings for the other person. We typically do not stand or sit close to persons whom we do not like, do not respect, or with whom we do not have common experiences. Physical proximity allows active listening to occur.

9.   *Use vocal responsiveness.* Change your pitch, rate, inflection, and volume as you respond to the speaker. Appropriate changes and choices will suggest that you are actually listening rather than responding in a standard, patterned manner that suggests that you are only appearing to listen. The stereotypical picture of the husband and wife at the breakfast table with the husband, hidden behind a newspaper, responding, ''Yes, yes, yes'' in a monotone voice while the wife tells him that their son has shaved the cat, that she is running off with the mail carrier, and that the house is on fire, provides a familiar example of the appearance of listening while you are actually far away from the speaker's message.

10.   *Provide supportive utterances.* Sometimes you can demonstrate more concern through nonverbal sounds like ''Mmm,'' ''Mmm-hmm,'' and ''uh-huh'' than you can by stating, ''Yes, I understand.'' You can easily provide supportive utterances while other persons are talking or when they pause. You are suggesting to them that you are listening, but that you do not want to interrupt with a statement or verbalization of your own at this particular time. Such sounds will encourage them to continue without interruption.

A study by Garland found that married couples could be trained to use active listening. Active listening was measured by categorizing the number of statements interactants used that repeated or paraphrased some aspect of the partner's statement *and* asked for feedback from the partner regarding the accuracy of interpretation (e.g., ''You seem to be saying . . . Right?'' or ''If I understand you correctly, you believe that . . . Is this what you meant?''). Other less competent forms of active listening were also examined in the study.

The results were intriguing. For example, those trained in use of active listening skills achieved higher levels of understanding and accuracy in their conversations. However, those who were trained in the use of active listening were observed to be *able* to use active listening, but did not *actually* use them more. Apparently, as the model of relational competence implies, they had the knowledge and the skill, but not the motivation.[21] That motivation is important to the use of listening skills has also been demonstrated by a study in which students who were told that they would have to write a report if they did not do well on a listening test after a lecture on better listening had significantly better test scores than those students given no such incentive.[22] The implication of these studies is that mastering the skills of listening alone is not enough; you must choose to use these skills if they are to make a difference in your communication.

Active listening requires a great deal of energy and sensitivity to the other person, but it is a reachable goal. The skills that were just outlined should assist you in your endeavor to listen more actively to others. In order to determine your understanding of these skills, complete the following exercise.

Mother-Daughter Interaction

One student felt that her mother provided a model of active listening. She recalled one example when she went home on a weekend early in a quarter. She had felt a great deal of frustration with one of her instructors and needed someone to talk with about the situation. She thought her mother would understand and she was not disappointed. The conversation that occurred follows. The comments in the right-hand column suggest the techniques used by her mother to demonstrate her concern through active listening.

Dialogue	Analysis
Jackie: Boy, I sure don't like Mrs. Smith, my new math teacher. She's really bad news.	
Mother: Why do you feel that way?	*Jackie's mother invites additional comments by asking questions.*
Jackie: She is so boring! All she talks about is herself and the way things were in the fifties. I want to tell her to be quiet or get lost!	
Mother: It sounds like you have a lot of anger toward her.	*She attempts to paraphrase the content of Jackie's message.*
Jackie: A lot of students don't like her. Who hires people like that anyway? She is so bad, I don't see how she can keep her job.	
Mother: It does make you wonder how anyone who is that bad could be allowed to teach.	*The mother restates Jackie's position.*
Jackie: Well, I guess there's not much I can do about it. I've got to study now for *her* class!	

Jackie's conclusion that her mother was a good active listener is probably correct if this short example is typical of her conversations. List the specific verbal skills that are demonstrated by her mother in this conversation. Did she vary her verbal responses? Did she trivialize Jackie's feelings? Were evaluative comments offered? What conclusions can you draw about dominating the conversation, affirming statements, and clear verbal responses? Finally, can you identify specific restatements and paraphrases? For each of the verbal skills that you identify in this conversation, provide at least one example from the dialogue. You may conclude that Jackie's mother responded with the kind of concern that most of us desire and need from other people.

Summary

You have considered the role of active listening in interpersonal communication in this chapter. You have distinguished listening from hearing, active listening from passive listening, and have determined that feedback demonstrates our skill in actively listening to others. You may have discovered barriers to active listening that have provided problems for you in your own communication with others. Perhaps you now recognize that your focus on yourself, your preconceived notions about the other communicator, or distractions in the message or environment have contributed to problems for you. You have examined some of the verbal and nonverbal skills associated with active listening. You are now prepared to study another component of effective interpersonal communication that builds upon active listening. Empathy, the ability to view the world of another person as though that view were your own, is the subject of the next chapter. Active listening and empathy, together, allow you to demonstrate concern for others in your interpersonal communication.

Notes

1. Larry L. Barker, *Listening Behavior* (Englewood Cliffs, N.J.: Prentice Hall, 1971).

2. Robert Bostrom, "The Kentucky Comprehensive Listening Test," unpublished manuscript, Kentucky Listening Research Center, University of Kentucky, 1983.

3. Dominick Barbara, "On Listening—the Role of the Ear in Psychic Life," *Today's Speech* 5 (January 1957): 12.

4. Norbert Weiner, *Cybernetics* (New York: John Wiley & Sons, 1948), p. 33.

5. For a review of listener, speaker, and environmental factors related to listening ability, see Kittie Watson and Larry Barker, "Listening Behavior: Definition and Measurement," *Communication Yearbook* 8(1984): 178–97.

6. C. Derber, *The Pursuit of Attention: Power and Individualism in Everyday Life* (Cambridge, Mass.: Schenkman, 1979).

7. Stuart Chase, *Power of Words* (New York: Harcourt, Brace, & World Inc., 1954), p. 173.

8.   G. Ledger, "To Hear, or Not to Hear: What Was the Question?" *Dallas Times Herald,* March 8, 1987.

9.   Ralph G. Nichols and Thomas R. Lewis, *Listening and Speaking: A Guide to Effective Oral Communication* (Dubuque, Ia.: Wm. C. Brown Company, 1954), p. 2.

10.   See R. O. Hirsch, *Listening: A Way to Process Information Aurally* (Dubuque, Ia.: Gorsuch Scarisbrick, 1979).

11.   P. T. Ranking, "The Measurement of the Ability to Understand Spoken Language," *Dissertation Abstracts* 12(1926): 847.

12.   See, for instance, D. Bird, "Teaching Listening Comprehension," *Journal of Communication* 3(1953): 127–30; and Larry L. Barker, *Listening Behavior* (Englewood Cliffs, N.J.: Prentice Hall, 1971), p. 3.

13.   M. Gibbs, P. Hewing, J. E. Hulbert, D. Ramsey, and A. Smith, "How to Teach Effective Listening Skills in a Basic Business Communication Class," *The Bulletin* 48(1985): 30–34.

14.   G. T. Hunt and L. P. Cusella, "A Field Study of Listening Needs in Organizations," *Communication Education* 32(1983): 393–401.

15.   Maxim Maximovich Litvinov, *John Bartlett's Familiar Quotations,* 14th ed. (Boston: Little, Brown, and Company), p. 941.

16.   Lewis Carroll, *Through the Looking Glass and What Alice Found There* (Macmillan, 1872).

17.   Dean Rusk, *Just for You: 365 Days* (Norwalk, Conn.: The C. R. Gibson Co., 1977).

18.   Erma Bombeck, "At Wit's End," *Des Moines Register,* December 19, 1978, p. 16.

19.   See, for instance, Edward J. J. Kramar and Thomas R. Lewis, "Comparison of Visual and Nonvisual Listening," *Journal of Communication* 1(November 1951): 16–20; James I. Brown, "The Objective Measurement of Listening Ability," *Journal of Communication* 1(May 1951): 44–48; Paul W. Keller, "Major Findings in Listening in the Past Ten Years," *Journal of Communication* 10(March 1960): 29–38; Sam Duker, *Listening Bibliography* (New York: Scarecrow Press, 1964); and Sam Duker, ed., *Listening: Readings* (New York: Scarecrow Press, 1966).

20.   Ralph Nichols and Leonard Stevens, "Listening to People," *Harvard Business Review* 35(1957), no. 5.

21. D. R. Garland, "Training Married Couples in Listening Skills: Effects on Behavior, Perceptual Accuracy and Marital Adjustment," *Family Relations* 30(1981): 297–306.
22. L. R. Smeltzer and K. W. Watson, "Listening: An Empirical Comparison of Discussion Length and Level of Incentive," *Central States Speech Journal* 35(1984): 166–70.

Additional Readings

Barker, Larry L. *Listening Behavior.* Englewood Cliffs, N.J.: Prentice Hall, 1971.

Benward, Bruce. *Ear Training: A Technique for Listening,* 3d ed. Dubuque, Ia.: Wm. C. Brown, 1987.

Duker, Sam. *Listening: Readings.* New York: Scarecrow Press, 1966.

Glenn, Ethel C. "A Content Analysis of Fifty Definitions of Listening." In *Journal of the International Listening Association* 3 (1989), pp. 21–31.

Gordon, Thomas. *Parent Effectiveness Training.* New York: Peter Wyden, 1970.

Longheed, Lin. *Listening between the Lines: A Cultural Approach.* Reading, Mass.: Addison-Wesley, 1985.

McGregor, Graham and White, Robert S., eds. *The Art of Listening: The Creative Hearer in Language, Literature, & Popular Culture.* New York: Routledge, Chapman & Hall, 1986.

Moray, Neville. *Listening and Attention.* Baltimore, Md.: Penguin Books, 1969.

Morris, Jud. *The Art of Listening.* Boston: Farnsworth Publishing, 1968.

Nichols, Ralph G. and Stevens, Leonard A. *Are You Listening?* New York: McGraw-Hill Book Company, 1957.

Reed, Warren H. *Positive Listening: Learning to Hear What People Are Really Saying.* New York: Watts, 1985.

Rogers, Carl E. and Farson, Richard E. "Active Listening." In *Readings in Interpersonal and Organizational Communication,* edited by Carl E. Rogers and Richard E. Farson. Boston: Holbrook Press, Inc., 1969.

Weaver, Carl. *Human Listening: Processes and Behavior.* Indianapolis: Bobbs-Merrill, 1972.

Wolff, Florence I., Marsnik, Nadine C., Tracey, William S., and Nichols, Ralph G. *Perceptive Listening.* New York: Holt, Rinehart & Winston, 1983.

Wolvin, Andrew D. and Coakley, Carolyn Gwynn. *Listening,* 3d ed. Dubuque, Ia.: Wm. C. Brown, 1988.

Empathic Understanding

CATHY   by Cathy Guisewite

Communication is a fragile, uncertain venture much of the time. Cathy is able to traverse the maze of hidden meanings in her mother's questions because they share so much common experience and such an extensive relational history. In essence, Cathy "reads between the lines" by putting herself in her mother's role and predicting what her mother is actually interested in knowing. In the previous chapter, we considered the role of listening in actual oral communication behavior. In this chapter, we extend the notion of active listening into an area known as empathic understanding.

Empathy, like active listening, allows us to demonstrate concern for others. Empathy is related to genuineness or honesty in an interpersonal relationship. It is not an independent set of behaviors that may be viewed as superficial responses called upon in order to manage an interpersonal relationship. Empathy assumes respect for others or what has been termed "unconditional acceptance." To the extent that we are able to understand and appreciate the fundamental similarity of all persons, we are able to empathize with them.

219

In this chapter you will discover the nature of empathy and the numerous skills that are involved in demonstrating empathy to others. You will find that empathy is distinct from sympathy and neutrality. Among the benefits that empathy includes are an increased understanding of others and deeper relationships with other people. Although empathy is not simply a set of verbal and nonverbal skills, you will learn some specific skills that are behavioral manifestations of this important component of interpersonal communication. An understanding of this chapter will allow you to demonstrate greater concern for those persons with whom you interact.

The Nature of Empathy

Definition of Empathy

Empathy comes from the German word, *Einfühling,* which means "to feel with." We typically define empathy as the ability to perceive another person's view of the world as though that view were our own. The religious injunctions, "Thou shalt love thy neighbor as thyself," and "Do not judge your fellow until you have come into his place," as well as the Sioux Indian Tribe's prayer, "Great Spirit, help us never to judge another until we have walked for two weeks in his moccasins," all express the nature of empathy in particular subcultures.

Empathy is closely related to two forms of role-taking, or putting yourself into the role of another person. *Affective role-taking* can be viewed primarily as a reaction to, or experience of, the emotional states of others. *Cognitive role-taking* is defined as the ability to view the world as others view it. Both these abilities are involved in the process of empathy. *Empathy* is the process of experiencing feelings or thoughts in reaction to the attributed internal state of another person and demonstrating an active concern for, attention to, and interest in the other person. You are no longer fully "centered" upon your own personal state, but you are being influenced by the attributed feelings and thoughts of another entity. You can never fully experience another person's thoughts or feelings, and your experiences are always interpreted in light of your own past experiences. However, when you make another person the center of your attention and attempt to demonstrate positive regard for that person, you are engaging in empathy. While it is possible to talk about empathy with a variety of referents (e.g., to imagine what a caged animal is thinking or to react emotionally to seeing a mighty redwood felled), in this chapter we will be concerned only with interpersonal empathy, in which we center attention on another person's thoughts or feelings.

Empathy is difficult to achieve and requires a number of different abilities. First, you must be sensitive to yourself and be able to vividly recall your past experiences. Empathy involves the process of recalling our past emotions and feelings in order to see common experiences with others. Second, you must be able to recall how particular feelings were translated into behaviors for you. To the extent that we can relate particular behaviors to specific feeling

We show our concern for others through empathy. Empathy is more difficult to achieve when the other person is considerably older or younger, of a different gender, or of a different background than ourselves.

states within ourselves, we can recognize the same or similar behaviors suggesting shared feelings. Third, you must be a sensitive perceiver of those cues offered to you by another person. The empathic person is alert to subtle, as well as blatant, cues in the environment. An empathic person possesses insight, perceptiveness, and social acuity. Fourth, you must be able to separate your own intellectually reflective response and your emotional or feeling response from those of the person with whom you are empathizing and hold your responses in temporary suspension. In other words, inferences about self and others are kept distinct. Fifth, you must interpret the available cues assisted by your past knowledge of the other person, similar experiences, and cognitive ability. The empathic person is able to generate creative hunches, adequate explanations, and correct inferences. Finally, you must communicate your understanding to the other person through clear and specific feedback.[1]

Empathy can break down in any of these abilities. We may not be viewed as empathic because we fail in our sensitivity to those cues offered to us by our environment and the other person. Polite conversation that we initiate may not be viewed as polite if we miss important cues. Similarly, we may be unable to separate our own feelings from those of the other person. None-theless, empathy is possible. We must recall our own past experiences and their attendant behaviors, perceive the cues offered to us by another person, separate our own responses—including, perhaps, a negative judgment—from those of the other person, interpret the available cues, and respond with an appropriate message demonstrating that we understand the other person's feelings.

Differentiating Empathy from Neutrality and Sympathy

Empathy is distinct from neutrality and sympathy. Neutrality occurs when a person refuses to take any position or any side in a dispute. Persons who appear to be indifferent or occupying a middle position are viewed as neutral. Neutrality suggests a lack of involvement, participation, or concern. Gibb has identified neutrality as one of six behaviors that results in a climate of defen-siveness. In other words, if you behave in a neutral manner toward another person, that individual will probably feel defensive in his or her reaction toward you. Gibb contrasts neutrality with empathy and suggests that empathy frequently results in a supportive climate in which defensiveness is reduced.[2] Neutrality may result in defensiveness or it may result in withdrawal on the part of the other person. In either case, it is potentially destructive in the in-terpersonal communication setting.

Sympathy is generally viewed as a broad-based concept that is synonymous with pity. Although sympathy is often viewed to be a response that occurs in sorrowful or difficult circumstances, we also sympathize with others when we share their joy or excitement. When we sympathize with other people, we demonstrate our concern by participating in the same emotion they are ex-periencing. We cry over their loss, show anger about their frustrations, and laugh at their joy. Sympathizing with others may be less than useful to another person if we are limited by the strong feelings of the moment. If we are blinded by tears or deafened by the shouts of joy, we may be less than sensitive to the feelings of the other person. Support may be difficult to demonstrate when we are participating in the same emotion. In general, sympathy connotes spontaneous emotion rather than a conscious, reasoned response.

Two examples may clarify the difference between sympathy and empathy. For instance, you may be tempted to sympathize with another person if that person fails an exam. Your sympathetic response would be to join in the dis-paraging remarks being made about the instructor, the method of grading or the particular area of study. Or, you might join in with a friend who has just disclosed that her husband is unfaithful and is considering divorce. You might sympathetically agree that the man is no good and does not deserve his present wife. Your sympathetic response may seem particularly inappropriate two weeks later when the couple is happily reunited and views you as an enemy to their happiness.

Sympathy may also provide difficulty in the interpersonal setting if the recipient of the sympathy feels that the sympathizer views himself or herself to be in a superior position. In other words, sympathy may suggest that one person is stronger, more capable, more advanced, or beyond the need for sympathy. Sympathetic responses can be viewed as patronizing by those who receive sympathy. The person who failed the exam may feel even worse if you say, "I am sorry for you." The spouse may wonder about your credentials as a marriage counselor in offering free advice to her. Sympathy may include advising and recommendations for future action; empathy does not.

Empathy, unlike neutrality, connotes involvement, participation, and concern. Unlike sympathy, it is not the mere reflection of emotion; instead, it suggests conscious, deliberate involvement. When we empathize, we do not become so emotionally involved that our judgment is affected; we are involved with another person's situation in the sense that we identify vicariously with that person. Empathy does not require that we experience the same fear, anxiety, or frustration that others are experiencing; rather, it requires that we communicate our awareness and appreciation of their emotions. Empathy includes sensitivity to others and an ability to communicate that sensitivity. Our involvement with another person when we empathize with that person is not based on shared emotions, but on feelings that are understood.

Models of Empathy

Examine your interactions with other people and attempt to identify a person who appears to be particularly adept at understanding your feelings. Specify the behavior of those persons. Consider those people who must regularly demonstrate empathy to others: counselors, teachers, ministers, and people who answer emergency or crisis telephone calls. What behaviors do they demonstrate? After you have identified behaviors that are associated with empathy, name some people whom you know who appear to be particularly poor at understanding other people's feelings. What behaviors do you associate with them? The primary benefit of exploring the behaviors associated with empathy and the lack of empathy is that you will have added the possibility of behavioral empathy to your repertoire. If you wish to behave in a manner that suggests empathy to another person, you will know the related behaviors. If you are told that you do not demonstrate understanding, you can examine your own behaviors and determine why this perception is held by another person. In either case, you will be able to operationalize the concept of empathy.

The Importance of Empathy

It may be readily apparent to you that empathy results in increased understanding of others. It may be less apparent that empathy allows a deeper understanding of the person who is emphathizing. One writer explains the benefits of empathizing for the empathizer. He writes:

Through empathy a man may closely identify himself with anyone he may wish to understand. He may seek inspiration from the gifted, the

Empathic Understanding

When we fail to empathize, we lose the opportunity to understand another person. Empathy is not a difficult skill when we have long-established relationships with other people and can predict their responses to particular situations. In addition, we oftentimes agree with people with whom we have related for some period of time. Empathy is more difficult when the other person is a stranger, having experiences that are significantly different from our own, or when we disagree with that person. In order to extend your ability to empathize with others, try the following exercise.

1. Identify an experience that you *have* never had or *can* never have. Talk with someone in your class, at work, or in a social situation who has had this experience. Continue your conversation until the other person is satisfied that you truly understand his or her perceptions. Examples of experiences you might choose are having a baby, being a member of a minority, losing your job, divorcing, having an abortion, serving in the military in Viet Nam, having a love affair, or flunking out of college.

2. Identify a topic on which you have a well established point of view. Talk to someone who holds an opposing point of view until that person is convinced that even though your point of view is different, you can completely understand the other's position. Examples of topics include the effectiveness of the current president, the role of women in society, premarital sex, abortions, legalization of marijuana, the abuse of valium, alcoholism, pornography, health foods, death penalty, or hunting.

3. Initiate a conversation with a stranger on campus. Tell him or her that you are completing a project for a course in which you are enrolled. If he or she is willing, engage in a conversation. Attempt to understand the attitudes, values, and beliefs of this new acquaintance. When the conversation is completed, tell this person what you perceive to be his or her perception of the world. Try to account for any differences between your perception of the other's perspective and what he or she tells you is a correct interpretation.

victorious, the happy. He may develop a deep comprehension of the problems of the blind, the crippled, the sorrowing, and the defeated. . . . Empathy is the key to leadership. It unlocks the dreams in the hearts of men so the leader can help to make those dreams come true.[3]

Understanding other people allows us to discover the common humanity that we share. As we unravel the intricacies of their experience, we discover the complexities and contradictions that define ourselves. For instance, we may gain some insight on our own security, based on positive experiences as a child, as a result of empathizing with a person who is highly egocentric and insecure and has determined that negative experiences with his or her parents appear to account for these feelings. Or, we may be able to view our high task orientation within a larger context as we begin to understand another person's lack of motivation to achieve.

Empathy also has been found to facilitate a number of valuable processes. For example, people who are higher in empathy have been found to reveal greater levels of prosocial behavior. Prosocial behavior includes giving help to people in need, volunteering behavior and contributions to social causes, and cooperative behavior in conflict situations.[4] Persons higher in empathy are generally viewed by others as more interpersonally skilled.[5] Finally, therapists who are more empathic tend to be more successful in their therapies than those demonstrating lower levels of empathic behavior.[6] Clearly, being able to demonstrate empathy benefits a variety of social processes.

Finally, relationships with others also result when we open ourselves to empathic understanding. An allusion is suggested by the proverb, "He is so full of himself that he is quite empty."[7] Most of us desire the understanding of others and recognize that only superficial relationships occur when we fail to empathize.

Competence in Empathy

Verbal Skills of Empathy

Your ability to empathize with another person can be demonstrated in a variety of verbal skills. Listed below are some practices that will show others your concern. You will recall that some of these skills were listed in chapter 8 and are cross-referenced here. How many of these skills are already part of your repertoire in interpersonal communication?

1. *Invite additional statements.* Offer the other person the opportunity to elaborate on his statement. Encourage additional self-disclosure. Ask questions or use phrases like "Go on," "Tell me more," "Can you add anything?," and "What other feelings do you have?" Notice the use of this verbal technique in the dialogue that follows. These two college students had this conversation

during midterm time. Carol continually demonstrates her concern through questions that invite additional information from Bob.

Bob: I just bombed out on my organic test.

Carol: Was it really that bad?

Bob: Well, considering I got a score fifteen points below the mean, yeah, I would say it was that bad.

Carol: You were surprised by the results of the exam?

Bob: I'll say I was—I studied for two days for this test.

Carol: Do you know how any of your friends did on the exam?

Bob: No, I was so upset when I saw my grade, I just wanted to get out of there.

Carol: How do you feel now?

This conversation continued with Carol inviting additional information from Bob in order that he could disclose his feelings. You will notice that Carol is careful not to impose her own feelings on Bob nor does she advise him about what he should do in the future. Empathy is at the other end of the spectrum from advising and monitoring others.

2. *Identify areas of agreement or common experience.* Share similar experiences and explain how you handled the situation. Establish a common base of "something shared." In *Stuart Little,* empathy is demonstrated through the sharing of experiences as Stuart discusses a pillow, belonging to a student:

> *"I suppose it was given you by a boy you met at Lake Hopatcong last summer, and it reminds you of him," murmured Stuart dreamily.*
> *"Yes, it was," said Katherine, blushing.*
> *"Ah," said Stuart, "summers are wonderful, aren't they, Katherine?"*
> *"Yes, and last summer was the most wonderful summer I have ever had in all my life."*
> *"I can imagine," replied Stuart.*[8]

In the following cartoon, Charlie Brown questions whether Lucy will be able to show no concern for children when she is older since she will have the memory of a similar experience.

A conversation that occured in a fraternity house den provides an example of a communicator identifying common experiences. Bob was sitting in a corner of the room alone when his roommate, Bill, walked in. The conversation follows:

Bill: Hey Bob, what's the matter?

Bob: Ah, nothin'.

Bill: Come on, something is bugging you. Tell me about it.

Bob: Cindy kind of dropped me and went out with some other guy tonight.

Bill: Oh, I understand now.

Bob: Yeah, she meant a lot to me.

Bill: Not too long ago, I was in the same situation.

Bob: You were?

Bill: You bet, and it's not pleasant.

Bob: I can't believe anyone who is as good looking as you ever had anyone drop him.

Bill: I think everyone has experienced being dropped by another person at one time or another.

Bob: Yeah, I guess you're right. I just felt like I was the only one it ever happened to. It helps to know that I'm not alone. Thanks, Bill.

Bill demonstrates empathic ability by inviting additional comments from Bob and asking him pertinent questions at the beginning of the conversation and by sharing a similar experience with him as the conversation ensues. When he felt that Bob had discussed the situation sufficiently, he suggested an alternative activity.

3. *Provide clear verbal responses.* Avoid long, complicated statements. Do not rely on clichés, euphemisms, or other ambiguous terminology. Instead of replying, "That's the way it goes," "You can't get ahead," or "Nothing comes easy," try to

respond with a specific statement that focuses on the matter at hand. Stereotypical responses are not only unclear, they also suggest a lack of sensitivity to particular problems.

4. *Use descriptive, nonevaluative statements.* Avoid patronizing sarcastic, cynical, threatening, trivializing, or judgmental statements. Avoid giving advice. When you tell the other person what should be done, you put yourself in a superior position and decrease your ability to see the other person's point of view. Statements like "I see that you are angry today," "I can tell that something is bothering you," or "You seem in a good mood," are descriptive and are preferred over evaluative comments like, "I don't know why you're so angry," "What's the matter now," or "You'd better wipe that smile off your face!"

5. *Provide affirmative and affirming statements.* The use of praise and positive comments demonstrates concern. Positive feedback demonstrates a level of empathy. Reassuring and comforting statements including "I know you can do it," "It will be all right," and "It's okay" provides assurance. Empathy is demonstrated in this way in *Charlotte's Web:*

    > *"Charlotte?" he said, softly.*
    > *"Yes Wilbur?"*
    > *"I don't want to die."*
    > *"Of course you don't," said Charlotte in a comforting voice.*
    > *"I just love it here in the barn," said Wilbur. "I love everything about this place."*
    > *"Of course you do," said Charlotte. "We all do."* [9]

    Statements that respond to the other person's need to be acknowledged serve as affirming statements. Comments like "You have feelings, too," "You're worth a lot to your company," "Your point of view should be heard," and "You can add to this conversation" are affirming.

6. *Provide understanding through reflective statements of the other person's perceptions and through verifying feedback.* Your understanding can be shown through explicit statements such as "I know how you feel," "I understand," and "I've been there, myself." Reflective statements of the other person's perceptions may be shown through the comments, "Do you feel so happy that you want to kiss everyone?," "Your anger causes you a great deal of frustration," or "Your anxiety seems to be overwhelming." We demonstrate a lack of empathy when we deny other people's feelings by telling them that they do not really feel a particular way.

Empathy in Business

You may feel that empathy is an important interpersonal skill in your personal life, but has relatively little to do with your business or professional dealings. On the contrary, empathy is as important to successful interactions in your work as it is in your personal relationships. In the following dialogue, two people are engaged in an appraisal interview. The employee is given an evaluation of her work for the past three-month period. Notice how the lack of empathy interferes with a successful appraisal interview. Rewrite the supervisor's responses to demonstrate empathy. Then, rewrite the employee's responses. After you have rewritten this dialogue, examine the original one and compare it with your version. In which interview would you prefer to be the employee? Are your current work relationships marked by empathic responses among supervisors, co-workers, and others? How can you alter these interactions to make them more humane and satisfying to all of the persons who are involved?

Supervisor: Come on in Chris, have a seat. As you know we evaluate each employee after he or she has been here for one quarter, or three months. I have filled out the evaluation form that we use and I would like you to examine it. Why don't you take a few minutes to read it and then we can talk about it if you wish?

Employee: (After she has read the document) Why did you mark me so low in my ability to take directions and get along with others?

Supervisor: Because you never follow the directions that are given to you; you always question the way we do things.

Employee: When I ask questions, it's because the directions don't make any sense or I think there's a better way of handling the problem.

Supervisor: That's part of the problem—you've been here three months and you already think you know more than those of us who have been here for ten years.

Employee: I think I do know some things that people who have been out of school for a long time don't know. There are new ways of doing things, you know.

Supervisor: What's happening right here is an example of your problem. I'm supposed to be conducting this interview and instead I'm being told how to do my job. You've got to learn what your job is and what another person's job is!

Employee: When I see a problem, I feel obligated to mention it. The most important thing is getting the job done!

Supervisor: You do the same thing with your co-workers. A number of them have complained about your know-it-all attitude.

Employee: Who?

Supervisor: Well, I don't want to name names, but more than you can imagine.

Employee: How can I improve my working relationship if I don't even know with whom I have poor relationships?

Supervisor: Well, Chris, a creative person would be able to handle that—or that person wouldn't have the problem in the first place.

Employee: What exactly do you want me to do to improve?

Empathy in Business continued

Supervisor:	That's up to you.
Employee:	Look, you bring me in here and tell me I've got problems. What solutions do you propose?
Supervisor:	That's not my job.
Employee:	Whose job is it?
Supervisor:	Chris, I think you'd better cool off and we'll talk about this later.
Employee:	Thanks for nothing.

We also may deny another person's feelings if we claim to "know what you're feeling" when we actually have little idea. If such statements are forced or said without genuine understanding or concern, they may seem patronizing. We have probably all encountered a time when someone said they knew how we felt, when we felt convinced that no one could possibly know our feelings at that moment. Consequently, such statements need to be made judiciously, and only when sincerely motivated.

Verifying feedback, providing information to the speaker about your level of understanding, also demonstrates empathy. Restatement of the content of the message, a paraphrase of the content or intent or other forms of feedback are useful. You may wish to review these three methods of verification feedback in chapter 8.

Finally, research in the counseling setting has provided fairly precise ways of observing the verbal demonstration of empathic communication.[10] In any given encounter, ask yourself to what extent you engage in the following behaviors or tendencies: Do you demonstrate that you make inferences about the other person's "between the line" meanings? To what extent do your interpretations of the other person's statements receive confirmation or agreement? Do your statements concern themselves primarily with the "here and now" of the conversation? Are you able to center in on the issues of most importance to the other person? Do you use words, expressions, and verbal style similar to the other person? Do you avoid interruptions and frequent topic shifts? Do you avoid saying things that deny or disconfirm the other person's feelings or right to have these feelings? An answer of yes to all of these questions suggests that you are demonstrating high levels of empathy in your verbal behavior.

Nonverbal Skills of Empathy

Empathy can be demonstrated through nonverbal communication as well as through verbal cues.[11] The following skills generally show empathy in interpersonal communication. You may wish to increase your ability to demonstrate concern to others by practicing these nonverbal behaviors.

1. *Demonstrate bodily responsiveness.* Movement and gestures show that you are listening attentively to the speaker and responding to the message he or she is presenting. The lack of feedback suggests lack of concern and an overabundance of movement may suggest boredom, anxiety, or mockery.

2. *Lean forward.* Your interest in the speaker and his or her message will be shown if you lean toward the speaker. In addition, you will be able to better observe the verbal and nonverbal cues offered by the other person.

3. *Use a direct body orientation.* As in leaning forward, a direct body orientation allows you to be a more sensitive observer of the other person. Also, a direct orientation suggests that you are focusing on the speaker rather than on other distractions in the room.

4. *Establish an open body position.* Sitting with your arms crossed in front of your chest and your legs crossed away from the other individual may suggest that you are closed off to him or her mentally and emotionally as well as physically. Complement your mental and emotional readiness to empathize and be open with its physical counterpart. Consistent nonverbal cues will clarify your intent and motivation. Inconsistent nonverbal cues may confuse the speaker.

5. *Use positive, responsive facial expression and head movement.* Smiling indicates warmth and acceptance and nodding suggests listening and approval. Avoid yawning, looking bored, staring, appearing shocked, angry, or unconcerned. You can communicate a great deal of understanding through your facial expression.

6. *Sit or stand close to the speaker.* You increase your demonstration of warmth and understanding as you move closer to the other person. Sit or stand so that you can adequately hear and observe him or her. Demonstrate your mental or emotional closeness to your partner by reinforcing it with physical closeness.

7. *Increase touching.* Increased closeness allows you to increase your touching of the other person. Put a friendly hand on his or her shoulder, give him or her a hug, or sit so that your bodies are touching. Sometimes reaching out and holding the other person's hand is appropriate. Touching is especially recommended when the other person is disclosing negative information or information that is difficult to discuss. When persons are experiencing pain or other difficulty, they often appreciate the warmth of touch.

Empathy can be demonstrated verbally or nonverbally. Touch can be a powerful non-verbal indicator of empathic understanding.

8. *Use vocal responsiveness.* Avoid a monotone response that suggests lack of interest and boredom. Change your pitch, rate, inflection, and volume in response to the speaker's message and intent.

9. *Use a sincere, warm voice tone.* Avoid a high pitch, a harsh quality, or an aggressive tone. One student reported the following conversation that occurred in a campus bookstore. She suggested that the clerk's tone of voice, more than any other quality, caused her to feel that the clerk was not interested in assisting her.

Campus Book Store Worker: May I help you?

Student: I'm sorry, what?

Worker: I said, may I help you? (Increasing pitch rather than volume.)

Student: Whoa! I didn't hear you. Please repeat yourself.

Worker: (Narrowing her eyes and glaring): I said, what do you want?

Student: I'd like to have a key made.

Worker: (Looking exasperated and in a high pitched, angry tone): Well, why didn't you say so in the first place!

Student: I would have, if I had heard you.

Worker: (Sarcastically): What are you, deaf or something?

Student: Yes, I am!

Worker: (Stepping closer and increasing her volume): Gee, I'm sorry.

Student: (Walking away): So am I.

The understanding that the clerk attempted to show came too late for the student to appreciate it. Instead, the student walked away feeling frustrated and insulted.

10. *Establish direct eye contact.* Direct eye contact, like some of the other nonverbal cues, facilitates more accurate utilization of the cues that others provide. Such direct eye contact indicates that the other person is clearly the focus of your attention. Try to be observing of the other communicator. Avoid looking away, staring at others, glancing around the room, or looking at your watch.

An Example of Empathic Understanding

Empathic understanding is demonstrated by a myriad of verbal and nonverbal cues. We are called upon to show empathy to our friends, family, and co-workers. In the dialogue that follows, Ann is empathic to Jane. The two women are co-workers in a small office. This conversation occurred after a confrontation with their boss in which Ann was severely criticized for a clerical error that had resulted in some financial loss for the company.

	Dialogue	Analysis
Jane:	Boy, he made me feel so small and stupid!	*Jane self-discloses her feelings.*
Ann:	Yeah, I know how you feel. He's yelled at me like that before.	*Ann reveals a similar experience and identifies an area of agreement. In addition, she provides a statement of understanding.*
Jane:	I can't imagine you ever feeling this way. You're so sure of yourself.	*Jane provides a validating statement to Ann.*
Ann:	Not really. I just don't let anyone see my emotions. When he yells at me, I go home and cry.	*Ann provides a clear verbal response and again identifies a common experience.*
Jane:	I think that if I see him again today, I'll break down and cry.	*This sharing of feeling creates a feeling of equality, which allows empathic understanding to occur.*
Ann:	I always feel better after I've talked with a friend, then had some time to be alone and think.	*A clear verbal response by Ann in which she identifies and describes a similar experience.*
Jane:	I hope I don't get fired.	
Ann:	You won't. He knows that you're a good worker. You've always been so conscientious! (Ann puts her arm around Jane and smiles at her.)	*Ann provides a validating statement and an affirming statement, which she complements with the nonverbal cues of touch and positive facial expression.*
Jane:	Thanks, Ann. I feel better already.	

Jane felt better about the conflict with her boss very soon because of the understanding that Ann provided. Empathy is a powerful interpersonal communication skill.

Opportunities for Empathy

One way that we can shift our thinking about empathy is that each of us is given opportunities in which we can behave in an empathic manner rather than believing that empathy is a skill that we must impose upon our current behavioral style. In the following situations of potential conflict, you have the opportunity of behaving in an empathic manner. For each situation, identify how you might respond if you were interested in demonstrating understanding and how you might respond if you were not concerned with showing understanding of the other person and the situation. After you have completed this exercise, discuss your most likely response, or your typical response in the past, for each situation.

1. You have left your car in the garage to have the tires rotated. The garage owner has promised that the car would be ready by 6 P.M. You arrive at the garage at 7 P.M. and you are in a hurry—you have a date at 8 P.M. and you are not ready to go out. The owner apologizes and explains that he has had an unusually busy day and that his mother was taken to the hospital with symptoms resembling a heart attack. Your car will be ready in less than an hour, but he has only begun to rotate the wheels.

    Your Empathic Response: _____

    _____

    Your Nonempathic Response: _____

    _____

2. Your parents have been planning on visiting you on the upcoming weekend. They made the arrangements about a week or two ago. Their visit on this weekend was not completely workable for you, but you cancelled a date and finished a paper early in order that you would be free to spend time with them. It's Friday afternoon and one of your parents calls. She explains that your younger sister has gotten into serious trouble at school. Your parents feel they must spend extra time with her this weekend in order to help her understand the importance of certain decisions that she has made. Your parent asks if the following weekend will work out just as well for you. You changed your date to the following weekend and you have two major tests on the Monday after that weekend. How do you respond?

    Your Empathic Response: _____

    _____

    Your Nonempathic Response: _____

    _____

3. You are talking on the telephone with a person you have just begun to date. Your roommate walks into the room and lies down on her bed. She begins to cry. You are surprised at this outburst since your roommate is not normally a very emotional person.

    Your Empathic Response: _____

    _____

    Your Nonempathic Response: _____

    _____

Opportunities for Empathy continued

4. You are in a restaurant with a group of friends. The service has been particularly slow and the food has been especially poor. For instance, the restaurant no longer has available the special items it advertised for the day, the food that is available is overpriced, and when you receive your food it is not hot. The person serving your table has been called over by one of the more assertive persons in your party. She explains that her husband, the manager of the restaurant, lost his lease on the building within the last week and that they are about to declare bankruptcy. The business has been in her husband's family for two generations.

Your Empathic Response: _____

_____

Your Nonempathic Response: _____

_____

5. You loaned an excellent hardback book to a friend. You have had the book for a number of years and it has always been a favorite of yours. You have never loaned it to anyone and felt some concern over letting another person use it now. Your friend kept the book for twice as long as he said that he would and now is returning it. You notice that the cover has mud on it and some of the pages are folded and torn. When you ask for an explanation, your friend shows surprise that you had not heard that he had been mugged. The book became soiled in the scuffle and was almost lost.

Your Empathic Response: _____

_____

Your Nonempathic Response: _____

_____

11. *Provide supportive utterances.* Sounds like "mmm," "hmm," and others are sometimes more appropriate than making a statement or using a short phrase. Such sounds allow the speaker to know that you are listening empathically, but do not interrupt his or her train of thought. Use such sounds to demonstrate your understanding.

12. *Use silence appropriately.* Just as it is sometimes too much of an interruption to make a statement or even respond with a few words, it is occasionally disruptive to make any sound. Use silence at these times. Do not be afraid to simply touch someone as he or she speaks or to hold someone without either of you speaking. Sometimes the most appropriate response is no response. Allow the saddened individual to express his grief, the excited person to share all of her story, and the anxious person to explain the cause of his anxiety. Do not rely on the "sounds of silence" at all times. When silence is used too frequently, it may suggest lack of concern.

Related to this, be careful not to dominate the conversation by talking too much of the time. If most of the time of the conversation is taken up by your own speaking, it is unlikely to appear that you care much about what the other person has to say.

Summary

In this chapter you have discovered the importance of empathic understanding in the interpersonal communication process. You can distinguish among empathy, neutrality, and sympathy. You know the many abilities that are involved in the act of empathizing with others and how difficult empathy is to demonstrate to others. The benefits of empathy—a greater understanding of others, a greater understanding of self, and the deepening of interpersonal relationships—make it well worthwhile. Empathy is based on an unconditional acceptance of other persons and is closely associated with honesty or genuineness in an interpersonal setting.

The ability to perceive the world of another person as though that view were your own is an essential element in effective interpersonal communication. Empathy and active listening, together, allow us to demonstrate our concern for other persons.

Notes

1. A similar set of processes is identified by D. J. Meyer, F. J. Boster, and M. L. Hecht, "A Model of Empathic Communication," *Communication Research Reports* 5(1988): 19–27, in which empathy is broken down into the components of humanistic orientation, perspective-taking, empathic concern, emotional responsiveness, and communicative responsiveness.

2. Jack R. Gibb, "Defensive Communication," *Journal of Communication* 11(1961): 141–48.

3. Wilfred A. Peterson, *The Art of Living Treasure Chest* (New York: Simon & Schuster, 1977), p. 75.

4. N. Eisenberg and P. A. Miller, "The Relation of Empathy to Prosocial and Related Behaviors," *Psychological Bulletin* 101(1987): 91–119.

5. N. Eisenberg and P. A. Miller, 1987; see also M. V. Redmond, "The Relationship Between Perceived Communication Competence and Perceived Empathy," *Communication Monographs* 52(1985): 377–82.

6. J. D. Matarazzo, and A. N. Wiens, "Speech Behavior As an Objective Correlate of Empathy and Outcome in Interview and Psychotherapy Research: A Review with Implications for Behavior Modification," *Behavior Modification* 1(1977): 453–80.

7. *The New Webster Encyclopedia Dictionary of the English Language* (Chicago: Consolidated Book Publishers, 1971).

8. E. B. White, *Stuart Little* (New York: Harper & Row, 1945), p. 91.

9. E. B. White, *Charlotte's Web* (New York: Harper & Row, 1952), pp. 62–63.

10. C. T. Cochrane, "Development of a Measure of Empathic Communication," *Psychotherapy: Theory, Research and Practice* 11(1977): 41–47; R. Elliott, H. Filopovich, L. Harrigan, J. Gaynor, C. Reimschuessel, and J. K. Zapadka, "Measuring Response Empathy: The Development of a Multicomponent Rating Scale," *Journal of Counseling Psychology* 29(1982): 379–87.

11. See Matarazzo and Wiens, 1977; M. A. Bayes, "Behavioral Cues of Interpersonal Warmth," *Journal of Consulting and Clinical Psychology* 39(1972): 333–39; R. F. Haase. and D. T. Tepper, Jr., "Nonverbal Components of Empathic Communication," *Journal of Consulting Psychology* 19(1972): 417–24; D. T. Tepper, Jr. and R. F. Haase, "Verbal and Nonverbal Communication of Facilitative Conditions," *Journal of Counseling Psychology* 25(1978): 35–44.

Additional Readings

Appleford, G. Burton. *Sensitivity: Agony or Ecstasy.* Bryn Mawr, Penn.: Dorrance, 1988.

Carkhuff, Robert R. *Helping and Human Relationships.* Vol. I, II. New York: Holt, Rinehart & Winston, 1969.

Danner, Jack. *People-Empathy: Key to Painless Supervision.* New York: Parker Publishing Co., Inc., 1976.

Egan, Gerard. *Interpersonal Living: A Skills/Contract Approach to Human Relations Training in Groups.* Belmont, Calif.: Brooks/Cole, 1976.

Eisenberg, Nancy and Strayer, Janet, eds. *Empathy and Its Development.* Cambridge Studies in Social and Emotional Development. New York: Cambridge University Press, 1987.

Fromm, Eric. *The Art of Loving.* New York: Harper & Row, 1956.

Gaylin, Willard. *Caring.* New York: Alfred A. Knopf, 1976.

Gazda, George M., Walters, Richard P., and Childers, William C. *Human Relations Development.* Boston: Allyn & Bacon, 1975.

Goldstein, Arnold P. and Michaels, Gerald Y. *Empathy: Development, Training and Consequences.* Hillsdale, N.J.: Laurence/Erlbaum and Associates, 1985.

Guerney, Bernard G., Jr. *Relationship Enhancement.* San Francisco: Jossey-Bass, 1977.

Ivey, Allen E. *Microcounseling: Innovations in Interviewing Training.* Springfield, Ill.: Charles C. Thomas, 1971.

Katz, Robert L. *Empathy.* New York: The Free Press, 1963.

Smith, Henry Clay. *Sensitivity to People.* New York: McGraw-Hill, 1966.

Stern, Edith. *On the Problem of Empathy.* The Hague, The Netherlands: Martinus Nijhoff, 1964.

Stewart, David. *Preface to Empathy.* New York: Philosophical Library, 1956.

Stotland, E., Mathews, K. E., Jr., Sherman, S. E., Hansonn, R. O., and Richardson, B. Z. *Empathy, Fantasy, and Helping.* Beverly Hills, Calif.: Sage, 1978.

Communication Rules

". . . and so I find our system can act as a cluster controller for PC networks . . . oh, excuse me, that's business talk—let me switch into cocktail chatter . . . we're weekending in Hilton Head next week. . . ."

Reprinted by permission: Tribune Media Services.

The gentleman in the conversation has realized that something is amiss in discussing computers at a cocktail party, even if it is occurring in an office penthouse. This realization seems to be based on a sense that the purpose of the situation is not task-oriented, but social in nature. Knowing what is appropriate behavior in various situations is a critical aspect of competent communication. Most communication episodes are facilitated by standards of appropriateness known as communication rules. These rules inform, guide, and are often the focus of communication behavior. They therefore play an important role in managing interaction and achieving a smooth flow of behavior within and across conversations. This chapter examines the nature, importance, and skills associated with communication rules.

The Nature of Communication Rules

Sometimes we are very aware that there are certain things we should, or should not, do in a given social situation. At other times, we seem to muddle through a situation, trying all the while to figure out what types of comments and behaviors are most appropriate. These issues revolve around the concept of communication rules.

241

A Definition of Rule

A communication rule is basically a prescription or proscription for behavior in a communicative context or episode. More formally, a *communication "rule is a followable prescription that indicates what behavior is obligated, preferred, or prohibited in certain contexts."*[1] This definition contains several important terms that each need to be considered before the nature of rules can be fully understood.

To say that a rule is followable may seem obvious. However, rules vary considerably in the extent to which they can be followed, and prescriptions that cannot be followed cannot properly be defined as rules. For example, it may seem relatively simple to follow a rule such as, "Do not disclose highly negative information about yourself while on a first date." This rule seems fairly clear and should not present too much of a problem in following its prescription. Following a rule becomes more problematic in other situations. The traditional rule "respect your elders" is probably too ambiguous to be followed. It does not specify context, relationship, or what constitutes either evidence of "respect" or "disrespect" (i.e., violation of the rule).

Such a rule becomes especially difficult to follow when placed in the context of a double-bind statement. A *double-bind* statement or context is one in which virtually any direction taken results in negative consequences for the interactant. The statement, "You argue with me too much," is a pure instance of creating a dilemma, or bind, for the respondent. Extending this example, consider the following conversation between an elderly person and a young attendant.

Attendant: How are you today? You're looking well.

Resident: As if you care. No one cares about people like me any more.

Attendant: I care. Would I be here if I didn't care? Why don't we go for a stroll today?

Resident: Why must you always contradict me? When I was your age, we were taught to respect our elders.

Attendant: But I do respect you.

Resident: Don't you sass me. There you go contradicting me again.

Such conversations place the conversant in an impression management dilemma, where following one prescription (respect your elders) seems to violate other prescriptions (defend your image against criticism). In such situations, the prescriptions are not easily followed and may need to be redefined.

A *prescription* is a statement of what *should* occur. To prescribe a drug or a diet is to tell someone what she or he should do in response to a condition.

Similarly, a rule indicates what behavior should happen and behavior that should not happen. Since one cannot not communicate in the sense that one cannot not behave, rules prescribe behavior in both inclusionary and exclusionary ways. That is, to prescribe that one "should use the salad fork for the salad at a formal dinner" is by implication a proscription that one "should not use other utensils for the salad at a formal dinner."

Rules concern behavior. It is insufficient to prescribe that a person should "be positive" or "be optimistic." These are attitudes and may not result in specifiable, observable behaviors. If the referent of the rule is not directly observable, then it is impossible to tell when the rule has been followed or violated. If it is impossible to know if a rule has been followed or violated, then it is also difficult to know how to abide by a rule.

The terms "obligated, preferred, or prohibited" indicate that there is some level of consensus or agreement that certain behaviors should be performed or avoided. Obligated behavior implies that some behavior is "required" by the context. Certain communication situations possess very strong rules for behavior. People who are scheduled to meet British royalty are often "schooled" by advisors on how to greet the prospective representative. The press is firmly instructed to address the present and past holders of the office as "President _____" or "Mr. President." Sometimes, however, behavior is not particularly obligated, but only preferred. Generally speaking, it is appropriate to thank a host of a party for the hospitality. Such behavior may be appreciated, but not considered particularly necessary, by the hosts. Finally, some behaviors are simply prohibited by the rules of a situation. Telling a sexually explicit joke at a formal dinner party with mixed company is often prohibited by the structure of the situation.

The phrase "in certain contexts" simply dictates that rules refer to behavior in particular situations. While there are some rules that apply across an enormous range of situations (e.g., never disclose information to others that was given in strict confidence to you), other rules apply in extremely narrowly defined situations (e.g., never refer to your fiancé's mother's culinary talents as "burnt offerings"). Again, if it is not clear exactly what contexts the rules apply to, it is impossible to know when the rule has been followed or violated. Thus, even when we refer to standard rules later in this chapter they may seem universal in the sense that they apply across an extremely large range of situatons or relationships. However, there are few, if any, rules that universally apply across all contexts.

Indeed, one of the more apparent features of rules and contexts is that they both vary in terms of their dependence on one another. Some contexts are bound by a large number of particularly rigid rules, whereas other contexts have relatively few rules. Similarly, some behaviors are appropriate across a wide variety of contexts (i.e., are not very rule-bound) whereas other behaviors are very rule-governed and only appropriate in a few contexts.

Behaviors and Situations

The following is a list of behaviors and typical types of situations. Rate the appropriateness of each behavior for each situation listed, from 1 (very inappropriate) to 5 (very appropriate).

Situation:	Classroom	First date	Interview	Elevator	Own room	Bar
Behavior:						
Talk	_____	_____	_____	_____	_____	_____
Kiss	_____	_____	_____	_____	_____	_____
Argue	_____	_____	_____	_____	_____	_____
Belch	_____	_____	_____	_____	_____	_____
Laugh	_____	_____	_____	_____	_____	_____
Cry	_____	_____	_____	_____	_____	_____
Shout	_____	_____	_____	_____	_____	_____

Several researchers have shown that most people rate these behaviors in systematically different ways. For example, in your own room you generally feel as if you can do virtually anything. It is a relatively rule-free context. However, elevators and classrooms tend to be highly rule-bound. Only a few of the listed behaviors are considered particularly appropriate in such situations. Similarly, talking is considered fairly rule-free, in the sense that it is generally appropriate across contexts. However, belching and kissing are fairly rule-bound behaviors, and only considered appropriate in specific situations.[2]

Differentiating Rules from Norms, Conventions, Morals, and Laws

Rules can be distinguished from *norms, conventions, morals, and laws.* *Norms* refer to behaviors that "normally" occur. This is almost a statistical sense of behavior. Whatever tends to happen most often is a norm. For example, greetings tend to reveal a declining elaboration over the course of a day in a context requiring proximity and frequent interaction. When you go to work where you will see someone several times during the day, your first greeting tends to be somewhat more elaborate and involved than latter greetings, where a simple nod or brief exchange of eye contact and grin may suffice. However, even though this may be a norm, a brief greeting in the morning may seem perfectly acceptable, especially if the person appears preoccupied or busy. A more elaborate greeting in the afternoon may also seem appropriate, as some object of discussion calls for a moment of conversation. In short, norms and rules are not necessarily the same thing.

Conventions may be viewed as arbitrary social customs that may or may not have implicit sanctions for violation. Clothing styles, hairstyles, and vernacular and slang concern trends and valued norms in various groups at various times. These conventions evolve over time within the groups and may be viewed as a somewhat loose collection of habits or tendencies that are collectively accepted by a group. People may or may not be aware of norms, but they are almost certainly aware of conventions.

Moral behavior and rule-governed behavior are not the same. Rules often reflect a sense of morality (e.g., "Do not insult your parents" is a reflection of "Respect your mother and father"), but are generally less intensely valued than morals. For example, the morality of avoiding violence in interpersonal conflict is likely to be far more important than the rule of avoiding name-calling in interpersonal conflict.

While it may seem obvious that laws and rules are not the same thing, it is informative to compare them. *Laws* are written, codified, and openly legislated prescriptions. Furthermore, laws indicate specific penalties for violation and are collectively enforced. Rules are often violated with widely varying forms of sanction for the violator. Rules may be extremely idiosyncratic and context- or relationship-specific, whereas laws tend to apply to a broad class of contexts and actions.

Functions of Rules

Now that we have a clearer understanding of rules as they compare to other forms of prescription, it is important to examine their function and form. At their most fundamental level, rules function to assist people in *achieving goals* through interpretations.[3] Societies, groups, and relationships develop rules for conduct because the rules facilitate efficient, cooperative, coordinated, and more satisfying interaction and goal accomplishment. To use a rough analogy, few of the goals of professional athletes would be easily accomplished if there were no clear rules to the games and competitive events being played. A football game with no rules would be chaotic at best. More specifically, however, rules serve a variety of identifiable functions relevant to managing interaction. Rules can serve a *regulative function.* Since rules are prescriptions for behavior, when they are violated some sanction (i.e., reward or punishment) is likely to occur. That is, rules imply a standard for evaluation and criticism of behavior. Evaluation, in turn, provides a basis for influencing and regulating behavior. If you insult the host at the dinner table, the glares and stares and silence or even the overt expression of disapproval all provide signs of "punishment" for rule violation. The "enforcement" of sanctions against rule-violators serves to regulate behavior so that future violations are less likely, and the presence and effect of the rule is reinforced.

Rules also serve an *interpretive function.* There are times when a person may not be aware of the presence of a rule. Upon observing sanctioning behavior when violating a rule, a person may be able to interpret what kind of context and episode are being enacted. A child learns to define certain situations as "noninteractive" when others "shhhh" talking (e.g., in movie theatres, in church, during weather alerts while viewing television, etc.). The discovery of the rule in effect "explains" the nature of the context.

Bowing in oriental countries and shaking hands in Western nations are two activities based on roles that serve an accounting function.

Rules frequently serve an *accounting function*. To account for something is to explain or justify it. People may explain why they did something because they were "supposed" to do it. If asked why people shake hands upon meeting someone for the first time, most people might be hard pressed to provide any more satisfying explanation than "it is the appropriate thing to do." Indeed, the "rule" of shaking hands in our culture seems to serve as an adequate explanation and justification for this behavior.

Finally, rules serve a *management function*. Knowledge of rules allows a person to predict others' behavior, comprehend how to weave the topical thread of conversational turns together, and adapt one's behavior to the requirements of the communicative context. To understand this latter function, it will be useful to examine three types of rules commonly encountered in our everyday behavior.

Types of Rules

Rules generally can be categorized into three classes: *standard, contextual,* and *coordinative.* These classes reflect the scope and object of the rules. *Standard rules* concern the most elementary requirements of social interaction. For example, *as a rule,* people understand that they should attempt to use a common language or signaling system when interacting, should position themselves in a position fairly close to the other interactant(s) when interacting face-to-face, avoid overly negative consequences for the other interactant(s) when possible (e.g., embarrassment, violence, denigration, etc.), and in a related vein, should be polite.[4]

Argyle and Henderson found four rules that were frequently mentioned across four different cultures across several types of relationships. While there were not many, four rules were endorsed by almost all people surveyed: respect the other's privacy, look the other person in the eye during conversation, do not discuss that which is said in confidence with the other person, and do not publicly criticize the other person.[5] In an earlier study of British university students, four rules were again found to be fairly general in acceptance: be friendly, do not try to make others feel small, try to make it a pleasant encounter, and do not embarrass others.[6] In short, while there are very few rules that apply to almost all situations, there are some important ones that are relatively standard across western cultures.

Contextual rules are rules governing appropriate behavior in particular situations or relationships. For example, it has been found that the vast majority of intimate couples develop rules of idiomatic discourse. That is, intimate couples develop terms and phrases that are unique to their own relationship. One study found that most idioms fell into one of eight different categories: teasing insults, confrontations, expressions of affection, sexual invitations, sexual references and euphemisms, requests and routines, partner nicknames, and names for other persons.[7] In a related study, sexual idioms, nicknames, and terminology not only varied by gender of user but also by context. Thus, as would be expected, respondents generated the highest frequency of idiosyncratic idioms regarding sex in the spouse/lover relationship, compared to relationships such as parent/guardian, same-gender, and mixed-gender contexts.[8]

Contextual rules have been found in a variety of contexts. Baxter found that the reasons people give for breaking up with their intimate partners reveal a variety of implicit rules. For example, the *autonomy rule* could be stated: "If parties are in a close relationship, then they should acknowledge one another's individual identities and lives beyond the relationship." The *similarity display* rule implies that "If parties are in a close relationship, then they should express similar attitudes, beliefs, values, and interests." Other discovered rules concerned the expectation that partners should provide support and reinforcement of self's sense of self-worth, be open and honest, be loyal and faithful, share time and activities with one another, invest resources and

Table 10.1   Conversational Rules*

Generally speaking, and especially in initial interactions, *communicators* should:

1. Adapt messages to the partner's characteristics, personality, experience, etc.;
2. Speak honestly (i.e., convey the "truth" as it is perceived);
3. Speak coherently and understandably;
4. Be neither overinformative nor underinformative;
5. Make statements relevant to the topic in general;
6. Make statements relevant to the immediately preceding statement;
7. Make statements appropriate to the situation and relationship;
8. Make statements consistent with the communicator's purpose(s);
9. Distribute speaking time somewhat equally among interactants;
10. Assume that your conversational partner is following the same rules of communication.

Generally speaking, and especially in initial interactions, *listeners* should:

1. Take into account the communicator's characteristics, personality, experience, etc.;
2. Take into account the communicator's purpose;
3. Take into account the situation and relationship;
4. Attend (in actuality and appearance) to the message;
5. Attend (in actuality and appearance) to the communicator;
6. Attempt to comprehend and understand the message;
7. Accept the existence of linguistic and stylistic variation;
8. Accept the need for occasional within-turn pauses (to search for words, ideas, and phrases);
9. Provide informative and consistent feedback;
10. Assume the communicator is following the same rules of communication.

*Adapted from H. P. Grice, "Logic and Conversation," in P. Cole and J. L. Morgan (eds.), *Syntax and Semantics,* vol. 3: Speech Acts (New York: Academic Press, 1975), pp. 41–58 and C. D. McCann and E. T. Higgins, "Individual Differences in Communication: Social Cognitive Determinants and Consequences," in H. E. Sypher and J. L. Applegate (eds.), *Communication by Children and Adults,* (Beverly Hills, Calif.: Sage, 1984), pp. 172–210.

obtain rewards relatively equally, and provide a sense of romance for the relationship. Violations of these rules were the most common reasons attributed for breaking up in relationships.[9]

Argyle and Henderson studied rules in same-sex friendships and found many commonly accepted rules, including: volunteer help in time of need, respect the other person's privacy, address the other person by his/her first name, do not discuss that which is said in confidence with the other person, trust and confide in the other, stand up for the other person in his/her absence, etc.[10] These rules obviously have some cross-contextual applications, but many are also obviously not standard (e.g., addressing the other person by first name is *not* a consistently appropriate rule for romantic intimate relationships, since personal idioms seem a more appropriate sign of bonding and affection in such relationships).

The final type of rule is coordinative. *Coordinative rules* refer to the procedural aspects of managing conversational interaction. These rules help coordinate the many complex behaviors involved in the sequencing, topical flow, and initiating and terminating of conversational turns and episodes. These are probably the rules of which communicators are least consciously aware, and yet may be the most advanced and complex of the rule systems. A sample of these rules is provided in table 10.1

Like all communication rules, these rules are guidelines for behavior. We tend to behave according to such rules because they make interaction more efficient, more successful, or more satisfying. We are not bound by them. Consequently, we may often find ourselves violating such rules, either intentionally or unconsciously. Nevertheless, across most conversations, especially in informal, nonintimate, social relationships, we tend to abide by these rules and express disapproval when they are not followed. Such disapproval may be very indirect, as in choosing to interact less with the other person than we might otherwise. More direct sanctioning might involve interruptions, frowning, or open discussion of the violation. Still, *as a rule,* communicators tend to follow these conversational rules.

The Importance of Rules

The reasons *why* communicators have developed and follow rules such as those outlined in table 10.1 will be dealt with more completely in the next chapter. For right now, it is only important to point out that without such guidelines for coordination of conversational behavior, communication might be virtually impossible. What, for example, keeps people in a group of interactants from constantly interrupting and piling unrelated statement upon unrelated statement? What keeps the lapse of time occurring between speaking turns to an average of approximately two to three seconds? Humans, with their unique capacity for communication, have evolved complex yet collectively unrecognized rules for engaging in conversation. Without these rules, conversation might resemble the city streets if there were no traffic signs, signals, or regulations. Chaos would ensue until a system of rules was developed.

As a subtle but vital illustration of the importance of rules, consider the conversational rule that requires people to speak honestly (as Lewis Carroll might say, they should mean what they say and say what they mean). Without this simple assumption underlying our day-to-day interaction with others, it would be an enormous challenge to ever accomplish anything through communication. Consider the alternatives to assuming that people speak honestly. Either they do not say what they mean, or they may or may not mean what they say. At this point, it should be clear that statements as mundane as "I hope you have a nice day" and "Take care of yourself" become challenging and problematic. If such straightforward statements as these become difficult to interpret, then such communication events as corporate negotiation, international diplomacy, and interpersonal conflict, where interactant motives may already be questionable, become truly tangled webs of symbols.

Many of us have experienced the problems that can occur when conversational rules are not followed. If you have ever tried to carry on a conversation with a person who constantly interrupts you while you are talking, you recognize how frustrating it can be to have someone "invade and capture" your conversational "territory." Some of you will have encountered "conversational entrapment," where someone insists upon keeping you in a conversation in which you do not want to partake. You feel trapped to the extent that you make several moves to exit or end the conversation (e.g., orienting body away from conversant) decreasing eye contact, and providing minimal response feedback, and yet the other person seems oblivious to your desire to remove yourself from the conversation. Events such as interruptions and conversational entrapment are likely to lead to very dissatisfying interactions, and ultimately, may lead to failed interpersonal relationships.

In addition to the awkwardness of interacting with others who violate communication rules, it seems that we tend to be victims of rule violations ourselves. For example, rule violation is one of the major sources of embarrassment for people.[11]

Embarrassment is an uncomfortable feeling of heightened self-attention resulting from a recognition that rules of conduct have been violated in a manner that negatively reflects upon self in the eyes of valued others. Embarrassment is in turn closely associated with feelings of social anxiety, shyness, shame, and even self-blame and lowered self-esteem. We have all experienced times of embarrassment, and, while not all such experiences are necessarily devastating, for some people these encounters have lasting psychological effects.

Conversational entrapment occurs when one person insists upon keeping the other engaged in talk and is oblivious to the situation.

One of the possible results of rule violation, and perhaps the resulting embarrassment, is a sense of regret. In a study of regrettable messages, Knapp, Stafford and Daly found that people had no shortage of examples of regrettable events. A regrettable message was viewed as a statement that threatened the "face" or intended image of a person. In all, eleven types of regrettable messages were identified, most of which can be viewed as rule-violating statements: blunder, direct attack, group reference, direct criticism, reveal/explain too much, agreement changed, implied criticism, lie, behavioral edict, expressive/catharsis, and double entendre.[12] Most of us can think of times when we violated rules with such statements, and these episodes continually haunt our memories for years into the future. Since communication is not reversible, once something is said it can never be unsaid.

Rules may also be important because they help achieve a certain enforceable order or structure in our relationships with others. Since rules are prescriptive or proscriptive, and therefore carry sanctions for violators, rules help maintain predictability and order in relationships. For example, in a study of "moral violations" shown in soap operas (e.g., bigamy is wrong, rape is wrong, blackmail is wrong), "deceit" was the most commonly shown moral addressed (and a rule rather than a moral, according to our definition). Most of the occurrences of deceit were "actual" rather than only intended or attempted. Interestingly, in the clear majority of instances, violation of rules led to an episode in which the violation was sanctioned by opposition, warning, or punishment by other characters and resolution of the violation occurred that was consistent with the original rule.[13]

In a related study, Baxter and Wilmot studied the concept of "taboo topics" in interpersonal relationships. A *taboo topic* is some area of discussion that is perceived "off limits" to the relationship partners. As such, taboo topics reflect interactants' evolution of relationship-specific rules for managing certain subject areas. The researchers found that most taboo topics fell into one of the following categories.

By far the most common type of taboo topics concerned the *state of the relationship*. These were topics that dealt with the current or future nature of the relationship. A second type of taboo topic regarded *extra-relationship activity,* in which activities and network involvement outside the immediate relationship were considered off limits for discussion. *Relationship norms* formed a third category, including explicit rules for behavior within the relationship (e.g., an understanding not to talk about each others' parents-in-law). Many people indicated that *prior relationships* (e.g., especially discussions of previous opposite-sex relationships) were to be avoided as a topic of discussion, as were *conflict-inducing topics* (e.g., topics that indicate the dissimilarity of the parties) and *negative self-disclosures* (e.g., disclosures that cast one in a negative light).[14]

The implicit rules underlying these taboo topics are clear. These topics were found to be contextual, in that they varied in their frequency across relationship types (e.g., platonic, romantic potential, romantic) and the reasons for keeping the topics taboo. In each case, the most common reason why the topic was taboo was the perception by the interactants that discussion of the subject would be destructive or damaging to the relationship. Rather than constantly having to renegotiate and resolve these issues over and over, the relationships found a way to develop rules against even discussing these potential danger areas. Thus, the rules serve to make the relationships more manageable and possibly more satisfying.

Competence in Using Rules

Competence in communicating requires attention to the rules that interactants apply in various contexts. There is no easy or simple way of assuring skill at applying, adapting, and developing rules for social interaction, but there are several factors that an interactant should try to be sensitive to when facing a prospective communication encounter.

1. *Analyze the context.* Spitzberg and Cupach indicate that contexts can be understood according to four specific questions.[15] First, what culture is this? Obviously, the culture influences what behavior is appropriate. Even something as straightforward as a greeting ritual varies significantly across cultures. Whereas a

handshake is appropriate in North America (although shaking hands with a female is a somewhat less rigid expectation), in many Pacific rim countries a bow is appropriate. Interpersonal distance during interaction, personal grooming habits, gestures, colloquialisms, and a plethora of communicative routines vary radically across cultural contexts. If you are "in" another culture, careful observation of those around you should assist in knowing how to adapt to the extant rule system.

The second question to ask is "Where is this?" We all intuitively recognize that certain environments call for different behaviors. A library or church tends to call for fairly subdued behavior, whereas a family room in one's home may allow for virtually any type of behavior. Certain environments tend to be more public than private, more formal than informal, more quiet than busy, etc. These types of distinctions generally imply different rules regarding behavior within those situations.

The third question in analyzing contexts is "What type of situation is this?" This question involves ascertaining what is "going on," or what the interactants are primarily attempting to accomplish in a communication episode. There may be many types of situations contained within a given cultural and environmental context. Thus, during an evening at home with your family, there may be a conflict episode, a time when someone is instructing someone else how to do something, a casual get-acquainted conversation with a sibling's friend who drops by, a formal ritual of saying a prayer before dinner, and a group discussion regarding family finances. Each of these episodes varies in terms of its function, or what the interactants are attempting to accomplish through their interaction. As a result, the appropriate behavior is different for each situation because different rules are being applied to each.

The fourth question concerning contexts is "What is my relationship to others in this context?" As indicated throughout the text, the relationship you have with someone strongly affects the type of behavior you engage in with that person. You behave very differently with a superior at work than you do with a romantic intimate. You interact differently with a friend than you do with your parents. People evolve idiosyncratic, or unique, rules for their ongoing relationships. You may have a certain greeting ritual or nickname for a given person that you do not use in other relationships. You may have worked out a way of engaging in conflict with a parent that you do not consider appropriate with a boss. Attending to the expectations and behavioral rules of your particular relationship allows you to adjust your behavior more carefully to the interaction context.

2. *Know the various features of rules.* Simply knowing what the rules are is only one way in which you can fully comprehend the rules of a context. Indeed, there are at least four ways in which you can "know" a rule or set of rules. First, you can articulate some form of the rule itself (e.g., when at a party, one should express appreciation or thanks to the host). Second, you should be able to recognize what constitutes evidence of rule violation or infringement (e.g., by not talking to the host, leaving the party without saying goodbye, or recognizing a nonverbal display of disappointment or anger by the host, one may conclude that the appreciation rule has been violated). Third, you can understand the nature of sanctions applied upon violating the rule (e.g., by violating the appreciation rule, one risks not being invited to future parties). Fourth, you can infer the existence of rules through observation of complex behavioral patterns of others (e.g., through observing others departing the party, you notice that all give their thanks and regards to the host, albeit in a variety of ways to different degrees of elaboration). This latter way of knowing a rule is simply a way of noticing sometimes subtle regularities in behavior and determining an implicit rule of conduct from those regularities.[16]

3. *Anticipate remedial strategies.* Occasionally, almost regardless of how skilled you are or how attentive you are to social rules, you are likely to violate a valued rule. When rules are violated, most people engage in attempts at remediation. That is, people try to repair the damage that was done or that is thought to have been done. There are a variety of strategies for repairing possible harm due to rule violation and embarrassment. One may *apologize* by expressing guilt about violating a rule, expressing remorse about having disturbed a "victim," and expressing embarrassment. One may attempt to repair a violation by *accounting* for the violation. An account may attempt to excuse the behavior (i.e., deny responsibility) or justify the behavior (i.e., accept responsibility but deny the negative aspect or effect). A person may simply *avoid* a rule-violation situation through exiting the context or by preventing the rule violation through careful monitoring of the situation and making behavioral adjustments. Finally, a person may rely on *humor* to manage impressions resulting from rule violation by diffusing or recasting the evaluation.

Cupach and Metts recommend that a person facing an embarrassing incident should proceed along three steps in remedying the situation. First, regain poise immediately after the incident. This means that the order of the context should be smoothly reestablished. This demonstrates that you have enough composure to let the embarrassing incident pass without debilitating your performance. By restoring "normal" action, you also demonstrate understanding of what the situation is supposed to be about, implying that the rule-violation was not reflective of your ignorance or inattention. Second, attempt to manage the negative attributions of others. Excuses and apologies appear to be relatively effective at accomplishing this step, partly because they demonstrate an attention to the importance of others' evaluations and standards. Third, in extreme rule-violations, attempt to repair the "face" of others.[17] In cases of bizarre or extremely rude behavior, those in attendance are likely to be "embarrassed for" the violator. Thus, appropriate remediation is likely to involve the expression of guilt or remorse, perhaps the denial of any role of the others in causing the incident, and an offer to make restitution in some way if the harm can be repaired. Generally speaking, justification is not likely to be very effective when the offense is severe.

4. *Recognize when rules should be negotiated, adapted, or violated.* In the vast majority of instances, the more a person conforms to the rules of a context, the more competent that person is likely to be. However, there are instances in which rules need to be altered or violated in order to accomplish certain objectives or to be viewed as competent in the long term. Generally speaking, you should work to redefine or develop *new* rules in a relationship when the existing rules are no longer functional for the participants. This can often be done simply by calling attention to aspects of behavioral tendencies that hurt or impair relationship satisfaction or productivity. In the process of examining the behavior, new agreements or understandings can be reached.

In some instances, there are actually reasons to violate a rule. Generally speaking, violating an extremely important and valued rule greatly threatens a person's impression of competence. However, there may be times when violation of relatively minor rules may actually be allowed or preferred. In an interview situation, the interviewee may be able to violate, and then transform, the context into a get-acquainted episode. On a first date, a person may disclose something very personal and subsequently find out that the other person had a very similar experience to tell and can appreciate an opportunity to get it out in the open. Some research has found that minor pratfalls or slip-ups can often enhance a person's interpersonal attractiveness, apparently by making the person seem more human and like us.[18]

Other research indicates that people who expect to fail in a social encounter (e.g., interview) may sometimes engage in *strategic failure* so as to create lower expectations and standards of evaluation.[19] In this way, a person may violate a rule so that high standards of competence will not be applied, and it will be easier to live up to the lower standards applied. This form of achieving competence through incompetence is not the most preferred approach to communication, but it does illustrate the complexity of the process, as well as the many ways in which a person can adapt behavior to the context to achieve valued outcomes.

Summary

In this chapter, you discovered that underlying most interpersonal transactions are rules that govern the conduct of communication. The nature and characteristics of communication rules were identified and distinguished from norms, conventions, morals, and laws. Rules were found to facilitate the accomplishment of goals, regulate interaction, interpret messages, explain behavior, and manage the specific aspects of communication transaction. Three types of rules were identified: standard, contextual, and coordinative. The importance of rules in competently handling conversation and avoiding embarrassment was examined. Finally, a number of general principles of applying rules were outlined, suggesting that careful attention to the context and the opportunities for rule clarification and negotiation will usually enhance one's competence in interpersonal communication.

While rules are the general prescriptive standards underlying everyday conversation, there are also specific behaviors that actually implement the moment-to-moment processes of interpersonal transaction. Furthermore, there are forms of knowledge that inform these processes, allowing us to competently perform such specific behaviors as turn-taking, topic management, and conversational initiation and ending. These processes comprise the subject of conversational coordination, which will be taken up in the next chapter.

Notes

1.   S. B. Shiminoff, *Communication Rules: Theory and Research* (Beverly Hills, Calif.: Sage.)

2.   R. H. Price and D. L. Bouffard, "Behavioral Appropriateness and Situational Constraint as Dimensions of Social Behavior," *Journal of Personality and Social Psychology* 30(1974): 579–86; see also M. Argyle, A. Furnham and J. A. Graham, *Social Situations* (Cambridge, England: Cambridge University Press, 1981).

3. M. Argyle and M. Henderson, *The Anatomy of Relationships* (London: Heinemann, 1985).

4. See P. Brown and S. Levinson, "Universals in Language Usage: Politeness Phenomena," in E. N. Goody (ed.), *Questions and Politeness* (Cambridge, England: Cambridge University Press, 1978).

5. See Argyle and Henderson.

6. See Argyle, Furnham and Graham.

7. R. Hopper, M. L. Knapp, and L. Scott, "Couples' Personal Idioms: Exploring Intimate Talk," *Journal of Communication* 31(1981): 23–33.

8. J. S. Sanders and W. L. Robinson, "Talking and Not Talking About Sex: Male and Female Vocabularies," *Journal of Communication* 79(1979): 22–30.

9. L. A. Baxter, "Gender Differences in the Heterosexual Relationship Rules Embedded in Break-up Accounts," *Journal of Social and Personal Relationships* 3(1986): 289–306.

10. M. Argyle and M. Henderson "The Rules of Friendship," *Journal of Social and Personal Relationships* 1(1984): 211–38.

11. See R. J. Edelmann, "Social Embarrassment: An Analysis of the Process" *Journal of Social and Personal Relationships* 2(1985): 195–213; R. J. Edelmann, "Dealing with Embarrassing Events: Socially Anxious and Non-socially Anxious Groups Compared," *British Journal of Clinical Psychology* 24(1985): 281–88.

12. M. L. Knapp, L. Stafford, and J. A. Daly, "Regrettable Messages: Things People Wish They Hadn't Said," *Journal of Communication* 36(1986): 40–58.

13. J. C. Sutherland and S. J. Siniawsky, "The Treatment and Resolution of Moral Violations on Soap Operas." *Journal of Communication* 32(1982): 67–74.

14. L. A. Baxter and W. W. Wilmot. "Taboo Topics in Close Relationships," *Journal of Social and Personal Relationships* 2(1985): 253–69.

15. B. H. Spitzberg and W. R. Cupach, *Interpersonal Communication Competence,* (Beverly Hills, Calif.: Sage, 1984).

16. P. Collett, "The Rules of Conduct," in P. Collett (ed.), *Social Rules and Social Behaviour,* (Oxford England: Basil Blackwell, 1977).

17. W. R. Cupach and S. Metts, "Remedial Strategies in Embarrassment," Unpublished manuscript, Illinois State University. See also W. R. Cupach, S. Metts, and V. Hazleton, Jr., "Coping with Embarrassing Predicaments: Remedial Strategies and Their Perceived Utility," *Journal of Language and Social Psychology* 5(1986): 181–200; C. A. Riordan, N. A. Marlin, and R. T. Kellogg,

"The Effectiveness of Accounts Following Transgression," *Social Psychology Quarterly* 46(1983): 213–19; M. B. Scott and S. M. Lyman, "Accounts," *American Sociological Review* 33(1970): 42–62.

18. R. Helmreich, E. Aronson and J. LeFan, "To Err is Humanizing—Sometimes: Effects of Self-esteem, Competence, and a Pratfall on Interpersonal Attraction," *Journal of Personality and Social Psychology* 16(1970): 269–78.

19. A. H. Baumgardner and E. A. Brownlee, "Strategic Failure in Social Interaction: Evidence for Expectancy Disconfirmation Processes," *Journal of Personality and Social Psychology* 52(1987): 525–35.

Additional Readings

Argyle, Michael, Furnham, Adrian, and Graham, Jean Ann. *Social Situations.* Cambridge, England: Cambridge University Press, 1981.

Chomsky, Noam. *Rules and Representations.* New York: Columbia University Press, 1980.

Cooper, David E. *Knowledge of Language.* New York: Humanities Press, 1975.

Harré, Rom and Secord, Paul F. *The Explanation of Social Behaviour.* Totowa, N.J.: Littlefield, Adams, 1973.

Harré, Rom. *Social Being.* Totowa, N.J.: Littlefield, Adams, 1980.

Pearce, W. Barnett and Cronen, Vernon E. *Communication, Action, and Meaning.* New York: Praeger, 1980.

Pfeiffer, J. William, ed. *A Handbook of Structured Experiences for Human Relations Training.* Vol. X. Human Resources Development Series. San Diego: University Associates, 1985.

Potter, Jonathan and Wetherell, Margaret. *Discourse and Social Psychology: Beyond Attitudes and Behavior.* Newbury Park, Calif.: Sage, 1987.

Schlenker, Barry R. *Impression Management: The Self-concept, Social Identity, and Interpersonal Relations.* Monterey, Calif.: Brooks/Cole, 1980.

Shimanoff, Susan B. *Communication Rules: Theory and Research.* Beverly Hills, Calif.: Sage, 1980.

Smith, Dennis and Williamson, L. Keith. *Roles, Rules, Strategies, and Games,* 3d ed. Dubuque, Ia.: Wm. C. Brown, 1985.

Conversational Coordination

Drabble   by Kevin Fagen

© 1981 United Feature Syndicate, Inc. Reprinted by permission.

Any American-born speaker of English is immediately able to sense that something is odd about Norman's family conversation. Most would even be able to articulate a reason for the oddity. The characters' statements seem to go in different directions simultaneously. The conversation begins on track, but as the father begins a new dyadic conversation with the younger son, Norman continues on in a single-minded sequence of statements as if he were still in conversation with the father. Further, Norman's statements at first seem intent upon being polite and not taking the last morsel of food. The facade of this politeness is ultimately dropped in favor of hunger. Thus, although his last statement seems inconsistent with his former statements, this oddity does not seem too disruptive, since politeness rituals often are performed merely to "go through the motions."

These types of issues are involved with managing the ebb and flow of speaking turns in conversational interaction; that is, coordinating communication. This chapter will examine the skill of conversational coordination. Its nature and importance will be examined, and techniques for improving your conversational coordination will be outlined. Finally, the relationship of communicative knowledge and conversational coordination will be examined.

The Nature of Conversational Coordination

Imagine trying to dance with someone who is attempting to dance a slow dance step while you are attempting something more akin to a twist. Such a bizarre event would not only be embarrassingly tedious, it probably could not even be sustained for more than a brief moment. Now imagine watching the first rehearsal for a play in which the actors have all received independent instruction on where to move onstage. The resulting chaos would be comical in its lack of coordination. These imaginary visions illustrate the importance of synchrony, or meshing, of action when people are attempting to accomplish a coordinated plan of action.

We often do not think of conversation as being a "coordinated plan of action," although if you consider it carefully, successful conversation must conform to this notion. Conversations must be coordinated in much the same sense as the previously mentioned dance and play if they are to succeed in sharing any common meaning between interactants. True, most of us have at some time or another been taught how to dance, and actors in a play tend to receive fairly specific direction in their movements. However, as we found in the last chapter, conversations have their own set of general directions in the form of rules. In addition, since these rules specify that statements should be topically related and interruptions should be avoided, coordination is required among participants to assure that such rules can be followed.

The fact that conversations maintain some level of coordination is most apparent when such coordination is absent. Norman's statements are not coordinated with those of his father, and the lack of this coordination is immediately apparent. Most of us have had interactions with people with whom we just could not seem to connect or get in sync. Most of us have encountered conversations in which we want to end the conversation, but the other person seems completely inattentive to the cues we provide toward this end. And most of us have experienced the aggravation of someone interrupting us while we were in the middle of saying something. You may even have experienced an episode in which someone utters a statement such as, "Well, if you're not going to let me speak, I may as well leave, because it's obvious you don't want to *discuss* the issue." The disruption, resentment, conflict, and occasional fights that ensue from such lack of coordination are clear evidence of the extent to which we rely on conversational coordination in our day-to-day conversation.

Conversations are also plans of action in the sense that participants are attempting to accomplish something through their conversations. Goals underlie virtually all our communication, even when we are not particularly aware of them. Thus, to *have* a conversation requires that at least two interactants attempt to implement certain plans for achieving goals in a coordinated manner.

We have been referring to conversational coordination without defining it. *Conversational coordination* is the process of managing speaking turns and the initiation and conclusion of conversational episodes to the mutual satisfaction of participants. Although the notion of a speaking turn itself may seem fairly obvious, it is not easy to precisely define. For example, if a person says something to reinforce what you are saying while you are saying it, is this a speaking turn? Normally, such behavior fits into a class of behavior known as backchannel responses.

Backchannel responses consist of behavior, usually brief and relatively nondisruptive, that a listener uses to provide feedback to the person speaking. There are six general types of backchannel responses. *Verbal reinforcers* are short utterances that provide feedback to the speaker on the listener's understanding of the statements (e.g., "m-hm," "yeah," "right," "sure," "I see," etc.). *Completions* are instances in which a listener fills in the speaker's utterance with a phrase or word without disrupting the speaker or keeping the speaker from continuing. *Clarification requests* are verbal (e.g., "huh?," "what?") or nonverbal (e.g., a puzzled facial expression) responses indicating a need for elaboration, repetition, or clarification of some sort. *Restatements* are backchannels when a very brief summary or rewording of some aspect of the speaker's statements is provided in a questioning manner (e.g., the speaker saying " . . . and next Wednesday we are . . ." while the listener simultaneously says "You mean next Thursday?"). *Head movements* can be considered a separate class of backchannels, given their potential for indicating agreement and approval or disagreement and disapproval without verbally disrupting the speaker's turn. Finally, *smiles* constitute a form of backchannel, since listeners frequently use such responses to indicate not only appreciation and approval but also an implicit acceptance of the speaker's turn ownership.

Understanding backchannel responses makes it a little more clear what is considered a true speaking turn and what is not. However, before speaking turn can be defined, another form of communicative behavior needs to be examined: silence. At first, silence seems to be easily understood. It is, in fact, easy to define and measure. When no one is talking, it is silence. However, the occurrence of silence in interaction makes the understanding of turns very difficult. When silence occurs, such questions as "Is the speaker *giving up* a turn, or is it simply a pause?", "If two or more conversants simultaneously start to speak after a silence, and only one continues, is this considered an interruption?," or "If there is a long pause of silence in the middle of a speaker's turn but between two clear sentences or grammatical utterances, should this be considered one turn or two?" arise. Obviously, the implications of silence are not as straightforward as they might seem.

Conversational coordination is like the subtle choreography of a well executed dance.

For purposes of understanding the concept of a speaking turn, two types of relevant silence are defined. A *hesitation pause* is the occurrence of silence in which the speaker talks before and after the silence. This is a silence usually associated with thinking and planning what is about to be said.[1] A *switching pause* is a silence in which different speakers occupy the time before and after the pause. This type of pause is the silence for which turn-taking is most relevant and important. It is in such brief pauses that control of the conversation is usually relinquished and captured.

Given these considerations, a *speaking turn* may be generally defined as a verbal utterance bounded by at least one switching pause. That is, a turn is the time a person talks that is bracketed between the verbal utterances of another speaker or speakers. You may wonder why the definition only requires a minimum of *one* switching pause. The reason is that interruptions can involve simultaneous talk and therefore no pause. Whether or not the interruption is *successful* (i.e., gains a speaking turn for the interrupting person) is then defined by whether or not the interrupting utterance is then bounded by a switching pause at its end. Sometimes interruptions are unsuccessful, and a brief flurry of statements or words are used by the interactants before control of the turn is returned to the original speaker.

Like so much of communication, when these definitions are specified, they seem to be "common sense." However, it is rare that a person is able to identify and articulate these concepts. The practical benefit of identifying these concepts is that they allow a more precise understanding of the processes through which interactants manage the microscopic aspects of their conversations. For example, your ability to manage the turn-taking and topic development aspects of conversations dramatically influences others' impressions of your competence.[2] These processes, and the rules and norms that are reflected in the processes, are more fully developed in the next two sections.

Basic Behaviors and Processes

Components of turn exchanges.   Conversational coordination is the subtle choreography of social interaction. It is what keeps our conversations from evolving into complete chaos of people speaking simultaneously or the tragedy of not speaking at all. Although most of us are relatively adequate at negotiating the turn-taking of conversations, few of us would be able to identify *how* we are able to accomplish this. That is, most people are not very aware of the specific cues and behaviors they use to regulate turn-taking in conversations. Indeed, we may process many of these cues at a level of low cognitive awareness. Over time, as we develop from infancy to adulthood, we seem to learn to coordinate our speaking turns without knowing that we are learning. To illustrate this, try the following "On Knowing When To Take a Turn" activity.

On Knowing When to Take a Turn

The following list contains several behaviors that may or may not be essential and commonly used in the process of conversational coordination. In addition, there are a few blanks, in the event that you believe that there are important behaviors not listed. In the next column, briefly note in what specific way you think the behavior may be used by conversationalists, if at all. Two examples are provided.

Behavior	How the behavior is used
Audible inhalation (i.e., taking a breath of air)	Ex. Taking a breath indicates that a statement is about to be made
Coughing	Not used for turn-taking
Head Nods	
Establishing Eye Gaze	
Verbal Reinforcers (e.g., "uh-huh," "yeah," etc.)	
Raising Finger	
Smiling	
Paralanguage (e.g., drawl on the final syllable)	
Fillers (e.g., "um," "uh," "you know," "like," etc.)	
Gesturing	

The process of smooth turn-taking and exchange appears to be comprised of two interrelated components. The first is a *turn-relevant period* in which a state of "transition readiness" is created. That is, there are certain places or times in a conversation when the exchange of speaking turns is much more likely than others. Since interactants generally exchange speaking turns fairly smoothly, there must be behaviors that somehow signal that an exchange of turns is appropriate at a certain point in the stream of interaction.

There are five types of behavior that appear to be most important to signalling certain periods during which a turn transition is likely. One of the most important cues is also one of the most obvious: *verbal turn termination cues*. People tend to relinquish speaking turns when they have finished saying what they wanted to say, and what they wanted to say is completed by a recognizable sentence structure. Since people only occasionally speak in formally correct grammatical sentences, interactants come to recognize when

On Knowing When to Take a Turn continued

Sentence Completions (i.e., completing a
   grammatical phrase)

Questions

Pitch/Loudness (e.g., a noticeable drop in pitch/
   loudness)

Intonation Pattern (e.g., any melodic pattern of
   tone or volume)

Interruption

Fidgeting (i.e., adaptors such as hair-twirling or
   tapping fingers)

Averting Eye Gaze

As it turns out, all of these behaviors (as well as a few others) have at one time or another been implicated as influencing turn-taking (with the exception of coughing), although the exact nature of their functioning, and their importance in the entire process of coordination, is not yet entirely clear.[3] There is, however, substantial evidence regarding the importance and functioning of a specific subset of the listed behaviors.

"thoughts" are completed by the adequacy of a statement in getting an idea across. In the following brief conversation, notice how unnecessary formal grammar is to understanding the statements. Material needed for grammatical completion is provided in brackets.

Jan: "I'm goin' [home for the weekend]. See ya [Monday]."

Tom: "[Have you] Got anything [that you're] doin' [this weekend]?"

Jan: "[I was thinking that] Jack an' I may catch a movie. [Have] You [got anything going on this weekend]?"

Tom: "[I will be] Studying for a midterm. Sunday may be open [for me to do something other than studying]. [Do you and Jack] Need a double [date for the movie]?"

In this conversation, it is apparent that Jan and Tom are acquainted and have an intuition of how to "fill in the blanks" of each other's statements. But even without the bracketed material, you can probably understand fairly precisely what they imply, and you can probably tell by the nature of their statements when their speaking turns are being turned over to the other person.

There are two common forms of verbal turn termination cues. The first is grammatical completion, just illustrated. This refers to conversational grammar rather than formal grammar. Generally, such completions can be thought of as "thought units." *Thought units* represent something a communicator is thinking and wants to get across through verbal utterances. When a listener recognizes that a thought has been expressed verbally, it often indicates that the speaker is ready for the listener to respond by taking over the turn.

The second verbal turn termination cue is more difficult to define. It involves an almost ritualistic or stereotyped expression that consistently tends to evoke a certain set of expected responses. Such expressions are referred to as *sociocentric sequences.* Some of these phrases are easy to recognize, such as in the greeting ritual (e.g., "Hi." "Hi. How are you?" "Fine. You?"). In this example, certain statements, though they may express little in the way of an idea and even less in the way of grammatical completeness, still signal a clear time for the other person to respond. Other examples are phrases tagged to the end of statements, such as "you know," "or something," or "you see."

The next type of cue associated with turn-relevant periods is the *switching pause.* The most opportune time for any prospective speaker to initiate or take a turn is when no one else is currently talking. Thus, pauses present the most obvious and unambiguous time at which others can obtain a speaking turn.

The third type of cue is any form of *gesticulation* or gesture. There are two common forms of gesturing, and only one is a cue for turn-taking. *Body-focused* gestures are often called adaptors and involve some type of touching of the person's own body (e.g., twirling hair, scratching, rubbing nose, tapping feet, drumming or playing with pencil, etc.). You may think of these gestures as forms of fidgeting or signs of anxiety.

The only way in which this type of gesticulation has been found to be related to turn exchange is by excluding object-focused gestures. *Object-focused gestures* are those that illustrate, complement, or substitute for verbal statements. If you ask someone directions for getting somewhere nearby, they are likely to supplement their explanation with a number of gestures involving pointing, turning, etc. More subtle forms involve such moves as motioning your open palm up in a partial arc or directing your index finger toward the listener when trying to make a point. The relaxation of a tensed hand is itself an indication of completion of the gesture, which was part of the speaking turn.

Such gestures seem to provide a sense of completion to verbal utterances by supplying enough information to allow sufficient interpretation of the speaker's statement. However, gestures also cancel out other turn-taking cues. That is, a speaker can retain a speaking turn by using a gesture during an internal pause. Such action seems to communicate the message that "even though I am not talking, I am still communicating, so please keep listening while I formulate my next statement." Such gestures would be expected to accompany what is referred to as dramatic pauses, in which the speaker wants to emphasize a point by a pause but not relinquish the speaking turn.

The fourth cue associated with turn exchange involves *intonation*. There are two intonation patterns that appear to cue turn termination. First, deviations from a level, or relatively constant, pitch toward the last syllables of a phrase or word appear to indicate the completion of an utterance. Second, a paralinguistic drawl on final syllables tends to indicate that the turn is not relinquished. Such a drawl seems to imply that the speaker is holding the turn by elongating the previous utterance until the next statement can be formulated and uttered.

Finally, although the evidence is not entirely consistent, *eye gaze* apparently plays a complex role in coordinating the exchange of speaking turns. When gaze is directed at the listener by the speaker, it cues that a turn is being yielded. In addition, an aversion of eye gaze toward the speaker by a listener at the point of verbal interruption appears to signal an actual attempt at turn-taking rather than backchannelling. That is, listeners who intend to actually become speakers are more likely to turn their heads away from the current speaker when interrupting the speaker. Such behavior makes it more difficult for the interrupted speaker to regain immediate control because there is less access to the new speaker's perceptual field.

The importance of these verbal turn termination cues is obvious, but their interrelationships are extremely complex. For example, Duncan and Fiske found one or more of these cues to have occurred in over 99 percent of the smooth turn transitions they studied.[4] In a small sample of conversational behavior, Beattie found that some 61 percent of turn exchanges involved clause completions, and almost 95 percent of turn exchanges involved changes in pitch level. However, Beattie also found in his research that approximately 14 percent of exchanges constituted "silent interruptions," in which a listener capitalized on an incomplete utterance of the speaker in the apparent absence of any of the other turn termination cues. In addition, there appears to be no specific threshold or combination of cues that clearly signals that a turn-relevant period is occurring.[5] The key is that, across most conversations and conversational partners, it appears that the smooth transition of speaking turns is accomplished through the mastery of these five turn-exchange cues. The better you attend to and perform these behaviors, the more likely it is that you will be viewed as a competent communicator.

Turn-exchange rules.   Now that we have a better understanding of turn termination cues, it is possible to examine the second basic process involved in turn exchange: *turn exchange rules.* Turn exchange rules help coordinate the smooth transition of turns by providing an essential logic to turn exchange during turn-relevant periods. These rules have been extensively studied and

Gazing at a particular person at the end of a thought likely designates that person as the next speaker.

illustrated by Sacks, Schegloff, and Jefferson. These researchers identified what appears to be a relatively simple system that communicators use during conversation. This system consists of four relatively straightforward rules.

1. *The current speaker may designate the next speaker.* This may be accomplished through a variety of means. For example, directing a question to a particular person essentially nominates that person to be the next speaker. Directing eye gaze to a particular person at the end of a thought unit is likely to designate that person as the next speaker. The selected person is assumed to have exclusive speaking rights until relinquished through the normal processes of turn exchange.

2. *Failing rule number one, a listener may or may not choose to initiate a turn.* At the end of the speaker's turn, in the event that the speaker has not designated a particular person to take the next turn, any interactant present may elect to begin speaking. Upon so choosing, the new speaker is assumed to hold all the same speaking prerogatives as the previous speaker. Generally speaking, the first person to utter words during such a turn-relevant period is assigned the role of speaker.

3. *Failing rule number two, the original speaker may or may not choose to continue.* If no listener chooses to initiate a turn, the speaker may decide to reinitiate his or her speaking turn. At this point, as in rule two, the new turn begins the sequence of rules back at rule one. That is, once anyone has successfully accepted the role of speaker, the rule sequence restarts at rule number one.

4. *Failing rule number three, the floor remains open until a turn is initiated according to rules one through three.* By this time, we might expect that there would be a fairly noticeable switching pause, and if the previous speaker chooses not to continue, then the rules again apply in sequence to the next prospective speaker.[6]

As indicated in our discussion of rules in Chapter 10, interactants may not be particularly aware of these rules. Furthermore, although these rules have a clear sequence, it is possible that they can be implemented in the virtual blink of an eye. The fact that most turn transitions are handled smoothly and efficiently indicates the quickness with which such complex processes are managed.

In summary, there are two basic processes involved in the coordination of conversational speaking turns. Speakers may indicate a turn-relevant period by displaying any single cue or combination of cues of turn termination. When such cues indicate that a turn may be accessible to others, interactants proceed to implement a sequence of turn exchange rules that regulate which particular interactant will take the floor.

Thus far, the study of turn-taking and exchange may seem relatively trivial, given how specific and particular the skills and processes seem to be. However, the importance of mastering such skills and processes cannot be overestimated. The following section examines the ways in which we come to know about and implement means of conversational coordination.

The Role of Knowledge in Conversational Coordination

Conversation is obviously a very complex process. We have discovered that it is influenced by a myriad of subtle factors, such as rules and speaking-turn dynamics. Yet, we seem only vaguely aware of many of these important factors. This raises the important question of *how* we know how to manage the subtle and complex processes of interpersonal communication. Communicative knowledge may be thought of in terms of the knowledge you already possess and the ways of acquiring new knowledge.

Communicative knowledge functions.   In Chapter 1 we saw how interpersonal communication can be viewed as a system. One of the characteristics of a system is that its components function in some coordinated manner to accomplish certain goals. Since conversations must achieve some minimal level of interpersonal coordination for any other goals to be accomplished, coordination itself becomes a goal for interactants. Thus, communicators must organize and utilize their knowledge of how to communicate in such a way that they can engage in relatively smooth and harmonious interaction.

One comprehensive approach to explaining how we know what to do and how to do it in conversations has been developed by John Greene. Greene identifies seven procedural functions around which communicative knowledge may be organized.[7] These functions represent subgoals of the knowledge system. In other words, when a "macro" goal is established (e.g., to ask someone for a date), a number of subroutines must be performed. Each of these subroutines is further explained.

Interaction functions reflect the more macro level goals of the interactant. An infinite number of particular objectives may be attained, but most interpersonal communication attempts to accomplish one or more of the following functions: pleasure (e.g., to be excited or entertained), affection (e.g., to show support or caring), control (e.g., to influence or obtain something), inclusion (e.g., to have someone to talk to or reduce loneliness), appropriateness (e.g., to do what is expected or proper) and relaxation (e.g., to unwind or diminish stress).[8] These macro goals serve to guide the other processing functions of knowledge search and utilization.

Content formulation functions assist in mentally searching for knowledge regarding what will be discussed and what forms of speech activity will be performed. Knowledge of topics, current events, and people will be accessed to serve these functions. This type of knowledge is referred to as *substantive knowledge,* which refers to the content of what one knows. Interactants probably retain information in at least these eight areas: the drives and goals of people, rules of interaction, roles and role systems, skills and behaviors, sequences of behaviors, situation types, relationship types, and semantic or linguistic content.

Management functions assist in maintaining continuity of topics and initiating and closing conversations, as discussed in chapter 10. Presumably, we possess knowledge of certain rules of conversation. For example, one of the most generally adhered to rules is one of Grice's conversational maxims: make your response topically relevant to the preceding statement (you may want to review table 10.1). This rule, and others like it, function to manage the conversation.

Utterance formulation functions refer to the linguistic requirements of constructing meaningful sentences. This is knowledge in the sense that Chomsky referred to as linguistic competence. It involves our implicit understanding of the rules of syntax, grammar, and semantics involved in generating sentences that can be understood by our conversational partners. We know, for example, that the sentence "Chris is easy to please," is meaningfully different from "Chris is eager to please," even though they are syntactically identical. We also know that a change in syntax from "You can accomplish anything," to "Can you accomplish anything?" creates a very different message, despite the same grammatical elements.

Regulatory functions are relevant to the mechanics of turn-taking and maintaining smooth flow of interaction. Although interactants are rarely aware of the process, they are constantly making minor adjustments to each other in the process of maintaining a flowing conversation. Long pauses generally are avoided by monitoring minute behaviors of eye gaze, inhalation patterns, gesturing, sentence completion, theme coherency, and posture.

Homeostatic functions are those that regulate the balance and overall level of activity in the conversation. For example, two of the basic processes of adaptation in conversation are complementarity and symmetry. *Complementarity* describes a process in which conversationalist B behaves in a style dissimilar to A. Thus, if A is an active communicator (e.g., frequent gesturing, vocal variety, forward lean, etc.), then a complimentary orientation by B would be a fairly inactive or passive style (e.g., rigid posture, monotonous voice, backward lean, etc.). *Symmetry,* in contrast, describes a matching response style. Thus, if A is active, B becomes active. If A leans forward, B leans forward. Homeostatic functions influence these types of "balance" in conversations.

Congruency functions involve the integration of verbal and nonverbal behaviors. When verbal statements (e.g., "That's a very interesting outfit") are stated with inconsistent nonverbal expression (e.g., with a slightly surprised or pained face with pauses punctuating the statement as if it is difficult to find terms that would not sound like insults), one mode will tend to be believed more than the other.[9] Coordinative functions assist in maintaining consistency among the modes of communication.

Each of these functions serve to "instruct" knowledge processing. When the overall goal, for example, is to manage a conflict, each of these functions is coordinated to assist in retrieving only the most relevant knowledge from the memory for use in the encounter. Together, the appropriate verbal and nonverbal behaviors are reproduced in some content form, and the corresponding procedural routines are generated to perform the content.

Procedural knowledge represents another basic form of knowledge. If substantive knowledge is the "what" of communicative knowledge, then procedural knowledge is the "how." Procedural knowledge is the comprehension of how behaviors are performed. For example, consider your application for a driver's license. The written test attempts to assess your knowledge of the content of traffic laws, situations, and practices. The driving portion of the test determines whether you can *use* this content knowledge in actually driving a car. The behaviors you perform in the driver's seat not only rely upon your content knowledge but also involve a fundamentally different set of knowledge processes. Thus, in conversations you may be very knowledgeable regarding the topics discussed, the other person, the context, etc., yet be at a loss concerning how to behave. You have probably encountered a time when you "knew what to say, but couldn't seem to get the words out right." Such experiences reflect the difference between substantive and procedural knowledge.

While it is perhaps difficult to imagine your mind working through all these levels at all times during a typical conversation, it is also hard to imagine all of these functions *not* being performed in a conversation. If your knowledge fails in any one of these functions, the coordination level of the conversation is likely to fall dramatically.

Thus far, we have been primarily discussing knowledge about *how* to engage in communication. Obviously, without such knowledge, conversations might well indeed look like downtown rush-hour traffic with no traffic regulations and drivers who do not know how to drive. However, there is another form of knowledge that can improve the coordination of interpersonal transactions. There is also knowledge *about* the context, the other person, the topic areas, etc. The idea that the ideal communicator is well-versed on a wide variety of subjects dates back to the ancient Greek philosophers. Basically, their premise was sound. The more you know about various topics, people, and places, the easier it is to introduce conversational ideas, expand upon topic areas, ask relevant questions, and predict the flow of the conversation. Further, the more you know in particular about the other person with whom you are conversing, the more you can adapt your communicative style, verbal statements, and actions to mesh with those of your conversational partner. Thus, the more you know in general and the more you know about the other person in particular, the more you are able to coordinate the conversational encounter.

When you interact with someone you know very well, you probably have already developed a conversational style that feels comfortable. However, you may often find yourself in conversations with people you know relatively little about. How do you obtain information or knowledge about such people? Typically, you will try to acquire knowledge through the process of interaction itself. Some of the many ways in which we commonly acquire interpersonal knowledge through communication are described in the next section.

Processual knowledge acquisition.   Doug and Wendy have been in a study group in their communication class for about half of the semester. Doug finds Wendy attractive and wants to ask her out, but he has little idea about how she feels about him. The context of their meetings has always been somewhat constrained by the presence of others and the task-orientation of the group. He has tried to have lunch with her a couple of times after class, but she always seemed to have perfectly legitimate demands on her time that kept her from accepting. Doug thinks she has been friendly to him, but not necessarily any more or less friendly that she is with the other group members.

Doug would like to start dating Wendy, but he does not want to have her refuse, since it might make working with her awkward for the remainder of the semester. Doug has dated before, but he has never really tried to date someone he was also working with on an important project. He also feels that most of those with whom he has initiated relationships in the past had provided fairly clear cues as to their mutual interest.

In this situation, Doug simply does not feel very confident that he knows what to do. He possesses some general knowledge regarding what his communication options are, but these options were derived from encounters that were different from the current situation in important ways. So how does Doug know what to do in this predicament?

Up to this point we have been discussing knowledge as if it is a property that someone "possesses." Yet, it is obvious that people often do acquire knowledge about what to say and do, as well as how to say and do it, over very brief periods of time. An understanding of the means by which people find out about others and situations would seem to be an important area of interpersonal communication.

People tend to have a strong desire to know how to behave appropriately and effectively, so they seek knowledge that facilitates their performance. Since communication is such a complex and subjective process, few clear and unambiguous guides to behavior exist. Books tell a person how to behave in a particular situation. Only occasionally will we find someone we can simply talk to and expect an articulate and legitimate explanation of what to do. And generally speaking, when we are socialized and educated throughout life through family and school, rarely are we formally or explicitly taught about how to communicate better, or how to *find out* how to communicate better. So we are left to a process of trial and error to learn, and learn how to learn, about communication.

People somehow do learn a variety of strategies for acquiring knowledge relevant to communication.[10] These strategies can be viewed as distinct from the substantive and procedural knowledge previously discussed in the sense they involve the acquisition of knowledge rather than its storage, interpretation, and use. In examining the ways in which we gain knowledge in interpersonal settings, we will use the metaphor of espionage. While the world of espionage tends to be viewed either with disdain or intrigue, we use it simply to help understand the various means by which one party comes to know something about the other party.

Interrogation. The most obvious and direct way of finding out information about another person is to ask the person. During initial encounters, questions become one of the primary means of obtaining information about the other person. Such information provides a basis for predicting the other person's responses, determining if a continued relationship is desirable, and a means for maintaining the conversation itself. Questions also serve an ingratiation function, since people perceive questions asked of them to imply interest, concern, and caring on the part of the questioner.

Surveillance. Some interpersonal relationships lend themselves to overt or covert observation over time. In the metaphor of nations, satellites record the activities of other nations. In interpersonal relations, we sometimes have the opportunity to observe another person in a variety of situations that provide a rich source of information about the person. The person who is attracted to a student who plays a sport, is a member of the student senate, and is active in a church organization has ample opportunities for learning about the student. Doug may even be able to observe Wendy in various informal encounters around campus in order to learn more about the kinds of people she knows and with what "groups" she identifies closely.

Exchange. Nations sometimes decide to exchange information. President Reagan promised to share "Star Wars" or Strategic Defense Initiative (SDI) technology with the Soviet Union. In arms talks, the parties generally must exchange information regarding their relative levels of armaments, or the talks are virtually meaningless. In interpersonal relations, people often obtain information through a process of giving information. Generally speaking, and especially in the early stages of relationship development, people tend to match the quantity and intimacy of self-disclosures. This process is commonly referred to as the norm of *reciprocity.* Reciprocity is a strong force in initial interactions. If you want to find out about another person, you can usually do so by disclosing appropriate information about yourself. The norm of reciprocity typically will motivate the other person to disclose information in a similar fashion.

A relatively unexplored form of exchange is the gaming in which people engage. Games such as "Scruples" and "Twenty Questions" provide somewhat artificial formats for obtaining actual information about others. For example, in Scruples, people indicate how they would respond to a problematic ethical or social dilemma, after others in the game have predicted how the respondent would behave. Nations sometimes engage in "war games" with their allies to assess their ability to work together in some future conflict. People may seek out games with others in a similar fashion to explore their compatibility with each other.

Posturing. When nations are posturing, they are behaving in ways that, in effect, test the waters. It involves making moves that are generally compatible with self-interests yet are distinct enough to evoke reactions from others. By observing the reactions of others, information about their values and propensity for action is obtained. In interpersonal relations, a variety of posturing moves is available.

For example, *deviation testing* would involve behaving in a different way than usual, to see the reactions of others. When Anwar Sadat decided to visit Israel, it was a radically surprising occurrence. When Israel welcomed his visit, it set the stage for peace talks and demonstrated that a state of hostility was, in fact, *not* in existence. In interpersonal relationships, initiating a particularly intimate topic for discussion early in an initial encounter may allow the discloser to assess the listener's acceptance of certain rule violations and personal openness. Or, for example, were Doug to be assigned to engage in a class project with Wendy, he might bring up topics about social activities that have nothing to do with class to observe her acceptance of such preludes to personalizing their relationship.

Testing limits is a process in which a person "pushes" another to see their reaction to adverse or difficult dilemmas. For some time, the U.S. response to acts of terrorism was to threaten that its own limits were being pushed too far. Nations may test such limits to examine just how firm another nation's foreign policy is. Similarly, dates who survive their first dinner with the other person's family or parents are often considered to have passed a strong test of relational commitment. Some people have even admitted to bringing a conflict to the surface with their partners as a prelude to relational escalation to see if the relationship could withstand such a strain.

Related to these strategies is the process of *laying traps,* in which situations are devised to test a person's motives or tendencies. Historians have long speculated that many international conflicts have occurred in part because one nation set a stage in which the other would agress and provide an excuse for war. The sinking of the *H. M. S. Lusitania,* the Gulf of Tonkin incident, and even Pearl Harbor have been discussed as situations that may have been in part engineered because the resulting image of the enemy could be used to justify entering into war. In less militaristic settings, a person suspicious of his girlfriend's affection for a previous boyfriend could arrange a party that they both attend. By observing her reactions to the former boyfriend, the trapster may glean information regarding her motives.

Bluffing includes a variety of techniques involving false or ambiguous fronts for the purpose of observing the reactions of others. It is distinguished from posturing in that it usually involves putting forward a partially false front, usually one of strength, whereas posturing behavior is more representative of the party's true interests, whatever they might be. Bluffing typically will involve some sort of subterfuge or ambiguity that allows the bluffer a way out if things go badly. There are at least three kinds of bluffing: joking, hinting, and martyrdom.

Joking frequently allows one the opportunity to observe reactions to serious issues. In the movie *Patton,* General Patton is portrayed in a scene in which the victorious Soviets and Americans are celebrating the victory over Germany in World War II. When the Soviet General offers a toast to General Patton, Patton says he has no intention of drinking with a "Commie !#©%*# !" The potentially explosive situation is calmed when the Soviet General returns the insult, and Patton then treats the entire episode as a humorous event. The humorous form of the probe permits the joker a way out if it is misinterpreted. For example, in trying to find out if Wendy is already committed to another relationship, Doug might make a remark about how "*some* people never have to worry about getting dates" in a mock tone of voice. If Wendy responds "Hey, I'm no better off than anyone else" or "Well, some people have it, and some don't," the bluff worked. If, instead, the person takes it too seriously, the joker can always respond that "it was only a joke." The offhand joke by the person picking up his date that "his Mercedes is in the shop" may well evoke reactions to the concepts of wealth and status that are informative about the person's basic values or even her ability to engage in sarcasm.

Another form of bluffing is *hinting,* in which suggestive but noncommittal statements are made that lead into certain topics or reactions. Labor unions frequently will let statements and rumors surface that they are considering a strike if certain conditions are not met by management in order to see how management reacts. In an interpersonal example, a person sitting on a park bench watching schoolchildren playing might make such a remark to his partner as, "Aren't those little kids cute?" Such a statement could be intended to find out the other person's attitudes to having children and a family. A person on a first date might remark about what a "gorgeous night" it is in order to see how resolved the other person is to returning home immediately.

A slightly more devious form of bluffing involves martyrdom. By *martyrdom* we mean presenting a statement that is intended to be rebuffed by the other person. Nations will occasionally make a statement about how they are being persecuted by another more powerful nation, just in order that the more powerful nation will then have to go on record as not intending any harm to the less powerful nation. Whether or not a rejection is made indicates something about the party's attitudes toward the martyr. If Doug claims, "I really don't think I'm very attractive," it may well simply be attempting to hear Wendy's opinion on the subject.

Of course, these strategies for international intrigue in the interpersonal realm are not the only sources of communicative knowledge in ongoing interaction. People can also rely on creativity, innovation, decision-making, problem-solving, and perspective-taking to assist their search for information and understanding. The point is that interactants rarely have to rely solely upon their existing knowledge of how to behave. Knowledge is a resource, and it is more available to those who know how to acquire it.

The Importance of Conversational Coordination

The image of attempting to drive around a town completely devoid of traffic laws, signs, and regulations is a frightening one. There would be no mutual understanding of what to do at intersections, pedestrians would be on their own, and even the simplest of actions such as changing lanes and regulating your own speed would become new adventures in danger. To some extent, the process of conversation can be likened to a traffic system in which various signals and rules exist for the mutual satisfactory management of action and interaction. Conversation is much more complex than traffic in many ways, and its rules are not as precise or formal. But without some system of rules and competence in working with these rules, conversation might seem as chaotic and psychologically hazardous as the traffic situation with no laws.

Competence in conversational coordination is essential in at least four areas of social functioning. The first area is apparent in the very definition of speaking turns. We cannot fully devote our communicative energies to both speaking and listening simultaneously. Although communicators can simultaneously *process* information at various levels, it appears that it is almost impossible to simultaneously *attend* to more than one train of thought. In addition, the mental activities associated with formulating verbal statements take at least some attention away from actively processing the listener's feedback. Thus, the existence of a coordinated system for exchanging speaking turns is necessary for interpersonal communication to even function at all.

The second area of importance is not as obvious as you might at first think. Studies of infants have increasingly revealed far more complexity and variation in communicative skills than generally assumed by experts in the past. The concept of "taking turns" becomes essential to the infant immediately after birth in such processes as breast feeding. The principle of crying followed by some form of attention reinforces the concept, as in a baby crying to be fed and then being fed.

Turn taking in a somewhat more explicit form has been observed as soon as twelve days after birth in the form of imitation of facial and hand behavior.[11] Such imitation requires a primitive form of turn taking, in which observation of a behavior is followed by an attempt to mimic the behavior. Caretakers engage in a variety of actions to elicit a smile from the infant, and such actions frequently reveal an "on-off" turn taking appearance, as in the game of "peek-aboo." Such interaction between parents and infants has been referred to as a "proto-conversation," implying that it is the first beginnings of a more evolved form of conversational interaction. Mastering such essential forms of turn-taking may be required before language itself is allowed to develop, and certainly such skills seem necessary before interpersonal interaction is possible.

The third way in which conversational coordination skills are important is their influence on control and the perceptions of power. Clearly, to the extent that influence occurs through verbal means, competently managing turn-taking is undeniably vital to obtaining desired goals through interaction. Most experts agree that the skilled management of turn-taking is an integral and essential part of controlling interaction. As Capella forcefully states, "Without the ability to participate equally (or more) in conversations, the opportunity to persuade, argue, influence, decide, and lead does not exist. Participation in conversation may not guarantee power but nonparticipation guarantees powerlessness."[12]

Indeed, research reviewed by Capella and others consistently identifies three behaviors to be strongly related to the perceptions of power.[13] Specifically, frequency of speaking, average or total duration of speaking turns, and frequency of interruption are powerful predictors of impressions of dominance and power. In general, the more one speaks and the less one is successfully interrupted, the more powerful this person is perceived to be.

Even those who believe that the key to influencing others is to yield control to others must concede the importance of mastering the rules of turn taking. Influencing others requires that you participate in, present yourself as, and contribute to a predictable system of interaction.[14] Making the system predictable minimally requires the establishment and reinforcement of rules for

Very young infants have been observed engaging in primitive forms of turn-taking.

who talks when. When you can predict and anticipate who talks when, you can manage and control who talks when. To control sometimes requires letting another control, and to do this, you need to be competent in using the rules to allow others to take control.

The final area of importance for conversational coordination skills is in being viewed as a competent communicator. Research consistently indicates that the extent to which communicators are viewed as socially skilled and dominant depends strongly upon their interaction management skills.[15] Of course, like most skills, too much of a good thing is bad. In a review of this research, Capella estimates that as a person's percentage of time speaking increases relative to other interactants, the less socially attractive that person is viewed as being. As the percentage of speaking time approaches 100 percent, the person may even be viewed as somewhat less powerful relative to a slightly more equitable distribution of speaking times.[16]

Competence in Conversational Coordination

Not surprisingly, then, the extent to which communicators hope to master even the most elemental aspects of conversation, much less be perceived as powerful and competent, depends greatly on the skillful management of turn taking and exchange. While there is no magic formula for competent conversational coordination, there are some general guidelines for improving your turn-taking interaction.

1. *Be attentive to turn-taking and turn-exchanging cues.* The previously reviewed evidence indicates that there are five types of behaviors that cue a transition-relevant period in conversation. Attention to these cues, and their role in regulating speaking turns, should make you more aware of turn-taking dynamics.

2. *Be attentive to turn-taking and turn-exchanging rules.* Once certain cues indicate that a turn-relevant period has arrived in the conversation, it is important to recognize the normal sequence of options available to initiating a turn. Prerogative is generally given to the person relinquishing the turn to define who speaks next. If no choice is made, the turn tends to go to the first person to speak.

3. *Be attentive to how you are synchronizing your own cues.* We have learned that the cues of interaction management are often subtle. If you find yourself avoiding eye contact while simultaneously completing a statement, you may be sending inconsistent cues to others as to whether or not you are through speaking. Attempt to be consistent both within and across conversational speaking turns in your turn-yielding cues.

4. *Be attentive to how you synchronize your cues with others.* In other words, if you find that the person with whom you are speaking displays a particular type of cue upon yielding a speaking turn, you may want to adopt this behavior in your own interaction with this person. This type of adaptation is more likely to allow smooth exchange of speaking turns, as you will both be using the same signal and rule systems.

5. *Avoid disconfirming interruption of others.* Popular advice to the contrary, there are such things as appropriate interruptions. Kennedy and Camden found that 49 percent of the interruptions they studied could be considered "confirming" rather than "disconfirming." Confirming interruptions consisted of two backchannel responses termed "clarification" and "agreement." Clarification interruptions consisted of utterances intended to understand or elaborate the other person's message (e.g., "What do you mean?"). Agreement interruptions represent utterances providing support, reinforcement, or elaboration of the other person's message (e.g., "You ain't kiddin' "). Only approximately 32 percent of the interruptions were clearly disconfirming (i.e., changing the topic or minimizing the topic of the original speaker). These disconfirming interruptions are the type that are most likely to be viewed as disruptive or incompetent.[17]

6. *Avoid overlong speaking turns.* In general, people do not appreciate feeling excluded from conversation by virtue of another person's long-winded nature. Such unbalanced conversations may lead to a sense of conversational entrapment, in which a person feels constrained to stay in the conversation despite being unable or unmotivated to participate in the interaction. Furthermore, people who speak too much are often viewed by others as "being in love with the sound of their own voice" or just "egotistical." By being attentive to the feedback of listeners and by monitoring your own behavior, you can be more careful to avoid appearing too overbearing or domineering.

7. *Be attentive to sanctioning and repairing of rule violations.* People are capable of learning how to manage turn taking more smoothly. However, not everyone is going to know what is occurring that is contributing to the awkwardness of interaction. It is possible to sanction interruptions, for example, through such behavior as a stare, a silence, a statement of resentment, etc. And if you find yourself interrupting, you can seek feedback from the "offended" party regarding the seriousness of the offense (e.g., "Do you mind if I interrupt you here?"), apologize for the offense

(e.g., "I'm sorry for interrupting, but . . ."), etc. Such actions make it clear that smooth interaction, and the rules by which it is achieved, are important.

8. *Provide topical extension for other people's statements.* Competence in managing turn exchange involves more than simply knowing how to take turns. It also involves assisting others in continuing smooth flow of interaction. An interesting study by McLaughlin and Cody studied the occurrence of "awkward silences" in conversation. Awkward silences are those long silences that occur at turn-relevant periods when it seems that no one quite knows what to say and it is unclear who's turn it is to speak. While it may seem a very short time, silences of only three seconds and longer have been found to be awkward. The researchers found that almost 63 percent of awkward silences were preceded by a sequence of minimal responses. That is, turns leading up to the occurrence of an awkward silence tended to provide little new information or topical extension. Without new information or extension of the ongoing topic, the conversations "ran dry" of anything to say.[18] Pay attention to how your statements relate to, draw from, and extend the topic under discussion. By doing so, you are introducing "resources" into the conversation that can then be easily expanded upon without as much complex planning and reformulation of ideas.

9. *Recognize the dyadic nature of conversational coordination.* The research on awkward silences graphically illustrates the extent to which conversants are interdependent. Your partner's ability to smoothly initiate a turn after you have completed your turn depends in part upon your competence in providing something to which to respond. The term "turn taking" implies a somewhat monadic picture of a person simply grabbing a turn. In actuality, smooth interaction requires that both participants cooperate in maintaining a workable system of turn exchange. This means providing and interpreting turn-relevant cues in a consistent and clear manner.

10. *Attend to the contextual nature of conversational coordination.* Like all communication phenomena, turn taking and turn exchanging are influenced by the context. Obviously, household interaction reveals long periods of silence punctuated by periods of interaction. Intimate couples may spend relatively long periods of silence "looking into each other's eyes" and find that it is not unusual for a statement not to be immediately followed up by a topically relevant response. The key is that these examples

illustrate situations in which the communicators understand the rules, even though the rules are not typical of other, more normative social systems and groups. The cues and rules reviewed in this chapter are normative, and may not apply in a particular dyad or group. However, understanding these normative processes is likely to lead to a greater appreciation of, and sensitivity to, any idiosyncratic processes that have evolved. Ultimately, competent conversational coordination is likely to involve the ability to negotiate both normative and idiosyncratic turn-exchanging cues and rules.

Summary

The process of speaking at all in conversation presupposes an ability to exchange and take turns in a coordinated manner. We have found in this chapter that this process, although taken largely for granted, is highly complex. Turns are distinguished from backchannel responses and the role of different types of silence in defining turns is explained. The process of turn exchange is viewed as a product of mastering a set of turn-relevant period cues and turn-exchange rules.

The importance of mastering conversational coordination is demonstrated by the clear evidence that those who lack such skills are seen as less powerful and less socially skilled. Finally, competence in conversational coordination can be facilitated by being more conscious of the nature of the process and being more appreciative of your own role in assisting others in their turn-taking.

Notes

1. For a thorough examination of these definitions of silence, see M. L. McLaughlin. *Conversation: How Talk is Organized,* (Beverly Hills, Calif.: Sage, 1984). For an analysis of the role of planning and formulating in influencing pauses, see J. N. Capella, "Production Principles for Turn-taking Rules in Social Interaction: Socially Anxious vs. Social Secure Persons," *Journal of Language and Social Psychology* (in press).

2. J. M. Wiemann, "Explication and Test of a Model of Communicative Competence." *Human Communication Research* 3 (1977): 195–213.

3. See J. M. Wiemann and M. L. Knapp. "Turn-taking in Conversations" *Journal of Communication* 25 (1975): 75–92.

4. S. Duncan and D. W. Fiske. *Face-to-Face Interaction,* (Hillsdale, N.J.: Lawrence Erlbaum Associates, 1977).

5. G. W. Beattie. "The Skilled Art of Conversational Interaction: Verbal and Nonverbal Signals in Its Regulation and Management," in W. T. Singleton, P. Spurgeon, and R. B. Stammers (eds.), *The Analysis of Social Skill* (New York: Plenum, 1980), pp. 193–211.

6. H. Sacks, E. A. Schegloff, and G. Jefferson. "A Simplest Systematics for the Organization of Turn Taking for Conversation," in J. Schenkein (ed.), *Studies in the Organization of Conversational Interaction* (New York: Academic Press, 1978), pp. 7–56.

7. J. O. Greene. "A Cognitive Assembly Approach to Human Communication: An Action Assembly Approach," *Communication Monographs.* 51 (1984): 289–306.

8. R. B. Rubin, E. M. Perse, and C. A. Barbato. "Conceptualization and Measurement of Interpersonal Communication Motives," *Human Communication Research* 14, (1988): 602–28.

9. J. K. Burgoon. "Nonverbal Signals," in M. L. Knapp and G. R. Miller (eds.), *Handbook of Interpersonal Communication* (Beverly Hills, Calif.: Sage, 1985), pp. 344–90.

10. For a discussion of research on knowledge acquisition strategies, see C. R. Berger and J. J. Bradac. *Language and Social Knowledge: Uncertainty in Interpersonal Relations* (London: Edward Arnold, 1982).

11. See research reviewed by J. M. Wiemann. "Interpersonal Control and Regulation in Conversation," in R. L. Street, Jr. and J. N. Capella (eds.), *Sequence and Pattern in Communicative Behavior* (London: Edward Arnold, 1985), pp. 85–102.

12. J. N. Capella. "Controlling the Floor in Conversation," in A. W. Siegman and S. Feldstein (eds.), *Multichannel Integrations of Nonverbal Behavior* (Hillsdale, N.J.: Lawrence Erlbaum Associates, 1985), pp. 69–103.

13. See Capella (1985); and D. R. Brandt. "A Systematic Approach to the Measurement of Dominance in Human Face-to-face Interaction," *Communication Quarterly* 28 (1980): 31–43; J. P. van de Sande, "Cue Utilization in the Perception of Dominance," *British Journal of Social and Clinical Psychology* 19 (1980): 311–16.

14. See M. Athay and J. M. Darley. "Toward an Interaction-centered Theory of Personality," in N. Cantor and J. F. Kihlstrom (eds.), *Personality, Cognition, and Social Interaction* (Hillsale, N.J.: Lawrence Erlbaum Associates, 1981), pp. 281–308: S. R. Strong and C. D. Claiborn. *Change Through Interaction* (New York: John Wiley & Sons, 1982), pp. 30–51.

15. See J. P. Dillard and B. H. Spitzberg. "Global Impressions of Social Skills: Behavioral Predictors," *Communication Yearbook* 8 (1984): 446–63; M. T. Palmer. "Controlling Conversations: Turns, Topics and Interpersonal Control," *Communication Monographs* 56 (1989): 1–18.

16. See Capella (1985), p. 81.

17. C. W. Kennedy and C. T. Camden. "A New Look at Interruptions," *Western Journal of Speech Communication* 47 (1988): 45–58.

18. M. L. McLaughlin and M. J. Cody. "Awkward Silences: Behavioral Antecedents and Consequences of the Conversational Lapse," *Human Communication Research* 8 (1982): 299–316.

Additional Readings

Atkinson, J. Maxwell and Heritage, John, eds. *Structures of Social Action: Studies in Conversation Analysis.* New York: Cambridge University Press, 1985.

Craig, Robert T. and Tracy, Karen eds. *Conversational Coherence: Form, Structure, and Strategy.* Beverly Hills, Calif.: Sage, 1983.

Goodwin, Charles. *Conversational Organization: Interaction between Speakers and Hearers.* New York: Academic, 1981.

Haslett, Beth. *Communication: Strategic Action in Context.* Communication Series: Managing Conversations. Hillsdale, N.J.: Lawrence Erlbaum Associates, 1987.

McLaughlin, Margaret L. *Conversation: How Talk Is Organized.* Beverly Hills, Calif.: Sage, 1984.

Richards, Jack and Hull, Jonathan. *As I Was Saying: Conversation Tactics.* Reading, Mass.: Addison-Wesley.

Schenkein, Jim ed. *Studies in the Organization of Conversational Interaction.* New York: Academic, 1978.

Schiffrin, Deborah. *Discourse Markers.* Studies in Interactional Sociolinguistics: No. 5. New York: Cambridge University Press.

Street, R. L., Jr. and Cappella, J. N., eds. *Sequence and Pattern in Communicative Behavior.* London: Edward Arnold, 1985.

Yokoyama, Olga T. *Discourse and Word Order.* Pragmatics and Beyond Series: No. 6. Philadelphia: Benjamins North America, 1987.

Contexts

To this point, we have been examining interpersonal communication in terms of its basic or fundamental components, principles, and processes. You may have been asking yourself how and in what situations you can apply these components, principles, and processes. This section is intended to show you that there are important contexts within which interpersonal communication can be improved. Learning about interpersonal communication does not help you much if you do not know when and where to apply what you have learned. This section covers four of the most important contexts in which the skills you have been learning can be applied.

The first context includes those relationships we have with others that tend to be casual, nonintimate, and non-romantic in orientation. Strangers, acquaintances, and friends may comprise the majority of people with whom adolescents and adults communicate on a day-to-day basis, especially those of who work full-time, who are students, or who are not married or cohabiting. This chapter explains the similarities and differences among these types of relationships and the communication that characterizes each.

The second context examines intimate relationships and communication. Intimate relationships in this sense refer to those relationships that contain a romantic or sexual dimension. The various motivations and values of intimacy are discussed, and the characteristics of intimate communication are identified. Ways of improving communication in intimate contexts are also reviewed.

The third context is one that prevails as a social institution despite the trends examined in chapter 1. The family represents one of the most primary and influential contexts in which our identity is formed. The characteristics that distinguish the family from other social systems are also found to affect forms of communication significantly. Ways of improving family communication and systems are analyzed.

The final context is the interview context. While this context may seem very different from the others, it is similar in terms of its importance to quality of life. Few contexts can be so clearly and unambiguously identified that bear so significant an influence on your quality of life as the job interview. Distilled into one or two relatively brief encounters, a person's value is assessed and a decision is made on the basis of this judgment regarding what kind of organization and job in which this person is allowed to work, possibly for the rest of this person's life. Various characteristics and skills relevant to the interview context are examined, along with some advice in regard to improving your competencies in interview contexts.

Communication always occurs in a context. The contexts in this section represent four of the most common and important types of contexts in which you can communicate. To the extent that you can incorporate the knowledge and skills in the earlier parts of this textbook in understanding these contexts, you will have made an important step toward becoming a competent communicator.

Communication among Strangers, Acquaintances, and Friends

Reprinted with special permission of King Features Syndicate, Inc.

Introductions are indeed precarious. Though we engage in hundreds, perhaps thousands, of introductions to others during our lifetimes, seldom do we contemplate their importance. In this instance, the introduction seems less than optimal, and the character easily recognizes the awkwardness. Furthermore, such incompetence during introductions is likely to jeopardize the development or salvaging of any semblance of a further, satisfying relationship. Thus, if the introduction does not create a positive first impression, it is unlikely that strangers will ever get to be acquaintances, much less friends. This chapter is about the processes through which friendships develop, including the intermediate stages, and types of relationships between strangers and acquaintances.

The Importance of Communication among Strangers, Acquaintances, and Friends

Our culture values human communication. We participate in conversations with persons we have not met previously, persons we know casually, and persons we know very well and acknowledge as our friends. We engage in communication with strangers, acquaintances, and friends for a variety of reasons.

1. We may wish to initiate a relationship with another person. If you regularly ride a bus or a train at a certain time, you may notice that another person similarly uses that form of mass transportation at that time. You may notice that the other person is attractive, appears to have an occupation that is similar to yours, or reminds you of someone you knew some time ago. In any case, you wish to get to know the other person. In order to initiate the relationship, you speak to him or her. Your purpose is to call the other person's attention to yourself and possibly to begin a relationship of some kind with that person.

2. You may wish to demonstrate your cordiality or good will. You get on an elevator with an acquaintance and you engage in "small talk." You may discuss the weather, the administration at your university, or changing economic conditions in the state. Regardless of the topic, the purpose of your conversation is to show that you are friendly and cordial.

3. You may wish to exchange information. If you see a classmate on a street corner, you may stop and chat. You ask your classmate, in the course of a conversation, when you can begin the project that you agreed to work upon together. You agree on a time and place to begin your work. Although you may have exchanged some other information, the purpose of your conversation was to determine when you would begin work. Your purpose was not to establish your good will nor to begin a relationship; in this instance, you wished to exchange specific information.

4. You may simply wish to pass some time away. Perhaps you are waiting for a friend to get ready to go out for the evening and you talk with his or her roommate. Maybe you are waiting to see the dean of your college and you converse with the secretary. As you wait to see your dentist, you strike up a conversation with the receptionist. In each of these three cases, you are simply engaging in a conversation in order to pass time. You have no predetermined purpose, you do not wish to establish a long-term relationship with the other person, and you have no specific informational need.

The Nature of Communication among Strangers, Acquaintances, and Friends

Communication among strangers, acquaintances, and friends shares the generic characteristics that all interpersonal communication shares. This communication begins with self, requires that all communicators share immediacy and feedback salience, consists of communicators who are interdependent, is transactional, includes both content and relationship aspects, and is irreversible and unrepeatable. You may wish to review these characteristics in chapter 1. Communication that occurs with strangers, acquaintances, and friends is also unique because the context affects the interpersonal communication. In the following section, we will consider three characteristics of this type of communication.

Characteristics of Communication among Strangers, Acquaintances, and Friends

Importance of the relationship.   While communication with strangers, acquaintances, and friends includes both content and relationship aspects, *the relationship is frequently more important than the content.* For instance, after you have had an argument with a friend, you might decide that who was "right" and who was "wrong" is less important than the continuation of your friendship. Or, suppose an interesting looking person in one of your classes asks if he can walk you to your next class. This request is far different if the person is same-sex or opposite-sex, if you have talked to this person previously or not, or if you perceive the person as a potential friend or only as a classmate. Even though the content is the same, the relationship between yourself and the other person alters the meaning of the communication. The relationship appears to be more important than the content in these instances.

The primary purpose of communicating with a stranger may be to make contact with him or her. Our intent may be to establish a relationship with the other person rather than to share a particular message. The researcher, Gregory Bateson, writes:

> *When A communicates with B, the mere act of communicating can carry the implicit statement "we are communicating." In fact, this may be the most important message that is sent and received. The wisecracks of American adolescents and the smoother but no less stylized conversation of adults are only occasionally concerned with the giving and receiving of objective information; mostly, the conversations of leisure hours exist because people need to know they are in touch with one another. They may ask questions which superficially seem to be about matters of impersonal fact—"Will it rain?" "What is in today's war news?"—but the speaker's interest is focused on the fact of communication with another human being.[1]*

We appear to enjoy conversations with others whose ideas and beliefs are similar to our own. The social interaction in which we validate each other's perceptions and perspectives is rewarding. The specific messages may be less important than the act of establishing confirming contact.

Selections of persons for interaction.   While persons engaged in communicating with strangers, acquaintances, and friends must share a similar physical proximity, *everyone who shares a general space does not engage in communication.* In other words, we select those persons with whom we communicate. If someone speaks to us on a plane or a bus, we may turn away and not respond. If we are pressed together with a number of others on an elevator, we may deliberately choose to avoid conversing with any of them.

How do we select persons with whom to interact? You will recall that we discussed relationship development in chapter 2 and considered why persons attend to others and why they are attracted to some of them. You may wish to review that information at this point. In addition, we can glean some answers from the research literature that deals with this question. Interest in initial interaction is under close scrutiny and new answers appear to be emerging.[2]

Current research suggests that we make judgments about the relative cost/benefit of entering into an interaction.[3] If we determine that the encounter will probably result in more benefits than costs, we engage in conversation. Among the costs that we assess are the kinds of demands the interaction will place upon us, whether it will threaten other relationships that we wish to maintain, and the difficulty of disengaging from the conversation. We consider among the benefits the attractiveness of the other person, the reduction of uncertainty about the other person or the increased level of predictability about her or him, and the possibility of future interaction which includes the potentiality of a deepening relationship.

How do we analyze a potential interaction with another person into possible costs and benefits? A commonly accepted view is that we develop "implicit personality theories."[4] This means that we organize personality characteristics into specific sets; therefore our knowledge about a relatively small number of characteristics of a person will allow us to make fairly accurate predictions about other characteristics. The generalizations that we draw are based on observable characteristics of the other person and our own past experience with those characteristics. For instance, you notice that an individual in one of your classes regularly dresses in very expensive designer clothing. You might infer that he or she is wealthy, is concerned with appearances, and has a positive body image. On the other hand, another person with a different perspective may draw the generalization that he or she is highly insecure, has little depth, and is a conformist. We do not all view the same qualities or characteristics as belonging to the same sets, but we do appear to organize characteristics and qualities in certain ways. On the basis of relatively little information, we draw inferences and determine whether the benefits will outweigh the costs for us. We may believe that the person with designer clothing holds benefits because of his or her attractive appearance that outweighs potential costs in an initial interaction. Or, someone else may determine that an interaction with this person would cost more because of his or her apparent insecurity, lack of depth, and conformity than the benefit of becoming involved in a conversation.

Related to the implicit personality theory is the concept of person prototype. A prototype is a pure and abstract model of something. It appears that over time, people tend to develop mental prototypes of various things, including people. These prototypes will represent many possible categories. For example, you may have a prototype of a good parent that is largely based upon your experiences with your own parents, but it is also shaped by parents in the media, parents of relatives and peers, and even cultural norms about the role of parent. In initial interactions, people may possess prototypes of "ideal romantic partners," "friends," "colleagues," and even "competent communicators."[5] Prototypes are believed to develop by increasingly abstracting specific information into more general form. Thus, the more you interact with people and develop friends, the more you discover how they behave and the types of behavior that a "good" friend will typically display. After time, these behaviors become associated with an abstract prototype of a good friend. Initial interaction, therefore, becomes an opportunity to discover information and observe behavior to test whether the other person is likely to fit one of your prototypes. Very early in many initial interactions, you may start wondering to yourself, "What kind of relationship do I see this person developing with me?" The answer to this question is likely to be based in part upon the extent to which he or she matches your prototypes of relationships.

We do not communicate with everyone with whom we come into contact. Instead, we select people with whom to interact on the basis of perceived costs and benefits.

Other research has demonstrated that we tend to interact with persons who are similar to ourselves.[6] We interact with other people who appear to have something in common with ourselves. Occasionally the only thing that we have in common is our shared dislike or disapproval of a particular aspect of our culture, a specific person, or another feature of our lives. We begin talking to another person at the train station about the problems with mass transportation when the train is late for the third night in a row, we talk to co-workers about the seeming unfairness of the boss, or we talk to friends about the effects of inflation upon eating lunch on a regular basis in restaurants. We avoid speaking to the high self-discloser at a bar because we assume that he or she is inebriated and we are not; we do not continue talking to someone who responds negatively to all of our attitudes and values; and we may disengage from a conversation with someone who behaves in a manner that we judge to be deviant.

A recent study suggests that we may avoid interactions with persons who are dissimilar from ourselves because we must work so much harder at the interaction.[7] There are several reasons for this. First, when you agree with someone, the underlying reasons often do not need to be expressed. However, disagreement generally requires a formulation and expression of the basis for disagreement. Second, similarity of attitudes and experiences provides a ready-made set of conversational resources. That is, having similar backgrounds, experiences, and values permit you an immediate familiarity with topics for discussion and extension. Third, similarity tends to be positively reinforcing. When another person holds similar opinions and attitudes, it represents implicit confirmation for our own views.

The commonality that encourages conversation may be superficial or it may have more depth. We may choose a person with whom to begin a conversation because that person is physically attractive; we may continue the conversation if we find that the other shares similar interests. Nonetheless, it is the perceived commonality that encourages us to begin and sustain conversations.

Ritualized elements.   While communication is irreversible and unrepeatable, communication with strangers, acquaintances, and friends frequently has *ritualized elements*.[8] In the next section, we will consider the structure of conversations and you will observe that most conversations consist of the same three parts. Most conversations are predictable in how they begin and how they end. This structural similarity is part of the ritualized nature of conversations. Bateson, in the comment on page 293, similarly refers to this aspect of our conversations. Nonverbally, too, we engage in certain rituals in our informal interactions with others. We may shake hands when we meet, sit close together while we talk, or kiss when we leave each other.

Structure of Communication among Strangers, Acquaintances, and Friends

In the same way that we draw inferences about individuals on the basis of observable characteristics, we continue to draw inferences about them within a conversation. We may decide that the person wearing the designer clothes is actually quite insecure rather than satisfied with his or her body image. We may conclude that the interesting-looking person is really quite dull. Conversations occur within relationships. You will recall in chapter 2 that we considered the stages of relationship development and deterioration. As we develop a relationship, we move through the stages of attention, attraction, adaptation, and attachment. As our relationship deteriorates, we experience disregard, disinterest, divergence, and detachment. Conversations similarly go through these stages, although some of the stages are extremely brief. For example, you may glance at a person sitting next to you (attention); notice that this person is wearing a pin that symbolizes an organization in which you are interested (attraction); you might mention that you support the values espoused by the group and would be interested in joining it if the other person could supply you with the necessary information for becoming a member (adaptation); or you may disclose that you have been a member of a similar organization for a specified number of years (attachment). After additional conversation, you may glance around the room for another person with whom to talk (inattentiveness); you may experience boredom with the level of interaction between yourself and your conversational partner (disinterest); you may begin listening to a conversation that is occurring nearby (divergence); and finally, you may turn away and participate in the new conversation (detachment).

As we gather more information about the other person, we reassess the cost/benefit ratio.[9] In the previous example, we observe an interaction in which two people have moved through the stages of relationship development and deterioration. These stages are not all present in all interactions. For instance, you may determine after a brief exchange that the other person was wearing the pin because it was attractive and not because he or she believed in the organization it represents. From initial attraction you may move immediately to divergence and detachment. On the other hand, you may enter into an ever-developing relationship in which you develop a close friendship with the other person and the stages of deterioration are not present. Development of relationships appears to occur when persons believe the benefit is greater than the cost; deterioration accompanies the situation when the costs outweigh the benefits.

Most conversations begin on a fairly superficial level and only become more intimate if the conversation extends over a period of time or if the relationship deepens. Berger found that during the first few minutes of a conversation, participants exchanged typical biographical information including their name, major, class standing, hometown, and career choice. The little boy in this cartoon is attempting to bypass this initial stage of the conversation. He appears

"GOT A LOT OF RELATIVES
VISITING TODAY."

© 1979 GOOD HOUSEKEEPING. Reprinted by permission of Orlando Busino.

to recognize the basic demographic information that is usually shared in the early part of a conversation. Berger found that when he asked conversational partners to skip this part of their interaction, they showed discomfort and had difficulty in beginning the conversation. He concluded that the disclosing of nonintimate, low-risk information appeared pervasive and necessary.[10]

Most recent research suggests that conversations among strangers need not begin with demographic information and then proceed to more personal topics.[11] Rubin suggests that conversations follow the prescribed sequence only in situations in which ambiguity is present. In other words, if you are asked how you initially interact with any other person, you would probably respond that you include demographic information. However, if you were asked about a potential conversation in a group in which all of the persons were gathered because of a common interest in a specific issue, you would probably respond that you would talk about aspects of that issue. It is suggested that we bypass the exchange of superficial information when the context of the interaction is clear.

Conversational Analysis

The following conversation occurs in a college classroom just before class is to begin. Mark and Bob have been in classes together before this term and have been enrolled in this math course for about four weeks. At the beginning of the conversation, Mark is very confident and he is interested in getting to know Bob better. Bob is less confident about initiating interactions with others, but his competence in math allows him to become increasingly confident in this conversation. Read the dialogue and answer the questions at the end.

Mark: (Confident, smiling, projecting his voice) Hi—your name is Bob, isn't it?

Bob: (Nervous, distracted, looking around the room) Yeah, uh, I'm Bob Anderson.

Mark: I'm Mark Brown. I've noticed you in a couple of my other math classes.

Bob: Well, uh, I'm majoring in math.

Mark: Me, too, but the courses sure are hard here.

Bob: I came to this university because of the reputation of the math department.

Mark: I came for the fun!

Bob: I haven't been disappointed in the program so far.

Mark: How did you do on the midterm exam? I thought I'd studied, but I got a low "C."

Bob: I did all right on it.

Mark: But what was your grade?

Bob: Well, I got an "A."

Mark: Do you understand the material we covered during the last class?

Bob: Sure, I had something similar to that in an advanced math class in high school.

Mark: Oh, I guess my background isn't as strong as yours.

Bob: Well, would you like some help?

Mark: I don't know, I'm going to have to do something or else I'll have to change majors.

Bob: I'd be happy to help you study for the next exam.

Mark: That would be great—I'd really appreciate it.

You may have participated in a similar conversation at one time or another. Consider the following questions:

1. Identify those points in this conversation that appear to indicate the various stages in relationship development—attention, attraction, adaptation, and attachment.
2. Identify those points in this conversation in which the relationship appeared to deteriorate. Could the conversation have been terminated at that point? Why did the conversation not terminate?
3. What are the costs and benefits for Mark to developing an acquaintance or a friendship with Bob? What are the costs and benefits for Bob?
4. If you were one of the people involved in this conversation, would you have responded differently at any point? Specify where and how you would have responded differently.

Distinctions between Relationships among Strangers, Acquaintances, and Friends

In the same way that conversations appear to go through recognizable stages, depending upon whether they are being initiated or terminated, communication varies depending upon the relationship between the persons involved. In this chapter we are examining the conversations that occur between strangers, acquaintances, and friends. In order to understand the differences in communication that occur in each of these relationships, we will distinguish between each of these relationships and suggest how the relationship affects the interaction.

Strangers.   You will recall that in chapter 6 we discussed the finding that individuals may self-disclose a great deal more to strangers whom they will never see again than to close friends. The anonymity of the train ride or airline flight allows persons to offer personal details that they would not provide if they believed that they were going to interact further with the other person. Interactions with strangers whom we will never encounter again are less typical situations than are those interactions with strangers with whom we are to develop an acquaintance or friendship. The findings that follow are based on conversations among strangers in which the individuals may have future interaction.

In general, strangers converse on a fairly shallow level. They engage in what is sometimes termed "small talk." In the same way that the initial stages of a conversation may focus on demographic data, strangers frequently share nonintimate, low-risk information. For example, negative information, especially about self, is unlikely to be disclosed in initial interaction. This may be due to an implicit recognition that it would be attributed with excessive importance at such an early stage of relational development.[12] There is some evidence that in initial conversations common or typical information exchange quickly declines and the exchange of opinions increases as the interactants get to know each other better and are no longer complete strangers.[13] Strangers self-disclose less than do acquaintances or friends.[14] Finally, strangers tend to show less verbal and nonverbal interaction than do friends during the parting or terminating stage of a conversation.[15]

What are the implications of this research for your communication behavior with strangers? You may wish to show some discretion in your nonverbal behavior. You may choose to sit or stand farther away from strangers than you do from friends. You may choose to engage in less touching and less eye contact. You may keep in mind that some gestures are limited to a particular culture, subculture, or area of the country and may be confusing to the person you have just met. Similarly, your verbal communication should not be replete with language that is specific to an occupation, subculture, or specialized group (e.g., slang, jargon). Your self-disclosure will be most appropriate if it is about demographic or general information. If you feel that the stranger is behaving aggressively, you may want to demonstrate assertiveness skills. Active listening may be important in initial interactions, but empathic understanding will probably be more useful in more developed relationships. We will consider specific communication skills further.

Conversations among strangers may seem to be a relatively unimportant topic to you. You may incorrectly believe that your communication with persons who are unknown to you is irrelevant. However, every one of your friends, acquaintances, peers, and colleagues were once strangers. As you develop skill in the initial encounters that you have with individuals, you may be able to establish more relationships with others and relationships that have more depth. The transitional stage from stranger to acquaintance may be brief, but it may also form the foundation of a lasting relationship.

Acquaintances.   We have many conversations each day with acquaintances—individuals whom we have previously met, but with whom we have not established a friendship. These persons may be people with whom we conduct business—co-workers, colleagues, fellow students, instructors—or persons with whom we have superficial social relationships—joggers or other participants in intramural sports, persons who live on the same dorm floor, people in a car pool, people we regularly see in a bar or at church.

Acquaintances disclose more to each other than do strangers,[16] they stand closer together than do strangers,[17] and acquaintances begin to open themselves to the potential of disapproval by others.[18] In general, conversations among acquaintances appear to fall on a continuum between conversations among strangers and conversations among friends. That is, they are less intimate, less risk-taking, and less physically close than are conversations among friends and more intimate, more risk-taking, and more physically close than are conversations among strangers. These conclusions must be interpreted cautiously, however, for variations do occur. For example, a study suggests that subjects prefer to talk about nonintimate and moderately intimate matters with strangers, intimate matters with acquaintances, and moderately intimate information with friends,[19] while other research tends to support the previously drawn generalizations.

One of the reasons why interaction between friends cannot always be expected to be more intimate and disclosive is that friends generally spend so much time communicating and have a longer relationship history. By spending more time interacting, it is unlikely that the conversations are constantly about intimate or highly personal topics. Indeed, much of the talk among friends is likely to be about very nonintimate subjects, even if on average there is greater intimacy than with strangers and acquaintances. In addition, some intimate subjects will have already been discussed between friends and may be less likely to be repeated in any given conversation.

What generalizations can you draw from this literature on communication behavior with acquaintances? You may feel more freedom in your nonverbal behavior than you do with strangers. You may stand and sit closer to persons whom you consider to be acquaintances than you do to strangers. You may

Many of our conversations occur with people who are casual acquaintances. These interactions generally consist of "small talk."

look at acquaintances more than you look at strangers. You may feel that touching is permissible, under some conditions. Facial expression may be used to a greater extent and gestures may come to have a common meaning for both communicators. You may rely on verbal communication that is specific to the occupation, hobby, business, or other shared activity of the two of you. For instance, you might not discuss "tendonitis" with a stranger but you could discuss this affliction with a fellow jogger; you might reserve discussions of "capital gains" with a business partner; and you might initiate a discussion on the "Heisenberg Principle" with another student enrolled in a quantum mechanics course. Self-disclosure can become more personal with an acquaintance, but you would probably be well advised to limit your personal disclosures to information that is relevant to the context. Highly personal information would be out of place. Assertiveness skills are relevant to successful communication with associates and other acquaintances. Active listening is essential and some empathic understanding may be called upon.

Conversations among acquaintances are not only important because they contribute to relationship development, they also serve as important indicators of cohesiveness within communities. Bernstein demonstrated that public conversations in urban communities reflect the family orientations, the racial

Relational Influence on Openness

As we have already observed, the relationship between ourselves and others affects our communication with them. We will see in the next section that we are more trusting and more open with persons whom we classify as friends than we are with those who are our acquaintances. We have already determined that we are more open with acquaintances than with strangers. In order to determine how you alter your communication with others, depending upon your relationship, complete the following chart. Write a sample comment on each topic that is given for each of the three relationships.

	Stranger	Acquaintance	Friend
The Weather			
Money			
Extramarital Sex			
Occupational Choice			
Political Choices			

composition, and the economic status of its members. She showed that conversations extended beyond the small talk associated with strangers when ethnic and racial homogeneity were highest and when children were frequently observed on the street or in shops. Conversation ranged between small talk and somewhat more extensive conversation in those neighborhoods that were ethnically and racially mixed, but where small children were also present. Conversations came closer to superficial interactions where the black and white populations approached an approximately equal mix, where children were not observed, or where commercial buildings abounded.[20]

Friends.   The relationship that exists between friends has been examined poetically and scientifically more than the relationships that exist between strangers or between acquaintances. We might distinguish between friendships and acquaintanceships on the basis of *choice* and of *positive regard*. We choose our friends; we do not accidentally have friendships.[21] You might strike up a conversation with a stranger in a public place; you may have an acquaintance because you are enrolled in the same class, work at the same place, or have a similar hobby. Your friends are persons you have singled out with whom to have a relationship. Similarly, you generally show positive regard for your friends. You may talk to a stranger for whom you have little positive or negative feeling and you may have mixed feelings about some of your acquaintances, but your friends generally receive your positive regard. A recent definition of friendship seems particularly appropriate. Friendship is "an interpersonal relationship between two persons that is mutually productive, established and maintained through perceived mutual free choice, and characterized by mutual positive regard."[22]

On what basis do we choose our friends? You may have a variety of very distinctive people whom you consider as your friends. You may be able to account for your choice in selecting a person as a friend or you may be less certain about why your relationship with that person is so positive. In *The Heart of Friendship,* the authors suggest eight descriptors that identify a friendship.[23] A consideration of these eight characteristics is useful to our understanding of why we enter into friendships with others.

Characteristics of friendships.   One characteristic of friendships is *availability.* We expect friends to be available to us or we expect to have access to them. If we call a friend when we are in trouble, we expect that he or she will respond. Carole King probably popularized this concept best in her song, "You've Got a Friend":

When you're down and troubled
And you need some loving care,
And nothing, nothing is going right
Close your eyes and think of me
And soon I will be there
To brighten up, even your darkest night
You just call out my name
And you know wherever I am
I'll come running, to see you again.
Winter, Spring, Summer, or Fall,
All you have to do is call
And I'll be there—You've got a friend.

Similarly, the often-quoted sentiment, "You can't *make* friends, you have to be a friend and then others will make *you* a friend," suggests that our availability and access to others is why they may perceive us as a friend.

A second characteristic of friendships is *shared activities.* We expect to engage in common activities with our friends. A study provided some interesting results in this regard. The study examined whether friends and strangers could be distinguished from each other on the basis of shared activities or on the basis of shared attitudes. Perhaps surprisingly, the study demonstrated that friends can be identified by their shared or common activities, not by their shared or common attitudes. For instance, a friendship may develop between two people who enjoy jogging together, even though one is a staunch Republican and the other is an avowed Democrat. Or, a good friendship may include a person who was opposed to the national Equal Rights Amendment and a person who worked diligently in favor of it because they both are writers and enjoy co-authoring books and articles. Friends are more similar in their activities than in their attitudes and more accurate in estimating activity preferences of their friends than they are in identifying attitudes of their friends. For example, friends would be able to accurately predict the leisure activities but would be unable to predict the religious values of their own friends. In this study, attitudes tended to be as dissimilar among friends as among strangers.[24] Friends could belong to different churches, different political parties, and support entirely different causes, just as strangers might be expected to do.

A third quality that is associated with friendship is *caring*. We expect our friends to sincerely care about us. Caring is not necessarily the same as agreement. Caring involves such behaviors as attentiveness, interest, forethought, and watchfulness. We expect verbal and nonverbal sensitivity from our friends. We assume that they will observe the manner in which we behave and respond to our behavior. When persons neglect us, disregard our feelings, show indifference or inattention, we assume they do not care about us and are not among the group of people that we would identify as our friends.

A fourth quality of friendship is *honesty*. We expect our friends to be honest and open in their communication with us. If you make a serious error in judgment, if you drink too much alcohol, or if you have a smudge on your face, you would expect a friend to redirect, guide, or tell you. This does not mean that being someone's friend allows you the privilege of disregarding that person's feelings and beginning statements with, "I know this might hurt you, but . . . ," "I'm telling you this for your own good . . . ," and "You might be angry now, but some day you'll thank me for what I am about to tell you." We need to be cognizant of the other person's feelings and not take license to be brutally or hurtfully forthright. You may wish to recall the information in chapter 7 on self-assertion, keeping in mind that one of our goals in communication is to state our own perceptions and needs in a straightforward manner, but not to disallow the perceptions or needs of the other person. As a friend, we grant honest feedback and sincere responses that may result in improvement for the other person, but we do not show unnecessary cruelty or an imposition of our values on him or her.

We generally expect *confidentiality* from our friends. As you have learned from the discussion on strangers and acquaintances that precedes this section, we self-disclose more to our friends than to strangers with whom we expect to have future interaction and to acquaintances. One study examined the patterns of self-disclosure that existed between pairs of college roommates and college hallmates (non-roommates on the same floor) in first-year dormitories. The study determined that friendship was related to intimate self-disclosure and that proximity, or physical closeness, was related to superficial self-disclosure.[25] In other words, we self-disclose more personal information—how we feel about our body, our religious values, and our sexual behavior—to persons we consider friends while we self-disclose superficial information—our major, when we hope to graduate from college, and the places we have lived—to persons who are in our physical proximity. One of the reasons that we are able to make intimate and negative self-disclosures to our friends is that we expect them to consider the information confidential. We trust our friends not to disclose our idiosyncrasies and embarrassing moments to others. Jane Howard, in *Families,* recounts a meeting with one of her close girlhood friends:

> *"Do you still hold your wet head out the window on a cold winter's night so you'll catch cold and sound sexy like Tallulah Bankhead?"*
> *"I only did that once, when I was fifteen. Do you still hide your dirty dishes in the oven? Or was it the bathtub?" Our friendship is a cobweb of such frail legends.*[26]

Howard's reunion with her friend is filled with stories and experiences that the two have shared with each other, but before the publication of Howard's book, probably few other people knew of such stories. The proverb, "It is better to have friends learn of your faults than your enemies," alludes to the confidential nature of friendship that does not extend into the relationship between enemies.

A sixth quality associated with friendship is *loyalty.* We expect our friends to be loyal; we do not expect them to betray us or to show disloyalty, even under difficult circumstances. Perhaps we define those persons who stay with us "through thick and thin" as our friends while we define people who are only interested in us when we are successful as acquaintances. Friends remain loyal to us regardless of our circumstances.

We expect some level of *understanding* in our friendships. This understanding may be in the form of a friend recognizing why we respond in an unusual way to another person as a result of some past experience. Shared activities and relationship history lead to a background of understanding. Having been part of the same experiences allows the development of private jokes, idiosyncratic gestures and terms, shared stories, and a sense of mutual understanding regarding many similar experiences. Or, a friend may show his or her understanding of us by withholding negative judgments about idiosyncratic behavior on our part. Nonverbally, a friend may communicate understanding by a nod, a wink, or a smile that others do not notice or do not acknowledge.

Finally, we desire *empathy* from our friends. We discussed the importance of empathy in chapter 9. We want our friends to view the world as though they were seeing it from our perspective. We are very disturbed when we make a comment about an event, an idea, or another person and a friend appears unwilling or unable to perceive the phenomenon from the perspective that we offer. For instance, if you comment, "I think my physics professor is unable to teach in an interesting and effective manner," and your friend responds that he or she believes that you don't understand physics, that the particular professor is the best in the college, or that you don't know how to discriminate between an effective and an ineffective instructor, you would be surprised, and perhaps, upset. We expect our friends to attempt to see the world through our eyes, from our perspective.

We choose our friends and we have positive regard for them. Among the characteristics of friendship are availability, shared activities, caring, honesty, confidentiality, loyalty, understanding, and empathy. How do you communicate your friendship to others? Nonverbally, you can demonstrate your feelings of friendship by sitting and standing close to the other person. You may reach out and physically touch your friend. You may use increased facial expression and gestures to demonstrate your feelings. You may develop specialized gestures that have meaning for the two of you, but for no one else. You may look at your friend more than you look at a stranger or acquaintance. You may simply choose to spend more time with your friend than with others, or reveal greater involvement in those interactions you do have with your friend (as when you see a close friend who lives far away).

How is friendship transmitted verbally? You may develop special verbal codes with which to communicate. Words may be used in unique, but mutually understood ways, between friends. You may self-disclose more intimate information to a friend than to a stranger. You may discuss negative as well as positive aspects of who you are. You will want to behave assertively as you express yourself honestly and completely without imposing your views on your friend. You will demonstrate your understanding and empathy by those verbal skills that we listed in chapter 9. Topics of conversations with friends will include those shared activities or common perspectives that originally contributed to your friendship.

Some research indicates that relative to strangers, friends use more unique, unusual, or implicit greetings and openings, initiate more topics, ask more questions, and use more complex conversational closings. That is, persons with more knowledge of each other grow beyond the stereotypical forms of address, and they tend to develop habits of initiating and closing their conversations that are unique to their interpersonal relationship. In this research, acquaintances were more similar to strangers than to friends in conversational style.[27]

A number of other communication characteristics of friendship have been identified. In one study of relationships developing over twelve weeks, the conversations of those dyads who developed "close" friendships tended to be increasingly intimate compared to those who did not develop close friendships.[28] There is also reason to believe that "best" friends have more in common with intimates (e.g., those with whom they are dating or romantically involved) than they do with "friends" and "acquaintances." Specifically, best friends and intimates are most characterized by their tendency to accept the demands the other person may make without any question. Best friends, like friends, tend to be empathic and positive toward each other. However, best friends tend to be more similar to each other in interests, find more stimulation in their activities together, care more about each other, view their relationship as more exclusive and mutual, and are more aware of relationship potential than mere friends. In terms of relational potential, stimulation of activities, legitimacy of demands, and exclusivity, friends appear to be lower than the class of best friends and lovers and higher than the class of acquaintances and workers. In other words, friends seem to be a truly intermediate type of relationship.[29]

According to one study, friendships tend to abide by at least a few basic rules of behavior.[30] The most consistently held rules indicate that friends are expected to (1) share news of success with each other, (2) show emotional support for each other, (3) volunteer help in times of need, (4) strive to make each other happy in each other's company, (5) demonstrate trust in each other, and (6) stand up for each other in their absence. It seems that friendships do involve a certain degree of commitment and trust in each other's unconditional support.

Communicating Friendship

Do you communicate your friendship to others? Would others agree that you are a good friend? Write down the names of three or four friends in the left-hand column. Rate yourself on a scale from 1 = superior, 2 = excellent, 3 = good, 4 = fair, to 5 = poor for each of the characteristics in terms of how well you believe you demonstrate that particular quality of friendship to others.

Friend's name	Avail- ability	Shared activities	Caring	Honesty	Confiden- tiality	Loyalty	Under- standing	Empathy

Are you surprised by any of your responses? When you analyze the way you communicate your friendship to others, do you reach any new conclusions? Do you find that there are general areas of friendship that you do not communicate to those persons whom you identify as friends? Can you make improvements in your communication patterns to your friends? Why do you feel you are able to communicate some of these qualities and not others? Do your friends reciprocate your behavior? In other words, if you show little understanding and empathy, do you find that they do not demonstrate these qualities either? Or, do you find that you are particularly negligent at one of these qualities, while your friends are very good at them? For example, you are not good about keeping confidences, but your friends maintain a high level of confidentiality. Do you feel you can improve your ability to communicate friendship? In what specific ways?

Of course, rules are often violated. In a study of friendship relationship violations, 70 percent of the violations were never actually resolved.[31] The occurrence of these violations detracted from the satisfaction and survivability of the friendship. However, as discussed in chapter 10, rules are negotiable rather than absolute. It appears that friends often develop beliefs regarding exceptions to the rule that friends should lend aid, assistance, and support to one another.[32] Apparently, some friends are able to understand that friendship must allow license for occasional violations.

Many of the characteristics discussed thus far are summarized by Davis and Todd as follows. As a type of relationship, friendships are generally characterized by authenticity, affection and enjoyment, intimate disclosure, receiving and giving assistance, mutual trust, shared activity and companionship, mutual respect, and maintenance conflicts.[33]

When we do not communicate our friendship to those persons whom we classify as friends, what occurs? The relationship may deteriorate as was discussed in chapter 2, or one person may continue to maintain the relationship.[34] Friendships cannot occur in one-sided situations, however, and they frequently deteriorate if one person refuses to communicate his or her commitment to the relationship. Friendships may deteriorate to become acquaintances or they may change and become intimate or even family relationships, which we will discuss in the next two chapters.

Improving Communication with Strangers, Acquaintances, and Friends

We communicate with strangers, acquaintances, and friends every day. Our proficiency with conversational skills can affect the relationships that we develop or fail to develop, the tasks that we are able to accomplish or fail to accomplish, and the way that other people view or fail to view us. In this section we will offer some suggestions on how to improve in these contexts of communication. You have already read about some of the specific nonverbal and verbal skills you should rely upon in communicating with strangers, with acquaintances, and with friends.

Before we begin this discussion, we should dispel the myth about conversational ability that people are "naturally" good or poor conversationalists. The person who always has a ready illustration or an apt anecdote may be a popular guest at cocktail and dinner parties, while the person who "doesn't know what to say" or is reticent may find that he or she receives few invitations. Are good conversationalists born and not made? Research has yet to demonstrate that the ability to interact competently with strangers, acquaintances, and friends is inherited rather than a learned ability. It appears evident that persons can improve their informal interactions with others.

The nature of communication with strangers, acquaintances, and friends may cause us to believe that we cannot improve in this skill area. We may agree that public speaking skills, radio and television broadcasting, and even interviewing techniques can be learned, but may seriously question whether we can become better conversationalists. Some of the other communication skills appear to be more formal, that is, they are more ceremonial, more methodical, and more precise. Conversations, on the other hand, are more informal or common, ordinary, and conventional. The formality or informality of an activity should not be the determinant of whether improvement is possible, however. Consider other informal activities in which you engage. For example, a number of books have suggested that we can become better gardeners, better carpenters, and better "fix-it-up" people. We learn how to raise our house plants, how to purchase and return items more successfully, and even how to improve our eating habits. Similarly, we can learn more about and improve our ability to hold conversations with persons we consider to be strangers, acquaintances, and friends. We have already considered the importance of conversations with persons who fall into one of these three categories; let us now consider how we can improve our skills in these contexts.

Many factors are at work that interfere with effective conversations among people. In chapter 1 we considered the effect of society upon interpersonal communication and we noted that such features of our society as the large size, the increasing complexity, and the speed with which changes occur all affect our communication with others. In addition such features as the increasingly media-constructed culture, the changes in the family structure or unit, the increasing number of older people in our population, the great mobility of individuals, and the changes in the labor force all interact with our conversations with others. For example, our acquaintances and friends are replaced with strangers because of our society's mobility, and strangers become acquaintances with changes in the labor force. Nonetheless we can improve our communication with strangers, acquaintances, and friends.

Perspectives for Improving Communication

We may find that we are better able to communicate with others if we adopt three perspectives. First, we need to understand and operationalize differences in relationships. We cannot treat everyone in the same way—disclosing intimacies to new acquaintances, risking little with close friends, or using nonverbal gestures that have a special meaning for a small group of friends with everyone that we meet. We must be clear about the mutually understood nature of the relationship. Do you perceive another person as a friend while he or she views you merely as a business acquaintance? Is the person who delivers your mail considered to be a stranger or an acquaintance? Can you self-disclose intimacies to your roommate?

An important feature of relational definition lies in the mutually accepted definition of the relationship. In other words, one person cannot impose the definition of the relationship on both people. We cannot, independently, determine the nature of the relationship. As a consequence, we cannot introspectively determine what the relationship shall be and then impose that view

We communicate differently with people based on the relationship we have with them. Relational definition is mutually determined, however, and may be difficult to clearly and correctly ascertain.

on another. Clarification of a relationship often requires sharing your feelings with your partner, particularly when you feel that the other person is a friend, as opposed to a stranger or an acquaintance. We can rely on generally agreed-upon cues in the environment or situation in defining if another person is a stranger or an acquaintance. For instance, if you have just met, most people would qualify your relationship as two strangers in initial interaction. If you are co-workers, you can assume you are acquaintances. However, if disagreement about the relationship appears to exist—a stranger begins to ask you highly personal information, a friend shows no interest in a difficult situation that you experienced, or an acquaintance acts as though he or she does not know who you are—you may consider discussing the quality, depth, or focus of your relationship with the other person who is involved. Self-evaluation is important, but mutual evaluation of the relationship can result in greater understanding and growth.

Second, we need to be aware of, and practice, interpersonal skills. The four skill components of interpersonal communication discussed in chapters 4 through 11 are all important to competently managing conversations with various persons. Are you expressing yourself clearly? Are you demonstrating confidence and assertiveness? Are you communicating in a way that reflects concern, interest, and attentiveness in the other person? Do you handle the aspects of turn taking and conversational coordination smoothly? In addition, keep in mind the specific nonverbal and verbal cues that were recommended in the preceding sections of this chapter.

Third, we must accept change and adapt our behavior appropriately. You will recall the discussion of behavioral flexibility in chapter 1. It is important to understand that relationships *do* change. We do not remain friends with everyone for our entire lives. Both acquaintances and lovers can become friends while friends may become strangers. Our relationships with others need not be bound by age, sex, or other subcultural differences. You may find that a relationship with someone much older than yourself is very rewarding or that men and women can be "just friends." You may develop a more personal relationship with a colleague or classmate. You may find that a person with whom you ride to school every day has become a stranger when he or she moves to a different city. You may feel a sense of loss when a friend becomes merely an acquaintance or a stranger or you may feel exhilarated when a stranger becomes a close friend. The point is that relationships do change as they meet the expectations or fail to meet the expectations of the participants, as the partners grow at similar or different rates, as needs are satisfied or fail to be satisfied, and as pleasure is maximized and pain is minimized or as pleasure is minimized and pain is maximized. Our task is to be sensitive and responsive to those changes. To the extent that we are able to be creative in our definitions of relationships, caring in our interactions with others, and courageous in taking the first step, we will find satisfying interpersonal relationships with strangers, acquaintances, and friends.

Let us illustrate the importance of behavioral flexibility with an extended example. If you meet a person in a social situation, you will probably define your conversation with him or her as communication between strangers. You will probably make disclosures about demographic information. You may tell the other person where you are from, what your major is, where you currently live, and why you happened to be invited to this particular gathering. Two weeks later, the person is hired to work in the same office where you hold a part-time position. You become acquaintances and may engage in further conversations. You will discuss the place where you work, and you may make disclosures that are relevant to your shared employment. You will demonstrate more careful active listening skills and you may show empathy as the other person shares his or her feelings about fairly impersonal matters. Nonverbally, you will have more freedom to express yourself than you did when you initially met. After a period of time, you may begin to have lunch with the other person or arrange to meet him or her outside of work. Your relationship may develop into a friendship. At this point, you will have different expectations of the other person's behavior and you will communicate differently with him or her than you previously did. You will feel free to discuss topics that are unrelated to work and you will feel that it is appropriate to self-disclose more intimate information. Your nonverbal behavior will indicate a greater closeness, too, as you sit, stand, and move more closely to the other

Improving Conversational Skills

We can improve our conversational skills with strangers, acquaintances, and friends. In the conversation that follows a man and a woman who are friends are having a disagreement. After you have read the dialogue, analyze how this conversation could have been improved. The questions at the end of the conversation will direct your consideration. Robin and Tim met on campus and are walking back to the dormitories together. Their conversation focuses on the topic of running.

Robin: See that man moving out over there?

Tim: Which one? The old guy in the convertible?

Robin: No, no. The man who is running—he has on a tank top and yellow Nike running shoes.

Tim: Oh, him. Boy, does he have a funny running style.

Robin: What do you mean? I think he looks pretty good.

Tim: I'm on the track team and I run 10 miles almost every day, and I think he runs funny. Anyway, what makes you such an expert on running?

Robin: Well, I started running last week and my running form is a lot like that man's style. My friends have told me that I run with perfect form.

Tim: If you run with such perfect form, why don't you tell me what it is?

Robin: I just run perfect, I can't explain it.

Tim: Okay, tell me how do you step down, do you go heel-toe or toe-heel?

Robin: I don't know, I just put one foot ahead of the other. It doesn't make any difference, does it?

Tim: It most certainly does! If you always run on your toes for long distances, you could strain your Achilles tendon and you could also damage your calf muscles.

Robin: Well, is that all there is to know about running?

Tim: No, there's a lot more, like how do your feet land with each step?

Robin: My feet kind of point out.

Tim: You mean you run like a penguin?

Robin: Come on, Tim.

Tim: No, Robin, that's okay. I know a lot of women who run that way. It's really very common. It doesn't matter, anyway, because you are just a jogger.

Robin: If you know so much about running, why don't you tell me more?

Tim: Okay. Did you know that the way you hold your arms and hands is very important to the kind of runner you could become?

Robin: I know that. My friends told me to move my arms as fast as I could and to hold my hands in tightly clenched fists. It makes me feel like I'm moving faster.

Improving Conversational Skills continued

Tim:	Who are these friends of yours?
Robin:	Some people who live on the same dorm floor.
Tim:	They sure don't know anything about running. First of all, you don't move your arms fast, you move them in a rhythmic motion with your body. Also, you never move your arms across your body; you move each arm at your side and point them straight ahead. That's a typical woman for you—listening to everything some jerk tells you. Women get something in their minds and nothing you can say will change it.
Robin:	Personally, Tim, I think my friends have helped me a great deal, even more than you have. I don't want to be a great runner—I'm just running for fun.
Tim:	Sure, running for fun to lose weight. All women try running at some point in their lives, too bad it never works.
Robin:	I've already lost five pounds in a little over a week.
Tim:	That's really good, Robin, but I don't have time to get into a long conversation on women and their weight problems with you. I've got to have lunch. I'll walk you home from class tomorrow, though.
Robin:	Don't bother.

Have you participated in a conversation that is similar to this one? Did both Robin and Tim self-disclose in this dialogue? Give examples of self-disclosure that occur. Did Tim demonstrate empathic understanding? If not, identify those points in which he might have demonstrated empathy. Did the two persons have differing perceptions? How did these differences affect their conversation? Were both of the communicators assertive? Can you identify specific comments that appear to illustrate non-assertion or aggressiveness? What was the effect of each of these comments? Did both of the communicators demonstrate active listening? Were language choices appropriate for the two people? How would you improve this conversation? Rewrite the dialogue in a manner that you believe is realistic for two persons who are attempting to develop their friendship.

person and as you feel that it is appropriate to touch his or her arm or hand. Your empathic understanding of the other person will increase and you will engage in more active listening than you did at earlier stages in your relationship.

The person who is unable to exhibit behavioral flexibility in this situation might have responded inappropriately at any stage in the development of the relationship. For instance, the person might have inappropriately self-disclosed highly personal information upon first meeting. He or she might have stood uncomfortably close to the stranger and touched him or her freely. When the two persons were co-workers, he or she may have used words that were not mutually understood or used nonverbal gestures that confused the other person. As friends, and it is doubtful that the two would have become friends if one of the persons responded inappropriately at other stages in the development of this relationship, one of the persons may have been unwilling to either self-disclose or to show any understanding of the other person's situation. We must adapt our behavior to the changing nature of the relationships in which we are involved!

Summary

You may not have realized the importance of communication among strangers, acquaintances, and friends before you read this chapter. Or, you may not have recognized that we can improve our communication skills with persons whom we consider to be strangers, acquaintances, and friends. If you are typical, you probably have experienced some difficulties in the conversations that you have had in these contexts. You may have wondered about why you were unable to develop a friendship with one person or why you could not communicate to another with whom you only wished to be acquaintances. Few people have never experienced the situation in which they did not know just how to communicate with someone they have just met, someone with whom they work or share an activity, or with someone they consider to be a friend. This chapter should be useful in your skill development in these areas.

You are aware of the unique characteristics of communication that occurs with strangers, acquaintances, and friends. You know that the relationship is frequently more important than the content, that all persons who share the same physical proximity do not engage in communication with each other, and that communication with strangers, acquaintances, and friends frequently has ritualized events. We engage in different communication behaviors with strangers, acquaintances, and friends. For instance, we do not self-disclose to the same extent, about the same topics, or with the same level of intimacy in the three cases. We do not use the same nonverbal cues in the three settings. Our language choices, too, are guided by the relationship with the other person. Finally, the level of empathic understanding and active listening that we exhibit may be altered by the relationship that exists between us and the other person. Nonetheless, all of the skills that are discussed in chapters 4–11 are relevant to our success in communication with strangers, acquaintances, and friends.

We can improve our conversations by understanding the specific verbal and nonverbal cues that are appropriate for each of the different relationships in which we engage. In addition, we will know vast improvement if we (1) understand and operationalize differences in relationships, (2) are aware of and practice the interpersonal communication skills that are discussed in this text, and (3) accept change and adapt our behavior.

Notes

1. Gregory Bateson, "Conventions of Communication: Where Validity Depends upon Belief," in *Communication: The Social Matrix of Psychiatry,* Jurgen Ruesch and Gregory Bateson (eds.) (New York: W. W. Norton & Co., 1951), p. 213.

2. See, for example, Charles R. Berger, "Self-Consciousness and the Adequacy of Theory and Research into Relationship Development," *Western Journal of Speech Communication* 44(1980): 93–96; Jesse G. Delia, "Some Tentative Thoughts Concerning the Study of Interpersonal Relationships and Their Development," *Western Journal of Speech Communication* 44(1980): 97–103; Donald G. Ellis, "Ethnographic Considerations in Initial Interactions: Toward a Different Model," *Western Journal of Speech Communication* 44(1980): 104–7; W. B. Gudykunst, S. Yang, and T. Nishida, "A Cross-cultural Test of Uncertainty Reduction Theory: Comparisons of Acquaintances, Friends, and Dating Relationships in Japan, Korea, and the United States," *Human Communication Research* 11(1985): 407–55; K. Kellerman, "The Negativity Effect and Its Implications for Initial Interaction," *Communication Monographs* 51(1984): 37–55; and Marilyn B. Osterkamp, "Communication During Initial Interactions: Toward a Different Model," *Western Journal of Speech Communication* 44(1980): 108–13.

3. M. Sunnafrank, "Predicted Outcome Value During Initial Interactions: A Reformulation of Uncertainty Reduction Theory," *Human Communication Research* 13(1986): 34–38.

4. For further discussion of this view, see Walter H. Crockett and Paul Friedman, "Theoretical Explorations of the Processes of Initial Interactions," *Western Journal of Speech Communication* 44(1980): 86–92.

5. See C. Pavitt, "Preliminaries to a Theory of Communication: A System for the Cognitive Representation of Person and Object Based Information," *Communication Yearbook* 5(1982): 211–32; C. Pavitt and L. Haight, "The Competent Communicator as a Cognitive Prototype," *Human Communication Research* 12(1985): 225–42; C. Pavitt and L. Haight, "Implicit Theories of Communicative Competence: Situational and Competence Level Differences in Judgments of Prototype and Target," *Communication Monographs* 53(1986): 221–35.

6. See, for instance, James C. McCroskey, Virginia P. Richmond, and John A. Daly, "The Development of a Measure of Perceived Homophily in Interpersonal Communication," *Human Communication Research* 1(1975): 323–32. See also, R. A. Neimeyer and K. A. Mitchell, "Similarity and Attraction: A

Longitudinal Study," *Journal of Social and Personal Relationships* 5(1988): 131–48; M. Sunnafrank, "Communicative Influences on Perceived Similarity and Attraction: An Expansion of the Interpersonal Goals Perspective," *Western Journal of Speech Communication* 50(1986): 158–70.

7. Mark L. Knapp, Seminar paper on communication processes during the early stages of acquaintanceship. Speech Communication Association Convention, Minneapolis, November 1978.

8. See P. D. Krivonos and M. L. Knapp, "Initiating Communication: What Do You Say When You Say Hello?", *Central States Speech Journal* 26(1975): 115–25.

9. R. J. Eidelson, "Interpersonal Satisfaction and Level of Involvement: A Curvilinear Relationship," *Journal of Personality and Social Psychology* 39(1980): 460–70.

10. See C. Berger, "Beyond Initial Interaction: Uncertainty, Understanding, and the Development of Interpersonal Relationships," in *Language and Social Psychology,* H. Giles and R. St. Clair (eds.) (Oxford, England: Blackwell, 1979), pp. 122–44; C. Berger, "Communicating under Uncertainty," in *Interpersonal Processes: New Directions in Communication Research,* M. E. Roloff and G. R. Miller (eds.) (Newbury Park, Calif.: Sage, 1987), pp. 39–63; C. R. Berger and R. J. Calabrese, "Some Explorations and Beyond: Toward a Developmental Theory of Interpersonal Communication," *Human Communication Research* 1(1975): 99–112; C. R. Berger, R. R. Gardner, M. R. Parks, L. Schulman, and G. R. Miller, "Perceptions of Information Sequencing in Relationship Development," *Human Communication Research* 3(1976): 146–58.

11. Rebecca Rubin, Seminar paper on communication processes during the early stages of acquaintanceship. Speech Communication Association Convention, Minneapolis, November 1978.

12. K. Kellerman, "The Negativity Effect and Its Implications for Initial Interaction," *Communication Monographs* 51(1984): 37–55.

13. K. Kellerman, "Anticipation of Future Interaction and Information Exchange in Initial Interaction," *Human Communication Research* 13(1983): 41–75.

14. Jacquelyn W. Gaebelein, "Self-Disclosure Among Friends, Acquaintances, and Strangers," *Psychological Reports* 38(1976): 967–70.

15. A. B. Summerfield and J. A. Lake, "Nonverbal and Verbal Behaviours Associated with Parting," *British Journal of Psychology* 68(1977): 133–36.

16. Gaebelein, pp. 967–70.

17.   Carol J. Guardo, "Personal Space in Children," *Child Development* 40(1969): 143–51.

18.   Morris Axelrod, "Urban Structure and Social Participation," *American Sociological Review* 21(1956): 13–18.

19.   Myong, Jin Won-Doornink, "On Getting to Know You: The Association Between the Stage of a Relationship and the Reciprocity of Self-Disclosure," *Journal of Experimental Social Psychology* 15(1979): 229–41.

20.   Judith Bernstein, "Small Talk as Social Gesture," *Journal of Communication* 25(1975): 147–54.

21.   B. J. Palisi and H. E. Ransford, "Friendship As a Voluntary Relationship: Evidence from National Surveys," *Journal of Social and Personal Relationships* 4(1987): 243–59; J. P. Wiseman, "Friendship: Bonds and Binds in a Voluntary Relationship," *Journal of Social and Personal Relationships* 3(1986): 191–211.

22.   Joseph A. DeVito, *The Interpersonal Communication Book,* 2d ed. (New York: Harper & Row, Publishers, 1980), p. 477.

23.   Muriel James and Louis M. Savary, *The Heart of Friendship* (New York: Harper & Row, Publishers, 1976).

24.   Carol Werner and Pat Parmelee, "Similarity of Activity, Preferences Among Friends: Those Who Play Together Stay Together," *Social Psychology Quarterly* 42(1979): 62–66.

25.   Zick Rubin and Stephen Shenker, "Friendship, Proximity, and Self-Disclosure," *Journal of Personality* 46(1978): 1–22.

26.   Jane Howard, *Families* (New York: Simon & Schuster, 1978), p. 175.

27.   G. A. Hornstein, "Intimacy in Conversational Style As a Function of the Degree of Closeness between Members of a Dyad," *Journal of Personality and Social Psychology* 49(1985): 671–81.

28.   R. B. Hays, "The Development and Maintenance of Friendship," *Journal of Social and Personal Relationships* 1(1984): 75–98.

29.   J. Indvik and M. A. Fitzpatrick, "Perceptions of Inclusion, Affiliation, and Control in Five Interpersonal Relationships," *Communication Quarterly* 34(1986): 1–13; for similar distinctions and related research, see E. Kayser, T. Schwinger, and R. L. Cohen, "Laypersons' Conceptions of Social Relationships: A Test of Contract Theory," *Journal of Social and Personal Relationships* 1(1984): 433–58; W. K. Rawlins, K. Leibowitz, and A. P. Bochner, "Affective and Instrumental Dimensions of Best, Equal, and Unequal Friendships," *Central States Speech Journal* 37(1986): 90–101; S. Rose and F. C. Serafica, "Keeping and Ending Casual, Close and Best Friendships," *Journal of Social and Personal Relationships* 3(1986): 275–88.

30.   M. Argyle and M. Henderson, "The Rules of Friendship," *Journal of Social and Personal Relationships* 1(1984): 211–37.

31.   K. E. Davis and M. J. Todd, "Assessing Friendship: Prototypes, Paradigm Cases and Relationship Description," in *Understanding Personal Relationships: An Interdisciplinary Approach,* S. Duck and D. Perlman (eds.) (Beverly Hills, Calif.: Sage, 1985), pp. 17–38.

32.   L. O'Connell, "An Exploration of Exchange in Three Social Relationships: Kinship, Friendship and the Marketplace," *Journal of Social and Personal Relationships* 1(1984): 333–45.

33.   Davis and Todd.

34.   S. M. Rose, "How Friendships End: Patterns among Young Adults," *Journal of Social and Personal Relationships* (1984): 267–77.

Additional Readings

Brain, Robert. *Friends and Lovers.* New York: Basic Books, 1976.

Brenton, Myron. *Friendship.* New York: Stein and Day, 1975.

Carnegie, Dale. *How to Win Friends and Influence People.* New York: Simon & Schuster, 1939.

Derlega, Valerian J., ed. *Communication, Intimacy, and Close Relationships.* New York: Academic, 1984.

Derlega, V. J. and Winstead, B. A., eds. *Friendship and Social Interaction.* Springer Social Psychology Series. New York: Springer-Verlag, 1986.

Gottman, John M. and Parker, Jeffery, G., eds. *Conversations with Friends: Speculations in Affective Development.* Studies in Emotion and Social Interaction. New York: Cambridge University Press (Co-publisher with Maison des sciences de l'Homme).

Greeley, Andrew M. *The Friendship Game.* Garden City, N.Y.: Image Books, 1971.

Hafen, Brent A. and Frandsen, Kathryn J. *People Need People: The Importance of Relationships to Health and Wellness.* Evergreen, Colo.: Cordillera, 1987.

James, Muriel and Savary, Louis. *The Heart of Friendship.* New York: Harper & Row, 1978.

Leefeldt, Christine and Callenbach, Ernest. *The Art of Friendship.* New York: Pantheon Books, 1979.

Meacham, J. A., ed. *Interpersonal Relations: Family, Peers, Friends.* Contributions to Human Development: Vol. 18. New York: S. Karger, 1987.

Shelton, Robert. *Loving Relationships.* Elgin, Ill.: Brethren, 1987.

Intimate Communication

Boys and girls can be friends, as we discussed in the last chapter; however, they can also engage in intimate relationships. The "stirrings" that are referred to in this cartoon are often associated with intimate relationships. In our culture, intimate relationships occur between same-sex and opposite-sex persons and between persons of varying ages. In this chapter we will examine communication in intimate relationships. We will consider the importance of intimate communication, the basis of intimacy, which may include the self, the other person, or the situation, and ways of improving intimate communication through four stages—sharing the self, affirming the other, becoming "one," and transcending "one." Let us begin our discussion by examining the importance of interpersonal intimacy.

The Importance of Intimate Communication

W. S. Gilbert in *Iolanthe* stated, "It's love, it's love that makes the world go round," and popular songs stress our need for intimacy which appears to last throughout our lives. Consider James Taylor's "How Sweet It Is to Be Loved by You":

How sweet it is to be loved by you.
I needed the shelter of someone's arms and there you were.
I needed someone to understand my ups and downs
And there you were.
With sweet love and devotion . . .
You were better to me than I was to myself . . .
And everywhere I went it seems I'd been there before . . .
For me there's you and nobody else.
I want to stop and thank you, baby—
How sweet it is to be loved by you.

Before we consider why each of us desires intimacy and why we attempt to establish that intimacy through our interpersonal communication, let us consider a definition for intimacy. We may have heard the expression that when we encounter intimacy, we will know what it is. Some poets and philosophers suggest that we should not spend time defining intimacy, for fear that we will lose it. Nonetheless, for our purposes, a definition of intimacy will guide our understanding of this interpersonal phenomenon. According to Smith and Williamson, intimacy is "a loving collaboration between two people who both understand and feel understood by each other."[1] This definition is useful as it explains intimacy in a very broad way and does not exclude the variety of the kinds of intimate communication that occur today. However, we should note that this broad definition would allow some friendships and family relationships to be intimate. For the purposes of this text, we will consider only two-person relationships in which sexual intimacy is potential or realized. A platonic relationship, that is, a close relationship with an opposite-sex person with whom sexual intercourse is not salient, is not an intimate relationship; but a homosexual relationship, or a close relationship with a same-sex person with whom sexual intercourse is probable, is within our definition. An intimate relationship need not include sex, but the potential for a sexual expression of love is present. We will define *intimacy,* then, as a loving relationship

Selecting an Intimate

Complete the following chart by identifying where another person who might establish an intimate relationship with you would likely fall. Place an X in the space between the bipolar adjectives that most closely indicate your perception of this imaginary or real person. For example, in the first scale, if you think an intimate should be somewhat open-minded and somewhat close-minded, place an X in the middle blank. For the last item, if you believe an intimate should be highly gregarious and talkative, place an X in the blank closest to the term "extroverted."

	1	2	3	4	5	6	7	
open-minded	___	___	___	___	___	___	___	close-minded
dominant	___	___	___	___	___	___	___	submissive
kind	___	___	___	___	___	___	___	unkind
simple	___	___	___	___	___	___	___	complex
thoughtful	___	___	___	___	___	___	___	thoughtless
beautiful	___	___	___	___	___	___	___	ugly
self-confident	___	___	___	___	___	___	___	diffident
unsympathetic	___	___	___	___	___	___	___	sympathetic
active	___	___	___	___	___	___	___	passive
dull	___	___	___	___	___	___	___	bright
nervous	___	___	___	___	___	___	___	composed
introverted	___	___	___	___	___	___	___	extroverted

Compare your responses with a person with whom you have, or would like to have, an intimate relationship. Are your responses similar? Do you complement each other—that is, do you desire a partner who is dominant and she or he prefers one who is submissive? What conclusions can you draw?

between two persons in which understanding is both felt and offered and for whom a sexual relationship is salient. Intimate communication is that interpersonal communication that occurs between persons engaged in such a relationship.

Thus, intimate communication is not uniquely distinguished by any particular characteristics of behavior or process, but by the context in which it occurs. This is sensible because highly intimate couples frequently communicate in ways that appear similar to nonintimate dyads. Of course, intimate couples also display general tendencies and characteristics that are rarely observed in nonintimate dyads, and it is these characteristics that are the primary concern of this chapter.

An intimate relationship is a relatively closed system. The two people involved do not act independently. The behavior of one affects the other and affects the relationship. The interdependence that occurs in an intimate relationship has led some theorists to view this relationship as "two halves that equals a whole." In other words, one person is incomplete without the other and provides only half of the relationship. Harry Chapin expressed this sentiment:

> *I guess I took you for granted*
> *I thought of us as one*
> *But now the laugh's on me*
> *'Cause your half of me*
> *Just took off with the sun.*

© STORY SONGS LTD. 1972.

Intimate relationships foster communication that is more unique, less predictable, and generally less public than communication in less intimate contexts. They are more unique than conversations between acquaintances, less predictable than interactions among strangers, and less public than employment interviews. Loving relationships between two people exist in a variety of forms. Behaviors that occur in one relationship may not exist in another. For instance, some couples rarely verbalize their feelings for each other. Actions that might be viewed as hurtful to one couple may be beneficial to another. We have all observed the couple who appear to be in constant conflict, arguing over every detail of every event. If we would suggest to them that they do not appear to get along very well, they would be surprised and maybe angry. Generalizing about those behaviors that will lead to a successful marriage may not be true for all married couples. An additional problem in understanding intimate communication is that "no one knows what goes on behind closed doors." Intimate communication is often private. The couple in the cartoon depict the unique, unpredictable, less public nature of intimate communication.

Now that we have developed a definition of intimate relationships and intimate communication, we can return to the question that introduced this section. Why is intimate communication important? Clearly, intimate communication is important because it functions to allow us to engage in, maintain, and disengage from, intimate relationships. Why do we desire intimate relationships? Most of us appear to share the need to be loved and to love others. Similarly, many of us hold the need to be desired and to desire other people. These needs sometimes conflict, but they continue to tantalize us.

"Don't be so sure they're that happily married . . .
They could be saying the same thing about us!"

We may understand human needs more analytically if we consider the writing of Abraham H. Maslow. Maslow identified a hierarchy of human needs that are illustrated in Figure 13.1. Each of us holds physical needs, safety and security needs, social needs, self-esteem needs, and the need to be self-actualized. Maslow suggested that these needs form a "hierarchy," or an order of importance, with the physical needs being most basic, followed by safety and security needs, and the others. Self-actualization needs are only considered when the other more basic needs are already fulfilled. To some extent we may seek the fulfillment of these needs in our intimate relationships. For instance, a woman who is a single parent attempting to raise three children with a small income may be attracted to a wealthy man in order to help her manage the physical needs of herself and her family. Security needs may explain why people who face tragic and unexpected circumstances often enter into close personal relationships with others soon thereafter. The unattractive man may demonstrate his social acceptance, and thus fulfill his social needs, by marrying an attractive woman. Conversely, the spouse who complains of not doing things together and is offered the response, "Of course we do things together—we go to the marriage counselor together, don't we?" probably has unfulfilled social needs. Given such a response, it may not be surprising that the two require marital counseling!

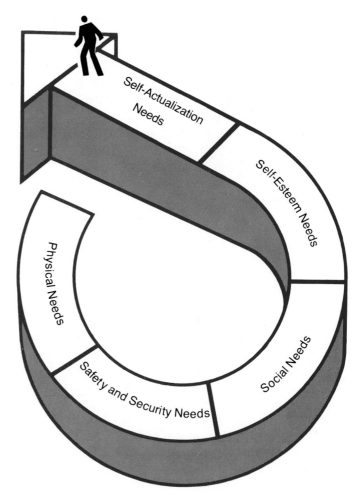

Figure 13.1

Maslow's hierarchy of needs.

Our self-esteem needs may be satisfied by entering into an intimate relationship with someone of high status, someone who is highly respected, someone who has a great deal of recognition, or someone who is highly appreciated by others. We can also be fulfilled by entering into a relationship in which the other person grants us status, respect, recognition, and appreciation. Many people have their self-esteem needs fulfilled by the responsiveness and empathic behavior they demonstrate toward their spouses or partners. The man on the television commercial who smiles at a beautiful woman and states, "She needs me," demonstrates that people feel loved because they are needed.

How do we feel self-actualized through intimate relationships? Self-actualization occurs when we are allowed to become the person we wish to be and is characterized by a greater acceptance of ourselves and others, increased spontaneity and creativity, increased autonomy and independence, and an increased awareness of, and identification with all others. Later in this chapter we will consider the stage of transcending "oneness" that occurs in intimate relationships and that corresponds to self-actualization. At this point we might exemplify satisfying our needs to be self-actualized in intimate relationships through the person who learns more about himself or herself as a result of the relationship and moves toward self-fulfillment.

Maslow's hierarchy of human needs is supplemented by Schutz's analysis of interpersonal needs. Schutz suggested that each of us needs (1) inclusion—the feeling that others include us in their activities and that we include them in ours; (2) control—an ability to be controlled by others and to control them; and (3) affection—being able to give and receive affection.[2] A number of studies have demonstrated the usefulness of Schutz's perspective in examining interpersonal relationships. Our intimate relationships allow us to feel included in a dyadic group. Similarly, by developing a relationship with another person we are extending our capability of including another person in our lives and our experiences. Varying amounts of control occur in intimate relationships. Some partners demonstrate minimal control over each other while other couples exhibit high levels of control. Some relationships are marked by one partner who does most of the controlling and another partner who is controlled. Finally, needs for affection are met in intimate relationships. You can offer your affectionate concern for another person and the other person can extend his or hers to you.

Now that we have considered our common needs for intimate relationships and the importance of intimate communication, let us explain some of the differences that appear to occur in intimate relationships as we turn to the basis of intimacy.

The Basis of Intimacy

Why do we seek intimacy with some people and not with others? Why do some people appear to move easily in and out of intimate relationships while others appear to never approach intimacy with anyone? Are intimate relationships a matter of "being in the right place at the right time"? Do particular personality characteristics contribute to an "intimate personality"?

Reduced to the most simple level, we may identify four bases for the development of intimacy: (1) the self, (2) the other, (3) the situation, and (4) the relational state. Each of these factors may contribute in a major way to an intimate relationship or one or two may be the primary bases for the relationship and the other one or two may serve as minor factors. Let us consider each of these components in more depth.

The Self

Our self-concept, composed of our self-image (who we view ourselves to be) and our self-esteem (how we feel about ourselves) contributes to the ability or inability to develop intimate relationships with others. Some researchers suggest, for example, that if we hold negative feelings about ourselves, then we are unable to establish positive feelings about others. We must love ourselves before we are free to love others. The explanation for this tendency is quite simple. If we have negative feelings about ourselves, we expect that others will similarly have negative feelings toward us. When others respond positively to us, we find that response to be disconfirming. Their positive judgment about us is not consistent with our own negative assessment. Since other persons do not validate our own perceptions, we reject their assessment and their positive regard. Ultimately, we reject them because of their inability to make valid judgments.

Each of us possesses unique personality characteristics that contribute to our ability or inability to develop intimate relationships. Some people are ambitious, task-oriented, aloof, and cold while others may be warm, empathic, yielding, and insecure. These personality characteristics influence our intimate relationships. For instance, if you are reticent and communicate with others only when absolutely necessary, your intimate relationships may be far different than those of the person who is highly gregarious. You may have fewer relationships if you are reticent; you may have shallow relationships if you cannot express your inner feelings, and you may have relationships that are short in duration if you are cold and aloof.

Your background, which is at least partly responsible for your personality, also affects your opportunities for intimacy. Unfortunately, we know of few proven causal relationships between background characteristics and present needs. Two women will illustrate this point: Mary is the youngest of three children. She has two older brothers—one is ten years older than her and the other is eight years older. Her parents wanted a daughter very much and were very pleased when she was born. Throughout her childhood, Mary was doted upon by her brothers and her parents. She was given every advantage. Mary was of average intelligence, but was sent to an expensive prep school and a private university. When she graduated from college, Mary married a man whom she had known only a short time. In general, Marv ignored her and focused on his own needs. Before their second anniversary, Mary and Marv were living apart; shortly thereafter, they divorced. Mary explained her terminated marriage through her background. She was accustomed to a great deal of affection and acceptance and could not be satisfied by an intimate relationship that did not include that basic factor.

June's background is quite different. She grew up in a two-career family. Both of her parents were very ambitious and very busy. They rarely spent time with their two children, particularly their oldest daughter, June. June developed ambition, was highly task-oriented, and was very talented. She had the lead in her senior class play, but her parents were away on business during the nights of the performances and did not see her play. June went to college and eventually received a Ph.D. in psychology. Highly accomplished, an expert in her area of inquiry before she was 35, June also divorced her first husband. The reason? He was unable to fulfill her high need for love. The lack of love that June received as a child, part of her background, created a void that she strongly desired to have filled in womanhood. These two women have decidedly different backgrounds, but their needs in an intimate relationship are remarkably similar.

The Other

The other person in an intimate encounter may similarly contribute to, and influence, the development of the relationship. Stop and think about the persons with whom you have had an intimate relationship. Do they share particular physical or personality characteristics? Do you always look for a man with a beard? Are brunettes more attractive than blondes? Are aggressive women more interesting? Are emotional men particularly attractive?

In most cases, intimate relationships do not occur unless the other person is someone whom we like and someone who is sexually attractive to us. "I love you, but I don't like you" may, under some circumstances, be a clichéd truth, but typically we do like the people we eventually love. Liking generally precedes loving. Anger and conflict are present to some extent in every relationship, but those relationships that are marked by strong dislike on a regular basis may be doomed. Consider the persons you like. Do they enjoy the ballet and theater? Have they shared difficult times in their past which they have overcome? Do most of the people you like share a common set of personality characteristics?

Sexual attraction is also present in intimate relationships. Sexual attraction is more difficult to describe than is liking. Nonverbal characteristics appear to be particularly important. The way a person wears his or her hair, dresses, walks, moves, gestures, and smells affect his or her sexual attraction for us. Interestingly, we may find that one person is attractive to us because he or she has a feature in common with someone else that we loved. The smell of an almost forgotten, but familiar, perfume or shaving lotion can cause us to turn around and look at the person who is wearing the scent; a person who holds our gaze in the same way that another person once held our glance may be startlingly attractive; or observing a person who walks with the same movement as someone from our past may be unnerving. Sexual attraction may also be caused by verbal behaviors: "babytalk," explicit sexual terms, or verbal aggressiveness, for instance.

While there is an almost infinite number of aspects about another person that might attract others, research has clearly shown that four principles influence much of our attraction to each other.[3] First, we are attracted to those persons who are positively reinforcing. In the case of intimacy, this reinforcement is likely to be in the areas of self-concept and affectional need fulfillment. Someone who fits our concept of "the kind of person I see myself with"

Sexual attraction is present in intimate relationships. We demonstrate the salience of our sexual responsiveness through a variety of cues.

and who is fun, exciting, and rewarding to be with is likely to attract us. Second, people are generally reinforcing when they share certain similarities with us. People who are similar in personality, various physical characteristics, attitudes, values and beliefs, intelligence, demographics, etc., are likely to be positively reinforcing. Since similar people tend to "see" the world in much the same way we see it, our beliefs and views are confirmed through interaction with these people.

Third, reciprocity of liking tends to enhance liking. That is, if someone responds to signs of attraction with similar signs of mutual attraction, we tend to be more attracted to them. Finally, proximity increases the likelihood that we will discover reinforcing, similar, and reciprocal relationships. Research has consistently found that we are most likely to become intimately involved with people we frequently interact with, and we are more likely to interact with those to whom we are environmentally close. If you think about the relationships you have developed, most are likely to have been with someone who was geographically close at the time the relationship began or who was in a situation that called for frequent interaction. Although there are many more options today for otherwise "geographically undesirable" relationships to be fostered (e.g., clubs, dating services, etc.), proximity is still likely to increase the likelihood of mutual attraction when other attracting factors are present.[4]

Understanding in Intimacy

Intimate relationships include the feeling of being understood and understanding the other person. When we understand another person, we are able to make predictions about his or her behavior. For instance, if you know that your partner dislikes large, crowded parties, you may refuse an invitation to such a party in his or her interest. Or, if your partner likes to relax and talk for an hour before dinner, you may provide something to drink or snack on and try to create a relaxing environment. But what occurs when the other person wants a change in the routine? Or, what if we have misinterpreted that person's wishes? Examine the following dialogue between a husband and a wife:

Husband: My egg is overcooked.

Wife: That's the way you like your egg.

Husband: That's not the way I like it—I like it over easy, not over hard.

Wife: It is exactly the way you like it. I know more about you than you know about yourself.

Husband: Do you mean that after a while, I am going to cease to be a person with my own perceptions?

Wife: Well, not exactly . . .

If you were the wife in this conversation, how would you respond to the husband? Can this conversation be improved? Is understanding shown in this dialogue? How does the concept of behavioral flexibility, discussed in chapter 1, relate to this example? Rewrite the dialogue, making the necessary improvements.

The Situation

The situation in which we find ourselves may similarly affect our intimate relationships with others. We should understand that the situation includes the larger situation, or culture, as well as the more immediate and obvious situation. The culture affects our intimate relationships in many subtle ways. Our own culture suggests that heterosexual intimate relationships are preferred, that a man and a woman who love each other should marry, that marriage should be postponed until one or both of the persons in the relationship can financially support the couple, that sexual intercourse should be reserved for the married or engaged couple, and that women should, at least in some ways, subjugate themselves to their husbands. It is particularly difficult to disagree with these cultural constraints because of their subtlety and their support. If, for instance, you have a same-sex affection orientation, you may find that you have little social support from your family or childhood friends. Or, if you have separated from your husband and children in order to complete an academic degree and your husband finds another love, many people suggest that it is "your own fault; a woman's place is with her husband and children."

One of the most obvious cultural influences is that related to male aggression, domination, or initiation and female nonassertive, submissive, or responsive behaviors. Past and current research suggests that these patterns of behavior remain pervasive in courtship.[5] Men typically ask women for dates and, in general, initiate the relationship. Men generally appear more assertive or aggressive in the intimate encounter than do women. Men usually take the initiative in contacts with the opposite sex and are reported to self-disclose first in the mixed-sex dyad. They also appear to dominate and initiate sexual encounters. On the other hand, women frequently self-disclose more in an opposite-sex dyad once self-disclosure has been initiated. In addition, women frequently take the lead in demonstrating concern for the other person through love and understanding. Women appear to place more importance on partner dependability, and prefer mates who are taller, older, and more intelligent than themselves, compared to males. Females also tend to view love more in terms as a special form of friendship, whereas males seem to view love as instrumental and game-like.[6]

Changes in role expectations in intimate relationships appear to be occurring, but this change is slow and somewhat confusing. Consider the excerpt from a popular recent article.

The traditional date is a sexist institution. The name of the game is male domination—the man asks the woman out, drives the car, decides where to go, pays the bill and—more often than not—attempts to extend his domination into the sexual arena.

At a time when sexism is under fire whenever it rears its unfashionably ugly head, it's not surprising that the old courtship patterns are being revised on college campuses. Equality in male-female relationships is a highly sought goal. Anne Peplau, assistant professor of psychology at UCLA, and two colleagues found in a study of 200 student couples that 95 percent of the women and 87 percent of the men thought both partners should have "exactly equal say" in a relationship.

But Peplau's study also found that less than half of those same students felt they had achieved their goal of equality in their own relationships. "There's a real difference between abstract ideals and how you run your everyday life," says Peplau. . . .

Because individual practices vary so widely, there is great potential for confusion—especially on the first few dates. Confusion is, in fact, a major difficulty for people who try to practice egalitarian ideals, says Barry McCarthy, a clinical psychologist and associate professor at American University. "Everyone pretty well agrees, especially in the area of sex, that the old double standard relationship was not good training for

*later adult relationships," McCarthy says. "The hassle is that what is re-
placing it is a more ambiguous, confused pattern. The rules are not as
clear, which raises anxiety. I don't know if it's any healthier."*

From Don Akchin, "Revising the Rules of the Dating Game" in *Nutshell, 1979–1980.* Copyright © 1980
Whittle Communications, Knoxville, TN. Reprinted by permission of the author.

You may determine that your intimate relationships are satisfactory, even
though your behavior does not match the research findings. Perhaps, you, as
a woman, initiate dating situations in which sexual relationships are salient.
Or, perhaps you, as a man, have a partner who generally initiates contact. We
need to keep in mind that subcultural differences are continually in flux and
that reported findings about the male/female dimensions of relationships are
regularly changing. The research results are useful only if they offer us normative or descriptive information and suggest possible rationale for failing
relationships. They are less than useful if we use them in a prescriptive way
and are unyielding in our judgments about relationships that do not completely adhere to them. Behavioral flexibility, rather than stagnant role expectations, should guide our interactions with others.

In order to better understand the impact of cultural norms on intimate relationships, consider these possibilities. How would your parents react to your
disclosure that you plan to marry someone of a different racial group? Would
your family accept your same-sex lover and allow the two of you to share a
bed? How often do you observe women with men who are significantly shorter
than they are? Would you consider dating a male who is fifteen years younger
than yourself (if you are a woman) or a woman who is fifteen years older than
you (if you are a man)? What is your reaction to a 45-year-old man who has
never married? Describe a woman of the same age who has never married. Do
you have preconceived ideas about a woman who has never married but has
two children?

A second way in which the situation affects the possibility of an intimate
relationship may be termed *timing*. One theory about the development of
love suggests that love may be viewed as a kind of imprinting. Konrad Lorenz
popularized the notion of imprinting when he showed that baby ducks would
follow any moving object if it was presented at the appropriate time, just as
though the object was its mother. The importance of timing was stressed in
imprinting. In the same way that the baby ducks would follow any moving
object as long as it came into their environment at a certain time, this theory
applied to loving suggests that people fall in love, not because of themselves,
or the other person, but because "the time is right." It is suggested that at
certain points in a person's life, he or she is ready to "fall in love" with whom-
ever is in his or her environment. You may initially scoff at this theory, but
consider how many of your acquaintances become engaged in their senior
year of college and marry soon after graduation compared with how many of
them become engaged in their first year in college and marry in their sophomore year. It is more than chance that so many people "meet the right person"

in their last year in college. Similarly, many unhappy married persons appear to find "just the right person" as they are preparing to divorce their first spouse. Timing appears to be related to the development of intimate relationships.

The Relational State

The quality of intimacy is not just a function of self, other, and the situation. Something happens when people become intimate. They adapt their patterns of behavior to each other. They evolve. Individually they evolve by learning from each other, influencing each other, developing expectations for their future, and even by creating a history that defines their present. But all these processes involve a relational system. Sometimes relationships become intimate by virtue of the dynamics that occur in day-to-day interaction that are unique to the relationship itself. In short, the special interplay of characteristics of two particular individuals in a relational system often creates a momentum, or movement, toward intimacy. The relationship itself stimulates the development of intimacy.

One of the ways of understanding how the relationship can influence and facilitate (or hinder) intimacy is to examine how interaction changes in intimate relationships. If intimacy is a meaningful state of relational being, then it should be reflected in the communication behavior of the partners. The following activity is designed to reveal some of these changes in relational behavior.

Research and scholarly speculation indicate that most of the behaviors or characteristics listed in the Intimacy Behaviors activity can be expected to increase overall as intimacy increases. These changes in behavior both produce and are produced by relational intimacy. Many of the listed behaviors are positively reinforcing and rewarding. The more rewarding a person is, the more you are likely to become attracted to her or him. Furthermore, the more that you observe the other person to be adapting behavior to you and you to the other person, the more you begin to see the relationship as a unique system. This perception means that you begin to perceive relational boundaries. These boundaries serve to "bracket" your relationship from other relationships in which you engage. You view your intimate relationship as being different from your friendship and acquaintance relationships. You begin to view your relationship as a particular form or unit—a romantically intimate relationship.

You may have noticed that we have described many specific behavioral facets of intimate relationships, yet we have not provided an explanation of its complex nature. In other words, we need to explore what constitutes the state of intimacy with another person.

Intimacy is not a simple, single feeling. Instead, intimacy appears to be comprised of several different types of perception and feeling. For example, a given relationship may involve intimacy and closeness on the emotional level, in social relations, in sexual relations, on an intellectual level, in terms of recreational activities, or across all these levels.[7]

Intimacy Behaviors

Presumably, intimacy reflects a basic orientation persons have toward one another. Thus, this orientation should be reflected in their behavior toward one another. The following list has several behaviors that may or may not change as relationships become more intimate. For each behavior, indicate whether you believe it will increase or decrease as relationships become highly intimate. Simply write "increases" or "decreases" in the blank beside each behavior, depending on how you think each will reflect increased intimacy.

As Intimacy Increases,

Frequency of interaction
Average duration of conversation
Average duration of discussion of particular
    topics
Variety of interaction settings
Attempts to restore proximity after separation
Typical proximity
Similarity of dress and appearance
Breadth of self-disclosure
Depth of self-disclosure
Communicative spontaneity
Disclosure of negative information
Idiosyncratic interaction
Development of unique sexual references
Development of nicknames
Accuracy in predicting behavior of partner
Synchrony or meshing of behavior patterns
Development and stability of behavioral rituals
Sharing of resources (e.g., time, activities)
Public displays of affection (e.g., touching)
Reference to possible shared future events
Expressions of relational commitment
Metacommunication
Frequency of long response latencies
Use of plural pronouns (e.g., "we," "our")

In addition to the previously listed behavioral characteristics, intimacy probably entails such perceptions and feelings as feeling close, a sense of obligation and desire to provide emotional support, a perception of similarity about core issues, a generally rewarding style of interaction, commitment to a shared future, interdependence, and a feeling of emotional closeness and affection.[8] When issues become problematic, individuals in satisfying intimate relationships are more likely to use cooperative conflict behaviors rather than destructive behaviors,[9] and are more likely to blame the issues on the

Your Basis for Intimacy

How do you develop intimate relationships with others? Each of us finds different people attractive and has differing needs. To determine some of the patterns in your basis for intimacy, try the following. First, select two or three intimate relationships that you have had. Then, go back over each of these, one at a time, very slowly. How did the relationship begin? What did you notice about the other person? Where did the relationship begin? What kinds of activities did you participate in? How did you feel about the other person? Were you particularly close immediately or did the relationship take time to develop? How were you feeling about yourself when you met the other person? Who made the first move to begin the relationship? How did the other person respond to you? What ended the relationship? Who ended the relationship? How did you feel when the relationship ended? How soon after the relationship ended did you find another person with whom to establish an intimate relationship? As you examine these three or four relationships, notice any similarities that occur. These similarities may represent the qualities of importance in an intimate relationship for you. We have no equation that works well for everyone, but to the extent that we understand ourselves and our own relationships, we can learn to improve our intimate relationships with others. We can increase the number of relationships we have, decrease the number we have, or improve upon existing intimate relationships.

relationship rather than on the other person.[10] Intimate couples generally believe that the rewards or satisfactions each member receives from the relationship are relatively equal.[11] Not surprisingly, therefore, persons perceive communication in intimate relationships to be generally more effective, personal,[12] and accurate.[13] While it should be obvious that not all interaction in highly intimate relationships can be characterized in these ways, the nature of the intimate relationship does seem to permeate much of the interaction that makes up the day-to-day encounters of relational partners.

Intimacy in relationships arises from a complex set of factors. Features of the self, the other, the situation, and the relationship all seem to play an important part in the development and evolution of intimacy. The extent to which the self and other uniquely tend to adapt their behavior to the situation and the relationship itself indicates the possibility of relational intimacy.

Improving Intimate Communication

In *Conjoint Family Therapy,* Virginia Satir explains that a wife's and husband's perceptions of his or her communication and of the other person's communication in the relationship are critical to the development or deterioration of the marriage. To the extent that perceived differences occur, the relationship will be unsatisfactory. If both persons believe that they talk effectively about subjects of mutual interest and use clear nonverbal cues, their relationship is more effective. Intimate relationships appear to be enhanced when the two members in the relationship share common perceptions of the communication and when both members appear to exhibit effective communication behavior.[14] Let us consider specific stages in the development of intimate communication.

Four stages appear to be particularly important to the development of intimate relationships. We may identify these stages as (1) sharing the self, (2) confirming the other, (3) becoming "one," and (4) transcending "one."

Sharing the Self

Self-disclosure, the sharing of self, was discussed in chapter 6. You may wish to review the information in that chapter. Self-disclosure is especially important in intimate communication. Frequently people equate intimate communication with self-disclosure because it is viewed as so central to the development of a relationship.

Research on self-disclosure verifies that it occurs more frequently in the dyad, or two-person group, than in larger group settings.[15] In addition, self-disclosure appears to occur more frequently in intimate relationships than in acquaintanceships.[16] Self-disclosure tends to be more open, personal, and direct as relationships develop. In intimate dyads, in which people express love for the other partner, more self-disclosure occurs than in dyads in which the two people have only expressed degrees of liking.[17]

If you are currently encountering difficulty in an intimate relationship, determine if the problem lies in your self-disclosure behavior or the self-disclosure behavior of the other person. Are you willing to express your feelings and thoughts in an open, direct, and personal way? Do you share your reactions to the current situation? Do you recall past experiences that have a bearing on current events? Are you sensitive to the self-disclosures of the other person and attempt to reciprocate? Do you self-disclose more to those persons you love than to those whom you like?

Confirming the Other

A second stage in the development of intimate relationships may be termed "confirming the other." *Confirming* means to provide support for the other person's self-concept.[18] When we confirm a person, we are validating who he or she is as a person. We are, in effect, acknowledging the other person's unique self and we are suggesting the importance of the other person. When we confirm another person, we need not agree with all of that person's perceptions, beliefs, or attitudes, but we do need to understand some of them.

In "Sometimes When We Touch," the writer expresses a commitment to a nonevaluative, empathic response:

And who am I to judge you
On what you say or do?
I'm only just beginning,
to see the real you.

In chapters 8 and 9, we discussed the importance of listening and empathy in interpersonal communication. These skills are at the base of confirming other people. You may wish to review these chapters and consider some of the applications to your own intimate relationships. A recent article described the importance of active listening to intimate relationships. The author suggested that good listening carried the inherent message that you cared about the other person. Active listening appears to break down a self-focus that interferes with relationship development.[19] *Empathy,* putting ourselves in someone else's place, is similarly important to the affirming process. Attempting to see the world from another's perspective and developing alternative ways of thinking about situations is highly useful.

Merging.   We need to merge with another if we wish to allow our interpersonal relationships to develop. In chapter 2 we discussed the development of relationships and the steps through which they appear to move. The final step in the development of a relationship, as you will recall, was attachment. When we attach ourselves to another person, we experience a kind of bonding, or "oneness." We may think of ourselves as a unit, rather than as two separate identities. Frequently the "one" that we create is considerably different than the "two" who are part of it.

Additionally, you should not conclude that two people actually *become* a single entity. Merging means that aspects of the two increasingly begin to appear like a single unit. However, the two individuals always retain some of their personal identities and uniqueness. Indeed, as a caveat, it should be noted that any attempts to "become one" need to be considered cautiously. Individuals should be aware that going too far toward becoming one with another person risks losing a sense of self. Relational intimacy should thus be viewed as involving a merging, but not a complete merger.

We create "us" from "you" and "me" in a variety of ways. Nonverbally, we become one by increased touching, less distance between us, using similar vocal patterns, dressing in similar ways, and moving in similar ways. Verbally,

An important step in the development of an interpersonal relationship may be termed "merging." This couple appears to symbolize two separate entities rather than a single unit.

we change our pronouns from "I" to "we" and "me" to "us." We also develop intricate sets of personal codes. Some current research focuses on the words and phrases that are given unique meanings in the context of specific relationships. This research suggests that we not only provide more information to those with whom we are intimate, as we have previously discussed with regard to self-disclosure, but we also use messages that are specially adapted to the interacting couple. A recent study summarized categories of personal idioms. They include partner nicknames such as "Boo," and "Duke," and teasing insults such as "animal," and "futtbutt."[20] Romantically intimate relationships usually develop a private code for sexual innuendo, or suggestive but indirect messages, as well.[21] By developing private codes we are able to exclude others and to develop greater closeness or "oneness" with our partner. This development of the single entity appears to allow the deepening of the intimate relationship.

Emerging.   Finally, we attempt to transcend by "emerging." This goal may appear to be in contradiction to the preceding section. You may wonder how an interacting couple can merge and yet go beyond that bonding. Transcending our bond to another person does not mean separating ourselves from the other person in a negative sense; it does suggest the avoidance of the dishonest communication that appears evident in these lyrics:

So here we stand, you and I
You are too kind, I'm too shy
To say what we really mean
So we make life a masquerade
Never showing all, only the parts we play.

Freedom, equality, and independence appear to be key concepts in the transcendence of the bond that we form in intimate communication. In the same way that our confirmation of other persons does not require that we accept their perceptions, attitudes, and values as our own, when we transcend the bond that we have with them, we find that we are free to hold unique perceptions, varying attitudes, and different values. Equality is the key to the functioning intimate relationship. One partner does not impose his or her will on the other because each holds an equal voice. Similarly, the individual does not forfeit his or her independence or separate "self" by bonding with another. When we are able to unite with another person and yet are able to go beyond that union, we find that "me" and "we" can live together in harmony.

The merging of selves in an intimate relationship permits the *emergence* of a new and stronger sense of self and relational unity. Such a relationship allows the individual a healthy context in which to grow and develop self interests, yet reinforces the bonds of the relational system of which she or he is a part. In this way, the individuals transcend the relationship through **emerging.**

These four stages, sharing self, affirming the other, becoming "one," and transcending "one," appear to be essential in the development of intimate relationships. A recent article summarized seven characteristics that distinguished happily married couples from those that were seeking counseling. You will notice that the first three are concerned with sharing self, the fifth characteristic alludes to affirming the other, characteristics four and six concern becoming a unit, and the last one deals with transcending the bond between an intimate couple.

1. They openly and frequently discuss their daily lives with each other regardless of whether the topic is pleasant or unpleasant;
2. They share their beliefs and concerns about sex and sacred issues with each other with little embarrassment or intimidation;
3. They do not express their emotions via the mystification process of sulking and pouting;

4. They select topics of interest to discuss with each other;

5. They know when to avoid certain subjects or conversation with a spouse, and know when not to tell things that put self in a negative light;

6. They discuss issues with each other before making important decisions that affect each other;

7. They understand the meanings of each other's nonverbal facial expressions and glances during conversation.[22]

Summary

In this chapter you became familiar with communication that occurs in the intimate relationship. You learned that intimate communication is different from conversations with friends in that sexual intimacy is salient in intimate communication and is not a potential in conversations with friends. Another difference between intimate communication and some other forms of interpersonal communication is that intimate communication occurs between only two people, that it provides a relatively closed system, is unique, unpredictable, and not always observable.

Most of us desire intimacy as we seek someone to love and someone who will love us. We seek the fulfillment of various needs through intimate relationships. As we examine Maslow's hierarchy of needs, we can determine that most of these needs can be fulfilled through intimate relationships. Similarly, Schutz's analysis of interpersonal needs offers us insight as to the importance of intimate relationships. The reason we seek intimacy at some time with some individuals and not at other times with other persons lies in our own background and personality, the characteristics of the others involved, the situation in which we find ourselves including the general situation of culture and the more specific situation which includes timing, and the relationship itself.

We can improve our intimate communication if we recognize the importance of the four stages through which interpersonal relationships should move and the related interpersonal communication skills that accompany each stage. We must share ourself with another person through verbal and nonverbal self-disclosure. We affirm the other person through the skills related to active listening and empathic understanding. We merge as we alter personal pronouns and engage in intimate nonverbal communication. Finally, we emerge through assertiveness skills. Intimate communication can be improved and the resulting satisfying intimate relationship is well worth the effort that we expend.

Notes

1. Dennis R. Smith and L. Keith Williamson, *Interpersonal Communication: Roles, Rules, Strategies, and Games* (Dubuque, Ia.: Wm. C. Brown Company, Publishers, 1977), p. 281.

2. William C. Schutz, *Firo: A Three-Dimensional Theory of Interpersonal Behavior* (New York: Holt, Rinehart & Winston, 1958). See also D. P. McAdams, "Personal Needs and Personal Relationships," in *Handbook of Personal Relationships,* S. Duck (ed.) (New York: John Wiley & Sons, 1988), pp. 7–22.

3. For an extensive discussion of physical attraction factors, see E. Hatfield and S. Sprecher, *Mirror, Mirror: The Importance of Looks in Everyday Life* (Albany, N.Y.: State University of New York, 1986).

4. For a thorough discussion of these attraction principles, see E. Berscheid and E. H. Walster, *Interpersonal Attraction,* 2d ed. (Reading, Mass.: Addison-Wesley, 1978).

5. See, for instance, John D. Davis, "When Boy Meets Girl: Sex Roles and the Negotiation of Intimacy in an Acquaintance Exercise," *Journal of Personality and Social Psychology* 36(1978): 684–92; J. G. Hollandsworth, Jr. and K. E. Wall, "Sex Differences in Assertive Behavior: An Empirical Investigation," *Journal of Counseling Psychology* 24(1977): 217–22; and B. I. Murstein, "The Relationship of Mental Health to Marital Choice and Courtship Progress," *Journal of Marriage and the Family* 29(1967): 447–51; M. L. Barnes and D. M. Buss, "Sex Differences in the Interpersonal Behavior of Married Couples," *Journal of Personality and Social Psychology* 48(1985): 654–61; F. Crosby, P. Jose, and W. Wong-McCarthy, "Gender, Androgyny, and Conversational Assertiveness," in *Gender and Nonverbal Behavior,* C. Mayo and N. M. Henley (eds.) (New York: Springer-Verlag, 1981), pp. 151–69; K. Deaux and B. Major, "Putting Gender into Context: An Interactive Model of Gender-related Behavior," *Psychological Review* 94(1987): 369–89; D. A. Dosser, Jr., J. O. Balswick, and C. F. Halverston, Jr., "Male Inexpressiveness and Relationships," *Journal of Social and Personal Relationships* 3(1986): 241–58.

6. These and other gender differences in intimate relationships are reviewed in R. A. Hinde, "Why Do the Sexes Behave Differently in Close Relationships?", *Journal of Personal and Social Relationships* 1(1984): 471–501.

7. M. T. Schaefer and D. H. Olson, "Assessing Intimacy: The PAIR Inventory," *Journal of Marital and Family Therapy* 7(1981): 47–60.

8. G. M. Maxwell, "Behaviour of Lovers: Measuring the Closeness of Relationships," *Journal of Social and Personal Relationships* 2(1985): 216–38.

9. S. Ting-Toomey, "Coding Conversation between Intimates: A Validation Study of the Intimate Negotiation Coding System (INCS)," *Communication Quarterly* 31(1983): 68–77.

10. G. J. O. Fletcher, F. D. Fincham, L. Cramer, and N. Heron, "The Role of Attributions in the Development of Dating Relationships," *Journal of Personality and Social Psychology* 53(1987): 481–89; H. Newman, "Communication Within Ongoing Intimate Relationships: An Attributional Perspective," *Personality and Social Psychology Bulletin* 7(1981): 59–70.

11. E. Hatfield, J. Traupmann, S. Sprecher, M. Utne, and J. Hay, "Equity and Intimate Relations: Recent Research," in *Compatible and Incompatible Relationships,* W. Ickes (ed.) (New York: Springer-Verlag, 1985), pp. 91–118; S. Sprecher, "The Relation between Inequity and Emotions in Close Relationships," *Social Psychology Quarterly* 49(1986): 309–21.

12. L. A. Baxter and W. M. Wilmot, "Communication Characteristics of Relationships with Differential Growth Rates," *Communication Monographs* 50(1983): 264–72; L. A. Baxter and W. W. Wilmot, "Interaction Characteristics of Disengaging, Stable, and Growing Relationships," in *The Emerging Field of Personal Relationships,* R. Gilmour and S. Duck (eds.) (Hillsdale, N.J.: Lawrence Erlbaum Associates, 1986), pp. 145–59.

13. J. M. Honeycutt, M. L. Knapp, and W. G. Powers, "On Knowing Others and Predicting What They Say," *Western Journal of Speech Communication* 47(1983): 157–74; J. L. Orlofsky, "Intimacy Status: Relationship to Interpersonal Perception," *Journal of Youth and Adolescence* 5(1976): 73–88.

14. Virginia Satir, *Conjoint Family Therapy* (Palo Alto, Calif.: Science and Behavioral Books, 1964).

15. Judy C. Pearson, "The Effects of Setting and Gender on Self-Disclosure," *Group and Organizational Studies: The International Journal for Group Facilitators* 6(1981): 334–40; and

Ralph B. Taylor, Clinton B. De Soto, and Robert Lieb, "Sharing Secrets: Disclosure and Discretion in Dyads and Triads," *Journal of Personality and Social Psychology* 37(1979): 1196–1203.

16. See, for instance, Charles Berger, "The Acquaintance Process Revisited." Paper presented at the Annual Convention of the Speech Communication Association, New York, December 1973; and Jin Myong Won-Doornink, "On Getting to Know You: The Association between the Stage of a Relationship and the Reciprocity of Self-Disclosure," *Journal of Experimental Social Psychology* 15(1979): 229–41.

17. Joseph W. Critelli and Kathleen M. Dupre, "Self-Disclosure and Romantic Attraction," *The Journal of Social Psychology* 106(1978): 127–28.

18. K. N. Cissna and E. Sieburg, "Patterns of Interactional Confirmation and Disconfirmation," in *Rigor and Imagination: Essays from the Legacy of Gregory Bateson,* C. Wilder-Mott and J. H. Weakland (eds.) (New York: Praeger, 1981), pp. 253–82.

19. Kate White, "How to Take the Emotional Leap of Getting Close to Someone," *Glamour,* August 1979, p. 80.

20. Robert Hopper, Mark L. Knapp, and Lorel Scott, "Couples' Personal Idioms: Exploring Intimate Talk," *Journal of Communication* 31(1981): 23–33.

21. J. S. Sanders and W. L. Robinson, "Talking and Not Talking about Sex: Male and Female Vocabularies," *Journal of Communication* 29(1979): 22–30.

22. P. Yelsma, "Marital Communication, Adjustment and Perceptual Differences between 'Happy' and 'Counseling' Couples," *American Journal of Family Therapy* 12(1984): 26–36. See also C. E. Larson, "Interaction Patterns and Communication Effectiveness in the Marital Context: A Factor Analytic Study," *Journal of Communication* 17: 342–53; B. E. Tolstedt and J. P. Stokes, "Relation of Verbal, Affective, and Physical Intimacy to Marital Satisfaction," *Journal of Counseling Psychology* 30(1983): 573–80.

Additional Readings

Bach, George R. and Deutsch, Ronald M. *Pairing*. New York: Avon Books, 1975.

Bach, George R. and Wyden, Peter. *The Intimate Enemy: How to Fight Fair in Love and Marriage*. New York: William Morrow & Company, Inc., 1969.

Crosby, John T. *Reply to Myth: Perspectives on Intimacy*. New York: Macmillan, 1985.

Hendrick, Clyde, ed. *Close Relationships*. Newbury Park, Calif.: Sage, 1989.

Lerner, Harriet G. *The Dance of Anger: A Woman's Guide to Changing Patterns of Intimate Relationships*. New York: Harper & Row, 1985.

Levinger, George and Raush, Harold L., eds. *Close Relationships: Perspectives on the Meaning of Intimacy*. Amherst, Mass.: University of Massachusetts, 1977.

McDonald, Robert. *Intimacy: Overcoming the Fear of Closeness*. Old Tappan, N.J.: Revell, 1988.

O'Neill, Nena and O'Neill, George. *Open Marriage: A New Lifestyle for Couples*. New York: Avon Books, 1973.

O'Neill, Nena and O'Neill, George. *Shifting Gears*. New York: Avon Books, 1975.

Perlman, Daniel and Duck, Steven. *Intimate Relationships: Development, Dynamics, and Deterioration*. Focus Editions series: Vol. 80. Newbury Park, Calif.: Sage, 1986.

Phillips, Gerald M. and Metzger, Nancy J. *The Study of Intimate Communication*. Boston: Allyn & Bacon, 1976.

Roloff, Michael E. and Miller, Gerald R., eds. *Interpersonal Processes: New Directions in Communication Research*. Newbury Park, Calif.: Sage, 1987.

Rubin, Zick. *Liking and Loving*. New York: Holt, Rinehart & Winston, 1973.

Vaughan, Diane. *Uncoupling: Turning Points in Intimate Relationships*. New York: Oxford University Press, 1986.

Zimbardo, Phillip G. *Shyness: What It Is and What To Do about It*. Reading, Mass.: Addison-Wesley Publishing Company, 1977.

Family Communication

the neighborhood™ Jerry Van Amerongen

2/27

Under stress, Mrs. Marley often slips back into old, unproductive and often painful family patterns.

Although most of us do not experience family patterns that are quite so overtly unproductive and painful as this cartoon portrays, it is clear that the ways in which our families interact greatly affect our well-being and quality of life. A number of books have been published that consider the communication that occurs in "normal" families.[1] As you might expect, a great deal of disagreement still occurs about what constitutes a "normal" family. Authors variously define the term to refer to "nondysfunctional," "functioning," "stable," and "homeostatic" families.

This chapter will examine the family as an interpersonal communication context. You will discover the many different kinds of families in our society and that each family unit has special communication needs. You will learn how the family is a system and, more specifically, a communication system. Family communication can be improved. Integral to the improvement of family communication is the establishment of the family members' need for autonomy, the maintenance of the family's need for interdependence, and the development of an awareness of the recurring interaction patterns and the changes within the family system. Let us turn now to a description of the family unit and a consideration of the effect of this context on communication.

The Nature of the Family

What is a family? Does a father living with his three children constitute a family? How about a couple whose children have "left the nest"? If a woman and man divorce and they are granted joint custody of their children, do they still comprise a family unit? The contemporary changes in the family unit provide problems in creating a definition that is broad enough to encompass the many different kinds of families in our society, but narrow enough to distinguish the family from other groupings of people.

A Definition of Family

Bochner defined the family in broad terms as "an organized, naturally occurring relational interaction system, usually occupying a common living space over an extended time period, and possessing a confluence of interpersonal images which evolve through the exchange of messages over time."[2] The family unit is organized in the sense that members generally fulfill particular roles—mother, sister, daughter—and that behavior among members does not occur in a random way. In other words, after a period of time, we can make predictions about how one family member will respond to another family member's interaction. When a small child becomes angry and demonstrates anger through crying, shouting, and similar disrupting behaviors, he or she may generally be sent to another room. Or, when the father tells an older son to mow the lawn, clean his room, or wash the car, a typical response from the son might be an argument, followed by a threat on the part of the father, followed by compliance. The family naturally occurs because it is not an artificially created group as friends and co-workers may be seen to be. The family is a relational interaction system that will be discussed further in the next section, but in its simplest form this means that relationships exist among the members and that the interactions among the members affect the other members. Families usually occupy the same living space, although they may live apart—at least for some portion of time. Families do not come into being and disintegrate at the same rate that other relationships can and frequently do.

Finally, families create a blending of images that are provided through interpersonal communication. In other words, families develop common ways of viewing the world that are shared among the family members. A family may agree that a certain level of cleanliness is necessary in order to have a satisfactory living environment and members may be disturbed when they visit a relative's home that does not meet that standard. A particular family might view nudity as healthy and not be concerned with the wearing of clothes when they are in the privacy of their own home. Using language that may be offensive to others may be appropriate within a particular family.

Bochner's broad definition of the family is useful as it does not exclude the variety of kinds of families that occur today. Nonetheless, we will limit the family to units in which at least one adult and one child are present. We will not consider two people who cohabit as a family; we have already described this interpersonal unit in chapter 13 on intimate communication. Similarly, the couple whose children have left home do not constitute a family as we will define it. The family may be as small as two persons—one parent and one child—or virtually unlimited in size. We will thus define a *family* as an organized, naturally occurring relational interaction system consisting of at least one parent and one child who occupy a common living space, existing for an extended period of time, and creating common images through communication.

Types of Families

This definition of the family is useful as it includes the varying sizes, shapes, and types of families that are present in our culture today. As we stated in chapter 1, only 16.3 percent of the 56 million families in our country are conventionally "nuclear" and include a father who works, a mother who stays at home, and natural children who live with the couple. Let us consider some of the other forms that families take, the terms that have evolved which refer to each of them, and how the form of the family may affect communication patterns. The *natural family* consists of two adults and their children. The natural family usually begins with a couple who then have children. The original communication unit is that created by the parents. The addition of a child or children can alter this arrangement. For instance, the mother may form a closer bond with the child or children replacing the former communication bond with the father. Or, the father may link with the children. Finally, the couple may maintain their strong communication bond and the children may form another communication unit.

The *blended family,* which is occurring with increasing frequency, includes two adults and step-, adoptive, or foster children. The unit provides particularly complex and difficult to analyze communication units. If a woman with children marries for a second time, she may have her allegiances torn between her new husband and her natural children. The communication patterns that were previously established in the earlier family unit may not be followed by the new father. Similarly, the father's previously understood notions about acceptable communication patterns may be disregarded by the others. Families that include foster children have different problems. In these cases, children may live with foster parents for an extended or shorter period of time, but they may leave the family unit unexpectedly. The uncertainty and lack of stability in foster families can cause a great deal of tension and anxiety and can interfere with satisfying interpersonal communication.

The *single parent family* has only one adult and may include children who are adopted, natural, step-, or foster children. The single parent family generally results when one parent dies or leaves the family unit. Research has found that, "of the children born in the early 1980s, 45% are expected to live with only one parent at some time before they reach age 18."[3] Stress is often placed on the communication in the single parent family. Children may accept the single parent to fulfill the role of both parents. The roles of "super mom" and "super dad" are untenable for most adults who are attempting to juggle two parenting roles and economic support for a family. The family member or members who formed especially close communication units with the missing parent experience particular pain. The adolescent boy who is without a father, the little girl who is without her mother, the baby who was primarily cared for by his father, or the husband who no longer has his wife's companionship experience a special loss that may be difficult for other family members to fully understand or to appropriately soothe.

The *institutional family,* which occurs in pockets throughout the country, includes groups of adults who share the parenting of groups of children. Communes and other groups that hold a distinctive religious or philosophical belief provide examples of the institutional family.[4] A wide variety of communication patterns are possible in these families. On the positive side, we recognize that a number of different communication units are possible. The kinds of family groupings that are available are nearly endless—a parent with a child, two parents, two adults who have not parented children, two children of the same or different ages. On the negative side, individuals in institutional families may experience a sense of loss of control or a lack of stability. They may feel that they really have no *one* person with whom to form an especially close unit. In other words, the flexibility of the institutional family that is one of its greatest benefits may provide a problem for some people.

Finally, we use the term *extended family* to refer not only to parents and children, but to grandparents, aunts, uncles, cousins, and others in the family unit. Occasionally people will use the term to refer to very close friends for whom they are attempting to demonstrate closeness. Extended family members may provide similar functions that others in the more traditional family unit provide. For instance, a grandmother may be able to establish a closeness with a child that neither of the child's parents have or an uncle can function as a father in a particular family. The rationale for calling close friends "a member of my extended family" may be just because they are fulfilling functions that are normally found in the family and they create a particularly close communication relationship with one of the family members.

The Family as a System

Earlier in this chapter we noted that researchers had not directed their attention to the "nondysfunctional" family until relatively recently. Similarly, the family has been viewed as an interacting communication system for little over twenty years. The suggestion that the family was a system was espoused as early as 1926 by Burgess, a sociologist, who called the family a "unity of interacting personalities."[5] Usually, however, Bateson and his colleagues at the Mental Research Institute are credited with the pioneering efforts on viewing the family as a communication system.[6] Donald Jackson contributed a great deal to the continued research on the family as a unit when he described families as closed communication systems that included feedback mechanisms that served to alter and correct the functioning of the system. Jackson also coined the term "family homeostasis," or equilibrium produced by a balance of functions, that has been shown to be helpful in current thinking about family communication.[7] The notion that a family provides a communication system is especially useful for our purposes. Viewing the family as a system suggests that the family unit is attempting to maintain stability or a sense of equilibrium. This balance is not inherently positive or negative, rather it suggests that the family is not in a state of major change or flux.

Family therapists helped solidify the idea that the family was a system. They noted that if one person in a family had a particular behavior problem and that person's behavior was altered, frequently another person developed the same problem behavior. In other words, the family unit appeared to "need" the behavior problem from some member in order to maintain balance. Or, conversely, the family was operating in a way that the problem behavior evolved from their patterns of interaction. For instance, if one family member had a dependency on drugs or alcohol and overcame this dependency, another family member might then develop a similar dependency problem. This dependency problem might be a result of the family unit "needing" a weak member who was dependent upon chemicals, or interaction patterns in the family encouraged a family member to develop such a dependency.

Transactional nature.   This example from family therapy emphasizes one of the features of the family as a system. Systems are *transactional* rather than based on an action or interactional model. You will recall that we distinguished among models of communication as *action, interaction,* or *transaction* in chapter 1. When we view communication as an interaction, we are tempted to determine causes and effects of behavior; when we view communication as a transaction, we recognize the futility of attempting to identify

Families may be viewed as interesting communication systems based on transactional models.

one event as a cause and another as an effect. When we view the family unit as a system we do not focus on cause-effect relationships, but rather recognize the interrelationships among events. Thus, in the example of the family that includes a person with a behavior problem, we neither identify his or her behavior as the cause of the family's pattern of interaction nor do we assert that the family's pattern of interaction is responsible for the person's behavior.

Holistic unit.   A second feature of viewing the family as a system, which is related to this first feature, is that the whole is greater than the sum of the parts. We view the family unit as the basic unit of analysis. We do not identify individuals in the family as responsible for the interaction patterns that occur; rather, we credit the family system with those interaction patterns. We recognize that when a problem occurs in the family, it is the family's problem rather than an individual's problem. We know that persons who are effective communicators in one setting may not be effective communicators in their family setting. Individuals may contribute to the interaction in a family, but they do not cause success or failure.

Disruption in the Family System

Disruptions occur in the family system. We should not blame individuals but examine the entire system. In the conversation below, we view an example of a fairly common disruption. The son has returned home from college during the fall semester.

Father: Mark, before you go back to school, there's something I'd like to talk with you about.

Son: What is it?

Father: Well, you know how important my fraternity was when I was in college. I've been wondering if you wouldn't find the same benefits in fraternity life as I did.

Son: There's no point in going any further—I'm not interested in fraternity life.

Father: Why?

Son: The guys are all conformists and snobs. All they care about is money, cars, and drinking.

Father: You know, son, some of the connections that you make in college can help you later on. Two of my best customers are people I met in my fraternity.

Son: I don't plan on going into business—I'm an education major, remember?

Father: Why do you always reject my ideas without even thinking them over?

Son: Why don't you ever try to understand that what I want is not the same as what you want?

Father: It's hopeless trying to talk to you.

Son: I feel the same way about talking to you!

Based on this conversation, we may guess that these two family members have had similar arguments at other times. We should not conclude, however, that it is the fault of either father or son. Each of them may be effective communicators with their own peers or their colleagues, but still find that each conversation that they share results in confrontation.

Have you had similar disagreements with one of your parents? Did you notice a pattern in these disagreements? Did you conclude that one of you was "wrong," and the other was "right"? Have you been able to successfully work through a similar disagreement? If you have, what strategies did you use? To what effect did differences in age contribute to the disagreement? Was the argument with your same-sex or opposite-sex parent? Do you think this is typical? Put yourself in the role of the son in the conversation and rewrite the conversation demonstrating empathic understanding of the father's perspective, but assertive responses regarding your own lack of interest in fraternity life.

Importance of feedback.   Finally, when we view the family as a system, we recognize that a feedback system is operative. This feedback system governs the behavior in the family in such a way that changes in the family are met with other changes. For every action, there is a direct reaction. The reaction to the change may positively reward the change or negatively punish the change. For example, if a family unit includes a homemaking mother who decides that she is going to become a full-time college student, the family may respond in a variety of ways. The other members may agree to do those tasks that she has previously done (positively rewarding) or they may all complain and criticize her behavior (negatively punishing). Changes in the family system may be large changes as the homemaking mother who resumes her college education or they may be more minor changes as depicted in this dialogue. The child altered his appropriate response pattern and received negative reinforcement.

Chris: (Watching television) I wonder what's going to happen to that dog?

Mom: It's time to eat—wash up.

Chris: (Still watching television) Okay.

Mom: Right now.

Chris: Yeah, I'm coming.

Mom: Chris . . .

Chris: I'm coming, Mom.

Mom: I am not going to call you again.

Chris: That's good news!

Mom: (Snapping off television) You're going to your room until you learn how to respond appropriately, young man.

In this instance, the lack of responsiveness resulted in punishment or negative feedback. Regardless of whether feedback is negative or positive, family members respond to changes in the family unit. For example, the mother in this dialogue responded to the child's trivializing of her command, which represented a change from his apparent compliance. With this understanding of the family as a system in mind, let us consider the family as a *communication* system.

The Family as a Communication System

Most of the current theories on family communication suggest that family members engage in the same interaction patterns again and again.[8] These patterns of interaction may be negative or positive. For instance, a family may include a wife who nags and a husband who drinks too much. We may view the pattern of interaction in which the wife nags and then the husband drinks and then the wife nags and then the husband drinks occurring almost endlessly. It is difficult to determine if the wife's nagging is the cause of the husband's drinking or whether the husband's drinking causes the wife to nag, as we recognize the transactional nature of the behavior. However, we can determine that this pattern of behavior recurs and that it appears to be detrimental to the family unit. On the other hand, we may view a family that includes a daughter who provides a great deal of nurturing for a newborn baby. The nurturing behaviors result in demonstrations of affection for the daughter from the parents. In this case, the recurring pattern of interaction appears to be beneficial to the maintenance of the family unit.

Labeling a pattern of interaction as positive or negative is not always such a straightforward matter, however. For instance, this interaction between an older sister and a younger brother may be positive or negative.

Kate: (Walking into the room where her 5-year-old brother is watching television) What are you watching?

Ben: Um, "Sesame Street."

Kate: (Changing the channel) I want to watch the rerun of "All in the Family."

Ben: (Running out of the room) I'm going to tell Dad.

Kate: (Watching television, and not responding to her brother)

Ben: Dad said he's going to settle this.

Kate: (Watches television and ignores her brother)

Ben: You always do this to me!

Kate: (No response)

Ben: When I get big, you won't be able to do this anymore!

Kate: (No response)

Ben: (Beginning to watch the program on television) I'll bet you think you can get away with this, don't you?

Kate: (No response)

Ben: (Watches television and appears to forget the argument)

You might label this typical pattern of interaction as negative because of the outcome for Ben; however, the interaction might be seen as positive because the two children solved their problem and resolved their differences. Similarly, interactions may be viewed as negative or positive from the viewpoint of one member, but in a different way from the perspective of another family member, or differently still if we consider whether the interaction pattern is detrimental or beneficial to the family unit.

Communication in Your Family

Every family has different rules or norms governing their communication patterns. Complete the following exercise in order to determine the patterns that exist in your family.

1. What communication topics *can* be discussed? _____
    _____
    _____

2. What topics *cannot* be discussed (for instance, sex, money problems, religious
    convictions, drug use)? _____
    _____

3. *When* can you communicate with others? _____
    _____

4. When can you *not* communicate with family members? _____
    _____
    _____

5. What emotions are you allowed to communicate (anger, hostility, sadness, hurt, joy,
    sorrow, fatigue, enthusiasm)? _____
    _____
    _____

6. What emotions are you *not* allowed to communicate? _____
    _____
    _____

    A second conclusion about family communication is that families establish agreements about what may and may not be communicated and how the content of what is communicated may be interpreted.[9] Families determine who can talk to each other and who can listen, what messages can be communicated, and how we may communicate those messages to each other. For example, in a particular family unit, the topic of how much money the wage earners make may be taboo for the children; the oldest son may not ask his father for use of the family car, but may ask his mother who, in turn, will ask his father; and the mother may not show her frustration through angry outbursts directed toward her husband. Perhaps each of us has made the error of telling a neighbor or a relative about some personal aspect of our family life,

Communication in Your Family continued

7. What verbal and nonverbal behaviors do you display in front of your family that you rarely, or never, display outside of your family unit? _____

_____

_____

8. Do you have family "secrets" that you are not allowed to discuss with others? _____

_____

9. List some specific words that you cannot use in your family (jargon, clichés, profanity, nicknames). _____

_____

_____

10. List some specific nonverbal behaviors that you cannot use in your family (nonverbal behaviors that have a specific meaning in one of your membership groups, nonverbal behaviors that have a profane meaning within your family, etc.). _____

After you have completed this inventory, compare your list with a person whom you trust. Do you see similarities? Explain why your family unit has different communication patterns than does another family unit. To what extent do nationality, region of the country, and other subcultural differences affect your family communication? Consider *who* the primary "rule maker" is in your family. Does this affect the communication patterns? What conclusions can you draw from this exercise?

only to be chastised by one of our parents later on. We also establish rules about *when* we can communicate with each other; we may not talk to a person watching a favorite television program, we may not communicate with someone who is trying to "sleep in," and we may not communicate with another family member when he or she has gone to the bedroom and shut the door.

Agreements about the communication patterns that can and cannot occur in the family may be stated directly or they may be merely implied by positively rewarding behavior when they are followed or negatively punishing behaviors when they are violated. While these agreements are normally tacit, rather than verbalized, they may be formally agreed upon. When we do verbalize our agreements with family members, rather than rely on assumed agreement, we are, in effect, communicating about communication. The term we reserve for referring to communication about communication is *metacommunication.*

Changes in Your Family's Communication

Re-examine the list that describes the communication in your family. Do you feel satisfied with the communication patterns that you have described? If you were to describe the "ideal family," would they communicate in the way that you have pictured your family's communication? List below the changes you would like to see in your family's communication patterns.

1. Communication topics that I would like to discuss or have discussed in my family are _____

   _____

2. The topics of conversation that I would not like to have discussed in my family are _____

   _____

3. The people with whom I would like to communicate more in my family are _____

   _____

4. The people with whom I would like to communicate less in my family are _____

   _____

5. The emotions that I would like to see expressed in my family are

   _____

6. The emotions that I would not like to see expressed in my family are

   _____

7. The times when I would like to communicate with other family members are _____

   _____

Finally, we should note that change is possible in the communication patterns that occur in the family. Theorists have suggested that the only changes that are significant in the family are those that alter the recurring systematic patterns of interaction.[10] Unless the change affects the basic premises that define the system, it is not a change. Change does not occur when a system moves from one state to another state, but when a system becomes a new and different system. This transformation occurs when the rules that govern the system are changed. For example, a death in a family may cause family members to feel the need to become closer. The traditional father who has seldom touched, held, or stroked his children may begin to engage in these activities. The busy mother who has rarely taken time to actively listen or empathize with her teenage daughter may begin to spend time engaged in conversation with her. The children, who previously spent a great deal of time alone in their rooms or with friends, may begin to spend more time playing games and watching television together. Thus the family has altered what may and may

Changes in Your Family's Communication continued

8. The times when I would not like to see communication occurring are

    _____

9. The verbal and nonverbal behaviors that occur in my family that I would like to extend

    beyond my family unit are _____

    _____

10. The verbal and nonverbal behaviors that I would like to reserve for my family unit are _____

    _____

11. The "secrets" that I would not like to discuss beyond my family unit are _____

    _____

12. The "secrets" that I would like to discuss beyond my family unit are

    _____

13. The words that I would not like members of my family using are

    _____

14. The nonverbal behaviors that should not be demonstrated in my family, given my point of

    view, are _____

    _____

Now that you have had an opportunity to identify the patterns of communication in your family and to suggest changes that you would desire, can you go further? Can you engage in metacommunication with other family members? Can you discuss these possible changes with your parents, brothers and sisters, or children? Is it possible for improvement to occur in the communication patterns in your family?

not be communicated and how the content of what is communicated may be interpreted. Change has occurred because the rules that govern the system have changed; the previous system has been transformed into a new system.

Family communication is complex because of the number of people involved and because of its systematic nature. All of us have observed family units that seemed to deteriorate before our eyes. Sometimes families are unable to adjust to major changes that occur—a suicide in the family, the loss of a job, or a person who refuses to play an established role. Sometimes barriers occur in family communication because we assume that everyone in the family understands us or we assume that no matter what we say, they will *not* understand us. The lack of flexibility in family relationships and the lack of clarity and honesty in verbal and nonverbal messages contribute to the problems that frequently occur in family communication.

Sometimes the deterioration of a family unit is desirable. If a family unit includes little love, respect, or honesty, the individuals involved may appropriately seek other relationships. The family in which one adult is deliberately dishonest with the other adult—through infidelity, gambling, or excessive drinking—may be better off if it is dissolved. A child or wife who is regularly and severely beaten may be better off if he or she is removed from the family unit. Family members must recognize that some family units are less desirable than is the deterioration of those families.

Most often, individuals in families wish to continue living with their families. We seek to improve the quality of our relationships with other family members. Family communication can be improved, allowing us deeper and more meaningful relationships with others in our family, and ensuring the stability of the family unit. Three skills seem particularly important in the improvement of family communication: (1) establishment of the individual's need for autonomy, (2) maintenance of the family's need for interdependence, and (3) development of an awareness of the recurring interactional patterns and the changes within the family system. These skills are similar to those we discussed in chapter 13 on improvement in intimate communication, but they are especially important in the context of family communication. Let us explore each of these skills further.

IMPROVING FAMILY COMMUNICATION

Establishment of the Individuals' Need for Autonomy

The family unit is composed of individuals. Each of the individuals has a need for independence and autonomy that precedes his or her need for the group. When we become a member of a family, we do not lose our essential self. Families that smother members or do not allow individuals to grow and develop in independent ways may be doomed. We need to establish our need for autonomy, even in the family.

Importance of self-disclosure.   Self-disclosure, which we discussed in chapter 6, is an important ingredient in establishing our need for autonomy. We should be free to intentionally and honestly tell others in our families how we feel. Our self-disclosure should not be forced or required, but voluntarily given. The adolescent who is forced to explain to his parents where he has been or the mother who must justify why she is pregnant when her oldest child is sixteen and embarrassed about the situation are not being given the opportunity to self-disclose nor to maintain their autonomy. An individual in a family should be free to self-disclose as much, or as little, as he or she desires. The length of the relationship among family members suggests that we should be able to self-disclose intimate information that is either positive or negative.

The family unit should provide a safe environment in which we can experiment with new ideas and different ways of perceiving the world. Sharing ideas with our family can result in a greater understanding and acceptance of ourselves. In addition, the self-disclosure in which we engage in our family can result in more satisfying relationships among family members. For example, you may be considering dropping out of college and getting a job for a year. By talking over this possibility with your parents, you may gain a different perspective of the idea, without risking commitment to it. In addition, your parents gain a better understanding of your values and ideas. The net result is more acceptance of you by your family and a better understanding of your own ideas.

Consider your own self-disclosure behavior in the family. Do you use "I" statements or hide behind generalized statements about how others feel? Do you speak directly and clearly to others in your family? Do you avoid meaningless qualifying words and phrases; words and phrases that negate your self-disclosure; and incomplete sentences? Do you go beyond the empathic level of communication to deal with your feelings and thoughts? Do you feel comfortable nonverbally with your family members? Do you exhibit openness with your body? Are you able to touch other family members when appropriate?

Assertiveness, which we discussed in chapter 7, is an additional skill that is useful in the establishment of self in the family. Clarity, straightforwardness, and honesty in communicating our needs, wishes, and desires without infringing upon the needs of other family members is important. Indeed, the process of influence, and the dynamics of power, interdependence, and conflict appear to be among the most ubiquitous and important aspects of family functioning.[11] Do you speak directly with your family members? Do you avoid threats, put-downs, and evaluative comments? Do you say "no" when appropriate? Do you communicate assertively through your nonverbal communication—by using a direct body orientation, an open body position, a relaxed, but attentive posture; continual, direct eye contact; and appropriate vocal characteristics?

Assertiveness problems.   Satir identifies two sets of behaviors that provide problems in family communication and that arise from a lack of assertiveness.[12] The first is labeled as *placating,* which means agreeing with the other people in your family simply to avoid conflict. The person who placates allows others to make choices that affect the entire family. This person appears to suggest from his or her behavior that any decisions made by others are acceptable and even desirable. The person who placates is very similar to the nonassertive person who was discussed in chapter 7. The person who placates may be the mother who responds that "I only live for my family; if they are happy, I am happy," the middle child who continually responds that she "doesn't care" when family decisions are to be made, or the father who is "seen, but not heard," who seldom voices an opinion, and who hides behind a newspaper or a television set.

At the other end of the continuum is the *blamer.* This individual places blame on others in an effort to appear stronger, wiser, or better in some way. The blamer uses the aggressive nonverbal and verbal behaviors that are discussed in chapter 7. He or she frequently disagrees with other family members and suggests, directly or tacitly, that no one else ever does anything right. The blamer attempts to gain his or her way without regard for the feelings of other family members. The blamer may be characterized by the child who regularly complains that all of his friends have a certain item, but he does not; by the father who ridicules his child's efforts to play ball, earn high grades, or develop friendships; by the mother who suggests that she had excellent career opportunities but she had to turn them down in order to care for her family.

Nonassertiveness and aggressiveness, in the form of placating or blaming, can seriously impair family relationships. Individuals who placate may be satisfied with the relationship for some time, but eventually become dissatisfied with not having their needs met. Sudden, drastic changes may then result that disrupt the family unit. A mother may abandon her children or a father may establish a new relationship with another person. Persons who blame may find that others do not respond positively to them, under any conditions. They may find short-term gains through this behavior, but eventually may find that others avoid them. The blaming father may discover that his children do not talk to him. The child who is a blamer may find that his siblings choose other playmates. Assertion difficulties often lead to negative family relationships.

Maintenance of the Family's Need for Interdependence

A family consists of individuals who have independent needs, motives, and goals. It is also a unit that requires interdependent behaviors. If persons in a family behave in a manner that is only cognizant of independent, individual needs, the family ceases to be a unit and becomes, instead, a collection of individuals who are each pursuing goals that may not be in harmony with maintaining the family as a unit. The family's need for interdependence must be maintained.

Active listening.   In order to maintain interdependence in the family, individual members must be responsive to each other's needs. You will recall that we discussed active listening in chapter 8. Active listening—hearing another person's message, attempting to understand that message, and then verifying your understanding by offering the other person appropriate feedback—is helpful in maintaining your need for interdependence in the family. Do you avoid defensiveness, experiential superiority, and egocentrism in dealing with family members? Do you allow other family members the independence to alter their behaviors and to play different roles at different times? Or, do you fail to listen to them because you perceive them always playing the same role? For example, do you assume that a younger sibling has nothing important to say or that a parent cannot understand how it is to be a college student?

When we view families as systems, we recognize that feedback systems are operative. Each change in the system, such as the addition of a new child or a child leaving home, is met with other changes in the interaction patterns.

How do you demonstrate that you are engaged in active listening with your family? Do you invite others to add other comments, do you ask relevant questions, do you share common experiences and identify areas of agreement? Do you offer descriptive, nonevaluative responses and provide affirming statements? Do you avoid complete silence, on the one hand, or avoid dominating the conversation, on the other? Do you restate the content of the message when a family member talks with you and attempt to paraphrase the content and the intent of his or her messages? Do you demonstrate responsiveness through your body, face, and voice?

Empathy.   Empathy is similarly important in maintaining the interdependence of the family unit. Our sensitivity to family members and our ability to communicate that sensitivity is critical. We can demonstrate that concern by providing validating statements, by providing reflective statements of the other person's perceptions, by providing statements of understanding, and by offering verifying feedback. Nonverbally, we can demonstrate our empathic understanding by a forward body lean, a direct body orientation, positive and responsive facial expression, physical proximity, and increased touching.[13] Consider your communication behavior with your own family. Do you demonstrate empathy?

Problem behaviors.   Satir's identifications of problem behaviors in the family include two behaviors that are barriers to responsiveness and concern for others in the family.[14] The first barrier is *computing*, which is behaving in a coldly logical way with no emotional response. Computing is overly reasonable behavior that suggests the person is calm and collected. Verbally, computing includes multisyllabic words; nonverbally, computing includes a voice with little inflection, proper posture, and appropriate gestures. In the movie, *Four Seasons*, the character played by Carol Burnett accuses the character played by Alan Alda of this tendency. At one point, in an argument, she asked him if he was angry and he responded that he was. She inquired, "How would anyone know," and continued, "When you're angry, I want to be able to tell that you're angry and not read about it in your diary three years later!" A lack of emotional involvement is communicated by the person who engages in computing. In the family unit, the computer is the person who spends a great deal of time in his or her room, the older child who regularly "talks down" to other siblings, or the parent who is unable to translate love and concern in human terms and must stand behind complicated concepts instead.

Distracting occurs when a person offers an irrelevant or meaningless comment. The person who always responds with a *non sequitur*—a comment that does not follow from the previous statement—is a distractor. He or she does not demonstrate having heard what the other person has said nor cares to understand what was stated. A lack of concern is what is communicated. Family members may occasionally be distracted by other concerns and not be able to listen actively or demonstrate empathy for others. The distractor uses this pattern of behavior regularly. An individual may be characterized as a distractor if he or she interrupts the other person, relates an anecdote from his or her own day in response to another person's story, brings up an entirely new topic, or shows no compassion for the other family member.

Rather than offer comments that show a lack of emotional involvement or a lack of understanding, we should practice our responsiveness on family members. It is especially important to be open to the feelings and perceptions of others when we are engaged in family communication. Parents need to demonstrate their concern for children and children should attempt to understand their parents. Family life is so much more satisfying when we are able to open ourselves to the others who are part of our family.

Development of an Awareness of the Recurring Interaction Patterns and the Changes within the Family System

Every family has recurring interactional patterns or themes. Surprisingly, many individuals cannot identify those patterns that characterize their own family. Nonetheless, the patterns of interaction that occur in the family in which we were born are often carried by us to the family that we create. Many people vow that they will not treat their own children in the way that their parents treated them; however, we frequently hear our parents' words echoing from our own mouths. Sometimes people are unaware that they are behaving as parents in the same way that their parents behaved.

Family Conflict

Conflict occurs in families because family members sometimes do not realize that individuals are growing and changing. This static notion of each family member playing one prescribed role is a special problem for children who become adults without acknowledgment by their parents. In some families, 30- and 40-year-old people are still treated as children. In others, preteenagers are given adult privileges. While these two approaches may be atypical, the following conversation between a mother and her 18-year-old daughter is common. The daughter in this conversation is a college student who is home because of a school vacation. Her mother has waited up for her and she has arrived home, after a date, later than normal.

Mother: Where have you been? Do you know what time it is?

Daughter: It's not that late, Mom. Besides, what I do is none of your business. I'm grown up and I can do what I want.

Mother: It is my business. I'm your mother. I was worried about you. I know you were out with that high school drop-out. I don't like the idea of your seeing him. You're better than that—you've already finished half a year of college.

Daughter: Rich is not a high school drop-out. He got his high school diploma last year. The only reason he was out of school for three months in his junior year was because his dad died and he had to work to help support his mom and his brothers and sisters. After he helped put some money in the bank, he went back to school and got his diploma. It doesn't matter what I say, you still don't think much of Rich. I'm going to bed, I don't want to talk about it any more.

Mother: If you don't come back here, I'm going to wake up your father.

Daughter: (Storms back into the room, sits down quickly, folds her arms across her chest, and sighs in disgusted way.)

Mother: (Approaches daughter, sits down next to her, puts her arms around her, and speaks softly.) I'm sorry, honey. I didn't mean to yell at you. It's just that I worry about you sometimes.

Daughter: Why do you worry about me, Mom? Don't you think I'm old enough to take care of myself?

Mother: It's just that when you're out that late I worry about your being in an accident or something.

Daughter: All we did was go out for pizza, sat and talked, and then he brought me home. That was it. I'm sorry. I didn't mean to worry you.

Mother: I know that. I'm sorry I blew up. It's just hard for me to accept the fact that you're not a little girl anymore. Well, let's try and get some sleep now. (She smiles as they both rise.)

Have you been involved in a similar conversation in your family? Recall that conversation and explain the sequence of events that occurred in the conversation. Did your parent and you resolve the conflict as the mother and daughter did in this conversation? Has this kind of conversation occurred frequently in your family? How could this situation have been reenacted without the conflict between the two family members? Explain how self-disclosure and empathy would have been valuable skills early in this conversation. Identify specific confidence and concern skills that would have eliminated or minimized the conflict here. Can you apply these skills to similar conversations of your own?

We need to develop an awareness of our recurring interactional patterns. We want to be aware of those patterns that are desirable and help us to maintain a healthy, functioning family unit. At the same time, we want to recognize destructive patterns that can eventually destroy the unity of the family. Our sensitivity to those regularly occurring patterns can make the difference between a long and enriching family life and one that is shallow or short-lived.

Similarly, we need to be sensitive to the changes that occur within our family. Giving birth to a new baby or adopting a small child, losing a family member as a result of death or dissolution, engaging in new work, or adopting a new role within the family all present major changes to the family unit. We should acknowledge such changes and recognize that other features of the family will change as well. For instance, a more time-consuming job for one of the adults will result in less time being spent with the children; the addition of a new baby or new adopted child will result in a reorganization of the relationships between the adult who is the primary parent and the other children; and the loss of a family member may cause irreparable harm to the family or may result in increased openness and understanding of the remaining family members. We should not expect the same behaviors from family members who are experiencing such changes. A change in one aspect of the system will result in changes throughout the system. We will be better able to cope with change if we understand and expect some of the major alterations that will likely occur among members in the family unit.

Summary

In this chapter we considered the family as a context in which interpersonal communication occurs. Family communication is ubiquitous and complex. We define the family as an organized, naturally occurring relational interaction system consisting of at least one parent and one child who occupy a common living space, exist for an extended period of time, and create common images through communication. Families may be natural, blended, single parent, institutional, or extended. Each of these types of families provide special communication features.

The family is a system that is transactional and has mechanisms for feedback. It is, in addition, a *communication* system and can be identified by recurring interaction patterns, agreements about what can be communicated and how the content of what is communicated may be interpreted, and continually changing patterns of interaction. How can we improve family communication? Family communication can be optimized if we allow individual need for autonomy, the family need for interdependence, and are sensitive to recurring interactional patterns as well as the changes that occur. Nearly everyone has a family and most of us feel we can improve our relationships within that family. Your understanding of the information in this chapter will assist you in that endeavor. You have now considered communication among strangers, acquaintances, friends, intimates, and family members. In the next chapter you will turn your attention to an interpersonal communication context that is more closely related to task-related needs, the interview.

Notes

1. See for example, S. Miller, (ed.). *Marriages and Families: Enrichment Through Communication* (Beverly Hills, Calif.: Sage, 1975); F. I. Nye, (ed.). *Family Relationships: Rewards and Costs* (Beverly Hills, Calif.: Sage, 1982); Judy C. Pearson, *Communication in the Family: Seeking Satisfaction in Changing Times* (New York: Harper & Row, 1989). J. Scanzoni and M. Szinovacz, *Family Decision-making: A Developmental Sex Role Model* (Beverly Hills, Calif.: Sage, 1980); E. J. Thomas, *Marital Communication and Decision Making: Analysis, Assessment and Change* (New York: Free Press, 1977); R. H. Turner, *Family Interaction* (New York: John Wiley & Sons, 1970). For good examples of work on "abnormal" families, see R. D. Laing, *The Politics of the Family and Other Essays* (New York: Vintage, 1971); E. G. Mishler and N. E. Waxler, *Interaction in Families: An Experimental Study of Family Processes and Schizophrenia* (New York: John Wiley & Sons, 1968).

2. Arthur P. Bochner, "Conceptual Frontiers in the Study of Communication in Families: An Introduction to the Literature," *Human Communication Research* 2(1976): 381–97.

3. Coleman, cited by D. Perlman and K. S. Rook, "Social Support, Social Deficits, and the Family: Toward the Enhancement of Well-being," *Applied Social Psychology Annual* 7 Family Processes and Problems: Social Psychological Problems, S. Oskamp, (ed.), p. 18.

4. For a somewhat dated but interesting collection of essays about alternative family systems and processes, see J. S. DeLora and J. R. DeLora, *Intimate Life Styles: Marriage an Its Alternatives* (Pacific Palisades, Calif.: Goodyear, 1972).

5. E. W. Burgess, "The Family as a Unity of Interacting Personalities," *The Family* 7(1926): 3–9.

6. G. Bateson, D. Jackson, J. Haley, and J. Weakland, "Toward a Theory of Schizophrenia," *Behavioral Science* 1(1956): 251–64. For an excellent discussion of the origins and principles of family systems theory, see A. P. Bochner and E. M. Eisenberg, "Family

Process: System Perspectives," in C. R. Berger and S. H. Chaffee (eds.), *Handbook of Communication Science* (Newbury Park, Calif.: Sage, 1987), pp. 540–63.

7. Donald D. Jackson, "The Question of Family Homeostasis," *Psychiatric Quarterly Supplement* 31(1957): 79–90.

8. See, for example, J. M. Sorrells and F. F. Ford, "Toward an Integrated Theory of Families and Family Therapy," *Psychotherapy: Theory, Research, and Practice* 6(1969): 150–60.

9. See, for example, R. D. Laing, *The Politics of The Family and Other Essays* (New York: Random House, 1969).

10. See, for instance, S. Minuchin, *Families and Family Therapy* (Cambridge, Mass.: Harvard University Press, 1974); and P. Watzlawick, J. Weakland, and R. Fisch, *Change: Principles of Problem Formation and Problem Resolution* (New York: W. W. Norton, 1974).

11. See M. A. Fitzpatrick and D. M. Badzinski, "All in the Family: Interpersonal Communication in Kin Relationships," in M. L. Knapp and G. R. Miller (eds.), *Handbook of Interpersonal Communication* (Beverly Hills, Calif.: Sage, 1985), pp. 687–736. S. L. Mills and J. E. Grusec, "Socialization from the Perspective of the Parent–Child Relationship," in S. Duck (ed.), *Handbook of Personal Relationships* (New York: John Wiley & Sons, 1988), pp. 177–91.

12. Virginia Satir, *Peoplemaking* (Palo Alto, Calif.: Science and Behavior Books, Inc., 1972), pp. 59–66.

13. Fitzpatrick and Badzinski.

14. Satir, pp. 68–72.

Additional Readings

Abramson, Jane B. *Mothermania: A Psychological Study of Mother–Daughter Conflict.* Lexington, Mass.: Lexington Books, 1986.

Ashwood, H. Lee. *Relationship Ideal and Family Forever.* Washington, D.C.: Relationship Family Communications, 1986.

Beebe, Steven A. and Masterson, John T. *Family Talk: Interpersonal Communication in the Family.* New York: Random House, 1986.

Cargan, Leonard and Melko, Matthew. *Singles: Myths and Realities.* Beverly Hills, Calif.: Sage, 1982.

Galvin, Kathleen M. and Brommel, Bernard J. *Family Communication: Cohesion and Change.* Glenview, Ill.: Scott, Foresman and Company, 1982.

Gilbert, Lucia Albino. *Men in Dual-Career Families: Current Realities and Future Prospects*. Hillsdale, N.J.: Lawrence Erlbaum Associates, 1985.

Gordon, Thomas. *P.E.T.: Parent Effectiveness Training*. New York: Peter H. Wyden, Inc., 1970.

Hinde, Robert A. and Stevenson-Hinde, Joan, eds. *Relationships within Families*. New York: Oxford University Press, 1988.

Kantor, David and Lehr, William. *Inside the Family: Toward a Theory of Family Process*. San Francisco: Jossey-Bass, 1975.

Laing, R. D. *The Politics of the Family and Other Essays*. New York: Random House, 1969.

Mishler, Elliot G. and Waxler, Nance E. *Interaction in Families: An Experimental Study of Family Processes and Schizophrenia*. New York: John Wiley & Sons, 1968.

Nye, F. Ivan, ed. *Family Relationships: Rewards and Costs*. Beverly Hills, Calif.: Sage, 1982.

Satir, Virginia. *Conjoint Family Therapy*. Palo Alto, Calif.: Science and Behavior Books, 1967.

Satir, Virginia. *Peoplemaking*. Palo Alto, Calif.: Science and Behavior Books, 1972.

Scanzoni, John and Szinovacz, Maximiliane. *Family Decision-Making: A Developmental Sex Role Model*. Beverly Hills, Calif.: Sage, 1980.

Interviewing

the neighborhood™ Jerry Van Amerongen

Once again Alex fails to overcome a poorly conceived resume.

Those of us who have suffered the painful outcome of rejection from a job interview know how Alex feels. We will find, however, that the resume is only a small part of the interview process and that how we behave before and during the interview is critically important to successful outcomes in the interview context.

The earlier sections on interpersonal communication contexts in this book have focused on social needs. We have examined communication with strangers, acquaintances, and friends, intimates, and family members. In general, we satisfy our loving and belonging needs in these contexts. In this chapter we will examine an interpersonal communication context that is related to our task-related needs. We engage in interviewing in order to receive information, in order to provide information to others, in order to sell goods, services, and ideas, in order to gain employment, in order to appraise or evaluate a person or product, and for counseling or advising.

Interviewing is central to many of our task-related activities, as you may have surmised from the lengthy list of occasions in which we engage in it. If you consider how frequently others interview you and even the interviewing that you do, you can appreciate its importance.

To the extent that interviews are designed to exchange information and create certain impressions, they are not unlike many more informal and social encounters.[1] More formally, you are interviewed by employers, administrators, accountants, physicians, sales personnel, persons of particular religious beliefs, individuals who belong to specific political parties, and even by your instructors. You may participate in interviews as the interviewer if your job involves persuasion of others, providing information to other individuals, gaining information from people, counseling others, evaluating the work of co-workers, or selecting personnel for specific jobs. You are probably no different from the college students and alumni who participated in a survey on the importance of assignments in interpersonal communication class. In this study, the college students identified the interview as the most important interpersonal communication assignment in the beginning communication course and alumni identified the interview as second only to the small group discussion.[2] You may find the information in this chapter as highly important to you now, as a college student, and even more important when you graduate.

In this chapter we will consider the nature of interviewing, including a definition of this kind of interpersonal communication, the purposes of interviewing, and specific features of the interview. We will discuss the role of questions and questioning in the interview, answers and answering in the interview, and a number of organizational patterns that may be used in the interview setting. Special attention will be paid to the informational and employment interviews. These two types of interviews may be especially relevant to your task-related needs.

The Nature of Interviewing

Interviewing is one of the more formal and preplanned kinds of interpersonal communication. Interviews are more structured than the conversations that occur with friends, strangers, acquaintances, intimates, and family members. Interviews are generally preplanned; we do not engage in interviews spontaneously without any prior thought as we sometimes do with conversations. Interviews usually have a specific purpose—to inform, to persuade, to appraise or evaluate, to counsel or advise, or to gain or offer employment. Interviews are typically well organized: they frequently are divided into an opening, body, and a closing just as most speeches are divided into an introduction, body, and conclusion. Most interviews occur between two persons, although they can occur between two parties. In other words, the interview in which one employer interviews one potential employee is most typical, but occasionally a few interviewers interview a single interviewee, as on "Meet the Press," and sometimes a single interviewer will interview more than one interviewee at a time, as in some sales situations. Interviews may involve more than two persons, but they never involve more than two parties—one representing the interviewer and one representing the interviewee. Interviews are typically not composed of comments or statements, as are other forms of interpersonal communication. Instead, interviews are based on the asking and answering of questions. Generally, the interviewer asks the questions and the interviewee answers them, although the interviewee may initiate questions.

Definition of Interviewing

We will combine these unique features of the interview to define the *interview* as a formal and preplanned form of interpersonal communication that has a specific purpose, is well organized, and involves two parties who ask and answer questions.

Generally speaking, behavior in an interview is organized around, or related directly to, one of four basic functions.[3] First, interview behavior functions to develop an organized exchange of information. The structure of most interview behavior is of a "question-answer" form. The employment interviewee is striving to find out if the organization is one in which he or she would like to work, and the employment interviewer is attempting to find out if the interviewee is the best available candidate for the position. These tasks call for optimum exchange of information and the development of coherent, accurate mutual understanding. Second, interview behavior is almost always intended to create certain impressions. Expressive nonverbal behavior, presenting primarily positive information on the part of the interviewee, appearing assertive yet deferent, all indicate the extent to which interactants in an interview are attempting to manage their impressions.[4] Third, much of any interview consists of influence or control-oriented behavior. This function tends to be more subtle than the others, but it is part of the process. The ways in which the interview setting and furniture are organized, questions are asked, interruptions are used, and vocal styles and nonverbal mannerisms are used all influence the process, comfort level, and "rules" of the interview. Finally, much interview behavior is performed to fulfill an affiliation, or rapport, function. Head nods, smiling, eye contact, friendly touch or handshake, facial expressiveness, and other such actions tend to develop a friendly and affable atmosphere within which the exchange of information can be facilitated. To the extent that you are aware of the functions that your behavior serves in the interview, the more likely it is that you will be able to succeed in accomplishing your personal goals in the interview process.

Before we leave the definition of the interview, one other characteristic should be noted. A good interview is an *inter*view, and not an *intra*view. In other words, the interview in which the interviewer controls the outcome and allows only a limited number of responses is not necessarily a good interview.

Similarly, interviews in which the interviewer is ill-prepared and allows the interviewee to talk without direction or focus are inappropriate.[5] For instance, if you are attempting to sell a product through door-to-door interviews, you will find little success if you do not engage in some preplanning and have some focus and direction to your interview. An interview allows the exchange of communication by both parties. Neither the interviewer nor the interviewee should totally control or dominate the interview.

Questions and Questioning in Interviewing

We previously stated that interviews involve the asking and answering of questions. All questions do not elicit the same kinds of answers. Some questions encourage the respondent to answer briefly, with a one- or two-word answer. Other questions encourage long, detailed answers. Similarly, some questions suggest an answer, while others allow the respondent to offer any answer. Finally, some questions change the topic or introduce a new area of inquiry while other questions serve as follow-ups to earlier questions that were not answered completely or adequately. We can categorize questions in at least three different ways. Our understanding of these categories will help us frame appropriate questions for specific circumstances. As we discuss each of the categories, we will attempt to delineate the specific use for each. You will see that the purpose of the interview may determine, to a large extent, the kinds of questions that should be asked.

Open or closed.   Open questions include those questions that are broad in nature and provide little structure for the respondent. The interviewee may reply in a number of equally correct ways. For instance, "Why are you looking for a job with our company?", "How do you feel the President is doing thus far?", "Tell me about your background in accounting," and "What was Amsterdam like?" are questions that allow the respondent to offer a number of different answers. Open questions are useful because they allow the interviewer to listen more than he or she speaks, because they demonstrate concern for the interviewee, and because they may offer a more complete picture of the interviewee than a closed question allows. If you are involved in an interview as an interviewer in which you wish to be especially cognizant of the interviewee's mood or feelings, such as the counseling interview, you may wish to use a large number of open questions. You may wish to use open questions during the early part of a persuasive interview, too, in order to determine what motivates the interviewee. Open questions may be less than useful if a short amount of time is available for the interview since open questions take more time than do closed questions. In addition, open questions lose their effectiveness if the interviewer is providing an abundance of feedback cues that suggest to the interviewee what the correct or desired answer may be. Finally, avoid open questions if you are interested in tabulating the responses you receive or you will be conducting statistical analysis on the information provided by interviewees.

Interviews, unlike conversations, consist primarily of questions and answers. Understanding the different kinds of questions that can be used may help you to become more effective in the context of interviewing.

Closed questions limit the possible answers that the interviewee may provide. Closed questions are restrictive and sometimes include all of the possible answers within the question itself. Closed questions range from less closed questions like "How many years have you been in college?", "When did you quit smoking?", and "How many cups of coffee do you drink each day?" to extremely closed questions such as, "If you were offered a salary of $20,000 per year with no fringe benefits or a salary of $15,000 with the benefits package I have outlined to you, which would you be inclined to accept?", "In what part of the country would you prefer to live—the North, the South, the West, or the East?", or "Do you agree or disagree with the extension for the ratification of the federal Equal Rights Amendment?" Despite the apparent limitations of this type of question, research indicates that most questions asked in interviews are closed.[6]

The most highly closed questions are those known as *bi-polar*. Bi-polar questions are those questions for which there are only two possible answers. Typical bi-polar questions include yes-no, agree-disagree, in favor-oppose, or other extremes that form the end-points on a continuum. When we rely on bi-polar questions, we are making the assumption that only two answers are possible for the specific question and that the two answers that we offer are significantly different. Answers between the extremes such as, *sometimes, maybe, don't know, agree in part, occasionally,* and *rarely* are not allowed when bi-polar questions are used. Bi-polar questions should not be overused nor used incorrectly, but they can be useful when a limited amount of time is available or when answers will be submitted to specific analysis.

In general, closed questions are useful when the interviewer wishes to control the outcome of the interview to a certain extent, when answers are to be recorded and/or coded, and when the interviewer is less experienced. Closed questions may be less than desirable under some circumstances. Closed questions do not allow you to secure a maximum amount of information, thus they may interfere with an attempt at persuasion on your part as the interviewer, since you may not know what motivates the interviewee. Closed questions may force respondents to provide an answer that is not the most accurate reflection of their attitude since they must select the *best* answer from a relatively small number of possible choices. Finally, the nature of such questions may mask more complete information. While open questions rely on interpersonal skills that fall in the areas of active listening and empathic understanding; closed questions rely on increased verbal clarity and specificity.

Primary or secondary. When a question changes the topic or introduces a new area of interest, we label it as a primary question. When a question seeks additional information about a topic already under discussion, we identify it as a secondary question. Some questions are obviously primary such as "I'd like to turn now to some questions about your experience in the Peace Corps," "What can you tell me about the changes in the stock market in the past few months?", and "Shall we begin our discussion by your sharing your feelings about your family?" Other questions are clearly follow-up or secondary questions such as "What else happened to you?", "How did you respond when that happened?", and "Could you go on?" Nonetheless, determining whether a question is primary or secondary is sometimes dependent upon the particular interview. For example, the question, "Tell me about your math scores," is secondary if it follows a relatively brief answer that included the comment, "I recently took the S.A.T. exams to enter college and received scores in English, math, science, and social studies." The question would be primary, however, if the interviewer had been asking questions about the interviewee's academic abilities in the language arts areas.

Primary questions are almost always preplanned. Secondary questions, on the other hand, are frequently added during the interview itself as a result of incomplete information or answers that are unexpectedly brief. Secondary questions are an important tool of the sensitive interviewer. If you are engaged in active listening as the interviewer, you will probably be able to add secondary questions as they are appropriate. For instance, if the interviewee begins to make a statement and then interrupts himself of herself with another point, you may wish to inquire about the original statement. If the interviewee provides a long and wandering response, you may wish to pick up some of the points that were made. When the interviewee uses language in an unusual way or when he or she relies on ambiguities rather than specific statements, you may wish to seek clarification with a secondary question. Finally, if the interviewee misunderstands your question, does not answer your question, or provides an incomplete answer, you may wish to rephrase your primary question into a secondary one. You do not need to follow up on every hint of additional information that the interviewee provides, but you can use secondary questions to capture the information that is central to your purpose.

Neutral or leading.   Questions can also be distinguished as neutral or leading. Neutral questions allow the respondent to provide any answer he or she wishes; leading questions suggest a correct or preferred answer within the question itself. Neutral questions are most often open while leading questions are frequently closed. The following questions are neutral:

"How do you manage to live on your current salary?"

"What plans do you have for redecorating your home?"

"How did you like living in Idaho?"

Contrast these questions with the following leading questions that are based on the same questions:

"You can't manage to live on your current salary, can you?"

"Your plans for redecorating your home include painting the walls off-white, don't they?"

"I'll bet you really enjoyed the open spaces and lack of crowding in Idaho. I know I did."

Leading questions typically have a prescribed and easily detected "correct" answer. For instance, in the three leading questions that were just listed, the first question is "correctly" answered negatively and the last two are to be answered positively. The interviewer would be surprised, at the least, and defensive, at the other extreme, if an interviewee answered these "incorrectly." Leading questions generally leave no doubt in your mind about how they are to be answered. An answer contrary to expectations generally results in tension between the two parties.

Neutral questions are most useful in interviews in which you are attempting to elicit information, especially if you are going to analyze your data and draw comparisons. Both neutral and leading questions can be useful in the employment interview, which we discuss later in this chapter. Leading questions are especially appropriate for the persuasive interview, when you are attempting to convince an interviewee that he or she should buy the goods or services that you are offering or alter beliefs according to your prescriptions.

Leading questions can interfere with the interview process when they encourage the interviewee to distort his or her perceptions, beliefs, or attitudes; when they result in the interviewee simply "parroting" the words and feelings of the interviewer; and when they cause negative or defensive feelings on the part of the interviewee. Neutral questions can be inappropriate when you are truly trying to convince someone of your point of view or when you want to stress a certain position.

Types of Questions in a Survey Interview

A person who was interested in the television viewing habits of women and their attitude toward the exposure of the female body put together a short survey interview. The six questions in her interview that was designed to elicit information are listed below. For each question, match whether it is open or closed, primary or secondary, and neutral or leading.

	Open or Closed	Primary or Secondary	Neutral or Leading
1. What is your age?	_____	_____	_____
2. What is your occupation?	_____	_____	_____
3. How many hours do you spend watching television each week? (a) Light (0 to 14 hours) (b) Mild (15 to 41 hours) (c) Heavy (42 hours or more)	_____	_____	_____
4. Do you have a favorite show?	_____	_____	_____
5. What is it?	_____	_____	_____
6. Do you think there is too much exposure of the female body on television?	_____	_____	_____

Answers and Answering in Interviewing

When we discussed active listening and empathic understanding in chapters 8 and 9, we pointed out that many people focus on what was *said* in a conversation rather than on what they *heard.* In other words, people frequently focus on the role of the speaker or the initiator of communication. In a parallel way, students of communication often concern themselves with the role of the interviewer in the interviewing context. We learn how to be effective interviewers and how to ask appropriate questions, but we do not learn how to be successful interviewees nor do we consider the role of answers and answering in the interviewing context. Nonetheless, for many people, the role of the interviewee is more important than the role of the interviewer. In short, most of us serve as the interviewee more frequently than we serve as the interviewer. Recognizing the importance of the answers that are offered by the interviewee, let us focus on appropriate answering in the interview. Answers cannot be divided neatly into categories as can questions; consequently, we will consider some general guidelines that should allow the interviewee to be a successful participant in the interview process.

We will include six recommendations for the answering of questions in the interview. Under some circumstances, interviewers may provide answers and interviewees may ask questions; however, typically the interviewer asks the questions and the interviewee provides the answers. As we discuss these guidelines, we will assume that we are considering the typical situation in which the interviewee is answering questions. First, an interviewee should answer the questions that are asked of him or her. This guideline may appear to be a statement of the obvious; however, interviewees occasionally have difficulty in answering specific questions and attempt to avoid them. An interviewee may look away, pretend that he or she has not heard the question, respond in a way that suggests that the question was not understood, or engage in other avoidance behaviors. Remember that we cannot *not* communicate. If we fail to answer a question, for instance, we are suggesting that we are confused, bored, or dishonest. None of these conclusions is useful to the interviewee. If you are tempted to refrain from answering the question because you are confused by the language or the focus of the question, explain your confusion or ask for clarification from the interviewer. If, for instance, you are reluctant to answer the question because you believe that it invades your privacy, is too personal, or is not within the legal guidelines recommended by the EEOC (Equal Employment Opportunity Commission), explain your concern. Offering a clear, specific explanation about your hesitation in answering a particular question is far better than stalling, offering a circumvented answer, or not responding at all.

Second, you should *not* answer questions that are not asked of you. In a sense, this guideline is a corollary of the first recommendation. Sometimes interviewees are anxious to please and may go far beyond the scope of the questions that are asked of them. In response to a question about courses he had taken in business at the college level, one interviewee detailed his entire college record and discussed, in general terms, his high school electives. When asked about her mobility, one woman explained, in great detail, that she had been recently divorced and was now free to travel. Her answer included reasons for the dissolution of her marriage, child custody, and other details that went far beyond the question that was asked. Do not go beyond the questions that you are asked and do not offer great detail when a simple, straightforward response is sufficient. Too much information or excessive self-disclosure will cause the interviewer to believe that you are inappropriately socialized, insecure, a poor listener, or trying too hard to create a certain impression. Also, lengthy answers that go far beyond the question waste valuable time for you and the interviewer.

Third, provide complete answers to questions. In this case, we may appear to be contradicting the previous recommendation. In fact, we are offering the limitation of the other extreme. In the second recommendation we suggested that you do not go far beyond the question; here we are cautioning against saying far too little. If you are asked if you have any experience as a salesclerk, you would be remiss in responding, "Yes," without any further explanation.

On the other hand, you would not be correctly advised to explain your work when you were eight years old selling Girl Scout cookies. Incomplete answers allow the interviewee to present a distorted picture of himself or herself. For instance, if you respond that you have extensive work in sales when your Girl Scout cookie sales comprises the bulk of your experience, you may be presenting a partial answer that is misleading. Be aware, too, that you and the interviewer may have a different perception of specific characteristics or particular information. A factor that you are willing to dismiss may be highly relevant to the interviewer. If you are uncertain about the relevance of prior experience, education, or other factors, ask the interviewer if he or she is interested in the specific information you can offer. A variety of factors can contribute toward your providing incomplete answers including the interviewer's apparent lack of patience, the short amount of time that is allotted for the interview, your own poor self-concept, your misunderstanding of the question, or your motivation in serving as an interviewee. Try to be aware of the factors that may be operating for you.

Fourth, related to the previous point, you should offer accurate and honest information in your answers. Do not say you have completed your college degree if you have not. Do not pretend to possess information that you do not have—"Yes, I know all about the Cuban crisis which occurred during President Kennedy's administration," "Of course I have read *The Brethren: Inside the Supreme Court* and understand all of the issues that it raises," or "I am aware of the economic program of President Bush's administration and exactly how it differs from that of the Carter administration." Do not be embarrassed to ask for clarification of concepts, terms, or phenomena. Inaccuracy and distortion should be avoided for ethical reasons as well as for effectiveness. Honesty pays!

Fifth, related to honest and accurate responses, you should provide specific, concrete answers. Avoid platitudes, clichés, emphemisms, jargon, and some of the other verbal distractors that we discussed in chapter 4. You may wish to review some of this material in order to recall the barriers that may interfere with clarity and specificity and to ensure that you are not relying upon some of these patterns. Avoid ambiguous "yes" or "no" responses when more information is clearly desired. Be descriptive and concrete in your language choices. Ambiguous language is confusing and may suggest to the interviewer that you are attempting to be deceitful.

Finally, provide relevant answers. Sometimes we fail to listen carefully to the other person and provide answers that fail to deal with the question. Or, perhaps, we attempt to "second guess" the interviewer and offer an answer to a question that we assumed that he or she was going to ask rather than the one actually asked. A number of factors interfere with active listening as we discussed in chapter 8. You may wish to review these before you engage in an interview as the interviewee. When we offer a *non sequitur,* a response that does not follow from the question, it may suggest that we are confused or attempting to deceive the interviewer. Again, neither of these impressions is desirable.

Skill in Answering Interview Questions

In order to improve your ability in the answering of questions in the interview setting, provide answers for the following questions from informational and employment interviews. Examine the differences between the answers that you provide.

1. "How did you happen to find out about our company?"

    A *complete* answer for this question would be _____

    _____

    An example of answering this question with a response that goes far beyond the question

    asked is _____

    _____

    A dishonest or inaccurate answer to this question is _____

    _____

2. "Do you have any background in sales?"

    An answer that is *not* specific and concrete would be _____

    _____

    An irrelevant answer to this question would be _____

    _____

    A complete, honest answer to this question would be _____

    _____

3. "Do you believe that all college students should take a beginning speech communication course?"

    The failure to answer this question would be exemplified as _____

    _____

    An incomplete answer to this question would be _____

    _____

    A specific, concrete answer to this question would be _____

    _____

4. "Why did you go to college?"

    An irrelevant answer to this question would be _____

    _____

Skill in Answering Interview Questions continued

A dishonest, or inaccurate answer would be _____

_____

An ambiguous answer would be _____

_____

5.   "Do you enjoy traveling?"

An honest and accurate answer would be _____

_____

A complete answer would be _____

_____

An answer that goes beyond the question would be _____

_____

Specific organizational patterns.   The body of the interview may be organized in a variety of ways. The most typical methods of organizing the body
include the funnel approach, the pyramid approach, the tube approach, the
hourglass approach, and the diamond approach. These descriptive labels arise
from a depiction of the organizational patterns as demonstrated in figure 15.1.

The organizational patterns of the body of the interview primarily refer to
the use of open and closed questions. The *inverted funnel approach* begins
with closed questions and at some point starts increasingly open questions.
This approach may be useful when there are certain crucial responses that
must be answered in a particular manner before it makes sense to even continue the interview further. This approach may also be beneficial in establishing a comfortable atmosphere if the initial questions are relatively simple
and nonthreatening. This pattern also assists the interviewer in setting a pace
and tempo for the interview. Of course, these objectives are served by limiting
the interviewee's input and opportunity to talk during the initial minutes of
an interview when the often all-important initial impressions are being formed.
Despite this limitation, this pattern appears to be the most commonly used
sequence in interviews.[7]

The *funnel approach* relies on broad, open questions at first, becomes increasingly restrictive as more closed questions are used, and concludes with
very tightly closed questions. The funnel approach may be especially useful
when the interviewer has done little preparation, when little is known about
the interviewee, or when the topic is not fully understood. The funnel approach may be particularly appropriate for the informational interviewer who
is interviewing a hostile or defensive interviewee since the openness of the

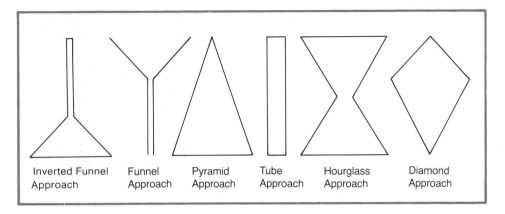

Organizational patterns for the body of the interview.   Figure 15.1

first questions should reduce the anxiety or defensiveness of the interviewee. This approach may be useful for the persuasive interviewer who is interviewing an interviewee who is not prone to accept the product or service that is being sold. Finally, the employment interviewer who is interviewing a novice applicant might find this approach useful.

The *pyramid approach* is similar to the inverted funnel. It relies on tightly closed questions at first and gradually becomes more open until the interviewer concludes with broad, open questions. The pyramid might be used when the interviewee is reluctant to speak because of nervousness, embarrassment, or because of the distastefulness of the topic. By eliciting short one- or two-word answers, the interviewer may gradually be able to encourage the interviewee to respond more completely.

The *tube approach* may consist of open questions or closed questions. The distinguishing feature of the tube approach is that all questions are relatively the same—all generally open or all generally closed. While the tube approach will generally not yield in-depth information, it is very useful if the interviewer plans on analyzing the information he or she receives in a statistical or scientific manner. For instance, the survey reported at the beginning of this chapter, in which it was determined that students identify the interview as the most important interpersonal communication activity, used a tube approach with all questions being closed. The information could thus be analyzed and comparisons could be made and conclusions could be drawn that had a measure of reliability.

The *hourglass approach* and the *diamond approach* are actually combinations of the other two approaches. The hourglass approach begins with open questions that become increasingly restrictive and then become increasingly open. The diamond approach begins and ends with closed questions but the middle of the interview includes unrestricted open questions. These approaches are sometimes suggested for motivational purposes or when the

Organizational Pattern of a Survey Interview

To determine if you understand the difference between the various organizational patterns of interviews, re-examine the survey interview in the exercise on page 378. Identify that short interview as a(n) inverted funnel, funnel, pyramid, tube, hourglass, or diamond approach. Why do you think that this structure was used? Do you think this interview could be reorganized in a more effective way? If you were to conduct this interview, how would you organize the questions?

purpose of the interview is more complex. For example, the diamond approach might be used in a persuasive interview when the interviewer begins with closed questions, opens the questions up to secure broad information from the interviewee, and then closes the questions in order to make the sale.

The types of questions that we have discussed, the overall three-part division of the interview, and the specific organizational patterns will become increasingly useful as we apply them to specific interviewing situations. In order to make these applications, we turn to a more thorough examination of two purposes of interviewing.

Two Applications of Interviewing

Interviews can have an endless list of purposes. They may serve the purposes of information-gathering, information-disseminating, problem-solving, appraisal, counseling, persuasion, reprimanding, interrogation, employment, journalism, surveying, and performance. We will not consider all of these types of interviews, but we will restrict our consideration to two basic purposes of interviewing: the informational interview and the employment interview. These two applications of interviewing are potentially most useful for the average college student.

As you consider these two applications of the interview, keep in mind that you can learn to become a better interviewer. Like the other communication skills that are discussed in this text, understanding the interviewing process and practicing the skills involved can allow you to become a more competent communicator. As Lopez, in his text, points out:

Interviewing is very much like piano playing—a fair degree of skill can be acquired without the necessity of formal instruction. But there is a world of difference in craftsmanship, in technique, and in finesse between the amateur who plays "by ear" and the accomplished concert pianist.[8]

Informational Interviews

Informational interviews occur in a variety of settings. Informational interviews are common when we are securing information about a particular event or product, when we are attempting to assess opinions, and when we are collecting data for a research project. A great deal of informational interviewing is done over the telephone, rather than face-to-face. However, studies that have compared the efficacy of telephone interviewing with the personal approach have suggested that the telephone interview does not have the same quality.[9] The primary problem with the telephone interview, as you may have surmised from your reading of chapter 5, lies in the lack of nonverbal cues. Additional difficulties include the lack of seriousness that interviewees sometimes exhibit in telephone interviews and the refusal of some persons to participate in telephone interviews.

We have all viewed the successful informational interviews of Barbara Walters, Gene Shalit, Jane Pauley, Merv Griffin, Johnny Carson, Tom Snyder, and other television celebrities. Informational interviewing, when done by professionals, looks easy. However, for those of us who have participated in informational interviewing, particularly with a reluctant interviewee, we know how difficult this task can be. If you find yourself involved as an interviewer with a less than verbose partner, you may want to try some of the techniques used by the professionals. First, you can rely on a nonstructured rather than a tightly structured interview. Allowing the interviewee to ramble at times may encourage him or her to open up to you. Second, you may attempt to maximize interpersonal relationships. Encourage the interviewee to relate to you on a personal, rather than on a strictly professional basis. Finally, if all else fails, you may need to consider alternative sources for your information. Are there other persons who may be able to supply equally useful information?

A final consideration in the informational interview is the role that you, as the interviewer, will play. Do you have biases or a distinct point of view about the outcome of the interview? Do you believe that you know the answers to the questions that you will ask? A recent study demonstrated that interviewer expectation can have a great effect on response rate and response quality.[10] We need to be aware of our perspectives and perceptions and the role they play in causing particular outcomes in the informational interview. As the interviewer with a potential bias, you can carefully scrutinize your questions to determine if they are leading rather than neutral or if they allow only one or two different responses rather than an array of different answers.

Sample informational interview.   The informational interview that follows was designed to determine a young state representative's opinions on a state proposition that would result in lower taxes. The interview was actually conducted as part of a class assignment. The interviewer was relatively successful

We are engaged in a variety of different kinds of interviews. The person conducting a consumer opinion survey is an informational interviewer.

in achieving her goals. You may be able to identify some of the reasons for the interviewer's success as you read the questions that she prepared.

> *Representative Crawford, I really appreciate your willingness to spend a few minutes today to talk about your feelings about proposition 12 which will be on the ballot this year. This interview should take no more than fifteen minutes.*
> *First, would you explain your understanding of what is involved in the proposition?*
> *Do members of your party generally support this proposition?*
> *Why (or why not)?*
> *Do members of the other major political party support this proposition? Why (or why not)?*

Do you support the proposition?
Why (or why not)?
What changes will occur if this proposition is passed?
What changes will occur if this proposition is not passed?
What advice do you have for the electorate when they come to the polls and must decide how to vote on this issue?
Thank you, Mr. Crawford, for your time and your views. I will be composing a news story which will be carried in the "Daily" on Friday. The story will contrast your view on the proposition with the view of your opponent. I will send you a copy of the article so you won't miss it. Thanks again.

The interviewer first assured that the representative understood the proposition about which she was interested. She asked closed questions about the support of the two major political parties for the amendment. She followed these closed questions with open questions that allowed the representative to detail rationale in support or in opposition. She then asked him for his stand on the proposition with a closed question and his rationale in a secondary, open question. She asked primary, open questions about the effect of this legislation. Finally, she provided the most open question in the interview as she allowed the state official to offer any advice to the electorate that he may wish to provide. Her opening was clear in stating the purpose of the interview and in suggesting a realistic time estimate of the interview while her closing provided a sufficient amount of orientation and appreciation for the interview.

Personal Informative Interview

One young woman was interested in interviewing a marriage counselor in a small town to determine if he felt there was a need for a women's crisis center. The interview guide that she used is printed below. Categorize each question as open or closed, primary or secondary, and neutral or leading. Determine the organizational structure of the interview. Based on your analysis of this interview, do you think the interviewer was successful in attaining her goal? Can you determine specific improvements that could be made in this interview? Are the opening and closing adequate or could they be improved? What improvements could be made? Do you think the interviewer asked too many questions or too few? How long do you think this interview would take? After you have thoroughly analyzed this interview, use it as your interview guide and role play the interview with another classmate. Do you have any different perceptions of the interview after you have reenacted it? Are you surprised by the adequacy or inadequacy of the questions?

OPENING: Hello, my name is Becky Meecham. I'm a college student and I am conducting this interview today for a class in which I am enrolled. I would like to get some general information about you and how you feel about initiating a women's crisis center in Middletown. I am going to be conducting a number of interviews with professionals in Middletown and if I determine a real need, I hope to assist in the institution of a women's crisis center.

Personal Informative Interview continued

	Open or Closed	Primary or Secondary	Neutral or Leading
1. Where did you receive your education?	_____	_____	_____
2. What was your major area of study?	_____	_____	_____
3. How do you keep up with your field?	_____	_____	_____
4. In your experience here in Middletown, have there been many cases of beaten women, unwed mothers, or rape?	_____	_____	_____
5. Which do you think occurs most often?	_____	_____	_____
6. Which do you think is the worst problem?	_____	_____	_____
7. What do you think can be done about it?	_____	_____	_____
8. Do you feel a women's center is needed here?	_____	_____	_____
9. Do you think a women's center is feasible here?	_____	_____	_____
10. Would you be willing to help with such a center?	_____	_____	_____
11. Do you think the public would help with such a center?	_____	_____	_____
12. How does one go about starting a center?	_____	_____	_____
13. Would you refer a person to a center if the center employed professional staff members?	_____	_____	_____
14. Would you refer a person to a center if professionals were not employed?	_____	_____	_____
15. In what instances?	_____	_____	_____
16. Do you think Middletown is ready for such a center?	_____	_____	_____
17. Taking everything into consideration, do you think a women's center is a good idea for Middletown?	_____	_____	_____

CLOSING: Well, I think I have taken up more time than I probably should have. I want to thank you for your time and for the opportunity to talk with you. You have been very open and helpful. If I do decide to work on the creation of a women's crisis center in Middletown, I will be sure to give you a call.

Employment Interviews: The Role of the Interviewee

The employment interview may be the most useful interview for you. You may already have engaged in employment interviews or you may anticipate interviewing for a job in the very near future. Applicants in the employment interview setting can do a great deal to enhance their employment opportunities.

Criticisms about employment interviewees.   Employment interviewers offer criticism that can be useful to potential employees. Among their most frequent complaints are that interviewees demonstrate poor communication skills, they are insufficiently prepared for the interview, they express vague or minimum interest, and they appear to demonstrate little motivation and express unrealistic expectations.[11] Let us consider each of these criticisms in more detail.

1. *Employment interviewees demonstrate poor communication skills.* By this, the interviewers mean that interviewees responded to simple questions with long rambling responses; that interviewees responded to direct questions with ambiguous, vague answers; that interviewees showed nonverbal and verbal signs of nervousness; that interviewees talked far too much or far too little. Poor communication skills may be perceived as dishonesty. A recent study showed that interviewees who used short answers with long time intervals between answers, were ambiguous, smiled consistently throughout the interview, shifted their posture frequently, and engaged in excessive grooming behavior, such as smoothing their tie or skirt or adjusting their hair, were perceived as lying.[12]

2. *Employment interviewees are insufficiently prepared for the interview.* The primary area of criticism with regard to preparation is that interviewees have only limited or no information about the company with which they are interviewing. They enter into the interview without knowledge of the product that the company produces or without an understanding of the services they offer. Interviewees are unable to ask knowledgeable questions about the company with which they are interviewing. Lack of preparation suggests minimal concern and minimal commitment to the company.

3. *Employment interviewees express vague interest.* When applicants are asked about their lifetime goals or career goals and express ambiguous, unclear responses, employers are less than comfortable. The applicant who cannot clearly and coherently state where she or he would ideally like to be in five years is suggesting a lack of specific goals.

4. *Employment interviewees demonstrate little motivation.* The interviewee who has little enthusiasm, excitement, or energy is viewed as lacking motivation. Similarly, the person who is apathetic, doesn't sell himself or herself, or is *too* agreeable may also be viewed as lacking in motivation.

5. *Employment interviewees express unrealistic expectations.* Potential employees who expect the salary or benefits afforded to senior members of the company are not being realistic. In general, persons who are overly concerned with salary and benefit packages may be rejected for their immaturity or lack of realistic expectations. While it is important to be clear about such matters as salary and benefits, placing these considerations ahead of other concerns results in a negative impression on the part of the employer.

Overcoming criticisms about employment interviewees.   You can overcome these criticisms offered by employment interviewers. When you consider that you will probably be spending about two thousand hours each year working at your career, or a total of over eighty thousand hours at your chosen profession in your lifetime, time spent in ensuring a successful job interview is well worth the effort. A recent study suggested that the interview preparation process may be divided into four steps for the interviewee. First, the interviewee should develop realistic expectations about the particular job. Second, the individual should develop interviewing skills. Third, the interviewee should be able to demonstrate her or his skills and determine how they meet the needs of the job. Fourth, the interviewee should be prepared for rejection since most interviews do not result in the applicant being hired.[13] Let us consider each of these steps in more detail.

1. *Develop realistic expectations about the job.* You can develop realistic expectations in two ways. First, you should know about employment opportunities in general. Although many people consider entering into a relatively small number of occupations, a thorough search of potential positions reveals over twenty thousand jobs available in the United States. You may wish to visit your local placement office or you may wish to examine the book, *Career Guide to Professional Organizations,*[14] in order to determine the broad range of options open to you. Second, you should know about the particular company with which you are interviewing. Take advantage of placement offices, the Better Business Bureau, the Chamber of Commerce, Dun & Bradstreet, and the Security Exchange Commission which will provide you with an Annual Corporate Report or a *10-K,* a statement that outlines the financial situation of a corporation. A specific

understanding about the company and the position that is available within the company will help you develop more realistic expectations.

2. *Develop interviewing skills.* The communication skills that are discussed in this book will be useful to you in the interviewing situation. Providing nonambiguous nonverbal cues, self-disclosing appropriately, demonstrating empathy and active listening, and being descriptive and clear in your verbal comments are essential.[15]

    Related to your interviewing skills is your ability to answer potential questions in a thorough and complete way. You can rehearse possible answers in order to be thoroughly prepared. While your placement office may be able to provide typical questions that are asked by employers, the following list includes some of the more common questions:

- What jobs have you held?
- Why did you leave your previous job(s)?
- What do you know about our company?
- Why do you wish to work for our company?
- What are your future career goals?
- Why did you go to college?
- What were your favorite courses in college (or in high school)?
- What extracurricular activities were you involved in in college?
- How did you choose your major?
- What are your salary expectations?
- Do you enjoy traveling?
- Are you willing to work overtime?
- In what city would you like to work?
- Do you prefer to work with others or alone?
- Do you have any unique skills?
- Where do you see yourself in ten years?
- Do you plan on doing any graduate work?
- Is your writing ability above average?
- Do you possess good oral communication skills?
- What percent of college expenses did you earn yourself?
- Could you tell me a good story?
- What are your best qualities?
- What are your worst qualities?

By providing answers to this set of questions, you can more thoroughly prepare yourself for the interview situation.

3. *Demonstrate your skills and determine how they meet the needs of the job.* As an interviewee in the employment setting, you should effectively present your qualifications. You should take the initiative to present your major personal characteristics that meet the job qualifications. You should provide specific details about your background and qualifications and skillfully, but honestly, stress your favorable characteristics. In addition, you should present questionable or weak factors in tactful, positive, and candid ways. An expert on employment interviewing expressed the concern that interviewees are sometimes coached rather than educated on employment interviewing. He explained that coaching students turns them into puppets who will eventually be unhappy employees. Educating interviewees, on the other hand, brings out an awareness of their unique capabilities and presents a more accurate and impressive image to the interviewer. He concludes that education results in benefits for all.[16]

In summary, you should present communication skills that include well-organized comments that are worded appropriately and presented smoothly with confidence and enthusiasm. You should listen carefully, maintain good eye contact, and generally present an effective style. In general, your physical and mental image should include a neat, clean, and conservative appearance. You should demonstrate a good knowledge of the employing organization and the position that is available. You should demonstrate a thorough knowledge of yourself including career objectives and personal goals. Nonetheless, with all this preparation, you must keep in mind that a very small percentage of employment interviews result in someone being hired. Be prepared for rejection, which is the most likely outcome in any single employment interview.

Employment Interviews: The Role of the Interviewer

The employment interview may be viewed from the perspective of the interviewee as we have done or from the point of view of the employment interviewer. You may be interested in learning about the employment interview because you expect to serve as the interviewer. But even if you do not visualize yourself as the interviewer, you may learn useful information that you can apply as the interviewee as you view the interview process from the employer's perspective. For example, if you find yourself being interviewed in an obviously incompetent manner, it may well be indicative of the quality of the organization that would allow such incompetence in such an important position. We have already discussed some of the employment interviewer's primary criticisms of the interviewee, let us now consider changes that have occurred in the interviewing process for the interviewer.

Not very long ago, and, to some extent, today, employers have used criteria such as personality characteristics, sex, personal style, and other irrelevant features by which to select people for their companies. Guidelines from federal and state levels and recommendations from experts in employment interviewing[17] suggest that such criteria are illegal and irrelevant. The Equal Employment Opportunity Commission (EEOC) has developed strict guidelines for interviewing and testing applicants. Five major provisions comprise the EEOC guidelines. They include that discrimination on the basis of sex, race, or ethnic group cannot occur, that one part of the interview cannot color the entire interview, that the validity of decisions must be demonstrated, that documentation of decisions must be provided, and that affirmative action, including the hiring of women and minority groups, should be taken to enact the guidelines. Nonetheless, unfair hiring practices still exist. You should familiarize yourself with the federal guidelines as well as the state laws that govern hiring and firing[18] and be informed about the signs of sexism and racism[19] as well as being considered on the basis of your personality characteristics rather than on how your skills and abilities match up with the needs of the job.[20]

Employment interviewers, like employment interviewees, must plan and prepare if they are to engage in successful interviews. The ideal model of the employment interview, according to one writer, assumes that the employment interviewer is well prepared for the interview, conducts it in an unhurried and uninterrupted manner, and devotes his or her full attention to the applicant.[21] Some research indicates that interviewers may actually benefit both the organization and the interviewee by providing balanced information on the negative or "realistic" aspects of the job. Despite the fact that a large portion of most interviews consist of talk about the job content and climate (e.g., duties, relations with coworkers, type of supervision, compensation and salary, etc.),[22] apparently interviewees frequently enter their jobs with overinflated or idealistic expectations. The obvious result would be job dissatisfaction later. Surprisingly, interviewers who provide negative or realistic information tend to be viewed as more credible and trustworthy by interviewees.[23]

Another author, discussing recruitment programs on college campuses, recommends that employers institute a number of steps to ensure better interviews. Among his suggestions are that interviewers interview on campus at least once or twice a year, that they provide personnel to speak in classes and at student professional organization meetings, that they work with the college placement office, that they maintain close ties to the university through special activities, and that they present retention figures and financial success reports of employees.[24]

The low reliability and validity of the selection interview can be improved. Suggestions for improving this interview are: (1) using a panel or board rather than one interviewer, (2) using a structured rather than an unstructured interview, (3) using the same chairperson for all interviews, (4) using persons who are similarly trained, (5) provide a briefing session before the interview for the panel members, (6) delegate specific topic areas to each of the panel members, (7) prepare a list of questions for each panel member, (8) record the applicants' responses by each panel member on a sheet and compare these at the end of the interview, (9) conduct all interviews within the same room with the same seating arrangement, and (10) train all panel members in interview techniques to minimize interviewer biases and to develop social skills.[25]

Employment interview guide.   Thorough planning can ensure a successful, legal interview. An employment interview guide can be very useful in the planning and conducting of the employment interview. The employment interview guide consists of the general purpose of the interview, the opening, a schedule of questions that comprises the body of the interview, and a closing. An example of an employment interview guide follows:

General Purpose: To find a competent analyst for the financial planning and analysis department of the Union Pacific Corporation.

Opening: Good afternoon. You must be Theodore Underhill. Do you go by Ted? I'm Lori Dearin from the personnel department of Union Pacific. Make yourself comfortable and we'll get started. First, I'd like to get to know some things about you and what you've done. Next, we'll get into Union Pacific Corporation and the analyst job. I have looked at your resumé, Ted, you have a very impressive military career. The work you did in the army sounds very interesting. Why don't you tell me about it? It appears that you have done some traveling, too. Was it all connected with your military service? What did you think of the U.S.S.R.?

Body:

1. When did you decide on your field of study?
2. Do you feel you received adequate preparation at State?
3. Which courses do you feel were particularly helpful to you?
4. Would you have taken any different courses if you had the opportunity of selecting your classes over?
5. Do you find analytical work easy?
6. Do you generally look at the big picture or at small, individual items?
7. Do you like working with figures and numbers?
8. Tell me about some of the campus activities you were involved in.
9. Did you hold any offices or have you done any major planning for the groups in which you are a member?
10. Do you do any public speaking?

11. How do you feel your work experiences helped you to communicate and relate to others?

12. Did you work while you attended college?

13. Did you feel your work and your other activities took a great deal of time?

14. Did you find it difficult to find adequate time to study?

15. What special qualifications do you have that you feel would make you successful in your field?

16. Tell me what you feel are your greatest strengths and weaknesses.

17. Tell me what you know about our company.

18. Do you have any specific questions?

19. Do you have any questions about the job?

20. Do you prefer to work for a large or a small company?

21. What size and location of city would you prefer?

22. Do you mind traveling?

23. Do you adapt fairly well to new environments?

24. Do you have any questions about anything we have discussed?

Closing: That is all that I have to ask. I want to thank you for coming in today. I have enjoyed talking with you. You have been very helpful in your answers. We have more applicants to talk with about this position and then I will get back to you about next Thursday or Friday. If you have any questions at all, feel free to give me a call. My telephone number is on this card and I will be in my office every morning from 8 A.M. until noon. Thank you, again.

The opening of this interview began with a few easy questions to develop rapport between the interviewer and the applicant. A congenial atmosphere was established and the interviewer and the interviewee were introduced to each other. The body of this interview consisted of 24 questions. The interviewer determined before the interview that five characteristics would define the competent analyst for this company. These characteristics are: well-educated, a motivated person with an analytical mind, relates well with others, well organized, and knows himself or herself. Questions #1 through #4 were designed to determine the applicant's education. Questions #5 through #7 were written to determine his or her analytical skills. Questions #8 through #11 were written to assess the person's ability to relate with others. Questions #12 through #14 were designed to assess the individual's organizational skills. Questions #15 and #16 were written to determine the applicant's knowledge of himself or herself. The rest of the questions, #17 through #24, were written to determine whether the applicant would fit the specific job. Finally, the closing of the interview is similar in length to the introduction. A congenial atmosphere is reestablished and the applicant is informed about what will

An Employment Interview Opportunity

Find a job description for a job for which you might apply or write a job description that would be appropriate for you. Exchange your job description with another person in class. Prepare an opening, a list of questions, and a closing for an employment interview in which you will serve as the interviewer and your classmate's job description will serve as the potential employment for which he or she is interviewing. In class, interview the classmate for the position. After about a 15–20 minute interview, exchange roles. You will now serve as the interviewee as your classmate interviews you for the position for which you wrote the job description. After you have each served as the interviewer and the interviewee, discuss this exercise. Were you surprised by any of the questions that the interviewer asked you? Do you believe that you had realistic expectations about the job? What interviewing skills were particularly useful? Did you demonstrate that your skills met the needs of the job? Did the interviewer appear to be well prepared? Did he or she conduct the interview in an effective manner? Did you feel that the interviewer was an active listener? Do you feel you are more effective as an interviewer or an interviewee? What can you do to improve your skills?

occur next. He is given specific telephone numbers and dates about when he can expect communication from the company. Employment interviewing can be a positive experience when both the interviewer and the interviewee are well prepared.

Summary

In this chapter you learned about the interpersonal communication context of interviewing. You may have already been involved in a number of interviews and the information in this chapter should allow you to be more effective in them in the future. While in the earlier chapters in this section of the book you learned about interpersonal communication contexts that assist you with your social needs, in this chapter you considered the importance of communication in assisting you in solving your task-related needs. You learned that interviewing is formal, preplanned, and has a specific purpose. Interviews typically include two persons and never include more than two identifiable groups of people. The asking and answering of questions is basic to the interview.

Questions may be categorized into open or closed, primary or secondary, and neutral or leading. Guidelines concerning answers in the interview are especially relevant to interviewees, but sometimes interviewers answer questions, too. Answers should address the question being asked, should not answer other questions, should be complete, should be accurate and honest, should be specific and concrete, and should be relevant. Interviews may be organized in a variety of ways, but all interviews should have an opening, a body, and a closing.

Interviews occur for a variety of purposes, but probably the most common for you are the information interview and the employment interview. You may have the need to secure information from others for class projects, term papers, or other assignments. You may engage in employment interviews as you attempt to gain summer or part-time employment or as you attempt to secure a position upon graduation. In any case, these two interviews are important to your task-related needs.

Notes

1. L. A. Baxter and W. W. Wilmot, "Secret Tests: Social Strategies for Acquiring Information about the State of the Relationship," *Human Communication Research* 11(1984): 171–201; C. R. Berger, R. R. Gardner, G. W. Clatterbuck, and L. S. Schulman, "Perceptions of Information Sequencing in Relationship Development," *Human Communication Research* 3(1978): 29–46; M. Snyder and S. Gangestad "Hypothesis-testing Processes," in J. H. Harvey, W. Ickes, and R. F. Kidd (eds.), *New Directions in Attribution Research* (Hillsdale, N.J.: Lawrence Erlbaum Associates, 1981) pp. 171–96.

2. Judy C. Pearson, Ritch L. Sorenson, and Paul E. Nelson, "How Students and Alumni Perceive the Basic Course," *Communication Education* 30(1981): 296–99.

3. See R. L. Street, Jr. "Interaction Processes and Outcomes in Interviews" *Communication Yearbook* 9(1986): 215–50.

4. For an analysis of impression management and influence functions in a counseling interview context, see M. L. Friedlander and G. S. Schwartz, "Toward a Theory of Strategic Self-presentation in Counseling and Psychotherapy," *Journal of Counseling Psychology* 32(1985): 483–501.

5. Leo Plotkin, "Interview or Intraview," *The Personnel Administrator* 15(1970): 13.

6. F. M. Jablin, "Task/Work Relationships: A Life-span Perspective," in M. L. Knapp and G. R. Miller (eds.), *Handbook of Interpersonal Communication* (Beverly Hills, Calif.: Sage, 1985) p. 620.

7. Jablin, p. 620.

8. Felix M. Lopez, *Personnel Interviewing* (New York: McGraw-Hill, 1975), p. 1.

9. Lawrence A. Jordan, Alfred C. Marcus, and Leo G. Reeder, "Response Styles in Telephone and Household Interviewing: A Field Experiment," *Public Opinion Quarterly* 44(1980): 210–22.

10. Eleanor Singer and Luane Kohnke-Aguirre, "Interviewer Expectation Effects: A Replication and Extension," *Public Opinion Quarterly* 43(1979): 245–59.

11. Cal W. Downs, G. Paul Smeyak, and Ernest Martin, *Professional Interviewing* (New York: Harper & Row, 1980), p. 147.

12. Robert E. Kraut, "Verbal and Nonverbal Cues in the Perception of Lying," *Journal of Personality and Social Psychology* 36(1978), pp. 380–91.

13. John P. Galassi and Merna Dee Galassi, "Preparing Individuals for Job Interviews," *Personnel and Guidance Journal* 57(1978): 188–91.

14. Staff of the Carroll Press, *Career Guide to Professional Organizations* (Cranston, R.I.: Carroll Press, 1976).

15. For very readable discussions of interviewing skills, see M. Gottlieb, *Interview* (New York: Longman, 1986); and D. Torrington, *Face to Face: Handling Personal Encounters at Work* (Toronto: Coles, 1980).

16. Richard K. Harwood, "Educating, Rather than Coaching, for the Job Interview," *Journal of Employment Counseling* 11(1974): 187–90.

17. See, for instance, John T. Hopkins, "The Top Twelve Questions for Employment Agency Interviews," *Personnel Journal* 59(1980): 209–13; and Jack Bucalo, "The Balanced Approach to Successful Screening Interviews," *Personnel Journal* 57(1978): 420–28.

18. The EEOC guidelines are clarified in two recent articles including William A. Simon, Jr., "A Practical Approach to the Uniform Selection Guidelines," *Personnel Administrator* 24(November 1979), pp. 75–79; and Robert D. Gatewood and James Ledvinka, "Selection Interviewing and EEOC: Mandate for Objectivity," *Personnel Administrator,* 24(December 1979), pp. 51–54.

19. Laura Garrison, "Recognizing and Combatting Sexist Job Interviews," *Journal of Employment Counseling* 17(1980): 270–76.

20. Bucalo, 1978, 420–28.

21. Richard M. Coffina, "Management Recruitment is a Two-Way Street," *Personnel Journal* 58(1979): 86.

22. F. M. Jablin and K. J. Krone, "Organizational Assimilation," in C. R. Berger and S. H. Chaffee (eds.), *Handbook of Communication Science* (Newbury Park, Calif.: Sage, 1987), p. 715.

23. F. M. Jablin and K. B. McComb, "The Employment Screening Interview: An Organizational Assimilation and Communication Perspective," *Communication Yearbook* 8(1984): 137–63.

24. Warren D. Robb, "How's Your CRP?" *Personnel Administrator* 25(1980): 101–6.

25. Ray Forbes, "Improving the Reliability of the Selection Interview," *Personnel Management* 11(1979): 36–39.

Additional Readings

Briggs, Charles L. *How to Ask: A Sociolinguistic Appraisal of the Role of the Interview in Social Science Research.* Studies in the Social and Cultural Foundations of Languages: No. 1. New York: Cambridge University Press, 1986.

Dunham, Randall B. and Smith, Frank J. *Organizational Surveys.* Glenview, Ill.: Scott, Foresman and Company, 1979.

Gorden, Raymond L. *Interviewing: Strategy, Techniques, and Tactics,* 3d ed. Homewood, Ill.: The Dorsey Press, 1980.

Gottlieb, Marvin. *Interview.* Longman Series in College Composition and Communication. White Plains, N.Y.: Longman, 1986.

Jennerich, Ellen Z. and Jennerich, Edward J. *The Reference Interview as a Creative Art.* Englewood, Colo.: Libraries Unlimited, 1987.

Kahn, Robert L. and Cannell, Charles F. *The Dynamics of Interviewing.* New York: John Wiley & Sons, 1957.

Lopez, Felix M. *Personnel Interviewing,* 2d ed. New York: McGraw-Hill, 1975.

McCracken, Grant. *The Long Interview.* Qualitative Research Methods Series: Vol. 13. Newbury Park, Calif.: Sage, 1988.

Milner, Cork. *The Art of Interviewing: How to Write and Sell the Personality Profile.* Santa Barbara, Calif.: Ronda House, 1987.

Nathan, Harriet. *Critical Choices in Interviews: Conduct, Use, and Research Role.* Berkley, Calif.: University of California, Berkley IGS, 1986.

Richardson, Stephen A., Dohrenwend, Barbara S., and Klein, David. *Interviewing: Its Forms and Functions.* New York: Basic Books, Inc., 1965.

Stano, Michael E. and Reinsch, N. L., Jr. *Communication in Interviews.* Englewood Cliffs, N.J.: Prentice-Hall, 1982.

Stewart, Charles J. and Cash, William B. *Interviewing: Principles and Practices,* 3d ed. Dubuque, Ia.: Wm. C. Brown, 1982.

Torrington, Derek. *Face to Face: Handling Personal Encounters at Work.* Toronto: Coles, 1980.

Webster, Edward. *Decision-Making in the Employment Interview.* Montreal: The Eagle Publishing Company, 1964.

Photo Credits

Name Index

Subject Index